Understanding

Second language acquisition

Understanding

Second language acquisition

Lourdes Ortega

**Understanding
Language Series**

Series Editors:
Bernard Comrie
and
Greville Corbett

HODDER
EDUCATION
AN HACHETTE UK COMPANY

First published in Great Britain in 2009 by
Hodder Education, an Hachette UK Company,
338 Euston Road, London NW1 3BH

Hachette UK's policy is to use papers that are natural, renewable and
recyclable products and made from wood grown in sustainable forests.
The logging and manufacturing processes are expected to conform to the
environmental regulations of the country of origin.

The advice and information in this book are believed to be true and
accurate at the date of going to press, but neither the author nor the publisher
can accept any legal responsibility or liability for any errors or omissions.

British Library Cataloguing in Publication Data
A catalogue record for this book is available from the British Library

Library of Congress Cataloging-in-Publication Data
A catalog record for this book is available from the Library of Congress

ISBN: 978 0 340 905 593

4 5 6 7 8 9 10
Extracts from *The Philosopher's Demise: Learning French* by Richard Watson are reprinted by permission of the
University of Missouri Press. Copyright © 1995 by the Curators of the University of Missouri.
Cover © Mark Oatney/Digital Vision/GettyImages
Typeset in 11/12pt Minion by Phoenix Photosetting, Chatham, Kent
Printed and bound in Great Britain by CPI Antony Rowe, Chippenham, Wiltshire

What do you think about this book? Or any other Hodder Education title?
Please send your comments to educationenquiries@hoddereducation.com

www.hoddereducation.com

A mis padres, Andrés y Lourdes, que tan bien me han entendido siempre en todas mis lenguas, aunque sólo compartamos una.

To my parents, Andrés and Lourdes, who have always understood me so well across my languages, even though we only share one.

Contents

Preface   xiii
Tables and figures   xvi

1 Introduction   **1**
   1.1   What is SLA?   1
   1.2   Whence language? Description, evolution and acquisition   2
   1.3   First language acquisition, bilingualism and SLA   3
   1.4   Main concepts and terms   5
   1.5   Interdisciplinarity in SLA   7
   1.6   SLA in the world   7
   1.7   About this book   9
   1.8   Summary   10
   1.9   Annotated suggestions for further reading   10

2 Age   **12**
   2.1   Critical and sensitive periods for the acquisition of human language   12
   2.2   Julie, an exceptionally successful late L2 learner of Arabic   14
   2.3   Are children or adults better L2 learners? Questions of rate   16
   2.4   Age and L2 morphosyntax: questions of ultimate attainment   17
   2.5   Evidence on L2 morphosyntax from cognitive neuroscience   20
   2.6   L2 phonology and age   22
   2.7   What causes the age effects? Biological and other explanations   23
   2.8   A bilingual turn in SLA thinking about age?   25
   2.9   How important is age in L2 acquisition, and (why) does it matter?   27
   2.10 Summary   28
   2.11 Annotated suggestions for further reading   29

3 Crosslinguistic influences   **31**
   3.1   On L1–L2 differences and similarities   31
   3.2   Interlingual identifications   32
   3.3   Besides the L1   34
   3.4   First language influences vis-à-vis development   34
   3.5   Markedness and L1 transfer   37
   3.6   Can a cup break? Transferability   38
   3.7   Avoidance   39

3.8   Underuse and overuse   41
3.9   Positive L1 influences on L2 learning rate   42
3.10 First language influence beneath the surface: the case of information   44
      structure
3.11 Crosslinguistic influences across all layers of language   46
3.12 Beyond the L1: crosslinguistic influences across multiple languages   48
3.13 The limits of crosslinguistic influence   51
3.14 Summary   52
3.15 Annotated suggestions for further reading   54

4   The linguistic environment   55
4.1   Wes: *'I'm never learning, I'm only just listen then talk'*   55
4.2   Acculturation as a predictive explanation for L2 learning success?   58
4.3   Input for comprehension and for learning   59
4.4   Interaction and negotiation for meaning   60
4.5   Output and syntactic processing during production   62
4.6   Noticing and attention as moderators of affordances in the environment   63
4.7   Two generations of interaction studies   64
4.8   The empirical link between interaction and acquisition   65
4.9   Output modification   67
4.10 Learner-initiated negotiation of form   69
4.11 Negative feedback during meaning and form negotiation   71
4.12 The limits of the linguistic environment   76
4.13 Summary   79
4.14 Annotated suggestions for further reading   80

5   Cognition   82
5.1   Information processing in psychology and SLA   82
5.2   The power of practice: proceduralization and automaticity   84
5.3   An exemplary study of skill acquisition theory in SLA: DeKeyser (1997)   85
5.4   Long-term memory   87
5.5   Long-term memory and L2 vocabulary knowledge   88
5.6   Working memory   89
5.7   Memory as storage: passive working memory tasks   91
5.8   Memory as dynamic processing: active working memory tasks   92
5.9   Attention and L2 learning   93
5.10 Learning without intention   94
5.11 Learning without attention   95
5.12 Learning without awareness   96
5.13 Disentangling attention from awareness?   97
5.14 Learning without rules   99
5.15 An exemplary study of symbolic vs associative learning: Robinson (1997) 100
5.16 An emergentist turn in SLA?   102
5.17 Summary   105
5.18 Annotated suggestions for further reading   108

6   Development of learner language   110

6.1   Two approaches to the study of learner language: general cognitive and   110
formal linguistic

6.2   Interlanguages: more than the sum of target input and first language   112

6.3   Cognitivist explanations for the development of learner language   113

6.4   Formula-based learning: the stuff of acquisition   114

6.5   Four interlanguage processes   116

6.6   Interlanguage processes at work: Ge's *da*   118

6.7   Development as variability-in-systematicity: The case of Jorge's negation   119

6.8   Interlanguage before grammaticalization: the Basic Variety of naturalistic   121
learners

6.9   Patterned attainment of morphological accuracy: the case of L2 English   124
morphemes

6.10 More on the development of L2 morphology: concept-driven emergence   126
of tense and aspect

6.11 Development of syntax: markedness and the acquisition of L2 relativization   129

6.12 A last example of systematicity: cumulative sequences of word order   130

6.13 Fossilization, or when L2 development comes to a stop (but does it?)   133

6.14 What is the value of grammar instruction? The question of the interface   136

6.15 Instruction, development and learner readiness   138

6.16 Advantages of grammar instruction: accuracy and rate of learning   139

6.17 The future of interlanguage?   140

6.18 Summary   141

6.19 Annotated suggestions for further reading   143

7   Foreign language aptitude   145

7.1   The correlational approach to cognition, conation and affect in   146
psychology and SLA

7.2   Learning and not learning French: Kaplan vs Watson   147

7.3   Language aptitude, all mighty?   148

7.4   Aptitude as prediction of formal L2 learning rate: the MLAT   149

7.5   Is L2 aptitude different from intelligence and first language ability?   151

7.6   Lack of L2 aptitude, or general language-related difficulties?   152

7.7   Memory capacity as a privileged component of L2 aptitude   154

7.8   The contributions of memory to aptitude, complexified   156

7.9   Aptitude and age   158

7.10 Does L2 aptitude matter under explicit and implicit learning conditions?   159

7.11 Most recent developments: multidimensional aptitude   161

7.12 Playing it to one's strengths: the future of L2 aptitude?   163

7.13 Summary   164

7.14 Annotated suggestions for further reading   166

8   Motivation   168

8.1   The traditional approach: the AMTB and motivational quantity   168

8.2   Integrativeness as an antecedent of motivation   170

8.3   Other antecedents: orientations and attitudes   171
8.4   First signs of renewal: self-determination theory and intrinsic motivation   175
8.5   Motivation from a distance: EFL learners' orientations and attitudes   178
8.6   Language learning motivation: possible in situations of conflict?   181
8.7   Dynamic motivation: time, context, behaviour   183
8.8   Looking forward: the L2 Motivational Self System   185
8.9   Behold the power of motivation   188
8.10 Summary   189
8.11 Annotated suggestions for further reading   190

9   **Affect and other individual differences**   **192**
9.1   Personality and L2 learning   193
9.2   Extraversion and speaking styles   196
9.3   Learner orientation to communication and accuracy   198
9.4   Foreign language anxiety   200
9.5   Willingness to communicate and L2 contact   202
9.6   Cognitive styles, field independence and field sensitivity   205
9.7   Learning style profiles   206
9.8   Learning strategies   208
9.9   The future promise of an all-encompassing framework: self-regulation   211
      theory
9.10 Summary   212
9.11 Annotated suggestions for further reading   214

10 **Social dimensions of L2 learning**   **216**
10.1   The unbearable ineluctability of the social context   217
10.2   Cognition is social: Vygotskian sociocultural theory in SLA   218
10.3   Self-regulation and language mediation   219
10.4   Some findings about inner, private, and social speech in L2 learning   221
10.5   Social learning in the Zone of Proximal Development   224
10.6   Negative feedback reconceptualized   225
10.7   Interaction is social: Conversation Analysis and SLA   227
10.8   The CA perspective in a nutshell   228
10.9   Some contributions of CA-for-SLA   229
10.10   Learning in CA-for-SLA?   232
10.11   Grammar is social: Systemic Functional Linguistics   233
10.12   Learning how to mean in an L2   234
10.13   Language learning is social learning: language socialization theory   236
10.14   The process of language socialization: access and participation   237
10.15   The outcomes: what is learned through L2 socialization?   239
10.16   Sense of self is social: identity theory   241
10.17   L2 learners' identity and power struggles: examples from circumstantial   243
        L2 learning
10.18   Close impact of identities on L2 learning: examples from elective   245
        L2 learning

10.19 Technology-mediated communication as a site for socially rich L2 learning 248
10.20 Never just about language 250
10.21 Summary 251
10.22 Annotated suggestions for further reading 253

References 255
Author index 290
Subject index 296

Preface

Writing a graduate-level introduction to SLA has been a challenge and, like all challenges, both a curse and a blessing in the effort. Perhaps part of the difficulty comes from the fact that I have always looked at textbooks with suspicion. Textbooks constitute an attempt to enshrine the official story of a discipline because they are, as Kuhn (1962/1996, p. 137) noted, 'pedagogic vehicles for the perpetuation of normal' disciplinary knowledge. In so doing, they can become unwitting tools for the inclusion and exclusion of what counts as validated work, and they portray disciplines as frozen in time and space. Good textbook authors also seek to tell an interesting story to their readers, and good stories always demand rhetorical sacrifices. Some of the rough edges of a discipline, the ambiguous trends, the less 'tellable' details, must be shunned for the sake of coherence and linearity, and a big story rather than a collection of 'small stories' (Georgakopoulou, 2006) must be produced. Good stories also tell as much about the narrator as they do about an event or a discipline. Textbooks are, therefore, one-sided views of any field, even when at first blush they may come across as perfectly innocent compendiums of available-to-all, neutral knowledge. I was painfully aware of these dangers as I wrote this textbook, although I cannot honestly say that this awareness has helped me avoid the pitfalls.

Another difficulty that made this challenge exciting but agonizing, and one that I only discovered as I put myself to the task, is that there is a certain schizophrenia in writing for an imagined audience of students (the real consumers of textbooks) while still feeling the usual presence of one's research community (the audience I was accustomed to addressing as a writer of research articles). Namely, what might appeal to and benefit our students versus our fellow researchers can be radically different. Thus, not only the language, but also the content, must be thoroughly calculated when writing a textbook. My strategy for dealing with this challenge was to constantly ask myself: What would my students benefit from hearing about this topic? How can I make the material more engaging, the story more palatable? How can I make my passion for studying L2 learning contagious to them? I also drew upon the frequent questions, comments, reactions, complaints and amazements that my students have shared with me over a full decade of teaching SLA during each and every semester of my career thus far. I have had the good fortune of teaching these courses across four different institutional cultures, and this has afforded me a special kind of cosmopolitan view of the world of SLA that I truly owe to my students' intelligence, enthusiasm and candour. Their names are too many to mention, their faces all spread across the geography of the United States that I have travelled. But all of them have been a strong presence as I wrote. I do not know if I have succeeded in writing this book for my students before my colleagues, but I can honestly say I have tried my best to do so.

I owe a debt of gratitude to many people who have supported me in this project. It has been a privilege to work with the Understanding Language Series editors, Bernard Comrie and Greville Corbett, whose astute comments and unflagging enthusiasm benefited me chapter after chapter. Norbert Schmitt suggested my name to them when they thought of adding a volume about SLA to the series, and so this opportunity would not have come my way without his initiative. At Hodder Education, the professionalism, kindness and savvy author psychology of Tamsin Smith and Bianca Knights (and Eva Martínez, initially) have been instrumental in helping me forward as I completed the project. Two of my students, Sang-Ki Lee and Castle Sinicrope, kindly volunteered their time to help me with comments and with tedious editorial and bibliographical details when it was much needed.

A number of colleagues lent their time and expertise generously when I asked them to read chapters of the book: Zoltán Dörnyei, Scott Jarvis, Alison Mackey, Sandra McKay, Carmen Muñoz and Richard Schmidt. Each of them took the request seriously and provided supportive and critical feedback that I have tried to incorporate. During the spring of 2008, Linda Harklau (at the University of Georgia) and Mark Sawyer (at Temple University in Japan) used a prepublication manuscript of the book in their courses, and so did Robert Bley-Vroman and myself in two sections of SLA at the University of Hawai'i. I am most grateful to Linda, Mark and Robert (and their students and mine) for the faith they showed in the book. Knowing how diverse their disciplinary interests are, their positive reactions gave me confidence that the textbook would be friendly for use in very different contexts, and this was an important goal I had set for myself. I cannot thank enough Mark Sawyer, in particular, who became a most knowledgeable and engaged interlocutor during the last months of drafting and redrafting, emailing me his detailed feedback on each chapter after reading it with his students in Japan. Many conversations with Kathryn Davis, Nina Spada (during an unforgettable summer spent at the University of Toronto) and Heidi Byrnes have also found their ways into small decisions along the writing process. Michael Long, as always, is to be thanked for his faith in me and for his generous mentorship.

How I wish Craig Chaudron, my friend, mentor and colleague, could have been here too, to support me as he had so many times before with his meticulous and caring feedback, his historical wisdom and his intellectual rigour. His absence was always felt as I was writing this book, locating and leafing through volumes from the huge SLA library that I have inherited from him with much sadness. I thank Lucía Aranda for many mornings of yoga and many moments of teaching me fortitude, giving me encouragement and keeping me sane. John Norris stood by me with his usual hard-to-find thoughtfulness, uncompromising intellect and warm heart. He was and is a vital source of inspiration and strength.

With such rich help from so many experts and friends, one would think all the imperfections and flaws that arose as the project unfolded would have been caught along the way, and surely amended by the end of the process. Much to the contrary, I am cognisant of a number of shortcomings, all of which are my exclusive responsibility. In the end, if nothing else, the experience of writing a textbook – this textbook – has humbled me, has renewed my passion for SLA in all its forms and has reminded me that in the making of a discipline, as in life, we should not take anything for granted. I have dedicated this book to my parents, who have never taken for granted my life- and language-changing decisions. They have always given me the two gifts of unconditional love and deep understanding.

Lourdes Ortega
South Rim of the Grand Canyon
7 July 2008

Tables and figures

Table 2.1 Critical and sensitive periods in animal learning, based on Knudsen (2004)
Table 2.2 L2 morphosyntactic knowledge along the age of onset continuum
Table 2.3 Differences between near-native and native morphosyntactic knowledge
Table 4.1 Four early L2 recast studies
Table 5.1 Memory tasks and benchmarks in the study of storage memory capacity
Table 5.2 How can awareness versus automatic attention be measured in SLA studies?
Table 6.1 Nora's use of 'How do you do dese' over a school year
Table 6.2 Jorge's development of English negation
Table 6.3 The Basic Variety summarized (based on Perdue, 1982; Klein and Perdue, 1997)
Table 6.4 Morpheme accuracy order, from earliest to latest mastery
Table 6.5 Three broad developmental phases in the expression of temporality
Table 6.6 Stages in the development of perfective (*pretérito*) and imperfective (*imperfecto*) aspect in L2 Spanish
Table 6.7 Relative clauses in L2 German following Keenan and Comrie's (1977) Noun Phrase Accessibility Hierarchy
Table 6.8 The emergence of word order in L2 German according to Meisel et al. (1981)
Table 6.9 The emergence of questions in L2 English according to Pienemann et al. (1988)
Table 7.1 Design of the MLAT
Table 8.1 Watson vs Kaplan on three dimensions of motivation
Table 8.2 Main antecedents investigated in L2 motivation research
Table 8.3 The L2 Motivational Self System according to Csizér and Dörnyei (2005b)
Table 9.1 Affect and L2 learning
Table 9.2 Three models of personality employed in SLA research
Table 9.3 Six of the ten dimensions in the Ehrman and Leaver (2003) Learning Style Model
Table 9.4 Self-Regulatory Capacity in Vocabulary Learning Scale illustrated (Teng et al., 2006)

Figure 6.1 The two L2s by two L1s design of the ESF project (adapted from Perdue, 1982, p. 47)

1

Introduction

Language is one of the most uniquely human capacities that our species possesses, and one that is involved in all others, including consciousness, sociality and culture. We employ the symbolic system of language to make meaning and communicate with other fellow humans. We mean and communicate about immediate realities as well as about imagined and remembered worlds, about factual events as well as about intentions and desires. Through a repertoire of language choices, we can directly or indirectly make visible (or purposefully hide) our stance, judgement and emotions both towards the messages that we communicate and towards the addressees of those messages. In characteristically human behaviour, we use language not only to communicate to specific audiences, but sometimes to address ourselves rather than others, as in self-talk, and other times to address collective, unknown audiences, as when we participate in political speeches, religious sermons, internet navigation, commercial advertisements, newspaper columns or literary works.

We take it for granted that all humans have the potential to accomplish all of these amazing feats in whatever language(s) they happen to grow up with. But many people around the globe also do many of the same things in a language other than their own. In fact, whether we grow up with one, two or several languages, in most cases we will learn additional languages later in life. Many people will learn at least a few words and phrases in a foreign language. Many others will be forced by life circumstances to learn enough of the additional language to fend for themselves in selected matters of daily survival, compulsory education or job-related communication. Others still will choose to develop entire communication repertoires and use literary or scientific discourses comfortably and with authority in their second language or languages. Indeed, many people around the globe may learn, forget and even relearn a number of languages that are not their mother tongue over the course of their late childhood, adolescence and adulthood. The details of people's L2 learning histories can vary greatly, depending on where their studies, their families, their jobs and careers, and wider economic and political world events, take them. How do humans learn languages after they learn their first? This is the fundamental question that we will explore in this book.

1.1 WHAT IS SLA?

Second language acquisition (SLA, for short) is the scholarly field of inquiry that investigates the human capacity to learn languages other than the first, during late childhood, adolescence or adulthood, and once the first language or languages have been acquired. It studies a wide variety of complex influences and phenomena that contribute to the puzzling range of possible outcomes when learning an additional language in a variety of contexts. SLA began in the late 1960s as an emerging interdisciplinary enterprise that borrowed equally from the feeder fields of language teaching, linguistics, child language acquisition and psychology (Huebner, 1998). During the 1980s and 1990s SLA expanded considerably in scope and methodology, to the point that by the end of the twentieth century, after some 40 years of exponential growth, it had finally reached its coming of age as an autonomous discipline (Larsen-Freeman, 2000). The growth of SLA continues to be prodigious today. This book is about SLA, its findings and theories, its research paradigms and its questions for the future.

In this first chapter I have three goals. First, I situate SLA in the wider landscape of the language sciences and introduce readers to the aims and scope of this field. I then present definitions of the main terms I will use throughout the text. Finally, I explain the rationale for the rest of the book.

1.2 WHENCE LANGUAGE? DESCRIPTION, EVOLUTION AND ACQUISITION

How can language as a human faculty be explained? This fundamental question guides a number of language fields that pursue three kinds of understanding about language: descriptive, evolutionary and developmental.

A number of disciplines within the language sciences aim to provide an accurate and complete **description** of language at all its levels, such as sounds (phonetics and phonology), minimal grammatical signs (morphology), sentences (syntax), meanings (semantics), texts (discourse analysis) and language in use (sociolinguistics, pragmatics). The overarching question guiding these subfields of linguistics is: What is language made of, and how does it work? Human language manifests itself in spoken, signed and written systems across more than 6,500 languages documented to date (they are catalogued in *Ethnologue*; see Gordon, 2005). Despite this daunting linguistic variety, however, all languages, no matter how different from each other they may seem (Arabic from American Sign Language from Chinese from English from Spanish from Swahili), share fundamental commonalities, a universal core of very abstract properties. Thus, linguistics and its various subfields aim at generating satisfactory descriptions of each manifestation of human language and they also seek to describe the universal common denominators that all human languages share.

A different approach to explaining language as a human faculty is to ask not *what* or *how*, but *whence* and *why* questions: Whence in the evolution of the human species did language originate and why? This is the line of inquiry pursued in the study of language **evolution**, which focuses on the phylogenesis or origins of language. A fundamental area of research for cognitive scientists who study language evolution (and a source of disagreement among them) is whether human language evolved out of animal communication in an evolutionary continuum or whether the two are fundamentally different biological capacities (Bickerton, 2007; Tallerman, 2005). It is well known that other animal species are capable of using elaborate systems of communication to go about collective matters of survival, nutrition and reproduction. The cases of species as different as bees, dolphins and prairie dogs are well researched. However, none of these species has created a symbolic system of communication that even minimally approaches the complexity and versatility of human language. Chimpanzees, however, possess a genetic structure that overlaps 99 per cent with that of *Homo Sapiens*. Although they do not have a larynx that is fit for human language or hands that could be physically modulated for signing, some of these animals have been taught how to communicate with humans through a rudimentary gesture-based language and through computer keyboards. Bonobos, if reared by humans, as was the case of bonobo celebrity Kanzi, can achieve the comprehension levels of a two-and-a-half-year-old human and develop human-like lexical knowledge (Lyn and Savage-Rumbaugh, 2000). The conclusion that apes can develop true syntactic knowledge remains considerably more controversial, however. As you can guess, language evolution is a fascinating area that has the potential to illuminate the most fundamental questions about language.

For a full understanding of the human language faculty, we also need to engage in a third line of inquiry, namely the study of the ontogenesis of language: How does the human capacity to make meaning through language emerge and deploy in each individual of our species? This is the realm of three fields that focus on language **acquisition** of different kinds.

1.3 FIRST LANGUAGE ACQUISITION, BILINGUALISM AND SLA

In some parts of our world, most children grow up speaking one language only. It should be underscored that this case is truly the minority in the large picture of humanity, although it is the norm in many Western middle-class contexts. Perhaps because many researchers also come from these same contexts, this is the type of language acquisition that has been studied the best (for a good review, see Karmiloff-Smith and Karmiloff-Smith, 2001). The field that investigates these cases of monolingual language acquisition is known by the generic name of **child language acquisition** or **first language acquisition**. A robust empirical research base tells us that, for children who grow up monolingually, the bulk of language is acquired between 18 months and three to four years of age. Child language acquisition happens in a predictable pattern, broadly speaking. First, between the womb and the few first months of life, infants attune themselves to the prosodic and phonological makeup of the language to which they are exposed and they also learn the dynamics of turn taking. During their first year of life they learn to handle one-word utterances. During the second year, two-word utterances and exponential vocabulary growth occur. The third year of life is characterized by syntactic and morphological deployment. Some more pragmatically or syntactically subtle phenomena are learned by five or six years of age. After that point, many more aspects of mature language use are tackled when children are taught how to read and write in school. And as children grow older and their life circumstances diversify, different adolescents and adults will embark on very different kinds of literacy practice and use language for widely differing needs, to the point that neat landmarks of acquisition cannot be demarcated any more. Instead, variability and choice are the most interesting and challenging linguistic phenomena to be explained at those later ages. But the process of acquiring language is essentially completed by all healthy children by age four of life, in terms of most abstract syntax, and by age five or six for most other 'basics' of language.

In many parts of the globe, most children grow up speaking two or more languages simultaneously. These cases are in fact the majority in our species. We use the term 'bilingual acquisition' or 'multilingual acquisition' to refer to the process of learning two or more languages relatively simultaneously during early childhood – that is, before the age of four. The field that studies these developmental phenomena is **bilingualism** (or **multilingualism**, if several rather than two languages are learned during childhood). Two key questions of interest are how the two (or more) languages are represented in the brain and how bilingual speakers switch and alternate between their two (or more) languages, depending on a range of communicative needs and desires. The study of dual first language acquisition is only one area of this wide-encompassing field, which also includes the study of adult and child bilingual processing and use from psycholinguistic, sociolinguistic and educational perspectives (good introductions to bilingualism are Romaine, 1995; Wei, 2000).

The third field devoted to the study of the acquisition and development of the language faculty is **second language acquisition**, the subject of this book. SLA as a field investigates the human capacity to learn languages once the first language – in the case of monolingual children – or the first languages – in the case of bilingual or multilingual children – have been learned and are established. Naturally, this happens later in life, whether in late childhood, adolescence or adulthood. Sometimes, however, the individuals learning an additional language are still young children when they start acquiring the L2, maybe as young as three or four years old (remember by this early age most of the essential pieces of their mother tongue may be all in place). Thus, bilingualism and SLA can overlap in the early years, making it at times difficult to draw the boundaries between the two fields. Nevertheless, they are clearly two distinct disciplines with their own journals, conferences and affiliations in academia. There are also some key differences between the two fields. SLA often favours the study of late-starting acquirers, whereas bilingualism favours the study of people who had a very early start with their languages. Additionally, one can say that bilingualism researchers tend to focus on the products of bilingualism as deployed in already mature bilingual capabilities of children or adults, whereas SLA researchers tend to focus on the pathways towards becoming competent in more languages than one. This in turn means that in SLA the emphasis often is on the incipient stages rather than on ultimate, mature competence. A third difference is that bilingual research typically maintains a focus on all the languages of an individual, whereas SLA traditionally orients strongly towards the second language, to the point that the first language may be abstracted out of the research picture. In this sense, SLA may be construed as the pure opposite of monolingual (first) child language acquisition. Indeed, in both fields monolingual competence is often taken as the default benchmark of language development. We will return to this issue in the next section.

1.4 MAIN CONCEPTS AND TERMS

In this book, I will use the acronym **SLA** to refer to the field and discipline and I will reserve the term **L2 acquisition** to mean the process of learning additional languages, that is, the object of disciplinary inquiry itself. This terminological distinction is not always kept by all SLA researchers, but it has the advantage of giving us added accuracy of expression. By the same token, **acquisition** and **learning** will be used interchangeably as synonyms in this book. This is because, as you will see in Chapter 6 (section 6.14), although in the early 1980s there was an attempt at distinguishing between the two terms, in contemporary SLA terminology no such distinction is typically upheld.

The various terms used in SLA discourse to refer to the so-called 'mother tongue' and to the 'additional' language being learned or acquired need some clarification. As a useful shorthand, SLA researchers use the terms **mother tongue, first language** or **L1** generically to refer to the language (in the case of monolingual acquisition) or languages (in the case of bilingual or multilingual acquisition) that a child learns from parents, siblings and caretakers during the critical years of development, from the womb up to about four years of age. Conversely, the terms **additional language, second language** and **L2** are used in SLA to refer to any language learned after the L1 (or L1s). Of course, things are a lot more complicated in real life. For one, in the case of very young children who are exposed to several languages, it may be impossible to determine whether the two or more languages in question are being learned simultaneously (that is, bilingually or multilingually) or sequentially (that is, as an L2). In addition, the term 'L2' or 'second/additional language' may mean the third, fourth, tenth and so on language learned later in life. Thus, these labels should be taken to reflect more of an analytical abstraction made within a disciplinary tradition and less of a black-and-white reality.

There is some danger in using these dichotomous labels and, as you embark on reading this book about SLA, I would like you to be aware of it. When we oppose L1 acquisition to L2 acquisition, a subtle but dangerous monolingual bias seeps into our imagination. Namely, with the L1–L2 dichotomy as a foundation, the phenomenon under investigation can be easily construed as efforts by monolingual adults to add on a monolingual-like command of an additional language. This bias has been the reason for criticism and self-examination among SLA researchers in the last decade or so, starting with Vivian Cook, who was one of the earliest voices in the field to raise these concerns (see Cook, 1991, 2008). This bias is in part reminiscent of the same monolingual orientation in first language acquisition research, a strong influence on SLA during its formative years as a field. It is slowly receding, as new research emerges in SLA that is strongly influenced by studies in bilingualism and by research that addresses social dimensions of L2 learning. Throughout this book, I will do my best not to perpetuate a monolingual bias in my portrayals of SLA findings and theories. I will also refer to the people who are investigated by SLA researchers as **L2 learners**, but will alternate that traditional term with several other terms: **L2 users, L2 speakers, L2 writers** and, when I explain empirical studies, **L2 participants**. And I will usually use the feminine pronoun *she* to refer generically to them.

SLA as a field is interested in understanding the acquisition of second languages in both naturalistic and instructed contexts. **Naturalistic** learners learn the L2 through informal opportunities in multicultural neighbourhoods, schools and workplaces, without ever receiving any organized instruction on the workings of the language they are learning. **Instructed** learners learn additional languages through formal study in school or university, through private lessons and so on. In our globalized world, multifarious opportunities for L2 acquisition arise from travel, employment, migration, war, marriage and other such happy as well as unhappy (and elective as well as circumstantial) life events. Most people, therefore, learn additional languages from a **mixture** of both naturalistic and instructed experiences.

Many language teachers make a sharp distinction between foreign and second language teaching and are mystified when they realize the same distinction is often obliterated in SLA studies, as if learning contexts were of little consequence. Yet, it is important to realize that in SLA the term 'second' (or 'L2') is often used to mean 'either a second or a foreign language' and often 'both'. This is because, for certain research questions and research programmes, it may be useful to temporarily suspend the contextual distinction, for the sake of the analysis at hand. For other research questions and research programmes in SLA, however, distinguishing among specific contexts for L2 learning is in fact important. In such cases, SLA researchers make three (rather than only two) key contextual distinctions: **foreign**, **second** and **heritage** language learning contexts. The issue of contexts for L2 learning, however, is more complex than it appears at first blush, and even this three-way characterization of language learning contexts is often not enough. Throughout the book I will make every effort to contextualize SLA findings and theories, evaluating what we know about L2 acquisition vis-à-vis specific contexts and learner populations.

One way to investigate humans' capacities for learning second languages is to inspect the oral and written records learners produce when people use the new language. Hence, a long tradition within SLA research has been the study of what we call **interlanguage**, or learners' mental grammar, and the special variety of language that it generates when they speak or sign, interact, write, negotiate and express themselves in the L2, based on the mental representations they forge of the new grammar. Throughout the book, and particularly in Chapter 6, I will discuss representative interlanguage findings that help us understand the nature of what is acquired. As you read each chapter, you will find that many of the illustrations are in English as an L2. This is because SLA researchers have often focused their research efforts on English. This excessively narrow focus on English should be acknowledged as a limitation, since SLA is about any language that is acquired other than the first, not just about acquiring L2 English. Nevertheless, important SLA findings have been generated in L2s as varied as Arabic, Chinese, Dutch, French, German, Italian, Japanese, Korean, Portuguese, Spanish and Swedish. Whenever possible, and in order to strike some balance across L2s, I have chosen a non-English illustration over an English one.

Many other specialized terms have been coined by SLA researchers, but the few presented here will suffice for now. As we delve into the various topics covered in this book, I will highlight new important terms by emboldening them when they are first introduced in the text.

1.5 INTERDISCIPLINARITY IN SLA

SLA has always been a porous, interdisciplinary field. For some, it is most intimately connected to theoretical linguistics and first language acquisition (White, 2003), and for others to cognitive psychology (Doughty and Long, 2003). Other academic and professional communities view SLA rather differently and associate it most directly with the teaching of languages (Kramsch, 2000). These four fields (language teaching, linguistics, child language acquisition, psychology) were the ones that originally converged into key initial developments that gave rise to the field. As we will see throughout this book, SLA has maintained close theoretical and methodological ties with all four. In addition, it has developed more recent ties with other disciplines, notably bilingualism, psycholinguistics, education, anthropology and sociology.

In general, SLA is seen as a subfield or branch of applied linguistics, a mega-field that concerns itself with problems that have their roots in the intersections between language and society, education and cognition (see good reviews of applied linguistics in Davies and Elder, 2004; Schmitt, 2002). Currently SLA enjoys the scholarly outlets typical of all autonomous academic disciplines, including refereed journals, book series in international publishers, specialized conferences, related professional and scientific associations, and university-based doctoral programmes. This high degree of specialization and autonomy notwithstanding, the field remains as strongly interdisciplinary now as it was in its origins.

1.6 SLA IN THE WORLD

Many of the questions that SLA researchers investigate are highly relevant in the real world. A few examples here can serve as illustrations of the potential impact that SLA scholarship can have on real-world problems:

- Parents who regard elective bilingualism as a social value wonder what the optimal age might be for their children to begin learning a foreign language.

This question is related to the **age of onset** of acquisition, or how early or late in life one should start to learn an additional language after the mother tongue.

- Policy makers and educators in different countries debate appropriate policies for minority children who speak other languages at home and need to be schooled in the societal language. They also wonder how long it should take them to learn the majority language. This speaks to many questions related to **rate** of acquisition, or how fast progress can be made in various areas of the L2, and how long is long enough to learn an L2.

- Sympathizers of anti-immigrant movements in various countries lament that newcomers to their societies allegedly refuse to learn the language of the majority and persist in settling for rudimentary survival language skills only, even after decades of living in their new country. These are prejudices that may be better countered if we knew more about **ultimate attainment** or the absolute potential for complete acquisition of the L2 for different people under various learning circumstances that entail diverse needs and goals.

- Language teachers across institutions all over the world hotly debate whether students in their classrooms need to be directly taught grammar and vocabulary in order to get the basic building blocks of a language first, or whether it is better to somehow approximate in their classroom the richness of natural language meaning-making processes. Which of the two broad approaches, or variations thereof, would better prepare language students for what they will encounter once they are to use the L2 for their own purposes beyond the classroom? This is the question of **effective instruction**, which plays out across many educational contexts in the form of tensions between formal and experiential approaches to learning. Whether in second, foreign or heritage language teaching, the battles have been for and against traditional grammar teaching and alternative meaning-oriented proposals, including communicative language teaching, task-based curricula, content-based instruction and focus on form instruction.

As you see, SLA researchers have many opportunities to generate knowledge about L2 acquisition that illuminates these public questions and makes the lives of people who learn and use second languages a little bit better. Therein lies the challenge of contemporary SLA as a discipline: on the one hand, to advance our understanding of theoretical conundrums about the human language faculty and of L2 acquisition phenomena in need of description and explanation; and, on the other, to connect such understandings to the real-world problems that arise for people who, by choice or by circumstance, set out to learn a language other than their mother tongue.

1.7 ABOUT THIS BOOK

SLA research has unveiled a number of **universal influences** that help shape the nature, pace, route and finish line in the path towards learning a second language. Among these, the most important and well-studied sources of universal influence are *age, mother tongue, environment* and *cognition*. These universal influences mutually interact and exert an impact on the internal processor system and the *learner language* it generates whenever learners speak or sign, interact, write, negotiate and express themselves in the L2. We will examine these universal dimensions of L2 acquisition in Chapters 2 through 6. A defining feature of L2 acquisition is that individuals vary greatly both in how fast and how far they will go in learning their second (or third, or fourth, and so on) language. We refer to these two aspects of L2 acquisition as rate and ultimate attainment. The high degree of individual variation in both has attracted the attention of SLA researchers over the years, because it contrasts sharply with the relatively much more uniform nature of monolingual first language acquisition. Factors that help explain such **individual differences** are reviewed in Chapters 7 through 9, with special emphasis on two essential ones: *language aptitude*, which has a cognitive basis, and *motivation*, which has a social psychological basis.

The body of knowledge about additional language learning mapped in Chapters 2 through 9 covers much of the scholarship contributed by SLA researchers in the first three decades of existence of the field. It encompasses universal and individual sources of influence that impinge on the linguistic and cognitive dimensions of L2 development. Attempts to understand L2 acquisition would be incomplete, however, if we did not consider how social forces also shape what gets (and does not get) acquired, and why. We will examine **social dimensions** of L2 acquisition in Chapter 10. Much of the research examined in this last chapter of the book has been generated since the mid-1990s.

While this is the reading sequence that I chose for the book, some readers may have a special interest in some topics over others, and in such a case reading Chapters 2 through 10 in a different order, or reading some but not all chapters, is perfectly possible. You will also see a Summary section at the end of each chapter. This section could be used as a review tool, if you read it after completing a given chapter, as much as an advanced organizer, if you read it before delving into each chapter. In inviting you to proceed with the chapters in the order I had in mind when writing this book, or to rearrange the material and reinstate a different kind of linearity that may work better for you, I am mirroring in the reverse the move made by Argentinean novelist Julio Cortázar in his famous 1963 novel *Hopscotch* (in Spanish, *Rayuela*). Cortázar was a remarkable intellectual, political activist, and multilingual and multicultural human being. *Hopscotch*, besides being my favourite novel ever, is an excellent illustration (written in a single language!) of what **multicompetence** (the distinct competence developed by people who function in two or more languages rather than one; Cook, 1991) feels like for those who work, live and function in more than one language.

I hope you enjoy reading and using this book, in whichever order and manner best serve your style and purposes. My intent with it is to help you craft a personal understanding of the fascinating field of SLA, and perhaps even to entice you to become a contributor to scholarship in L2 acquisition in the future. Above all, I hope with this book I can share some of the enthusiasm that I have for investigating L2 acquisition and the immense respect I feel for people who live in and with second languages.

1.8 SUMMARY

- Second language acquisition ('SLA' for short) is the scholarly field of inquiry that investigates the human capacity to learn languages other than the first, during late childhood, adolescence or adulthood, and once the first language or languages have been acquired. It encompasses the study of naturalistic and formal language acquisition in second, foreign and heritage learning contexts. It seeks to understand universal, individual and social forces that influence what gets acquired, how fast, and how well, by different people under different learning circumstances.

- Three fields investigate questions about the ontogenesis or origins of language in each new member of our species and thus seek to contribute knowledge about the human language faculty and its acquisition: first language acquisition, bilingualism and SLA. First language acquisition investigates the development of the first language in children who grow up monolingual. Bilingualism focuses on the mature bilingual capabilities of children or adults who grow up with two or more languages from birth. SLA investigates additional language learning in late childhood, adolescence or adulthood and focuses on the pathways towards becoming competent in the second language.

- Both first language acquisition and SLA have traditionally taken monolingual competence as the default benchmark of language development. This monolingual bias has been problematized in contemporary SLA and will not be endorsed in this book.

- SLA is strongly interdisciplinary. Four feeder disciplines since the inception of the field are language teaching, linguistics, child language acquisition and psychology. More recent influences come from bilingualism, psycholinguistics, education, anthropology and sociology.

1.9 ANNOTATED SUGGESTIONS FOR FURTHER READING

There are a number of textbooks and handbooks about SLA. For true beginners, particularly if your main interest is in language teaching, Lightbown and Spada

(2006) and Scovel (2001) offer authoritative and readable highlights of the knowledge generated in SLA that is most relevant to teachers. If you wish to further your theoretical understanding, Mitchell and Myles (2004) present an engaging overview of the field from the viewpoint of the main theories that have been proposed to explain L2 learning. A historical predecessor, but still unsurpassed when it comes to SLA theories during the formative years of the field, is McLaughlin (1987). A recent collection that explains nine contemporary SLA theories via authoritative but accessible chapters written by distinguished proponents of each is VanPatten and Williams (2007). Other introductory books offer an approximation to SLA from either social (Saville-Troike, 2005), school teaching (Freeman and Freeman, 2001) or psycholinguistic (de Bot et al., 2006) perspectives.

If you already have some knowledge of linguistics and want to become familiar with the research side of SLA, both Larsen-Freeman and Long (1991) and Gass and Selinker (2001) provide classic overviews of the theories and findings, with a focus on the 1980s and 1990s, respectively. If you are a linguistics student with a good background in Chomskyan generative grammar, then Hawkins (2001) and White (2003) are the best advanced introductions to SLA research in this area; if you are interested in linguistic approaches beyond Chomskyan grammar, then Braidi (1999) is a good introduction. For encyclopedic treatments of SLA and consultation at the most advanced level, the best three sources are R. Ellis (2008), Ritchie and Bhatia (1996) and Doughty and Long (2003).

2

Age

Children acquiring their first language complete the feat within a biological window of four to six years of age. By contrast, the ages at which different L2 learners may begin learning the new language range wildly. Thus, age emerges as a remarkable site of difference between L2 and L1 acquisition. Perhaps for this reason, understanding the relationship between age and L2 acquisition has been a central goal since the inception of the field of SLA. Two issues are hotly debated. One pertains to the possibility that a biological schedule may operate, after which the processes and outcomes of L2 acquisition are fundamentally and irreversibly changed. This is also known as the Critical Period Hypothesis in L2 learning. The other issue relates to the possibility that there may be a ceiling to L2 learning, in the sense that it may be impossible to develop levels of L2 competence that are isomorphic to the competence all humans possess in their own mother tongue. Although the topic of age has been investigated profusely in SLA, clear or simple answers to vital questions about the relationship between age and L2 learning have not been easy to produce. As you will see in this chapter, the accrued findings remain difficult to reconcile and interpret, and many questions to understand universal age effects on L2 acquisition remain open.

2.1 CRITICAL AND SENSITIVE PERIODS FOR THE ACQUISITION OF HUMAN LANGUAGE

The idea that there may be an optimal, maybe even critical, age period for the acquisition of language entered SLA research through the work in neurolinguistics of Penfield and Roberts (1959) and Lenneberg (1967). Their ideas quickly became influential in a time when the new field called SLA was emerging. These authors contributed neurolinguistic data supporting a natural predisposition in the child's brain for learning the first language, together with anecdotal observations that children were also adept foreign language learners, when compared to adults. The possible causes tentatively identified at the time were the loss of plasticity undergone by human brains by year nine of life (Penfield and Roberts, 1959) or perhaps the completion by the onset of puberty of the process of lateralization, the specialization in all right-handed individuals of the left brain hemisphere for language functions (Lenneberg, 1967). The hypothesis of a critical period for L1 acquisition, and as a corollary for L2 acquisition, seemed natural in the late 1960s and continues to be considered plausible today.

Indeed, critical periods have been established for several phenomena in animal behaviour and in the development of certain human faculties, such as vision. The hypothesis is that there is a specific period of time early in life when the brain exhibits a special propensity to attend to certain experiences in the environment (for example, language) and learn from them. That is, the brain is pre-programmed to be shaped by that experience in dramatic ways, but only if it occurs within a biologically specified time period. To be more precise, two different kinds of age-related periods for learning are typically distinguished: critical and sensitive. Knudsen (2004) offers useful illustrations of both cases from outside the SLA field, which are summarized in Table 2.1. In much of the SLA literature, nevertheless, the terms 'critical period' and 'sensitive period' are discussed as essentially synonymous. This is probably because the available evidence with regard to the acquisition of an additional language is still too preliminary for SLA researchers to be in a position to make finer distinctions between the two notions (see also discussion by Harley and Wang, 1997).

Table 2.1
Critical and sensitive periods in animal learning, based on Knudsen (2004)

An example of a **critical period** is ocular representation in the cortex of kittens. This neurological process develops according to a narrow window of opportunity between 30 and 80 days of life. If kittens are deprived from the experience of viewing during this time window (because one eye is forced to remain closed), they will lose vision, simply because the closed eye and the brain failed to connect, as it were. That is, even though the now uncovered eye is optically normal, it fails to convey the visual information to the axons in the thalamus, which in turn cannot convey it to the neurons in cortical level IV. Another well-known example of a critical, irreversible period is filial imprinting in the forebrain of ducks, which makes them follow the first large moving entity between 9 and 17 hours of hatching and bond with it as the recognized parent. An example of a **sensitive period**, on the other hand, is barn owls' ability to process spatial information auditorily (indispensable for catching mice in the dark!). Young owls develop the ability to create mental maps of their space based on auditory cues at a young age. If either hearing or vision is impaired during this sensitive period, auditory spatial information will not be processed normally later in life. However, problems can be compensated for and reversed, even well past the sensitive period, if the visual or auditory impairment is restored and rich exposure to sound input is provided

The evidence for a critical or sensitive period for first language acquisition in humans is strong, although it remains far less well understood than the critical period for the development of, for example, ocular representation in our cortex. Some of the evidence comes from research involving sadly famous cases of children who, due to tragic circumstances, were deprived from regular participation in language use and social interaction until about the age of puberty. This was the case of Genie (recounted from different perspectives by Curtiss, 1977; Rymer, 1993) and of several feral children (discussed in Candland, 1993). Under such seriously detrimental circumstances, these adolescents could not learn the mother tongue to the level of their peers, even after they were rescued and efforts were made to 'teach' them language.

Additional evidence comes from studies of so-called postponed first language acquisition in the deaf population. This case, although unfortunate, accounts for about 90 per cent of deaf babies who are born to hearing parents with knowledge of only an oral language. In essence, these babies grow up without experiencing regular exposure to either spoken or sign input for the first six years of life and, therefore, they learn no first language until they are sent to school, precisely at around that age. The findings contributed over the years by Canada-based researcher Rachel Mayberry (2007; Mayberry and Lock, 2003) suggest that these children will usually exhibit incomplete acquisition of their late-learned first language. A study in the United States by otolaryngologists Mario Svirsky and Rachael Holt (2005) augments this evidence. These researchers tracked the vocabulary, grammar and speech perception abilities of 96 deaf babies who had received cochlear implants at ages one through four. These babies' spoken language began developing once awareness of sound was made possible through the implants. However, babies who received the implant after the age of 2 exhibited slower progress and overall lower performance in vocabulary and grammar (but not in speech perception skills), compared to babies who had their hearing restored before the end of the second year of life. The researchers interpreted the evidence cautiously but suggestively as indication that a sensitive period for L1 acquisition exists, and one that is much shorter than once thought (see also Svirsky et al., *2007*). In light of the new cochlear implant evidence, we can speculate that it may end after the first two years of life, at least for some aspects of acquisition.

For L2 acquisition, as well, it seems plausible to posit that there are sensitive periods for a number of language areas. But what does the record of SLA research tell us?

2.2 JULIE, AN EXCEPTIONALLY SUCCESSFUL LATE L2 LEARNER OF ARABIC

Striking SLA evidence bearing on the sensitive period hypothesis for L2 acquisition comes from a study conducted by Georgette Ioup and her colleagues (Ioup et al., 1994). These researchers investigated the limits of ultimate attainment achieved by Julie, an exceptionally successful L2 user. The study is unique, as you will appreciate, because Ioup et al. employed a rich case study methodology that yielded in-depth knowledge of Julie's L2 learning history as well as a wealth of data probing several areas of her L2 competence.

Julie was an L1 speaker of British English who had moved to Egypt at the age of 21 due to marriage to an Egyptian. She settled in Cairo with her husband, became a teacher of English as a foreign language (EFL) and had two children. Julie had never received formal instruction in the L2 and could not read or write in Arabic. Yet, she was able to learn Egyptian Arabic entirely naturalistically and regularly passed herself off as a native speaker. In fact, her family and friends remembered she was able to do so just after two and a half years of residence in the country. According to Julie, Arabic became the dominant language at home after the third year of residence in Cairo (although she also reports her children grew up to be competent bilinguals). Julie had been living in Egypt for 26 years at the time of the research.

In order to test whether her accent was truly indistinguishable from that of a native speaker, the researchers mixed Julie's recorded explanation of her favourite recipe with recordings of the same oral task by another six native and advanced non-native speakers of Arabic. Seven of 13 judges rated Julie as definitely native, whereas the other six rated her as non-native, and commented that a few small differences in vowel and consonant quality and in intonation had given her away. In another task testing her speech perception abilities, Julie proved herself able to pick out Egyptian from non-Egyptian accents among seven different varieties of Arabic with 100 per cent accuracy. She was a little bit less adept at discriminating a Cairo-sounding Egyptian accent from two other Egyptian regional accents, but so were six of the 11 native-speaking judges.

In order to probe her tacit knowledge of the Arabic language, Julie, 11 L1 Arabic control participants and another very advanced non-native speaker of Arabic were asked to do three other tasks that tested morphosyntactic phenomena. The first task was translating 12 sentences from English into Arabic. Here, once again, Julie made very few mistakes. For example, she translated 'went to the club' as *raahit linnaadi*, without dropping the preposition *l-* (Ioup et al. explain that this is necessary in Arabic to indicate the meaning is not just 'to' but 'into'; p. 82). The second task involved judging the grammaticality of selected Arabic sentences. Julie's judgements diverged from those of the majority of native speakers on only five out of 37 sentences. Apparently, she preferred the unmarked word order choice for questions and rejected variable word order alternatives that are also grammatical in Arabic. In the third task, Julie and the others had to answer the question 'who did X' in response to 18 recorded sentences containing cases of **anaphora**, a syntactic phenomenon so subtle that it is unlikely to be learned through explanations or through conscious analysis of the input. Anaphora refers to the binding of a pronoun to the right preceding noun in a sentence. For example, who does *she* refer to in the following sentence (p. 89)?

(1)   'Nadia saw Mona when she entered the room'
   a.   *Nadya shaafit mona heyya daxalit il-ooda*
   b.   *Nadya shaafit mona lamma daxalit il-ooda*

Who entered the room – Mona or Nadia? The preferred answer would be 'Nadia' for the English sentence. In Arabic, if the pronoun *heyya* is used, as in (1a), the preferred interpretation is that 'she' refers to Nadia, the more distant referent. Conversely, if *heyya* is omitted, as in (1b), the preferred interpretation for 'she' will be Mona, the closest referent outside the embedded clause 'when she entered the room'. Julie was able to correctly interpret the anaphora pronouns in two-thirds of the 18 items. She performed less well on the remaining six items, which involved relative clauses such as 'Ahmad bought the dress for the girl that you went to the lady that she angered' (*ahmad ishtara il-fustaan li-l-bint illi inta ruht li-s-sit illi heyya'za alit-ha*, p. 90). Not only Julie, but the 11 native speakers too, found it difficult to answer the question 'who angered whom' after they heard this sentence! However, only Julie went on to answer in a way that would mean she interpreted the overt pronoun *heyya* to refer to the closest referent in the sentence.

In their study, Ioup et al. also included another exceptionally successful late adult learner, Laura, who like Julie was married to an Egyptian and typically passed off as a native speaker. Unlike Julie, however, she held a Master's degree in modern standard Arabic from a US university and was a teacher of standard Arabic at a university in Cairo at the time of the study. Laura performed by and large as well as Julie in all tasks except for the speech perception one. In other words, she was also exceptionally successful. However, Ioup et al. concentrate on Julie and leave Laura in the background of their report, perhaps because Laura was an instructed learner and hence many more factors come into consideration. Julie, by being a purely naturalistic late learner, provides a strong test case for the Critical Period Hypothesis. Or rather, some would say, against it! In the end, it is difficult to evaluate what the small degree of variability in Julie's L2 outstanding performance means, particularly given that there was definitely some variability for native speaker responses across all measures too. Interestingly, Ioup (2005) herself believes the preponderance of evidence supports the existence of age-related sensitive periods for L2 learning.

2.3 ARE CHILDREN OR ADULTS BETTER L2 LEARNERS? QUESTIONS OF RATE

We all tend to think that children pick up languages speedily and effortlessly. Like many apparently undeniable truths (e.g. the earth does look very flat to our plain eyes, after all!), this assertion was questioned once it was submitted to systematic investigation. When in the 1970s several SLA researchers compared children and adults' L2 learning rate in second language environments, the findings unexpectedly were suggestive of an advantage for adults over children. For example, in two oft-cited studies conducted in the Netherlands, Catherine Snow and Marian Hoefnagel-Höhle (1977, 1978) found that adults and adolescents were better than children in terms of what they could learn in a 25-minute instruction session or up to a year of naturalistic exposure to L2 Dutch. Although the advantage of the older learners began diminishing after ten months or so, the findings were surprising because they flatly contradicted assumed critical period effects.

In a seminal article, Stephen Krashen, Michael Long and Robin Scarcella (1979) put a grain of salt on these findings. They concluded that older is better initially, but that younger is better in the long run. They based this conclusion on a review of 23 studies of L2 learning in second language contexts published between 1962 and 1979, comprising the available findings at the time. The 18 studies that involved short-term comparisons (with lengths of L2 exposure in a second language environment between 25 minutes and one year, rarely up to three years) suggested that adult learners and older children learned at a faster pace than younger children. This may have been in part an artefact of instruction or tests that demanded cognitive maturity and involved metalinguistic skills, because adults may be able to use cognitive and metacognitive abilities and strategies to learn many aspects of the L2 initially faster. Findings were available also from five long-term studies, however, of which the most widely cited to date were dissertations conducted at Harvard University and New York University, respectively, by Susan Oyama (1976) and Mark Patkowski (1980). The five long-term studies revealed that when accomplishments in the L2 were compared after at least five years of residence in the L2 environment (often after ten or 20 years, and for some participants up to 61 years), then young starters were clearly better than adult starters. Long (1990) reassessed the evidence on rate and ultimate attainment a decade later and reiterated the same conclusions, arguing that the rate advantage for adults dissipates after a little more than a year, because children eventually always catch up and surpass late starters. More recent findings from a study by Aoyama et al. (2008) also lend support to the same conclusion.

Age findings gleaned in foreign language contexts in the last few years, however, have complicated this picture (see studies in García Mayo and García Lecumberri, 2003; Muñoz, 2006). Particularly in the context of English learned in Cataluña (Muñoz, 2006), when early starters studying English from the age of eight to 16 were compared to late starters studying English from the age of 11 to 17, the late starters actually maintained an advantage that persisted well after five years of instruction (seven and nine years, respectively). That is, younger starters do not appear to catch up in these foreign learning contexts, where the L2 is only available through instruction. This is actually not surprising if we remember that the same time length of five years entails an intensity and quality of exposure to the L2 that can be radically different in foreign versus second language learning contexts. At three hours a week by nine months of school a year, students enrolled in a foreign language in school may experience as little as 540 hours of actual instruction and L2 exposure over five years. By contrast, in the same chronological time window, learners in L2 environments may accrue about 7,000 hours of L2 exposure (if we calculate a conservative four hours a day). (A sobering comparison is that children learning their L1 may receive of the order of 14,000 hours of exposure, also based on a conservative estimate of eight hours a day!) Thus, as Singleton (2003) suggests, in foreign language contexts considerably more than five years would be needed to capture any lasting differences between differing starting ages. Age may exert universal influences on the learning of a second language, but context moderates these universal effects and needs to be considered carefully.

2.4 AGE AND L2 MORPHOSYNTAX: QUESTIONS OF ULTIMATE ATTAINMENT

Contemporary SLA researchers interested in the question of critical or sensitive periods now consider it essential to take a long-term view on ultimate attainment and to evaluate the end state of L2 acquisition (Long, 1990; Hylstenstam and

Abrahamsson, 2003). Two lines of recent research have investigated this question, both focusing on the area of L2 morphosyntax.

The first line is correlational. That is, it uses statistical analyses to determine the degree to which two sets of numbers (age and scores on some L2 test) co-vary or behave in a similar pattern. Building on the pioneering studies by Oyama (1976) and

Table 2.2

L2 morphosyntactic knowledge along the age of onset continuum

Studies comparing knowledge of morphosyntax associated with varying ages of onset for L2 acquisition.

- Main research question: Are age and morphosyntactic attainment systematically related?
- Researchers' interpretation of results: Johnson and Newport interpreted their data in support of a critical/sensitive period. Birdsong and Molis's replication did not support all of the original findings.

Johnson and Newport (1989)	46 L1 Chinese and Korean adult speakers of L2 English who were college educated and had been living in the US for at least five years took a 276-item grammaticality judgement task. There was a statistically significant negative correlation of $r = -0.77$ between age of arrival (which ranged from 3 to 39) and grammaticality judgement score. The correlation was larger when only the 3 to 15 age group was examined ($r = -0.87$) and disappeared for the 17 to 39 group. The youngest group (3 to 7 years old when they arrived in the US) scored within the range of the NS control group, the adolescent group (who had arrived between 8 and 16 years of age) showed scores linearly declining with age and the group of adults (who had arrived at between 17 and 39 years of age) scored variably, without age holding any systematic relationship with their grammaticality intuitions. One late arrival (at age 23 upon arrival) scored 92% accurate, as high as native speakers
Birdsong and Molis (2001)	Exact replication of Johnson and Newport: 61 college-educated L1 Spanish speakers of L2 English took Newport and Johnson's grammaticality judgement task. The 29 early acquirers had arrived in the US between age 3 and 16 and had a mean length of residence of 12.2 years in the L2 environment. The 32 late acquirers had arrived at age 17 or older and had a mean length of residence of 10.5 years. There was a statistically significant negative correlation of $r = -0.77$ for the full sample between age of arrival and grammaticality judgement score. The early arrivals exhibited no variation, as they obtained near-perfect scores. There was a statistically significant negative correlation of $r = -0.69$ between age of arrival for the late arrival speakers and grammaticality judgement score. 13 late arrivals obtained 92% or higher scores, 3 above 95%. (The study also examined reported amount of L2 use. Amount of current L2 use was strongly related to judgements)

Patkowski (1980), it looks at L2 learners sampled to represent a wide range of ages of arrival in the L2 environment, as early as 0 years of life and as late as 50. In most of these studies, the target language investigated is English. The key question asked is: Are age and morphosyntactic attainment systematically related? Ultimate attainment is usually measured by comparing L2 learners' responses on grammaticality judgement tasks along differing arrival ages and against a native speaker baseline. The accumulated findings suggest that, by and large, learners who began acquiring the L2 before a certain age, which these studies locate to be around puberty, will tend to exhibit intuitions that are very close to those of native speakers of that language. The late learners' intuitions, by way of contrast, are not likely to be in the native speaker range, and this holds true regardless of the number of years, since they arrived in the L2 environment past puberty. In the details, however, the evidence presents a consistent dissonance. A glimpse of this dissonance can be seen in Table 2.2, which summarizes a study of this kind conducted by Jacqueline Johnson and Elissa Newport that has become a classic, and a replication by David Birdsong and Michelle Molis that failed to support the original findings.

Two results in Table 2.2 are noteworthy. First, in Johnson and Newport (1989) the relationship between age and grammatical intuitions abruptly disappears after around puberty, whereas in Birdsong and Molis (2001) grammaticality scores keep gradually declining across all ages beyond puberty. Second, both studies turned up one or more learners who had begun to learn the L2 as adults but scored within the native speaker range. These two patterns recur in a number of other partial replications of Johnson and Newport. For example, DeKeyser (2000) produced findings that resonate with those of Johnson and Newport (1989) with 57 Hungarian US immigrants but Flege et al. (1999) obtained a pattern of results similar to that of Birdsong and Molis (2001) with 240 Korean permanent residents in the United States.

The second parallel line of work on age differences and L2 morphosyntactic development pertains to studies that are specifically designed to investigate the upper limits of successful late L2 learning. The focus is, like in Ioup et al. (1994), on exceptional learners who seem to have reached native-like ultimate attainment, often with L2s other than English. Even though these cases have traditionally been considered purely exceptional, Birdsong speculates that they may actually account for as much as 5 per cent to 25 per cent of cases of learners who are given 'a fair chance of success' (Birdsong, 1999b, pp. 14–15). The method of choice has been to compare their performance on grammaticality judgement tasks to that of native-speaking controls, sometimes using retrospective interviews to probe learners' explanations of their choices. The question at stake in this kind of study is: How native is really 'near-native'? Table 2.3 summarizes two oft-cited empirical studies of this kind, both with highly successful L2 French learners. R. Coppieters (1987) found strong evidence for the critical period but David Birdsong's (1992) replication of the same study found strong evidence against it. Interestingly, several studies, using a similar line of evidence but slightly different designs, have also replicated this pattern of conflicting findings. For example, Sorace (1993) found evidence favouring a critical period for morphosyntax among 44 L2 Italian learners,

Table 2.3
Differences between near-native and native morphosyntactic knowledge

Studies scrutinizing knowledge of morphosyntax in L2 speakers who achieve exceptionally high levels of ultimate attainment and are identified as near-native outside the laboratory (typically, cases of L2 acquisition after puberty)

- Main research question: Can some exceptionally successful L2 acquirers be indistinguishable from native speakers in their morphosyntactic knowledge?
- Researchers' interpretation of results: Coppieters: No, near-native speakers' L2 knowledge is different from true monolingual native speakers. Birdsong: Yes, some rare, exceptional near-native speakers cannot be distinguished from native speakers even under tight laboratory scrutiny

Coppieters (1987)	21 L2 French speakers, all of whom were highly successful and educated French users who had begun learning the L2 after puberty. They did a grammaticality judgement task and were interviewed. Their average grammatical intuitions on the task were three standard deviations away from the average of native speaker controls. Their rationalizations for their judgements during the interview were different from those of native speakers. Subtle syntactic-semantic and morphosemantic differences of knowledge distinguished nativeness from near-nativeness
Birdsong (1992)	Partial replication of Coppieters: 20 L2 French speakers all of whom were highly successful and educated French users who had begun learning the L2 after puberty. Their age of arrival in France was 19 to 48 and their L1 was English. Of these, 15 participants performed on a grammaticality judgement task within the native speaker range. There was a negative correlation of $r = -0.51$ between age of arrival and scores in this late-starter-only sample

but both White and Genesee (1996), with 89 L2 English learners, and Montrul and Slabakova (2003), with 64 L2 Spanish learners, found evidence against it.

The empirical dissonance illustrated in Tables 2.2 and 2.3 is persistent. Simply put, doubts as to whether a critical period for L2 learning really exists will not go away as long as studies continue to show that there is no sharp drop in grammatical intuitions after some supposedly critical age, and as long as cases of exceptionally successful late learners are discovered against the backdrop of the overwhelming tendency for early starters to 'succeed' and for late starters to 'fail'.

2.5 EVIDENCE ON L2 MORPHOSYNTAX FROM COGNITIVE NEUROSCIENCE

Knowledge about how the brain handles language is highly relevant to any discussions of critical periods for L2 learning. For a decade now, the new field of cognitive neuroscience has contributed interesting evidence on the issue. The data are elicited with neuroimaging techniques such as event-related potentials, which offer excellent temporal resolution and make it possible to measure in milliseconds the activation patterns of neural networks involved in different cognitive operations while the brain is processing language stimuli. The converging findings favour a critical period interpretation for L2 morphosyntax.

Some researchers have shown that localization of language functions in the brain is less lateralized in late bilinguals (more right hemisphere activation is observed) than in early bilinguals and monolinguals. This is the conclusion supported by research conducted in France by neuroscientists Stanislas Dehaene and Christophe Pallier (see Dehaene et al., 1997; Pallier et al., 2003). Likewise, Helen Neville and her lab in the United States have produced evidence that, when engaged in certain kinds of L2 syntactic processing, the bilingual brains of people who began learning their L2 later in life (eight years or older in most of these studies) show clear different activation patterns from those of monolingual and early bilingual brains. Such age-related differences disappear when brain activation is inspected during the processing of L2 semantic stimuli. For example, Weber-Fox and Neville (2001) investigated Chinese–English bilinguals who were first immersed in the L2 environment anywhere between age one and past age 15. Those bilinguals who were exposed first to the L2 after year seven processed closed-class words (i.e. **function words** like *with, the, some*) differently from the early bilinguals and the monolingual controls, whereas open-class words (i.e. **content words** like *nose, stored, glad*) yielded no major differences in brain activation patterns across groups. Germany-based researcher Anja Hahne (2001) also found that her Russian–German bilingual participants, all of whom had learned German as their L2 after the age of 10, processed syntactically anomalous sentences of the kind *Das Geschäft wurde am geschlossen* ('The shop was being on closed') statistically significantly different from monolinguals, whereas no differences were found between the two groups with semantically anomalous sentences. Based on such findings, these and other neurocognitive researchers (e.g. Ullman, 2001) have suggested that the learning of syntactic functions (in the L1 or the L2) is fundamentally different from the learning of semantic features. Specifically, they propose that syntax involves computational learning mechanisms and is constrained by a biological schedule, and that semantics draws on associative learning mechanisms and is free from critical period constraints.

Other neurocognitive scientists, however, offer different interpretations of the findings. For example, in the United States Lee Osterhout and colleagues (Osterhout et al., 2002) demonstrated that the different neural activation patterns uncovered for function versus content words could be also explained by the differential word length in both kinds of stimuli (content words are typically longer, and this naturally can affect processing). Italian researchers Daniela Perani and Jubin Abutalebi (2005) suggest that it is not the age of onset but the degree of active use of the L2 that matters when explaining degrees of brain activation. They argue that the neural systems serving L2 and L1 grammatical processing are the same, and that higher attained proficiency and higher daily exposure to the L2 are independently correlated to lower activation patterns. Furthermore, they report on studies that show that, even when attained proficiency is kept constant, the brains of L2 speakers who have less daily exposure to the L2 exhibit higher degrees of activation in the left prefrontal cortex. They claim this parallels the general neurocognitive finding that increased practice leads to lower levels of neural activation, because with more practice the same processing task will consume less resources (see Chapter 5, section 5.2). Along the same lines of reasoning, Osterhout and colleagues (Osterhout et al., 2008) have initiated a research programme that involves measuring the brain activity of zero-level beginning learners while they process L2 stimuli, longitudinally as they progress through their regular college-level foreign language courses. They have found that brain activation patterns can change in degree and location just after experiencing about four months or 80 hours of college instruction. At least for certain L2 forms, the brain's activation patterns become similar to the patterns observed in fluent L1 users.

Thus, the neuroscience findings, although fascinating, should not be interpreted hastily because, at this early stage of our knowledge about brain and language, it is difficult to evaluate what they may mean for the critical period discussion. As Marinova-Todd et al. (2000) pointed out, given what we know about the plasticity of the brain, any age-related differences in brain location and neural activity patterns may be as much a result of the brain's architecture shaping how subsequent linguistic experience is processed and used for L2 learning, as it could be the result of the brain having been shaped by previous experience. Evidence in favour of a critical period explanation will come only when neuroscientists can establish beyond doubt that the former, and not the latter, is actually the case.

2.6 L2 PHONOLOGY AND AGE

Unlike subtle morphosyntactic knowledge, which may be difficult to evaluate outside the laboratory, foreign accents are so conspicuous that they can often be detected by the untrained ear. Thus, we all tend to think that, if there are sensitive periods for some areas of L2 learning but not others, then phonology must be one of those areas.

This is Tom Scovel's (1988, 2000) position. For Scovel, speech has a special status when it comes to critical periods because 'pronunciation is the only part of language which is directly "physical" and which demands neuromuscular programming' (1988, p. 62). For example, one-third of the human brain's cortex is dedicated to controlling motor skills in the lower face, lips, tongue and throat, all involved in the production of speech. After reviewing a large number of early studies of foreign accent detection in his 1988 seminal book, he concluded that, in study after study, non-native speaking samples were consistently and accurately detected by native-speaker judges. Likewise, the evidence accumulated since 1988 overwhelmingly shows that foreign-sounding accents are likely to develop when the L2 is first learned later in life.

The study of 240 L1 Korean speakers of L2 English by James Flege and colleagues (briefly mentioned in section 2.4) also lends support to Scovel's suggestion that speech is different. Flege et al. (1999) found that the two moderating variables of self-reported amount of L2 use and amount of education in the L2 were more related to the morphosyntactic results than to the pronunciation results. This pattern of findings suggests that acquisition of phonology may be more impervious to non-biological influences such as L2 use and education, and therefore more strictly tied to biological schedules, than other areas of the L2. Nevertheless, Flege (e.g. 1987, 1999) proposes an explanation for the observed age-related phonology effects that is remarkably different from Scovel's.

According to Flege, phonetic categories or mental representations of speech sounds in the L1 are stabilized by age five to seven. After that point, new phonetic contrasts will be processed through such an L1 filter, and hence it is more difficult, although not biologically impossible, to detect and produce L2 categories that are not salient. Ironically, then, foreign accents may arise 'not because one has lost the ability to learn to pronounce, but because one has learned to pronounce the L1 so well' (Flege, 1999, p. 125). The older people are when they begin learning an L2, the more settled they may be in their L1 perceptions. In other words, instead of viewing neurophysiological maturational constraints as the main explanatory factor for the development of L2 phonology, as Scovel does, or as a result of neurofunctional reorganization during development, as cognitive neuroscientists do, Flege puts the explanatory emphasis on psychoperceptual and phonetic causes related to previous massive experience with the mother tongue.

We have said that there is clear evidence that accents are likely to develop when the L2 is first learned later in life. This notwithstanding, and paralleling the findings for L2 morphosyntax, there is also evidence in L2 phonology of exceptional post-pubertal learners whose accents are not recognized as foreign even under close scrutiny in the laboratory. Julie and Laura (Ioup et al., 1994) were the first cases, but several more have emerged by now. Notably, Theo Bongaerts and his colleagues in the Netherlands have produced a number of such studies involving very advanced, late L2 learners of English and, in subsequent replications, of French and Dutch (see Bongaerts, 1999). These exceptional learners shared two features. They had all received considerable amounts of high-quality L2 instruction and they all self-reported high levels of motivation and concern to sound native-like. Although her results are less dramatic, Alene Moyer (1999) also found that judges did identify as native the accent of one of 24 advanced L2 German users in the United States, all of whom had begun learning the L2 after the age of 12. In sum, in L2 phonology as in L2 morphosyntax, it is not impossible (although it is admittedly rare) to attain native-like levels. Indeed, it is remarkable that the feat has been attested with some exceptionally successful late L2 learners for target languages as different as Arabic, Dutch, English, French and German.

2.7 WHAT CAUSES THE AGE EFFECTS? BIOLOGICAL AND OTHER EXPLANATIONS

As you can surely appreciate by now, the interpretation of the evidence on age-related effects on L2 learning is far from being settled. For one thing, the interpretation of findings from correlational data on morphosyntax is subject to a number of methodological criticisms, particularly a discussion about whether an abrupt drop-off at around puberty or a gradual decline across ages is being observed in the data (see Table 2.2; see also discussion in Birdsong, 1999a, 2006). In addition, the critical period explanation does not sit well with the fact that one can always find exceptional learners who began learning the L2 after puberty, often in their twenties, and who perform within the range of native-speaker controls in their grammatical intuitions or go undetected as non-native speakers by multiple judges.

Furthermore, it is possible to conclude that age-related differences exist in how a skill or ability is learned, and to propose explanations that do not invoke pre-programmed biological changes in the brain as an underlying cause. One such explanation lies with previous and entrenched knowledge of the L1 and L1–L2 interactions, instead of biology. In L2 phonology, as we saw, James Flege takes such a position. In this view, 'age is an index of the state of development of the L1 system. The more fully developed the L1 system is when L2 learning commences, the more strongly the L1 will influence the L2' (Piske et al., 2001, p. 196). Other SLA researchers emphasize general socio-educational and motivational factors in connection to age effects on L2 learning. This is the position espoused by Ellen Bialystok and Kenji Hakuta (1999) and by Catherine Snow, Stefka Marinova-Todd and their colleagues (Marinova-Todd et al., 2000), among others. They argue that socio-educational and motivational forces are so radically different in the lives of adolescents and adults, when compared to children's lives, that language attainment differences can be expected, but they are probably a consequence of experience and socialization, and not biological or insurmountable in nature.

Other SLA researchers argue that the posited sensitive period (or periods) is indeed real (e.g. Hylstenstam and Abrahamsson, 2003). In their view, there is a not well-understood but nevertheless biologically determined impossibility, after a certain age, to continue using the implicit learning processes that are best suited for natural language learning during the early years of human life (e.g. DeKeyser, 2003; Ioup, 2005). This kind of explanation is compatible with Robert Bley-Vroman's (1990) well-known Fundamental Difference Hypothesis, which posits that the acquisition process undergone by children and adults is fundamentally different because children posses the innate ability to intuit the L1 grammar, whereas adults have lost this ability and thus need to resort to problem solving and conscious attention to handle L2 learning (see also further discussion in Chapter 7, section 7.9).

While those scholars who favour the critical period position may turn out to be right, thus far they have been unable to produce a clear answer as to what biological, irreversible changes may cause the brain to use implicit processes when learning language up until a certain age but not later. As mentioned in section 2.1, lateralization and plasticity are neurobiological processes that have been considered by various researchers. Another process is myelination, or the development during the first 10 or 12 years of life of white-matter substance around the brain's nerve fibres which protects the nerves and enables faster conduction of information across nerve cells (Pulvermüller and Schumann, 1994; Pujol et al.,

2006). An additional suggestion is pubertal increases in estrogen or testosterone (Ullman, 2004). To date, however, we lack sufficient evidence for neurological or neurochemical correlates that can support unequivocally a critical periods explanation (see Singleton, 2005, for more extended discussion).

In sum, it would be premature to proclaim that critical periods for L2 learning exist when so much discordant evidence keeps emerging across relatively diverse bodies of research. The preponderance of evidence suggests that late and adult L2 acquisition generally results in lower levels of ultimate attainment and more individual variability than is observed for L1 and very early L2 acquisition. However, the field is of two minds as to whether critical periods for L2 acquisition exist. Age effects on L2 learning are pervasive and undisputed, but satisfactory explanations, biological or otherwise, for the observed effects are yet to be conclusively produced.

2.8 A BILINGUAL TURN IN SLA THINKING ABOUT AGE?

Matters surrounding age effects on L2 learning have become even more complex in recent SLA discussions, as two threads of evidence have become available to the research community.

The first new thread of evidence pertains to the realization that age effects may be present in additional language acquisition much earlier than previously thought, perhaps by age four. The claim is far from conclusive but appears to be reasonably promising because it converges out of diverse research programmes. Thus, Hyltenstam and Abrahamsson (2003) noted that small but important morphosyntactic differences are detected in the written and spoken performance of extremely young L2 child starters, if researchers take care to recruit participants who began L2 learning at such early ages (e.g. below 6) and if they employ fine-grained elicitation and analysis procedures. Likewise, in L2 phonology Flege et al. (1995) found very young L2 starters who did not attain the native-like levels of pronunciation we all assume of pre-pubertal children learning other languages. In the neighbouring field of bilingual research, similar findings have been emerging for some time. For example, Catalan researcher Núria Sebastián-Gallés and her colleagues (Sebastián-Gallés et al., 2005) investigated lexical representations of early versus simultaneous bilinguals by asking them to tell apart Catalan L2 words and non-words on a lexical decision task. They found that participants who had started to be exposed to Catalan at age 4 or earlier, but not from birth, did less well on this lexical decision task than participants for whom both Catalan and Spanish were available from birth. As you will remember from an earlier discussion in this chapter, the case of postponed first language development among deaf babies after cochlear implants (Svirsky and Holt, 2005) is consistent with the view that there may be extremely early age effects for (first and second) language learning. Most of the SLA findings and associated explanations for age effects in L2 learning have been generated under the assumption of a much later biological window, namely around age 6 for phonology and perhaps around puberty or up to age 15 for morphosyntax. If age effects do set in as extremely early in life as age two or four, the long-held assumption that an early start guarantees complete and successful L2 acquisition loses much of its power. Moving the onset of age effects into the very first years of life also blurs the traditional distinction between L2 and bilingual learners. Thus, a new range of theoretical and empirical arguments in SLA may have to be considered in the future, and SLA researchers may need to turn to the study of bilingualism when reassessing the evidence.

A second recent realization for which increasing evidence is mounting is that the actual relative amounts of L2 and L1 use at the time of study may be central to the task of gauging age effects. This is the so-called issue of language activation (also called language dominance in bilingual studies) (see Birdsong, 2005; Perani and Abutalebi, 2005). For example, findings offered by Flege and MacKay (2004) suggest that young starters who do not live up to expectations of complete success in L2 pronunciation may present low L2-use profiles and spend much of their time using the L1. The study by Sebastián-Gallés et al. (2005) also revealed a similar effect for amount of L2/L1 use, even in the simultaneous (from birth) bilinguals they studied. Their participants did best in the language they were more actively and consistently using in daily activities at the time of study. When the putative critical age is pushed back to a much earlier point in life, and the age effects turn out to be entangled with language activation and practice effects, it becomes imperative to re-evaluate the extant evidence with a new lens.

Finally, the findings on age-related L2 learning effects are grounded in the widely held assumption in SLA that the obvious benchmarks for evaluating L2 acquisition and L2 competence are L1 acquisition and L1 competence. In light of the real possibility that bilingualism and language activation and dominance effects operate across all ages, beginning as early as age two of life, we may need to revise this assumption in the future. Quite simply, it may be that bilingual attainment, whether in early or late bilinguals, cannot be directly compared to monolingual attainment. At least David Birdsong (2005, 2006) in the United States, Birgit Harley and Wenxia Wang (1997) in Canada, Vivian Cook (1991, 2008) in the United Kingdom and David Singleton (2001, 2003) in Ireland have raised the possibility that such a comparison may be misguided. Cook (2008) explains the dangers of comparing L2 users with monolinguals eloquently:

> There is no reason why one thing cannot be compared to another; it may be useful to discover the similarities and differences between apples and pears. SLA research can use comparison with the native speaker as a tool, partly because so much is already known about monolingual speakers. The danger is regarding it as failure not to meet the standards of natives: apples do not make very good pears. Comparing L2 users with monolingual native speakers can yield a useful list of similarities and differences, but never establish the unique aspects of second language knowledge that are not present in the monolingual.

(p. 19)

What could, then, be taken as a fair point of comparison to gauge attainment in age studies? Citing the work on multicompetence and bilingualism by Cook (1991) and Grosjean (1989), Singleton (2003) suggests that:

> the appropriate comparison in the investigation of age effects in L2 acquisition is not between post-pubertal L2 beginners and monoglot native speakers but between post-pubertal L2 beginners and those who begin to acquire an L2 in childhood.
>
> (p. 10)

It may well be that the existing evidence on L2 critical periods will need to be reinterpreted as pointing at a fundamentally different state of language cognition for monolinguals and bilinguals, and a different state of overall readiness for language activation of the L1 and the L2 depending on current amount of use of each, rather than a fundamental difference between early monolingual and late L2 acquisition. If bilingualism and language activation/dominance effects operate across all ages, then the explanatory onus would subtly move away from biology and on to changes in the brain and in cognitive processing that are shaped by the experience that results from being exposed to more than one language simultaneously or sequentially and across varying ages. The putative impossibility to attain nativelikeness after a certain age, if reinterpreted under a bilingual lens by SLA researchers themselves, may turn out to mean that it is impossible for bilinguals to be monolinguals. This would be inconsequential both from a theoretical and a practical viewpoint. After all, saying that L2 learners cannot reach levels that are isomorphic with monolingual competence would be a non-issue in a world in which bilingualism would be considered the default state of the human language faculty.

In the end, these other recent strands of research suggest that a number of environmental (e.g. opportunities for exposure and use of high-quality L2 input and amount and quality of L1 use) and socio-affective factors (e.g. motivation, L2 instruction and overall education) may mutually interact and become important predictors of success at earlier as well as later starting ages. Thus, these additional variables deserve much more research attention in the future. We can also predict, or at least hope, that many more SLA researchers in the future will turn to new methods and designs that enable them to investigate the bilingualism of early and late L2 learners in their own right, not as deficient or deviant replicas of monolinguals.

2.9   HOW IMPORTANT IS AGE IN L2 ACQUISITION, AND (WHY) DOES IT MATTER?

As we have seen in this chapter, over its more than 40 years of existence the field of SLA has contributed a wealth of research on how age universally influences L2 acquisition. Having answers to the questions raised by age effects in L2 acquisition is important because it would make us go a long way in our quest for understanding the human language faculty as a whole. In addition, the main findings about age and L2 acquisition generated by SLA researchers to date can be used productively to advocate for various populations of L2 learners.

First, knowing that young children may have a slow start when acquiring an L2 can be an important research-based argument against harmful attempts to promote so-called sink-or-swim educational policies that attempt to reduce or even completely withdraw the first and second language support that is to be provided to language minority children by schools. Such policies have been dangerously gaining ground in the United States for some time now (see Crawford, 2000). Similarly, knowing that older children and adults can have an initial L2 learning advantage for rate over early starters, and that this advantage may last for about five years in second language environments and for even longer in foreign language settings, can also help problematize misguided attempts to mandate public schools to begin foreign language instruction in the first years of elementary education without first evaluating whether the local resources and conditions can appropriately sustain such efforts throughout the full length of schooling (see the discussion of these issues in the United States in Lally, 2001). This trend is regrettably expanding, particularly in areas of the world where English is seen as the default foreign language (e.g. Nunan, 2003). The third important age-related finding to remember is that amazingly successful late learners such as Julie and Laura exist, and that perhaps they account for as much as 5 per cent to 25 per cent of best-scenario learning cases (Birdsong, 1999b). This is hopeful for language teachers and educators. Indeed, knowing that many of them are highly motivated students who also enjoyed high-quality instructional experiences (Bongaerts, 1999; Moyer, 1999) is certainly good ammunition for lobbying in favour of increasing investment of material and human resources for the improvement of second and foreign language education.

2.10 SUMMARY

- In terms of L2 learning rate, adults and older children enjoy an initial advantage over young children that may last over up to one year, sometimes up to three years, particularly if they are tested through tasks that demand cognitive maturity and involve metalinguistic skills. After five years, however, early starters catch up and are better than late starters in second language contexts. In foreign language contexts, by contrast, the lagged advantage for an earlier start has not been observed, even after five years.

- In terms of L2 ultimate attainment, most learners who begin acquiring the L2 before a certain age, typically before puberty, will develop levels of morphosyntactic and phonological competence that are very close to those of native speakers of that language. Post-pubertal learners, however, are not likely to perform in the native speaker range, and this holds true regardless of the number of years they have resided in the L2 environment.

- Exceptions to the observed success and failure tendencies associated with age exist. Thus, some adult starters can achieve native-like levels in their L2, or at least extremely high levels that are near-native. Conversely, an early start does not guarantee complete and successful L2 acquisition in all cases, as some children who start learning the L2 at an age as early as four or even two may be found to differ from native speaker performance in subtle ways. In the former case, exceptions appear to be related to unusually high motivation and high quality of instruction, whereas in the latter case they appear to be associated with high L1-use levels (that is, with high L1 activation or L1 dominance).

- Several explanations for the observed age effects have been proposed and are considered plausible by different SLA researchers. Those in favour of a critical period explanation posit that, after a certain age, it is biologically impossible for the human brain to use the same processes that were involved in learning the L1. Instead, other processes, such as reasoning and problem solving, are summoned during post-pubertal L2 learning. Several neurological and neurochemical causes have been considered (including lateralization, plasticity, myelination and pubertal increases in oestrogen or testosterone) but the empirical evidence is still unavailable for any of them. Of the researchers who favour non-biological explanations, some have considered pre-existing knowledge of the L1 and others have emphasized socio-educational and affective-motivational forces.

- Recent research suggests that bilingualism effects (e.g. L1–L2 interactions) and language activation and dominance effects (i.e. relative amounts of L1 versus L2 use) operate across all ages, beginning as early as age two. This evidence suggests that it may be misguided to compare bilingual attainment to monolingual attainment. Thus, in the future, research programmes may need to shift away from the emphasis on a fundamental difference between monolingual child L1 acquisition and monolingual-like adult L2 acquisition and towards investigating changes in the brain and in cognitive processing that are shaped by the experience that results from being exposed to more than one language simultaneously or sequentially and across varying ages.

2.11 ANNOTATED SUGGESTIONS FOR FURTHER READING

Newcomers to the field of SLA are often overwhelmed by the many arguments and data that appear to equally support and contradict the Critical Period Hypothesis in L2 learning. It is important to maintain an open mind and an attentive eye when you delve into this literature. With a topic as controversial as this one, it is good to first read the brief overviews by Scovel (2000) and Singleton (2001). You can profitably compare these two articles published in the same journal and in contiguous years by two seminal experts in the area, the former representing the position in favour of a biological schedule explanation for the observed age differences and the latter espousing a more sceptical stance. At a more advanced level, it is good to read and compare the overviews by Hyltenstam and Abrahamsson (2003) and Birdsong (2006), which offer a more contemporary view, again the former definitely in favour of critical periods for L2 learning and the latter more cautious about making final interpretations.

An accessible treatment of possible reasons for scepticism regarding the Critical Period Hypothesis is Marinova-Todd et al. (2000), and I recommend you also read the rebuttal by Hyltenstam and Abrahamsson (2001) and the authors' response (Marinova-Todd et al., 2001). You could then deepen your understanding of the educational ramifications of age effects by reading Nikolov and Mihaljević Djigunović (2006).

If you are interested in gaining expertise in this topic, book-length readings are in order. The collection of papers edited by David Birdsong (1999a) is difficult to read but fascinating because of the balance between positions in favour and against biological explanations for age effects, and because of the range of theoretical and empirical arguments represented. Although specialized in treatment, the book by Julia Herschensohn (2007) offers a uniquely valuable window into the issue of age because it reviews in depth age effects in both L1 and L2 acquisition and it takes an innatist approach but ends up arguing in favour of a critical period for first but not second language acquisition. Tom Scovel's (1988) book is still a classic well worth reading if you are interested in foreign accents. The collections edited by García Mayo and García Lecumberri (2003) and Muñoz (2006) will be exciting reading if your main interest is in L2 learning in foreign language contexts.

I hope your interest in definitions and limits of nativeness in SLA has been spurred by our discussion in section 2.8. If this is the case, Grosjean (1989), Cook (1991, 2008) and Birdsong (2005) are good readings for you.

Finally, for readers who are or will be parents interested in knowing more about raising children with multiple languages, King and Mackey's (2007) book is engaging and directed to a lay audience but well rooted in the best research about the topic.

3

Crosslinguistic influences

All L2 acquirers, by definition, possess complete knowledge of an L1, and often knowledge of other languages, when they begin learning the additional one. Many of them, indeed, will begin acquiring their L2 after many years of being able users of another language. Thus, previous language knowledge is an important source of influence on L2 acquisition, and this holds universally true of all L2 learners. This chapter offers a synthesis of what we currently know about the following question: If knowledge and capabilities for competent language use are already available to L2 learners through the mother tongue and other languages they may know, how do they affect the development of the new language?

Research on this topic is often known by the rubrics of **transfer or crosslinguistic influence**. You may have also heard of 'interference', but this older term has been displaced by the former two in contemporary SLA discourse. This is to pre-empt the unwanted implication that knowledge of the first language hinders L2 development. Much to the contrary, as we will see in this chapter, crosslinguistic influences can have positive as well as negative consequences for L2 learning. In addition, knowledge of the L1 impacts on L2 acquisition subtly and selectively, sometimes resulting in strikingly different negative and positive consequences for different learner L1 backgrounds, at different stages of development or proficiency and for different areas of the L2.

3.1 ON L1–L2 DIFFERENCES AND SIMILARITIES

During the 1950s and early 1960s, it was initially hypothesized that differences between the L1 and the L2 were responsible for the L2 difficulties experienced by specific learner groups who shared a same L1. This assumption inspired a wave of research comparing similarities and differences between given language pairs, in what soon was known as the school of **Contrastive Analysis** (e.g. Stockwell et al., 1965). It was believed that systematic L1–L2 comparisons would eventually allow researchers and teachers to predict when negative transfer will occur and what errors will be produced by particular L1 background groups of L2 learners. During the 1960s and 1970s researchers in the emerging new field of SLA turned to analyses of actual learner language and began conducting studies using the new methodology of **Error Analysis** and later **Performance Analysis** (see Long and Sato, 1984). It soon became clear that neither the linguistic knowledge nor the linguistic behaviour of L2 learners was slavishly determined by externally catalogued L1–L2 differences.

For one, it soon became apparent that sometimes certain L1–L2 similarities do not seem to help. Let us look at the area of negation to illustrate this point (see also Chapter 6, section 6.7). Negation is achieved pre-verbally in languages such as French (*ne* + verb), Portuguese (*não* + verb), or Spanish (*no* + verb). By contrast, negation is done post-verbally in English, where we add the word *not* at the end of verbs like *is/are* or *can/should* or at the end of the auxiliary *do/does/did* for all other verbs. The same is true of other languages, such as German (verb + *nicht*), Norwegian (verb + *ikke*), and Swedish (verb + *inte*). Swedish SLA researcher Kenneth Hyltenstam (1977) investigated how 160 beginning learners of L2 Swedish handled negation after five weeks of study and again after eight weeks, when they had been in Sweden for little more than four months. He found that the general patterns of negation were the same for most of the 160 learners regardless of L1 background, which he took to mean that 'we are able to study one large interlanguage continuum instead of unrelated [L1–L2 pair] continua' (p. 401). He also reported that of six L1 Turkish learners in the sample, three seemed to benefit from the similarity between Turkish and Swedish (both are post-verbal negation languages), but the other three learners showed an initial preference for pre-verbal negation. It was only by week 8 that these three learners began to approximate the Swedish target in their negation choices. Why would these learners initially have trouble with something in the L2 that was done similarly in their L1, if it were true that the L2 is learned by simple reliance on the L1?

Conversely, it was also found that certain differences may result in no attested learning difficulty whatsoever and furthermore that learning difficulties do not possess a symmetrical or bidirectional quality. A good illustration here is the case of placement of pronouns in English and French, briefly discussed by Canada-based researcher Helmut Zobl (1980). English has post-verbal pronoun placement (*I see them*), whereas French has pre-verbal pronoun placement (*Je les vois*). This difference does not cause trouble for learners of English from an L1 French background, who seldom produce a logically possible transfer error like *I them see*. Why do L1 French speakers find no problem with this difference when they learn English? By contrast, for L1 English learners of French, the learning of what is essentially the same difference but in the opposite direction poses much more difficulty, and the error *Je vois les* is indeed attested. How can we explain that what is difficult to learn when moving from Lx to Ly is not necessarily difficult when moving from Ly to Lx, if it were true that it is mere L1–L2 differences that cause learning difficulty?

3.2   INTERLINGUAL IDENTIFICATIONS

Accumulated empirical evidence of this kind led the first generation of SLA researchers to conclude that not only differences, but even more often misleading similarities between the L1 and the L2 are at the root of attested learning difficulties. German SLA researcher Henning Wode (1976) called this principle the Crucial Similarity Measure. In the United States, Roger Andersen (1983) added the principle of Transfer to Somewhere, suggesting that not only the L1, but also the L2 must have some feature that invites the (mis)perception of a similarity. This is exactly what Klee and Ocampo (1995) discovered in an interesting study of L1 Quechua speakers of L2 Spanish in Peru. A site of difference between these two languages, among many, is **evidentiality**, that is, the degree of certainty with which a statement is believed or presented to be true. Spanish, just as English, encodes evidentiality lexically, through adverbs such as *supuestamente, evidentemente, al parecer* (*allegedly, evidently, apparently*), but Quechua encodes it in the morphology of the verb (for those of you who know German, this would be similar to the use of the Konjunktiv I as in *er sei nach Hause gegangen*, 'supposedly, he has gone home'). Klee and Ocampo discovered that many of their participants used the past perfect tense of Spanish verbs, among other devices, to mark the fact that the event has not been witnessed directly, thus signalling evidentiality rather than tense. They concluded that these bilingual Quechua–Spanish speakers had 'found a way of expressing an obligatory category of Quechua with Spanish forms' (p. 68). That is, they simply found in the verbal morphology of Spanish present and past tense a good formal recourse to encode evidentiality at the grammatical level, in a fashion congruent with their L1.

The findings contributed during the 1970s and 1980s also led to a second, even more general insight about crosslinguistic influence: in order to understand L1 transfer, one needs to go beyond L1–L2 formal correspondences. That is, in the end, a better understanding of the forces that shape crosslinguistic influence rests not with external language comparisons, but with learners' psychological perceptions of those L1–L2 similarities or differences. For transfer to occur learners have to make an **interlingual identification**, defined by Terence Odlin as 'the judgment that something in the native language and something in the target language are similar' (2003, p. 454). The judgement can be, but need not be, made as a conscious, strategic choice, for example, when there is a gap in L2 knowledge, and the best available solution is to rely on L1 knowledge. Singleton (1987) provides a striking illustration of such cases. He studied the transfer errors committed by Philip, an L1 English professional writer who had picked up French during three short visits to France (he already spoke Spanish fluently and he had studied Irish and Latin in school). In three half-hour interviews in French, 154 transfer errors were identified. About a third of them were accompanied by a hesitation, an apology, interrogative intonation, laughter or some other overt indication that Philip might have been conscious of the less than perfect transfer solution. When reviewing the interviews and commenting on a specific French choice retrospectively, Philip said: 'I knew that it probably wasn't right, but it was the nearest I could get to something that might be right' (p. 335).

Interlingual identifications, however, do not always involve a conscious judgement, as transfer will often occur at the subconscious level as well. Most importantly, as you will see in this chapter, interlingual identifications are influenced by at least three factors: (a) the nature of the specific L2 phenomenon and the universal forces that shape its natural development; (b) learners' perceived distance between the L1 and the L2 and their intuitions of what is transferable or not; and (c) their relative proficiency level.

3.3   BESIDES THE L1

By turning to analyses of actual learner language rather than comparing external L1–L2 differences, early SLA research also uncovered some fundamental similarities between the emerging language of children acquiring their L1 and young and old learners acquiring their L2. For example, as we will see in Chapter 6, the past tense form *runned* (rendered as *ran* in adult mature English language) or the utterance *the car was crashed* (when mature language speakers of English would say *the car crashed*) are used at certain stages by children who are learning English as their mother tongue. Exactly these same forms appear in the speech and writing of adults from a wide range of first language backgrounds who are learning English as their foreign or second language. These certainly are not forms that can be picked up from, say, caretakers and older siblings, or from co-workers and textbooks. Neither are they forms that could be traced back to the mother tongue, when one considers that children learning their first and only language have no pre-existing language they could rely on, and that adults regardless of first language background produce them too.

Rather, SLA researchers soon concluded these forms must be considered interim systematic solutions that both children and adults independently invent, as it were, when they are trying to figure out the workings of a new language system. Furthermore, they concluded that there are developmental solutions for a given area of the grammar that L1 and L2 learners must naturally and universally traverse on their path to final competence in that area. Although the details for how L1 and L2 learners do this may differ, in the most general sense the developmental constraints are undeniable in both L1 and L2 acquisition. In the end, therefore, the shift away from the cataloguing of external L1–L2 differences and towards analysing actual learner language contributed to the emergence of the notion of **interlanguage** (Selinker, 1972) and enabled the documentation of natural sequences, orders of acquisition and other rule-governed patterns of development across areas of the L2, a number of which we will examine in Chapter 6. But if there is so much evidence of systematicity and rule-governed interlanguage processes across all L1 backgrounds, then a new question arises: What is the role played by the first language in L2 development, vis-à-vis the role of other universal developmental forces?

3.4   FIRST LANGUAGE INFLUENCES VIS-À-VIS DEVELOPMENT

There is robust evidence that L1 transfer cannot radically alter the route of L2 acquisition but it can impact the rate of learners' progress along their natural developmental paths. This possibility was first formulated by Zobl (1982). He proposed that L1–L2 differences account for the pace or rate at which certain morphosyntactic structures will be learned by different L1 groups. All L1 groups will traverse the same series of approximations to the target L2 system, and will be challenged, broadly speaking, by the same aspects of the L2. However, certain L1 groups may stay longer in a given stage, add some extra sub-stage, or find it more difficult than other L1 groups to learn some aspect of the L2 system in question. Let us examine here three well-known examples.

The development of negation in English is a well-understood area, already introduced in section 3.1. As we will see in more detail in Chapter 6, section 6.7, it has been firmly established that at very early stages of development L2 English learners, regardless of L1 background, use pre-verbal negation (No/Not + Verb). In addition to the Turkish–Swedish cases uncovered by Hyltenstam (1977), robust additional evidence exists across L2s. For example, pre-verbal negation was amply attested by Cancino et al. (1978) with L1 Spanish learners whose L1 only allows pre-verbal negation, but also by Ravem (1968) with L1 Norwegian children who initially produced utterances such as *I not like that*, even though their L1, just like English, only allows post-verbal negation. The effects of the L1 become visible only when one considers **rate** of development. Speakers of languages where pre-verbal negation is the grammatical norm (e.g. Italian, Greek, Russian and Spanish) will remain in the first pre-verbal negation stage in English much longer than, for example, L1 Norwegian or L1 Japanese speakers, whose L1s, just like the L2 in this case, require post-verbal negation (Zobl, 1982). In other words, when the rules for negation in the L1 are incongruent with the L2 rules, L2 development in this given area is slowed down.

English question formation is another area for which a developmental path has been well mapped in SLA research (see Chapter 6, section 6.12). A research team led at the time by Manfred Pienemann in Australia (Pienemann et al., 1988) found that learners start off by marking their intended questions with a questioning rising intonation. They are able to do this first on fragments (stage 1: *a hat?*) and later on statements (stage 2: *you are tired?*). Still later, learners begin using a fronting strategy, that is, they build questions by placing question markers (e.g. *what, do, is*) in front of statements (stage 3: *what you want? do your daughter is here? is your daughter work there?*). Inversion does not occur until those three stages are acquired. Once inversion emerges at stage 4, it first appears simultaneously in *wh*-questions containing the copula *is/are* (*where is dog?*) and in yes/no questions containing the auxiliary *is/are* (*are you listening me?*). The two last, most advanced stages are inversion in *wh*-questions across all possible contexts at stage 5 and target-like question formation with special cases at stage 6, such as tags (*you are surprised, aren't you?*), negation within questions (*don't you see?*) and embedded questions (*I wonder why they left*). (You will find a more formal summary of these stages in Table 6.9.) Many years later, Canadian researchers Nina Spada and Patsy Lightbown (1999) found that L1 influence can lead to the addition of an unexpected sub-stage in this well-established developmental sequence. Their participants were 144 L1 French sixth-graders learning English, and the unexpected L1 influence arose in relation to the learning of inversion at stages 4 and 5. For example:

(1)   a.   Where can I buy a bicycle?
      b.   *Why fish can live in water?

Both (1a) and (1b) constitute examples of *wh*-questions that require inversion in English, and therefore (1b) is ungrammatical, as indicated by the asterisk. After eight hours of being exposed to a regime of English questions that were flooded into the instructional materials at school, many of the students began to accept (1a). This was a good sign, in that it indicated English inversion in questions was being learned. However, in apparent contradiction, the same students often accepted ungrammatical sentences like that in (1b). Upon closer inspection of the data, Spada and Lightbown concluded these Francophone learners of English were probably at a stage of development in which their internal grammar sanctioned inversion with pronouns (as in 1a) as grammatical but inversion with nouns (as expected in the native-like English rendition of 1b) as ungrammatical. This is exactly the pattern their L1 French follows. That is, an L1-induced interlanguage rule had emerged, and one that was delaying many of these learners in their path towards adopting the full target-like rule of inversion in English questions.

A third, well-studied area is the English article system, or the choice of whether 'a', 'the' or zero article is needed in front of nouns (for example, do we say 'I like Ø French fries', 'I like the French fries' or 'I like a French fry'?). This topic was investigated in depth by Thom Huebner (1983; see also Chapter 6, section 6.6) and Peter Master (1987), in dissertations at the University of Hawai'i and the University of California Los Angeles, respectively. English articles are notoriously difficult to learn for all L1 groups alike. However, the nature and magnitude of difficulties that learners face depends on their L1. For L2 English learners whose native languages do not have articles at all, there is a pronounced initial disadvantage in rate of acquisition, as Master (1997) details. For example, an early stage of article development in L2 English is characterized by the alternation of *one* or *this* with *the* to mark nouns that refer to entities already known to the hearer. For learners whose L1s have articles, like Spanish, the first stage of article development where *one* or *this* alternate with *the* is brief, and the former two non-target-like forms are quickly abandoned in favour of *the*. When L1–L2 similarities are present, a fast start is to be expected. For example, Jarvis (2002) found that Swedes with only two years of English instruction showed 86 per cent accuracy in their use of the English indefinite article and 98 per cent accuracy in their use of the English definite article. This can be in part explained by the similarities that English and Swedish exhibit in their article systems. Nevertheless, complete mastery of all functional subtleties of the English articles is difficult, even for such groups. Thus, English learners from a Spanish L1 background tend to overgeneralize the definite article *the* to certain generic contexts (*I like the French fries*) and may continue to do so for some time, even into upper-intermediate levels of L2 proficiency. This choice is induced by the semantic makeup underlying their L1 article system, which marks generic meanings with definiteness, where English selects zero article (e.g. *me gustan <u>las</u> patatas fritas* but *I like Ø French fries*). Of course, this particular overgeneralization error is less persistent and less frequent, if at all attested, among learners whose L1s do not have articles.

3.5 MARKEDNESS AND L1 TRANSFER

Markedness is another important source of universal influence when learning human languages that is known to interact with L1 influences. The term has been used by linguists in a number of different ways (Batistella, 1996). In SLA, it has been used to denote a closed set of possibilities within a linguistic system, where the given possibilities rank from simplest and most frequent across languages of the world, or unmarked, to most complex and most rare, or marked. In addition, a special characteristic of many but not all markedness sets is that each marked member presupposes the existence of the less marked members, and never the other way around (in other words, the markedness relationship is implicational and unidirectional).

Linguists have found markedness hierarchies across the world's languages in a number of key areas of morphology, phonology and syntax. A good example is relative clauses, which we will examine in Chapter 6, section 6.11. Another good case concerns the distinction between voiced and voiceless final stops. If you touch your Adam's apple while pressing and releasing your lips to pronounce a clean /b/, you will feel a vibration through your fingertip, because /b/ is a voiced consonant. By contrast, if you now do the same while trying to pronounce a clean /p/, you should feel no vibration at all, because /p/ is a voiceless consonant. Voicing is the main feature distinguishing the two sounds, otherwise both /b/ and /p/ are pronounced using the same articulation features of place (both lips) and manner (a sudden obstruction of air followed by a release accompanied by aspiration). Voiced stops (as in the sounds /b/, /d/ and /g/ in 'tab', 'seed' and 'bag') are more marked than voiceless (as in the sounds /p/, /t/ and /k/ in 'tap', 'seat' and 'back'). The evidence comes from multiple sources. All languages of the world have some voiceless stops, but only some have voiceless and voiced ones, and no language exists that has only voiced stops without also having voiceless ones. Children learning an L1 that has both voiceless and voiced stops will acquire the former before the latter. There is also a natural phonetic process operating in human languages called devoicing, by which voiced stops can be pronounced as voiceless in certain positions, so that a marked feature (voiced) becomes neutralized and the unmarked one (voiceless) is used instead.

In L2 acquisition, the markedness principle is particularly successful in explaining well attested directionality effects in the transfer of L1 features. Building on the case of voiced and voiceless stops, both English and German have the same set of voiced and voiceless consonants. However, in English both kinds of consonants can appear in word-final position, whereas in German voiced stops do not occur in this position, because the natural process of devoicing applies and all voiced consonants in final position are pronounced as voiceless. Thus, for example, the 'g' in *Tag* ('day') is actually pronounced as a 'k' in German. In the early stages of development, L1 German learners of English have some difficulty with English words like 'wave' and 'tab' that end in voiced consonants. They will often devoice the final consonant and pronounce these two words as *wafe* and *tap*, in what is a direct transfer of the devoicing rule from their L1. No such difficulty has ever been observed in L1 English learners of L2 German (Eckman, 2004, p. 531), who will quickly learn they need to pronounce *Tag* with a final /k/ if they want to sound 'more German'. This is because their L1 English is more marked and they are learning an unmarked situation in their L2 German. By comparison, L1 German learners of L2 English find themselves in a situation where they have to learn the more marked case coming from a less marked rule in their L1.

For L2 development, the general implication is that marked forms tend to be more difficult to learn and therefore cause more interlanguage solutions. Moreover, a form that is more marked in the L2 than the L1 will lead to difficulty, whereas a form that is less marked in the L2 than the L1 will present no particular learning challenge. In addition, a form that is more marked in the L1 (as in the case of English word-final voiced stops) is less likely to be transferred than a form that is less marked (as in the case of the German word-final devoiced stop). This in a nutshell is the Markedness Differential Hypothesis proposed in the pioneering work of SLA phonologist Fred Eckman (1977).

3.6 CAN A CUP BREAK? TRANSFERABILITY

In a series of seminal publications in the Netherlands, Eric Kellerman (1979, 1983, 1985) introduced an important notion in the study of L1 influences: **transferability** (you may also find the term **psychotypology** used in SLA to refer to the same concept). Transferability refers to the claim that L1 transfer is partly a function of learners' (conscious or subconscious) intuitions about how transferable certain phenomena are. Choices in the L1 that are perceived to be marked or more 'language specific' are less likely to be transferred to the L2 than choices that are perceived to be unmarked or more 'universal' by learners.

In Kellerman's (1979) study, the acceptability of transitive and intransitive meanings of certain verbs was investigated with three different groups of L1 Dutch learners of English. Consider, for example, the verb *break* (English) and its Dutch counterpart *breken*. Both the transitive (*breaking something*) and the intransitive (*something just breaks*) meanings are possible in English and Dutch, as shown in these translation equivalents:

(2)   a.   He broke his leg → hij brak zijn been
        b.   The cup broke → het kopje brak

The results of the study afforded the SLA research community a few interesting surprises. A first group comprised Dutch students who were taking English in high school and whose proficiency in the L2 was just incipient. They accepted both the transitive and intransitive uses of such verbs correctly, almost 100 per cent of the time. One can argue that these learners were correct despite their beginning L2 proficiency probably because they were aided by the similarity in this area between English and Dutch. However, the answers given by a second group of 17- to 20-year-old Dutch students were wholly unexpected. They were enrolled in the last year of high school or the first two years of university, and therefore their proficiency in English was intermediate. This group correctly accepted all the transitive uses of 'break' (as in 2a), but they accepted the intransitive ones (as in 2b) only about 60 per cent of the time. What could have prevented this intermediate group of learners from using the L1 knowledge about *breken* to their advantage, just like the beginning learners in the same study obviously had? Also surprisingly, a third group of Dutch students with advanced proficiency (they were studying English in their third year of university) correctly accepted all transitive items (as in 2a) and, over 80 per cent of the time, they correctly accepted the intransitive items as well (as in 2b: *het kopje brak*, 'the cup broke'). Granted, their performance was better than that of the intermediate group, but why would these advanced level students be correct at a rate that was lower than that of the beginning proficiency student group?

Kellerman suggested that the transitive option of verbs such as *break* (as in 2a) is intuited by learners to be semantically more transparent and syntactically more prototypical than the intransitive option (as in 2b). Things do not normally break on their own. Instead we naturally expect an animate or an inanimate agent (that is, someone or something) that does or causes the breaking. At the beginning stage of proficiency, Kellerman (1985) speculated, '[y]ounger learners, who have had less instruction and are less sophisticated metalinguistically, seem to be unconcerned about these distinctions' (p. 349). They rely on their L1 knowledge and successfully arrive at a fully target-like response. However, as learners develop a more sophisticated knowledge of the language, they develop 'a sensitivity to a pragmatic distinction (implicitly known) between the causative and the noncausative meanings of a single verb' (p. 348). They go 'beyond success' (an expression that Kellerman, 1985, borrows from child language acquisition researcher Annette Karmiloff-Smith) and abstain from transferring the intransitive meaning from their L1. It is as if the intransitive meaning were perceived as too 'marked' or too 'Dutch-sounding' to be judged as transferable material.

Clearly, Kellerman's findings demonstrated that the judgement of whether something in the L1 is similar enough be transferred to the L2 is partly influenced by other factors beside externally driven L1–L2 comparisons. Based on these data, and the surprisingly different behaviour of three groups that shared the same Dutch L1 background but varied along the proficiency cline, Kellerman (1985) also noted that transferability interacts with L2 proficiency in shaping what may or may not get transferred, beyond L1–L2 apparent similarities or differences.

3.7 AVOIDANCE

Most of the examples of negative transfer you have encountered thus far in this chapter involve so-called errors of commission during L2 speaking and writing: *I not like that, Why fish can live in water?, I like the French fries.* When we hear these conspicuous forms we can easily trace them back to some L1 apparent similarity or difference. Other times, however, negative L1 transfer does not lead to noticeable errors of commission or to ungrammaticalities in the L2. This is the case of **avoidance**, or errors of omission.

Avoidance as a systematic case of L1 influence was first identified in an oft-cited study by Jacqueline Schachter (1974). In an analysis of the relative clauses (clauses introduced in English by *who, which/that* and *whose*) produced in 50 English L2 compositions, she found that the Chinese and Japanese L2 writers made strikingly few errors in relativization (only 14 altogether), but, upon inspection, they also produced very few relative clauses. By contrast, the Persian and Arabic L2 writers incurred many errors related to relative clauses (74 in total), but they also employed many more instances of relativization than the other two L1 background groups (328 – more than double the number of relative clauses contributed by the Chinese and Japanese essays). Drawing on the seminal crosslinguistic typological work by linguists Keenan and Comrie (1977; see also Chapter 6, section 6.11), Schachter noted that in Chinese and Japanese relativization happens very differently from English, whereas in Persian and Arabic relative clauses follow patterns that are much closer to English. She concluded that the Chinese and Japanese writers might have consciously or unconsciously avoided relative clauses in their English essays, thereby making few mistakes. Thus, an interesting consequence of avoidance is that it may lead to more accurate production. However, because in such cases learners take fewer risks in the L2, avoidance may also delay their L2 development of the given area being avoided. This shows something that many SLA researchers take for granted and that may surprise many readers at first: making fewer errors is not always a good thing!

The notion of avoidance is intriguing and spurred considerable initial interest among SLA researchers. However, it gradually became clear that, once again, factors other than externally defined L1–L2 differences needed to be considered when explaining avoidance behaviours. Three studies offer relevant evidence for this claim. All three investigated English phrasal verbs, which are two- or three-word verbs (*let down, back up, look up to*) that typically have one-word Latinate synony-mous counterparts (*disappoint, support, admire*). In a first study by Dagut and Laufer (1985), L1 Hebrew learners of English, whose mother tongue does not have phrasal verbs, showed a strong preference for the Latinate alternatives and avoided phrasal synonyms. By contrast, in a later study Laufer and Eliasson (1993) did not see evi-dence of such a preference among L1 Swedish learners, whose mother tongue has phrasal verbs. Interestingly, an additional avoidance effect was uncovered in both studies, related not to the L1 but to the sheer complexity of phrasal verbs. Namely, learners in the Hebrew L1 and the Swedish L1 study alike were more likely to choose a phrasal verb with a literal or semantically transparent meaning over a figurative or semantically opaque meaning. For example, a verb like *turn up* (meaning 'arrive') would be less likely to be chosen than a verb like *come down* (meaning 'descend'). Complicating matters even more, in a different study with L1 Dutch learners of English, Hulstijn and Marchena (1989) found that many participants avoided phrasal verbs in their L2 English, even though their L1 Dutch also has them, and preferred one-word synonyms. Moreover, the items most avoided were precisely those that had a close equivalent translation through another phrasal verb in Dutch. The results resonate with those of Kellerman (1979) discussed in section 3.6. These verbs were apparently too Dutch-like to be judged as transferable by these learners.

The results of the three phrasal verb studies, if taken together, once again show that predictions of positive or negative transfer, including predictions of avoidance, cannot be made solely on the basis of external similarities or differences between the L1 and the L2. As Odlin (2003) points out, crosslinguistic influences will always be probabilistic, and they will always be shaped by mutually interacting forces that come from learners' psychological judgement of transferability, learners' current proficiency level in the L2 and the nature and relative complexity of the given L2 subsystem at hand.

3.8 UNDERUSE AND OVERUSE

While interest in avoidance has subsided over the years, perhaps because it implicitly invokes conscious choices that are difficult to prove, the related notions of underuse and overuse in L2 learner language have received much attention in recent SLA research. The hypothesis is that L1 knowledge can inhibit certain L2 choices and prime others, thus resulting in the **underuse** or **overuse** of certain L2 forms in spoken and written learner production.

This is what Scott Jarvis and Terence Odlin (2000) discovered when they reanalysed the L1 Finnish and L1 Swedish adolescents' written retellings that had been elicited by Jarvis (2002), a study we will return to in the next section. Underuse of prepositions in general was attested in the sample of English written retellings produced by the Finnish-speaking adolescents. Many of them (but none of the Swedish learners they also studied) produced instances of zero preposition, as in:

(3)   The girl stole a loaf of bread the car and run away

Finnish marks location usually by adding suffixes at the end of words (that is, it is what we call an agglutinative language), and this may make prepositions in English (i.e. self-standing words or so-called free morphemes placed before nouns to mark location) less salient to these learners. Thus, the agglutinative morphology of the L1 indirectly biased many learners to underuse prepositions in the L2. Together with the underuse of prepositions in general, Jarvis and Odlin found that the Finnish-speaking adolescents overused the preposition *in*, and when they did they overextended it to many contexts where this choice is non-native-like, such as:

(4)   When they had escaped in the police car they sat under the tree

In fact, Charlie Chaplin and his new girl friend had escaped *from* the police car. The Swedes never overextended *in* to denote the meaning *from*. Overuse of *in* among the

Finns seems to have been motivated by semantic transfer. Finnish has six different locative suffixes that neatly mark internal and external space in combination with goal, location and source. By contrast, English prepositions can conflate internal location and internal goal. Jarvis and Odlin suggest that this difference in the L1–L2 semantic mapping misled Finnish learners to collapse all the uses of *in* into a general internal location meaning.

Underuse and overuse patterns in L2 learner language have attracted attention in recent SLA research that draws on corpus linguistic techniques. This type of research involves quantitative comparisons of parallel corpora produced by L2 learners from different L1 groups, often also compared to a baseline of the same tasks by native speakers of the target language. A volume edited by Belgium-based SLA researcher Sylvianne Granger and colleagues (Granger et al., 2002; see also Cobb, 2003) features several such studies. The findings typically suggest that there are noticeable differences in the frequency of use for the forms investigated across L1 groups, and that the L1-induced underuse or overuse of certain forms may be typical at different stages of L2 development for certain L1–L2 learner groups.

3.9 POSITIVE L1 INFLUENCES ON L2 LEARNING RATE

Another important fact to remember about how L1 knowledge influences L2 learning is that the effects can be not only negative but also positive. For example, positive transfer explained the behaviour observed in Kellerman's beginning learners, in section 3.6. The facilitative effects of L1 knowledge can be all too easily ignored, perhaps because instances of positive transfer are difficult to identify. Particularly in production, they lead to successful choices that raise no flags for teachers or interlocutors. By comparison, negative effects of L1 knowledge are much more noticeable and therefore have been more often investigated. Both are important for a complete understanding of how second language acquisition works.

Knowledge of the L1 can often have a positive impact on the rate of L2 learning. For many years now, Håkan Ringbom (1987, 1992, 2007) has been a strong advocate of the idea that relevant knowledge in the L1 can accelerate the rate of L2 learning. His research programme has focused on school-aged L2 English students in Finland. This country presents a special language ecology that has allowed him to investigate how English will be learned by two co-existing groups. The majority population consists of Finnish speakers who also learn Swedish in school starting in grade 3, 5 or 7. The minority population comprises Finnish Swedes who are L1 Swedish speakers and also learn Finnish in school from grade 3 onwards. Ringbom demonstrated that, in matters of English learning, Swedes have a great rate advantage over Finns, even though both groups speak the other group's language, and even though they share many cultural realities because both live in the same sociopolitical and national landscape. This advantage, Ringbom suggests, accrues from the **genetic and typological closeness** of Swedish to English, as both are Germanic languages in the Indo-European family and thus share many typological features. Finnish, by way of contrast, is an agglutinative language (that is, a language that glues morphemes or pieces of words together) belonging to the Finno-Ugric family, and thus is genetically unrelated and typologically more distant to English.

The rate advantages afforded by knowledge of the L1 have been documented across diverse areas of L2 learning. A good example is a carefully designed study by Scott Jarvis (2002), where he investigated the use of the English article system (Swedish, like English, has articles, whereas Finnish does not). The study was conducted also in Finland, with Finnish-dominant and Swedish-dominant students learning English at school. Jarvis elicited from them written retellings of a short silent video clip modified from the famous 1936 film *Modern Times* by Charlie Chaplin. He found that L1 influences from Swedish provided the Finland Swedes with an overall advantage in accuracy of use of *the* and zero article over the Finnish-speaking learners, and that the advantage narrowed but still was noticeable at higher proficiency levels after two, four and six years of L2 instruction.

The case of L1 crosslinguistic benefits in the learning of L2 grammatical gender is an even more striking illustration. For example, Bialystok (1997) found that L2 French learners of a German L1 background were better at marking French gender than L1 English background learners, whose language does not mark gender on nouns or adjectives. (Interestingly, and in connection to Chapter 2, she argued that, in this study at least, the L1 background factor explained more of the observed variability than the age at which learners in either group had begun learning French.) In the area of phonology, Wayland and Guion (2004) conducted a short-term laboratory study to examine the possibility of training L2 listeners to identify and discriminate between low and mid Thai tones. They found that the participants whose L1 was a tonal language (Taiwanese and Mandarin) benefited from the 30-minute training session more than participants who were speakers of an intonation language (English). In other words, the former participants' prior L1 experience with tones gave them an extra advantage.

There are also attested occasions where the benefits accrue from rather abstract similarities, as when a grammatical category in the L1 sheds light on a different grammatical category in the L2, thus facilitating the discovery and learning of the new category. Interesting evidence of this was gleaned in two experiments conducted in the United Kingdom by John Williams (2005). The study was designed to investigate the extent to which participants from various L1 backgrounds would be able to discover by induction alone (that is, without any explanations) a difficult artificial rule for article use. This rule was motivated semantically by the animacy of the noun following each article and roughly took the following lay formulation: '*gi* and *ro* both mean *the-near*; but we say *gi cow* because "cow" is a living thing and *ro cushion* because "cushion" is a non-living object.' For the participants, this rule must have been rather mysterious, as they were never provided with any explanation for it. Williams uncovered a systematic, facilitative relationship between knowledge of a language which encoded gender grammatically (as, for example, all Romance languages and German do) and ability to learn the *gi/ro* rule by induction. More specifically, the participants whose L1 had gender and article–noun agreement performed consistently better on the learning of this rule than participants from an L1 background without gender or noun–article agreement.

Finally, the same L1 fact may accrue both a disadvantage and an advantage for learning the corresponding area in the L2. Thus, Collins (2004) found that the attainment of accuracy in the use of simple past in English was slow for 91 college students in Quebec who were L1 French speakers because a single L1 form (the *passé composé*) corresponds to two forms in English, the past simple and the present perfect. This present perfect overlap (or crucial similarity, in Wode's terms; cf. 3.2) is misleading and primes L1 French learners of English to overuse the present perfect, supplying it in contexts where English speakers would use the simple past. At the same time, she also observed that the same crucial similarity enables the English present perfect to be mastered earlier by French L1 learners of English when compared to other L1 groups (Collins, 2002).

3.10 FIRST LANGUAGE INFLUENCE BENEATH THE SURFACE: THE CASE OF INFORMATION STRUCTURE

It would be inaccurate to imagine that L1 transfer, whether positive or negative, always leads to a direct translation of an L1 form into the L2 or to a glaring absence or excess of a form. The findings by Williams we have just discussed attest to this. More often than not, crosslinguistic influences yield interlanguage solutions that look very different from surface errors of either commission or omission. Often, knowledge of an L1 results in subtle influences that remain beneath the surface and are easy to miss or can be readily misinterpreted or misdiagnosed. We will illustrate this point with a well-researched case of subtle L1 transfer: **information structure**.

Languages are known to be of two kinds with regard to this feature. Topic-prominent languages organize information in sentences through the statement of a topic, followed by the new information. Subject-prominent languages typically organize sentences around a subject and verb and mark topics only when pragmatically needed and through other exceptional means. Thus, for example, Mandarin Chinese, Japanese, Korean and Somalian are topic-prominent languages, whereas Arabic, English and Spanish are subject-prominent languages. In Japanese, topics (whether they are subjects, objects and so on) are marked with the particle *wa*. In English, by contrast, if we want to structure a sentence around a topic, we may use a construction such as *As for my lost wallet, Peter finally found it*, or we may use intonation and pauses (*Noisy, those neighbours!*). Information structure of the L1 can have a profound influence on grammatical and discursive choices learners make in their L2, but the effects are difficult to diagnose. Findings contributed by William Rutherford and Jacqueline Schachter (Rutherford, 1983; Schachter and Rutherford, 1979) provide a well-known illustration.

Certain non-target-like choices are typical of the essays written by Chinese L1 learners of English, as the following sentence from Schachter and Celce-Murcia (1971) shows:

(5)   There are so many Taiwan people live around the lake

At first blush, this L2 writer appears to have omitted the relative pronoun (*who/that/which*) of a relative clause she arguably intended. Her writing teacher may think 'the problem' with this wording is caused by a relative clause error. Yet, through a detailed analysis of such interlanguage cases, Schachter and Rutherford were able to show that in fact in these cases L2 writers may be unconsciously attempting to organize information following principles of their L1. If they were right in their analyses, then the Chinese L1 writer in (5) may have meant to say something like 'Many Taiwanese people, they live around the lake' or 'As for Taiwanese people, many of them live around the lake', which is a topic-prominent way of organizing the information in this sentence. Having discovered that English has an existential construction (*there is/there are*) that enables information to be structured in this way (first topic, then comment), this writer may be skilfully using it to fulfil an L1-induced preference in this area.

More specifically, and if we expand on the analysis proposed by Rutherford (1983), sentence (5) above can be understood as an intermediate solution placed in the middle of the following developmental continuum, from most L1-like to most L2-like information structure:

(6)   a.   Many Taiwan people, they live around the lake
        b.   There are so many Taiwan people live around the lake
        c.   There are many Taiwanese people who live around the lake
        d.   Many Taiwanese people live around the lake

If Rutherford and Schachter are correct, then, a writing teacher who offers (6c) as a correction for (6b) may 'teach' this L2 writer something interesting about relative clauses in English, but the real benefit for this learner would probably be to realize that, in order to sound more natural in her English writing, she needs to begin topicalizing less (reducing the use of sentences like 6a through 6c) and to organize information around subject–predicate sequences more (using more sentences like 6d).

It should be noted that moving in the reverse direction, that is, away from the information structure of a subject-prominent L1 and towards devices that favour a topic–comment structure in the L2, is also difficult for L2 learners. This is what Jin (1994) found in a study of 46 L1 English speakers who were learning L2 Chinese. Participants at early stages of proficiency had difficulty adopting a topic-prominent orientation to syntax and discourse. The same finding was corroborated with 23 L2 Korean learners from an L1 English background by Jung (2004). These learners initially transferred subject-prominent clause structure from English, and only those at the more advanced levels produced the Korean topic marker *(n)un* to signal given or known information. The Korean double-nominative construction was even more rare. These topicalization devices were underused by beginning L2 learners even though they are common in the target language (as in *khokkili-nun kho-ka kilta*, 'as for the elephant, its nose is long').

With time and increasing proficiency, the tendency to transfer the information structure of the L1 in order to frame ideas in the L2 may gradually diminish, but the process may be rather slow. This is what Patricia Duff (1993) found in her longitudinal study of JDB, a Cambodian learner of English in Canada. JDB was at a stage before the (6a)–(6d) continuum, in that he had yet to discover the existential English construction. Instead, to preserve the topic-prominent information structure of Cambodian, he used the possessive construction *have* for both possessive and existential meanings, as in (7), which Duff paraphrased as meaning (7a) or (7b):

(7)   **Khao Larn Camp the King of Thailand they has a small camp about three thousand people**

      a.   'There is a Thai camp at Khao Larn with about three thousand people'

      b.   'The Thai government has a camp at Khao Larn with about three thousand people'

This use of *have* or *has* as an invariant form that means *there is/there are* has been amply documented across SLA studies. At the end of two and a half years of observation, JDB suddenly began using an interlanguage form *'s* (pronounced as a voiced /z/), shown in this utterance from Duff's recordings:

(8)   **And 's many rock by the river**

Duff interprets this form as a precursor of the existential topic marker *there is*. That is, after two and a half years of immersion in an L2 environment, JDB managed to advance to a stage that has the potential to evolve into stage (6b) in the developmental continuum presented earlier. While this can be considered an important sign of progress in JDB's interlanguage, it came after a considerable long time of stable use of *has*, the form that helped him preserve in the L2 the L1-preferred information structure.

Not only is the process slow, but Carroll et al. (2000) argue that information structure in the L1 continues to exert an important if subtle influence on the L2 even at very advanced stages of proficiency. They noted that English and Romance languages will prefer existential constructions for the introduction of new referents as in *There is a fountain on the square*, whereas German will favour locational constructions of the kind *Auf dem Platz ist ein Brunnen* ('On the square is a fountain'). They found that the existential construction preference was transferred by 10 L1 English speakers even though they were at very advanced levels of L2 German. This L1-influenced way of structuring information in their sentences had consequences for other narrative and discourse choices as well.

3.11 CROSSLINGUISTIC INFLUENCES ACROSS ALL LAYERS OF LANGUAGE

Another fact about L1 transfer that is well worth remembering is that crosslinguistic influences go well beyond form–form or form–function correspondences, and that L1 knowledge across all layers of language can influence L2 solutions at the levels of form, meaning and function.

Crosslinguistic influence in the area of **pragmatic competence** offers a good illustration of this point. Sometimes the L1 influence on L2 pragmatic choices is obvious and rather local. For example, Takahashi (1996) studied the perceptions of transferability of requests held by 142 learners of English as a foreign language at two universities in Tokyo. She found that many chose the following formulas in English as highly appropriate for polite requests, and that this preference was related to the existence of close L1 counterparts:

(9) a. Would/Could you please... → V-te itadak-e-nai-deshoo-ka
     b. Would/Could you... → V-te mora-e-nai-deshoo-ka

Other times, however, what gets transferred is more subtle and holistic, for example, sociopragmatic valuations of what is socially offensive, face threatening and so on. Thus, Elite Olshtain (1983) studied crosslinguistic influences on apologies and found that learners' sociopragmatic judgements about what situations and offenses warrant an apology were transferred from their L1. As a consequence, L2 English speakers of an L1 Hebrew background were at risk of sounding too impolite and, conversely, L2 Hebrew speakers of an English background were at risk of sounding overly polite. Similarly, Yu (2004) found that 64 L1 Taiwanese learners of English, half residing in Taiwan and half in the United States, were much more likely to reject compliments than to accept them, in a pattern that was consistent with the L1 Taiwanese baseline group and reverse to the responses of the L1 American English baseline group. Yu attributed these results to transfer from the L1 of a Taiwanese interactional style that values modesty over agreeability.

Another area which illustrates how L1 influences can cut across layers of language pertains to the semantic-functional ways of expressing thought or what first language acquisition researcher Dan Slobin (1996) called **thinking-for-speaking**. This refers to the fact that languages offer specific sets of resources to frame meaning, or to schematize experience, and speakers are known to be constrained by such language-specific ways at the time when they are putting together their thoughts into language. A widely researched case is the expression of motion. In so-called satellite-framed languages, motion is typically expressed via a verb that encodes manner and some other external element, such as an adverb or a gerund, that encodes path (e.g. English *to fly out*). In verb-framed languages, by contrast, the path is typically encoded in the verb, whereas the manner gets expressed in the external element (e.g. Spanish *salir volando* or 'to leave flying'). Slobin (1996) suggested that thinking-for-speaking in an L1 will be transferred into the new language by L2 learners and, furthermore, that they may never be able to restructure their L1-acquired ways of thinking for speaking when using an L2. Although he did not investigate the issue empirically, his suggestion has spurred great interest among L2 researchers. The rapidly accumulating research for the expression of motion in an L2, for example, has been reviewed by Cadierno (2008), who concluded that the results are mixed thus far. More research will be needed before we can know more about the nature of the challenges encountered when L2 learners learn to think for speaking anew in their additional language.

3.12 BEYOND THE L1: CROSSLINGUISTIC INFLUENCES ACROSS MULTIPLE LANGUAGES

Acknowledging that in many cases people bring knowledge of multiple languages to the process of learning an additional language, SLA researchers in the last ten years have begun to ask two new questions: How will knowledge of two (or more) pre-existing languages influence acquisition of the L3 (or L4, and so on)? Will the L1 still play a privileged role in L3 acquisition?

The accumulating evidence suggests that knowledge of two (or more) languages can accelerate the learning of an additional one. Research on lexical transfer in L3 acquisition has found substantial vocabulary rate advantages for multilinguals (several of the studies can be found in a pioneering volume published by Jasone Cenoz and other colleagues in Europe; Cenoz et al., 2001). The benefits are particularly clear if one of the previous languages is typologically related to the L3, because in such cases there are many relevant cognates, that is, words that have a common origin and therefore have similar form and meaning in the two related languages (e.g. *redundant* in English and *redundante* in Spanish). Even in the case of unrelated multiple languages, moreover, already knowing several languages can give an overall advantage, simply because better vocabulary learning strategies have already been developed by the time the L3 is being learned. For example, Keshavarz and Astaneh (2004) reported that pre-university female students in Iran who were speakers of either Armenian and Persian or Turkish and Persian outperformed a comparison group of L1 Persian–L2 English students on an English vocabulary test, even in the absence of any cognates that would be useful for learning English vocabulary. The same general conclusion that bilingualism generally facilitates L3 acquisition rates has been reached in the area of morphosyntax. Thus, for example, Elaine Klein (1995) observed a general advantage for multilingualism when 15 high-school speakers of L3 English were asked to judge whether the separation of a preposition or a postposition from its noun phrase, or what is known as **stranding** (e.g. *What are the boys waiting for?*), was grammatical. They did considerably better than another group of learners of L2 (as opposed to L3) English. This was despite the fact that this phenomenon was absent from their L1s or L2s, since most languages of the world do not allow stranding (they favour the option *For what are the boys waiting?*, which is also possible in English but is rather formal-sounding).

Evidence slowly accumulating from a number of diverse perspectives strongly supports the conclusion that not only the L1, but all previously learned languages, can influence additional language learning. Which language will become the source for transfer does not appear to be random. Typological closeness is one powerful factor when competing sources of knowledge (L1 and L2) are available in the learning of the L3. Odlin and Jarvis (2004) mention examples such as the learning of English in the Basque country or in Finland, where many students are likely to be bilingual in Basque and Spanish and in Finnish and Swedish, respectively. Not surprisingly, the influence of Spanish and Swedish, which are the languages typologically closer to English, is stronger, whereas documented cases of transfer from Basque and Finnish are less pervasive. Typological closeness was also found to be the deciding factor for predicting the source of transfer in L3 acquisition in a study by Suzanne Flynn and colleagues (Flynn et al., 2004). These researchers investigated whether L3 learners of English who knew Kazakh as L1 and Russian as L2 would behave with English relativization in ways that were more similar to previous data from L1 Japanese or from L1 Spanish learners of English. The comparison was interesting because their L1, Kazakh, is typologically closer to Japanese, whereas their L2, Russian, is typologically closer to Spanish and English. The data came from an elicited imitation task in which participants were asked to repeat English relative clauses of several kinds. According to the researchers, the learners' repetition of sentences such as *The lawyer who criticized the worker called the policeman* revealed developmental patterns similar to the patterns attested with the previously studied L1 Spanish learners. They concluded that these L3 English learners were transferring relevant knowledge from the typologically closer language, in this case Russian, their L2. Importantly, they concluded that the L1 does not hold a privileged status in the acquisition of additional languages.

Predicting what the source language for transfer will be demands that we go well beyond external typological relations, however. In a large study with over one thousand participants who were trilingual users of Swedish, Finnish and English, Ringbom (2001) found that the language that was typologically closer to L3 English, Swedish, was the source for transfer motivated by formal similarity between languages (so-called false friends) for both groups. Thus, for example, the lexical invention *stedge*, which originates in the Swedish word *stege* ('ladder') was attested in the interlanguage of Finnish-dominant as well as Swedish-dominant L3 English participants. By contrast, cases of transfer of semantic knowledge (for example, translating *matches* as *firesticks*) were traced back to the L1 of participants, whether Finnish or Swedish. Interestingly, therefore, it appears that formal or surface transfer of words can come from the L1 or the L2, whichever is typologically closer to the L3, but semantic transfer is likely to have the L1 as its source.

Another interesting documentation of differential L1 and L2 influence on L3 learning involves codeswitching across the three languages of a learner. Sarah Williams and Bjorn Hammarberg (1998) showed this in an oft-cited case study of the L3 Swedish oral production by the first author over the first two years of her stay in Sweden. Williams was a speaker of L1 English and L2 German, which she had studied in college and subsequently developed to near-native degrees while living in Germany for six years prior to moving to Sweden. The researchers discovered that switches to the L1 were intentional and had a metalinguistic self-regulatory function (asking for help, clarifying the intended meaning); they gradually declined after the first eight months of study. By contrast, switches to the L2, the most active language in the beginning of the study, were unconscious and involved mostly function words that aided in language production; these switches also showed a decline after the first four months. Thus, both the L1 and the L2 influenced the L3, but the functional roles played by the each language in L3 production were not interchangeable, and their presence gradually receded over time, as the L3 developed.

In fact, proficiency is another factor that must be taken into account, in that L3 learners may be more prone to transferring aspects of whichever language they are more proficient in, and they will gradually show different crosslinguistic sources of influence as their L3 proficiency increases. Margaret Thomas (1990) studied the acquisition of the Japanese reflexive pronoun *zibun* ('self') in a group for whom Japanese was an L3 ($n = 6$) and compared their behaviour on a multiple-choice comprehension test to that of an L1 English–L2 Japanese group ($n = 27$) and an L1 Chinese–L2 Japanese ($n = 8$) group. She found that the six L3 Japanese learners behaved more like the L1 English–L2 Japanese group than the L1 Chinese–L2 Japanese group. This was the case, even though the six L3 participants' first language, Chinese and Korean, have reflexive pronouns that work more like Japanese *zibun* and less like English *herself.* That is, knowledge from the L1 that was congruent with the L3 did not afford them the expected advantage. In this case, positive transfer from the L1 failed to happen, and instead negative transfer originated from the L2. Thomas speculated this was possibly because they were dominant in their L2, English.

There are possibly other additional factors to consider in the mix when transfer influences in multilingual acquisition are investigated. The order of acquisition may play a role, in the sense that perhaps the most recently learned language (especially if it is learned as a 'foreign' language) shows a stronger influence than the language learned earlier. In other words, perhaps the L3 is affected by the L2 more, other things being equal, because both conjure the same psychological mode of 'talking foreign', as Selinker and Baumgartner-Cohen (1995) call it. These are cases where the language psychologically associated as 'foreign' intrudes in the L3. In such scenarios, the L2 may remain nevertheless more affected by the L1, even after an L3 has been learned (Dewaele, 1998). Another observed influence is the formality of the context, as it appears that informal communication favours the intrusion of lexical choices from the L1 or L2 alike in the L3 production (Dewaele, 2001).

The study of crosslinguistic influence during L3 acquisition has only begun to flourish in SLA, but the available evidence clearly points at two conclusions: that bilingualism generally facilitates L3 acquisition rates and that transfer does not always come from the L1. The discovery that the L1 does not need to have a privileged status across the board in additional language acquisition opens the door to the novel suggestion that crosslinguistic influences may occur in the opposite direction, from the L2 (or L3 and so on) to the L1. L2 effects on the L1 have indeed been documented in a collection edited by Vivian Cook (2003), and Pavlenko and Jarvis (2002) have called attention to **bidirectional transfer**, or the fact that 'crosslinguistic influence can simultaneously work both ways, from L1 to L2, and from L2 to L1' (p. 190). However, much more research is needed before conclusions can be reached in this new area of universal crosslinguistic influence.

3.13 THE LIMITS OF CROSSLINGUISTIC INFLUENCE

As you have seen in this chapter, over its 40 years of existence the field of SLA has contributed a wealth of research on how knowledge of the first and other languages universally influences L2 acquisition. Let us conclude with an evaluation of the findings presented in this chapter and what they might mean beyond research contexts.

First, from an intuitive standpoint, it is all too easy to conclude the L1 is a major explanatory factor in learner language. If we hear *How I do this?* from a Punjabi or a Spanish learner, whose languages do not have inversion, we may conclude it is the L1 that is causing this choice. This explanation is indeed compatible with the description of these two particular L1s. However, if we sampled learners from other L1 backgrounds where inversion does exist, we would find that at some early stage of development in the L2 they use uninverted questions in their English interlanguage (Pienemann et al., 1988; see also Table 6.9 in Chapter 6). Thus, many errors that at first blush might be attributed to the influence of the mother tongue can be, in fact, unrelated to the L1 and instead reflect developmental universal processes that have been attested in the acquisition of human language in general (and often in L1 acquisition as well, where no pre-existing knowledge of a specific language can be assumed to influence the process). In addition, many interlanguage phenomena are motivated by simultaneous L1 transfer and linguistic universal influences that conspire together to promote certain L2 solutions. For example, Spanish and Punjabi speakers of English at a given developmental level may more often produce such uninverted questions than speakers from other L1 backgrounds at the same developmental level.

It is intriguing to ask ourselves: Just how much of learners' obvious errors in production (that is, errors of commission) might one be able to explain away as caused by L1 transfer? In 1985, Rod Ellis tried to answer this question by polling the findings reported across seven studies of L2 English published between 1971 and 1983 (Ellis, 1985). The typical amount seemed to be in the range of 23 per cent to 36 per cent, as contributed by four studies, all involving English as a second language (ESL) adult learners of various L1 backgrounds (Arabic, German, Spanish and mixed). However, the full range across the seven studies was striking, from a low 3 per cent in the only sample of children, whose L1 was Spanish, to a highest of roughly 50 per cent in two studies involving adult learners of Chinese and Italian L1 background, respectively. This wildly varying quantitative estimation of the importance of transfer in L2 development has been cited by other researchers since then. However, by the late 1980s most SLA researchers were in agreement with Ellis's caution that trying to ascribe all interlanguage forms attested in a given data set to either the L1 or universal influence may be a futile enterprise. There are too many variables that can affect the amount of L1 transfer that materializes for a given learner. To the ones reviewed in this chapter, we can add external variables. Interlocutors, for example, may affect the degree to which L1 transfer occurs (Beebe and Zuengler, 1983; Young, 1991).

Another area that has occasionally intrigued SLA researchers and language teachers is whether we can assume that L1 transfer effects are subtle and selective in some areas of language but more robust and prominent in other areas. For example, is it possible that the L1 has a less massive and more fleeting influence on an area like L2 morphosyntax than on an area like L2 phonology? Might it be that transfer of pragmatic formulas (e.g. Takahashi, 1996) occurs more sporadically and at lower levels of proficiency, whereas the transfer of L1 sociopragmatic values (e.g. Olshtain, 1983; Yu, 2004) is more common and persists for a longer time in development? In his authoritative review of L1 transfer, Terence Odlin (2003) notes that it may be futile to pose such questions because seeking to make such comparisons across subsystems of a language is to try to 'compar[e] the incomparable' (p. 440). He explains that comparisons that try to quantify the incidence of L1-to-L2 transfer across subsystems are difficult, among other reasons, because certain phenomena are of high frequency in any language (e.g. sounds and articles cannot be avoided for very long in production), whereas other features of the grammar may be of very low frequency. For example, relative clauses are much less frequent than noun clauses, particularly in speech, and inversion in non-question contexts (as in *Not only did I warn him, I warned him repeatedly*) is of even lower frequency in English. Attempts at quantifying and comparing the amount of transfer observed across these areas and for different types of L1 knowledge would be difficult to interpret.

Odlin (2003) makes an important and seldom-voiced point that helps put transfer phenomena into a wider perspective. He notes that the macro context can also shape the nature and magnitude of crosslinguistic influences. He contrasts the case of L2 learning in postcolonial contexts, such as English in India and Nigeria, with the case of L2 formal instruction of a foreign language in expanding circle countries, such as English in China or Spain. In the latter contexts, teachers may warn students against false friends, literal translations and the dangers of relying on the mother tongue when learning a foreign language. In postcolonial contexts, by contrast, transfer occurs frequently and freely. In such contexts the learning and use of an L2 is characterized by a great degree of creativity involving crosslinguistic influences, and L1-induced transfer seems to be a major strategy for the indigenization or appropriation of a language by the postcolonial speech community. It should be also noted that in a variety of contexts learners may not wish to be identified with speakers of the L2, and creative L1 transfer processes may be a form of resistance and appropriation of the target language (see, for example, Seidlhofer, 2004). As with the topic of age and critical periods that we examined in Chapter 2, it may be that a more bilingual orientation and a less intent comparative approach of native (monolingual) and non-native (bilingual) speakers may bring further advances in the area of crosslinguistic influences in future SLA generations.

3.14 SUMMARY

- By definition L2 acquisition takes place in humans who already possess one or more languages. This being so, the mother tongue (and any other known languages) universally influences the processes and outcomes of L2 learning.

- Transfer is a highly complex phenomenon. It can be caused by perceived L1–L2 similarities as well as by large differences, and it goes well beyond strident calques and awkward transliterations from the L1.

- The influence of the mother tongue cannot explain all phenomena in interlanguage development, because universal influences that operate in all natural languages exercise a powerful effect also on L2 development. Knowledge of the L1 interacts with such developmental forces but does not override them.

- Pre-existing knowledge of the mother tongue influences interlanguage development by accelerating or delaying the progress learners make along the natural, developmental pathways (e.g. orders of accuracy, natural sequences and developmental stages), but it neither predetermines nor alters such pathways.

- What gets or does not get transferred is also in part determined by:
  - universal constraints and processes, such as developmental sequences and markedness, that apply across all natural languages and play a role in L1 as well as L2 acquisition
  - psychological perceptions of transferability
  - inherent complexity of the L2 subsystem in question
  - proficiency level.

- Crosslinguistic influences, even in cases of negative transfer, may or may not lead to ungrammatical solutions. Transfer can be manifested in errors of commission, errors of omission (avoidance) and L1-patterned frequencies (underuse and overuse). It can also result in subtle effects beyond form–form or form–function misidentifications and can occur at all levels of language, from information structure, to pragmatics, to thinking-for-speaking.

- L1 transfer does not happen mechanistically or deterministically. Rather, it is about tendencies and probabilities. Consciously or unconsciously, learners seem to operate on the basis of two complementary principles: 'what works in the L1 may work in the L2 because human languages are fundamentally alike' but 'if it sounds too L1-like, it will probably not work in the L2'.

- Knowledge of two (or more) languages can accelerate the learning of an additional one, and all previously known languages can influence knowledge of and performance in an L3.

3.15 ANNOTATED SUGGESTIONS FOR FURTHER READING

The study of crosslinguistic influence has for many years been bounded by the influence of a few seminal edited volumes and monographs, all published in the 1980s and early 1990s. It has only been recently that two publications devoted to the topic have appeared and gathered contemporary knowledge about crosslinguistic influence: Ringbom (2007) and Jarvis and Pavlenko (2008). Reading these two volumes can offer the best entry point into this fascinating field.

The seminal volumes can nevertheless be good follow-up reading. In Gass and Selinker (1983), you will find many key empirical and theoretical studies of transfer mentioned in this chapter, including Andersen's, Kellerman's, Rutherford's, Schachter's and Zobl's. A subset of the same papers plus a number of new ones (most still conducted in the early 1980s) appeared in a revised edition (Gass and Selinker, 1993). Other two oft-cited edited volumes are Kellerman and Sharwood Smith (1986) and Dechert and Raupach (1989). Two monographs are worth reading for their extensive and authoritative treatment even today: Ringbom (1987) and Odlin (1989).

For article-length readings, the most updated review on the topic is Odlin (2003), and a perusal of any of the journals that publish SLA research will yield additional empirical studies on various topics related to crosslinguistic influence.

Finally, you can read about transfer in multiple language acquisition in Cenoz et al. (2001) and L2-to-L1 transfer in Cook (2003). The two volumes have become early classic citations in these two new burgeoning areas of crosslinguistic transfer that promise to generate high volumes of research in the future.

4

The linguistic environment

Much of our knowledge about how people learn additional languages was forged during the 1980s and 1990s under a cognitive-interactionist perspective on L2 learning. Cognitive-interactionism is associated with the work in developmental psychology by Jean Piaget (e.g. 1974) and refers to the position that multiple internal (cognitive) and external (environmental) factors reciprocally interact (hence the word 'interactionist') and together affect the observed processes and outcomes of a phenomenon – in this case, additional language learning. It is noteworthy that internal cognition is assumed to be the locus of learning (hence the word 'cognitive' in the term) and that a clear separation between cognitive-internal and social-external worlds is presupposed, since how the two interact is the object of inquiry. More recent SLA research influenced by a number of related sociocultural perspectives has challenged the assumptions of cognitive-interactionism, and we will discuss these other ways of conceiving of language learning in Chapter 10. In the present chapter and the following one, however, we will examine findings about the environment and cognition that have been gleaned using a cognitive-interactionist prism.

Languages are almost always learned with and for others, and these others generate linguistic evidence, rich or poor, abundant or scarce, that surrounds learners. Knowing about the language benefits afforded by the environment is thus important for achieving a good understanding of how people learn additional languages. In this chapter, we will examine environmental influences on L2 learning. We open with the story of Wes (Schmidt, 1983), who is probably the most frequently cited, admired and puzzled-over exemplar in the long gallery of learners that SLA researchers have mounted to date through the methodology of case study (Duff, 2008). He stands for someone who became particularly adept at 'initiating, maintaining, and regulating relationships and carrying on the business of living' in his additional language (Schmidt, 1983, p. 168) but remained unable to master the L2 grammar despite what seemed to be sufficient time and ideal environmental conditions. His story illustrates well the selective impact that the linguistic environment exerts on L2 learning.

4.1 WES: *'I'M NEVER LEARNING, I'M ONLY JUST LISTEN THEN TALK'*

Wes was a young Japanese artist who learned English without instruction in Honolulu. His progress over the first three years of intermittent but increasingly prolonged residence in the L2 environment was chronicled by Richard Schmidt (1983) at the University of Hawai'i. Schmidt kept rich field notes over the duration of the study and collected 18 hours of English oral data, in the form of letters that Wes tape-recorded over three years during his visits to Tokyo, to update people back in Honolulu about personal and professional matters. Towards the final months of the study, Schmidt also recorded an additional three hours of casual conversations in Honolulu.

In his early thirties, Wes emigrated from Tokyo to Honolulu by choice, in a financially and socially comfortable position, in pursuit of expanded international recognition in his already well-established career. Perhaps two features can be singled out as most defining of Wes's personality. One is his strong professional identity as an artist, captured in excerpt (1) from an oral letter recorded into the third year of the study (Schmidt, 1983, p. 158):

(1)   you know I'm so lucky / because ah my business is painting / also my hobby is painting / ... this is my life / cannot stop and paint / you know nobody push / but myself I'm always push /

The second defining feature is Wes's predisposition towards communication. His was the kind of social personality that avidly seeks people and engages in skilfully designed reciprocal interaction. This is illustrated in excerpt (2), also recorded around the same time as the previous excerpt:

(2)   well / I like talk to people you know / um / I'm always listen then start talk / then listen / always thinking my head / then talk / some people you know only just talk, talk, talk, talk /

(Ibid., p. 160)

Schmidt describes Wes as someone who was confident and felt comfortable in his own identity as Japanese and at the same time showed extremely positive attitudes towards Hawai'i and the United States throughout the three years of study. Most of his acquaintances and friends, and most of his clients and art brokers, were L1 English speakers, and he had an L1 English-speaking roommate. In Schmidt's estimation, by the third year of study, he was using English in his daily interactions between 75 and 90 per cent of the time.

Wes had arrived in the United States with 'minimal' communicative ability in English (p. 140), and within three years he was able to function in the L2 during 'promotional tours, exhibitions of paintings [... and] appearances and demonstrations by the artist' that demanded of him whole-day, around-the-clock interactions and a mixture of demonstration painting and informal lecturing, all in English (p. 144). This transformation of his second language capacities seems remarkable. A close analysis of his language production in the recorded letters and conversations, however, revealed a more ambivalent picture. Evidence of the greatest strength and improvement was found in the area of oral discourse competence. Wes quickly became skilful and expressive in his conversations and grew able to narrate, describe and joke in rather sophisticated ways. Most interlocutors considered him a charming conversationalist who never ran out of topics and often took charge of steering conversations. At the other extreme, in the area of Wes's grammatical competence, Schmidt uncovered puzzling stagnation.

For example, the findings for verbal tense morphology are telling. For all three years, Wes's verbs were characterized by overuse of *–ing* attached consistently to certain verbs denoting activities (e.g. *joking, planning, training, touching*), the use of past in only high-frequency irregular forms that can be memorized as items (e.g. *went, sent, told, saw, said, met, bought*), a complete absence of *–ed* and an overwhelming preference to make interlocutors understand the intended tense and aspect of his messages via lexical means such as adverbs (e.g. *all day, always, right now, yesterday, tomorrow*). In other words, over three years of rich exposure to and meaningful use of English, Wes's temporal L2 system remained rudimentary, stuck in the transition between the lexical marking stage and the next stage of development, where tense and aspect morphology begins to deploy (Bardovi-Harlig, 2000; you will appreciate the significance of these findings better if you read Chapter 6, section 6.10). Likewise, his articles and plurals improved minimally, from practically no occurrence in the beginning of the study to accuracy in up to a meagre third of the relevant cases, but even then in great part because of repeated occurrence of these forms in chunked phrases like *n years old* or *n years ago* (for plural *–s*), and *a little (bit) X* (for use of the indefinite article *a*).

Regarding progress in the two areas of sociolinguistic and strategic competence, Wes presented a mixed profile, less extreme than the positive picture of discourse competence or the negative picture of grammatical competence. On the one hand, he developed a certain sociolinguistic repertoire that enabled him to issue requests, hint and make suggestions, if often strongly couched in indirectness:

(3)   maybe curtain
       [maybe you should open the curtain]
(4)   this is all garbage
       [put it out]
(5)   uh, you like this chair?
       [please move over]

Since Japanese is well known for its indirect politeness (Ide et al., 2005), this preference may have been transferred from his L1.

On the other hand, this repertoire, constrained by his limits in sheer grammatical resources, remained formulaic. That is, the formulas and chunks that Wes so adeptly used did not serve him as a springboard into the process of analysis towards rules, or what is known as bootstrapping from formulas to rules. As we will see in Chapter 6, section 6.4, this gradual process has been posited to occur with successful L2 development (e.g. Wong Fillmore, 1979; Myles et al., 1999; Wray, 2002), but did not happen in Wes's case. Likewise, his strategic competence to solve communication problems developed rapidly, as he availed himself of heuristics that helped him solve immediate meaning-making needs, driven as he was by his intense social and conversational will to communicate. By comparison, over the three years of study Schmidt never caught Wes using the kinds of strategy that would foster longer-term learning, such as consulting a dictionary or asking his interlocutors metalinguistic questions about subtle differences or idiomatic appropriacy. Furthermore, in the many conversational excerpts that Schmidt (1983) offers, we find no trace of interactional moves like the ones we will discuss in this chapter, and which have been posited to foster learning of the language code. For example, Wes does not appear to incorporate into his utterances new language or more precise wordings that are offered by interlocutors, and when faced with signals of non-understanding from others, he repeats exactly what he just said or he explains what he meant with entirely new utterances, unable or unwilling to revise and fine-tune his language choices.

How can Wes's mixed success story of language learning be explained? Schmidt proposed that 'sensitivity to form' or the drive to pay attention to the language code (p. 172) seems to be the single ingredient missing in Wes's efforts to learn the L2. Despite optimal attitudes towards the L2 and its members and plentiful and meaningful participation in English interactions, Wes was driven as a learner by an overriding investment in 'message content over message form' (p. 169). As he himself puts it, '*I know I'm speaking funny English / because I'm never learning / I'm only just listen / then talk*' (p. 168). Schmidt concluded that positive attitudes and an optimal environment will afford the linguistic data needed for learning, but that the learning will not happen unless the learner engages in active processing of those data. In other words, grammar acquisition cannot be successful without applying 'interest', 'attention' and 'hard work' (p. 173) to the task of cracking the language code.

With this conclusion, the kernel of the Noticing Hypothesis was born (discussed in section 4.6). Nevertheless, cognitive-interactionist SLA researchers interested in the environment spent most of the decade of the 1980s exploring the four ingredients of attitudes, input, interaction and output before the insights finally converged into an emerging consensus that attention was the needed fifth ingredient to consider. Let us examine each ingredient and its associated hypothesis.

4.2 ACCULTURATION AS A PREDICTIVE EXPLANATION FOR L2 LEARNING SUCCESS?

Obviously, the L2 environment engenders in learners certain **attitudes** that have affective and social–psychological bases and that must be considered if we want to understand L2 learning. In the late 1970s, John Schumann at the University of California Los Angeles focused on attitudes and proposed the Pidginization Hypothesis, also known as the Acculturation Model (explained in Schumann, 1976). The proposal was inspired by his case study of Alberto, a 33-year-old immigrant worker from Costa Rica who appeared to be unable to move beyond basic pidginized English after almost a year and a half in Boston, and even after he was provided with some individualized instruction. Schumann predicted that great social distance between the L1 and L2 groups (as is the case of circumstantial immigrants, who speak a subordinate minority language and are surrounded by a powerful language of the majority), and an individual's affective negative predispositions towards the target language and its members (e.g. culture shock, low motivation) may conspire to create what he characterized as a bad learning situation that causes learners to stagnate into a pidgin-like state in their grammar, without inflections or mature syntax. Conversely, he predicted that the more acculturated a learner can become (that is, the closer to the target society and its members, socially and psychologically), the more successful his or her eventual learning outcomes will be.

Schmidt's (1983) study of Wes was originally designed as a test case of the Acculturation Model and, as we have seen, it provided strong evidence against attitudes being the only or most important explanatory mechanism for L2 learning success. In response to the new evidence, Schumann eventually modified his model in important ways (Schumann, 1990, 1997). It should also be recognized that explanations that make acculturation into the target society a necessary prerequisite for successful language acquisition lend themselves to dangerous interpretations. Success and failure in L2 learning are too complex to be explained by static membership into a group or by individual choice alone. Furthermore, meritocratic explanations that everyone can learn an L2 well, if they only want it badly enough and try hard enough, do not stand research scrutiny. Nevertheless, affective and social–psychological variables that arise from non-linguistic dimensions of the environment remain important when explaining L2 learning. We will examine them in Chapters 8 and 9, through a social–psychological prism, and in Chapter 10, through a sociocultural and poststructuralist lens.

4.3 INPUT FOR COMPREHENSION AND FOR LEARNING

The environment affords learners **input**, or linguistic data produced by other competent users of the L2. Also in the late 1970s, Stephen Krashen at the University of Southern California formally proposed a central role in L2 learning for input in his Comprehensible Input Hypothesis (best formulated in Krashen, 1985). This proposal drew on his extensive educational work with English-language learners in California's schools and communities.

According to Krashen, the single most important source of L2 learning is comprehensible input, or language which learners process for meaning and which contains something to be learned, that is, linguistic data slightly above their current level. This is what Krashen termed **i+1**. Learners obtain comprehensible input mostly through listening to oral messages that interlocutors direct to them and via reading written texts that surround them, such as street signs, personal letters, books and so on. When L2 learners process these messages for meaning (which they will most likely do if the content is personally relevant, and provided they can reasonably understand them), grammar learning will naturally occur. Krashen proposed this role for input on the assumption that the mechanisms of L2 learning are essentially similar to the mechanisms of L1 learning: in order to build an L1 grammar, children only need to be exposed to the language that parents or caretakers direct to them for the purpose of meaning making.

The strong claim that comprehensible input is both necessary and sufficient for L2 learning proved to be untenable in light of findings gleaned by Schmidt (1983) and by many others, who documented minimal grammatical development despite ample meaningful opportunities to use the language, even with young L2 learners – for example, children attending French immersion (Swain, 1985) and regular English-speaking schools (Sato, 1990). Input is undoubtedly necessary, but it cannot be sufficient.

In addition, the expectation that more comprehension necessarily brings about more acquisition has not been borne out by the empirical evidence. Several researchers have noted that comprehension and acquisition are two distinct processes (e.g. Sharwood Smith, 1986), and some studies (e.g. Doughty, 1991; Loschky, 1994) have shown that learners can comprehend more than they acquire and can acquire more than they comprehend. In later years, Krashen himself has only indirectly engaged in research that would shed light on the relationship between comprehension and acquisition, placing his efforts on public advocacy of extensive reading (or voluntary reading, as he prefers to call it; Krashen, 2004) and bilingual education (Krashen and McField, 2005). Nevertheless, the suggestive evidence of a dissociation between comprehension and acquisition points at the need to understand the relationship between the two processes better in the future. The need is particularly important in connection with knowledge about optimal schooling conditions for linguistic minorities in mainstream classrooms, where educational goals related to the learning of content and of language are equal in importance (Mohan et al., 2001; Valdés, 2001; Schleppegrell, 2004).

4.4 INTERACTION AND NEGOTIATION FOR MEANING

Much in the linguistic environment, particularly in naturalistic settings, but also in today's communicative classrooms, comes to learners in the midst of oral **interaction** with one or more interlocutors, rather than as exposure to monologic spoken or written discourse. In the early 1980s, Michael Long proposed the Interaction Hypothesis (best explained and updated in Long, 1996). The hypothesis grew out of work conducted for his dissertation at the University of California Los Angeles, in which college-level ESL learners were paired to interact with English native-speaking pre-service and in-service teachers of ESL. It extended Krashen's proposal by connecting it in novel ways with studies in discourse analysis that had entered the field via the work of SLA founder Evelyn Hatch (1978) and work done on caretaker speech and foreigner talk in neighbouring disciplines. At the time, Long agreed with Krashen that learning happens through comprehension, and that the more one comprehends, the more one learns. However, he departed from the strong input orientation of the times by focusing on interaction and proposing that the best kind of comprehensible input learners can hope to obtain is input that has been interactionally modified, in other words, adjusted after receiving some signal that the interlocutor needs some help in order to fully understand the message.

Interactional modifications are initiated by moves undertaken by either interlocutor in reaction to (real or perceived) comprehension problems, as they strive to make meaning more comprehensible for each other, that is, to **negotiate for meaning**. Typically, negotiation episodes begin with **clarification requests** if non-understanding is serious (e.g. *whaddya mean? uh? pardon me?*), **confirmation checks** when the interlocutor is somewhat unsure she has understood the message correctly (e.g. *you mean X? X and Y, right?*) and **comprehension checks** if one interlocutor suspects the other speaker may not have understood what she said (e.g. *you know what I mean? do you want me to repeat?*). Following signals of a need to negotiate something, the other interlocutor may confirm understanding or admit non-understanding, seek help, repeat her words exactly or try to phrase the message differently. Often this two-way process makes both interlocutors modify their utterances in ways that not only increase the comprehensibility of the message but also augment the salience of certain L2 forms and make them available to the learner for learning (Pica, 1994). This is illustrated in (6):

(6) Jane: All right now [reading from the script], above the sun place the squirrel. He's right on top of the sun.
     Hiroshi: What is ... the word?
     Jane: OK. The sun.
     Hiroshi: Yeah, sun, but
     Jane: Do you know what the sun is?
     Hiroshi: Yeah, of course. Wh-what's the
     Jane: Squirrel. Do you know what a squirrel is?
     Hiroshi: No.
     Jane: OK. You've seen them running around on campus. They're little furry animals. They're short and brown and they eat nuts like crazy.

(Gass and Varonis, 1994, p. 296)

When interlocutors like Jane and Hiroshi work through messages in these ways, engaging in as much (or as little) negotiation for meaning as needed, we might say that they are generating tailor-made comprehensible input, or learner-contingent i+1, at the right level the particular interlocutor needs to understand the message. It was for this reason that Long predicted interactionally modified input would be more beneficial than other kinds of input. For example, it may be better than unmodified or authentic input (as in the listening or reading of authentic texts) but also better than pre-modified input (as in graded readers), which often means simplifying the language, thus risking the elimination of the +1 in the i+1 equation. Interactional modifications have the potential to bring about comprehension in a more individualized or learner-contingent fashion, with repetitions and redundancies rather than simplification. Thus, an important general benefit of interactional modifications is their contingency, in that learners are potentially engaging in what educational researchers would call just-in-time learning, or learning at the right point of need.

4.5   OUTPUT AND SYNTACTIC PROCESSING DURING PRODUCTION

Where there is interaction, learners engage by necessity not only in comprehending and negotiating messages but also in making meaning and producing messages, that is, in **output**. By the mid-1980s, it was becoming apparent to SLA researchers that positive attitudes and plentiful input and interaction, while important, were not sufficient to guarantee successful grammatical acquisition. It was at this juncture that Canadian researcher Merrill Swain (1985) at the University of Toronto formulated her Pushed Output Hypothesis (you will also see the terms Comprehensible Output Hypothesis and Output Hypothesis used interchangeably). She did so drawing on results of large-scale assessment of the linguistic outcomes of French immersion schools in Ontario, an English-speaking province of Canada.

Specifically, she compared the oral and written performances of children who had studied in immersion schools against the performances on the same tasks by same-age L1 French peers. She found patterns that remarkably resonate with Schmidt's (1983) findings for Wes (see section 4.1). School immersion from kindergarten to sixth grade afforded these children optimal development in discourse competence (as well as optimal comprehension abilities and school content learning), but not in grammatical competence or in sociolinguistic competence for aspects that demanded grammatical means (as opposed to formulaic means) for their realization, such as the French choice between *vous/tu* (formal/informal 'you') and the use of conditional as a politeness marker (Swain, 1985). She concluded that the missing element in this school immersion context was sufficient opportunities for the children to actually use the language in meaningful ways, through speaking and writing.

Comprehension does not usually demand the full processing of forms. During comprehension (e.g. when children read textbooks and listen to teacher explanations in school), it is possible to get the gist of messages by relying on key content words aided by knowledge of the world, contextual clues, and guessing. For example, in *yesterday I walked three miles*, we may hear 'yesterday' and not even need to hear the morpheme *–ed* in order to know our interlocutor is telling us about something that happened in the past. By the same token, reliance on this kind of lexical processing is less possible during production, because the psycholinguistic demands of composing messages force speakers to use syntactic processing to a much greater extent. Thus, Swain proposed that 'producing the target language may be the trigger that forces the learner to pay attention to the means of expression needed in order to successfully convey his or her own intended meaning' (p. 249). This is particularly true if interlocutors do not understand and push for a better formulation of the message, if learners push themselves to express their intended meaning more precisely or if the nature of what they are trying to do with words (i.e. the task) is demanding, cognitively and linguistically.

Swain's pushed output hypothesis created a space to conceive of a competence-expanding role for production that had not been possible before the mid-1980s, when most researchers could envision a causal role in L2 learning only for comprehension. Even to this date, many scholars view production as merely useful in building up fluency (e.g. de Bot, 1996; VanPatten, 2004). Yet, a focus on pushed output allows for the possibility that production engages crucial acquisition-related processes (Izumi, 2003; see section 4.9). Optimal L2 learning must include opportunities for language use that is slightly beyond what the learner currently can handle in speaking or writing, and production which is meaningful and whose demands exceed the learner's current abilities is the kind of language use most likely to destabilize internal interlanguage representations. By encouraging risk-full attempts by the learner to handle complex content beyond current competence, such conditions of language use may drive learning.

4.6 NOTICING AND ATTENTION AS MODERATORS OF AFFORDANCES IN THE ENVIRONMENT

Can we then conclude that acculturated attitudes, comprehensible input, negotiated interaction and pushed output are the four ingredients we need to explain optimal L2 learning? Not quite. As you will well remember from section 4.1, Wes enjoyed all four ingredients to no avail, at least for the mastery of the L2 grammar. **Attention** to formal detail in the input seemed to be missing and perhaps needed. The insights Schmidt gained from studying Wes and from a later case study of himself learning Portuguese during a five-month stay in Rio de Janeiro (Schmidt and Frota, 1986) led him to formally propose the Noticing Hypothesis in the early 1990s (best explained in Schmidt, 1995). He claimed that, in order to learn any aspect of the L2 (from sounds, to words, to grammar, to pragmatics), learners need to notice the relevant material in the linguistic data afforded by the environment. Noticing refers to the brain registering the new material, with some fleeting awareness at the point of encounter that there is something new, even if there is no understanding of how the new element works, and possibly even if there is no reportable memory of the encounter at a later time (see Chapter 5, sections 5.11 through 5.13). Since it is difficult to distinguish absence of noticing from inability to remember and report the experience of noticing at a later time, Schmidt (2001) concluded cautiously that the more L2 learners notice, the more they learn, and that learning without noticing (that is, subliminal learning), even if it exists in other domains of human learning, plays a minimal role in the challenging business of learning a new language.

The capacity to attend to the language code can be internally or externally fostered. Instances of noticing can be driven from within the learner, as when she struggles to put a sentence together and express her thoughts and in the process discovers something new. They can also be encouraged by external means, for example, through a lesson orchestrated by a teacher, a question or reaction from an interlocutor, and so on. Through such internal and external means, learners pay attention to the existence of new features of the L2 (Schmidt, 1995), become aware of locatable gaps between their utterances and those of interlocutors (Schmidt and Frota, 1986) and discover holes in what they are able to express with their given linguistic resources in the L2 (Swain and Lapkin, 1995). Thus, attention and noticing act as filters that moderate the contributions of the environment. We will scrutinize attention and noticing in more depth in Chapter 5, when we examine cognition.

4.7 TWO GENERATIONS OF INTERACTION STUDIES

Of the five environmental ingredients examined by cognitive-interactionists, the most exhaustively studied has been interaction. A first generation of interaction studies can be situated in an intellectual space between Long's dissertation in 1980 and the mid-1990s. It focused on negotiation for meaning and comprehension and concentrated on three goals: (a) describing how negotiation for meaning unfolds; (b) specifying the contextual factors related to interlocutor and task that stimulate the greatest amounts of negotiation for meaning; and (c) investigating benefits of interaction for comprehension. The first goal yielded a long lineage of process-oriented investigations, authoritatively reviewed by Pica (1992, 1994), that described the discourse of dyads interacting orally and developed a methodology for the identification and quantification of not only negotiation moves but also learner responses to them. This line of research also established that not only adults, but children as well, are capable of L2 negotiations using the same range of strategies as adults, although they disprefer comprehension checks and instead rely heavily on self- and other-repetition (Oliver, 1998). The second goal was fuelled by the reasoning that if negotiation-rich interaction facilitates L2 learning, we will want to ensure learners engage in negotiations by design. Its pursuit resulted in a wealth of findings regarding interlocutor and task elements that engender high amounts of negotiation, reviewed by Pica et al. (1993). The final goal to establish links between negotiated interaction and improved comprehension also met with success in a number of studies that showed that the more interlocutors negotiated, the more they comprehended, and that opportunities to negotiate led to better levels of comprehension than providing exposure to either unmodified or pre-modified input (e.g. Pica et al., 1987; Yano et al., 1994).

This first generation of interaction work was vibrant during the 1980s and early 1990s. Two oft-cited publications in the mid-1990s, a study by Gass and Varonis (1994) and another by Loschky (1994), marked the prelude towards a second generation.

Following Long's seminal work, researchers had always looked at learner reactions to negotiation moves on the fly. In 1994, Susan Gass at Michigan State University and her colleague Evangeline Varonis helped advance thinking about the acquisitional consequences of interaction by inspecting, for the first time, the benefits in subsequent production. They investigated 16 dyads of native and non-native speakers who had to work through a task that involved giving instructions for placing 20 objects on a board depicting an outdoor scene. In the first trial, the native-speaking member held the information to be read and the non-native-speaking member was the receiver of that information. Only half of the dyads were allowed to interrupt the reading of the script and interact, as Hiroshi and Jane did in excerpt (6) earlier. Following the first task, which lasted about 20 minutes, there was a similar second task, in which the researchers asked the dyad members to reverse roles. Now the L2 speaker was to hold all the information, whereas the native-speaking member of the dyad was responsible for placing the same 20 objects correctly on a different board. During the second trial, learners who had been allowed to interact were observed to recycle and incorporate input afforded by their interlocutors during the first task. The same kind of transfer of discourse strategies did not occur in the data of the remaining eight dyads who had not interacted. Gass and Varonis conclude encouragingly that negotiated interaction 'focuses a learner's attention on linguistic form, on ways of creating discourse' (1994, p. 298).

Ironically, Lester Loschky's (1994) contribution to the advancement of interaction work was motivated by disappointing findings when, for the first time, he directly examined the relationship between comprehension and acquisition in a quasi-experimental study carried out for his Master's thesis at the University of Hawai'i. He targeted the acquisition of a set of L2 Japanese vocabulary and a locative grammar rule and included three treatment groups. When the groups were compared on pre- and post-tests, he found that interactionally modified input resulted in better comprehension than no opportunity to interact plus either authentic or pre-modified input, yet all three conditions led to similar amounts of learning of the targets. Loschky attributed the equal learning to the attentional demands that arose from the tasks used in the study. Specifically, he argued that the task design made the use of the vocabulary set and the locative structure so singularly useful and salient to the participants that all of them apparently were able to show gains on the post-tests regardless of condition. In a related publication, Loschky and Bley-Vroman (1993) coined the term 'task-essentialness' to refer to such a desirable quality in task design.

4.8 THE EMPIRICAL LINK BETWEEN INTERACTION AND ACQUISITION

The next quasi-experimental interaction study, a doctoral dissertation at the University of Sydney by Alison Mackey (published in Mackey, 1999), was the first to report positive findings for the link between interaction and acquisition. She found that out of 34 intermediate ESL adult learners working with native speakers in dyads, only the learners in the 14 dyads who were allowed and encouraged to interact showed substantial improvement in their use of English questions on the immediate post-test. These gains were maintained on two delayed post-tests a week and again a month later.

Mackey (1999) opened the way for more and more studies that have turned to the cognitive rationale of the updated interaction hypothesis (Long, 1996) and have examined the link between interaction and acquisition directly. This second generation of interaction work has yielded a substantial number of studies characterized by: (a) product-oriented designs that include pre- and post-tests; (b) the measurement of learning gains on particular forms targeted during task-based interactions; and sometimes (c) the inclusion of measures of noticing (see Chapter 5) that may help clarify the posited causal link between interaction and acquisition. In fact, the second generation has now been synthesized in two meta-analyses that have furnished robust evidence for the facilitative role of interaction with the learning of L2 grammar rules and vocabulary.

Meta-analysis is a methodology that enables the researcher to combine the quantitative findings accumulated across many similar studies into statistical aggregations that are more than the sum of the parts and aim to reveal the pattern of evidence in a given research domain (Norris and Ortega, 2006). When the studies that make up the meta-analysis contribute comparisons of an experimental group and a control or baseline group, the results are usually reported in an effect size index called Cohen's d, which shows how many standard deviation units separate the average performance of one group from the other. A difference in favour of the treatment group of about half a standard deviation unit ($d = 0.50$) can be considered of medium size, and it is the equivalent of an increase in score from the 50th percentile to the 67th percentile for that group. A difference of 0.80 or higher, equivalent to raising scores from the 50th to the 77th percentile or higher, suggests that the impact of the treatment is large.

The first interaction meta-analysis was conducted by Keck et al. (2006), who combined the empirical evidence yielded by 14 task-based interaction studies published between 1994 and 2003 investigating English, Japanese and Spanish as target languages. They found that the gains for groups who used the targeted L2 forms during task-based interaction were substantial, with an average effect size around $d = 0.90$, that is, almost a standard deviation unit better than the baseline groups. These gains were sustained and even grew somewhat stronger for the ten interaction studies that featured delayed post-tests, scheduled as soon as one week and as late as two months after the interactional treatment. Keck et al. also found that in a few cases when primary researchers had striven by design to make the targeted forms and vocabulary essential for completion of the tasks (in Loschky and Bley-Vroman's 1993 sense), the effects not only endured but grew stronger ($d = 1.66$) over a lag period of up to about a month. The second meta-analysis was conducted by Mackey and Goo (2007). It incorporated an additional 14 studies and covered publications up to 2007. The researchers found an overall average effect size of $d = 0.75$ for interaction groups when compared to minimal or no interaction groups. In addition, with more studies to aggregate, an interesting difference emerged regarding the effects of negotiation on grammar learning, as opposed to vocabulary learning. Namely, average grammar benefits were initially of medium size ($d = 0.59$) and only grew stronger and became large ($d = 1.07$) when measured up to a month after the interaction had taken place.

An important insight from both meta-analyses, and one that lends support to early claims by Gass and Varonis (1994) and Mackey (1999), is that the benefits of interaction on L2 learning may need some time to manifest themselves. Judging from the insights offered by the two meta-analyses, a long-term view on the benefits of interaction may be particularly important in the future, when a new generation of interaction researchers may become interested in assessing longitudinally the L2 grammar learning that occurs through task-essential use of the new L2 material.

4.9 OUTPUT MODIFICATION

Work on the acquisition value of productive language use, initiated by Swain (1985), has been pursued by a number of cognitive-interactionist researchers. A dual focus on negotiation for meaning and output has been increasingly more common, for example, in the work of Teresa Pica at the University of Pennsylvania and, more recently, in the studies conducted by Kim McDonough at Northern Arizona University. Both contributors have paid close attention to how learners respond to negotiation for meaning moves, or what initially Pica called interlanguage modifications (see Pica, 1992, 1994) and is more frequently known today as **output modification** (McDonough, 2005). Swain herself has somewhat departed from this line of work by reconceptualizing her Output Hypothesis into a sociocultural framework (Swain, 1995, 2000) that we will examine in Chapter 10. Nevertheless, work by Belgian researcher Kris Van den Branden, Syrian researcher Ali Shehadeh and Japanese researcher Shinichi Izumi has continued to build on three competence-expanding functions for output that Swain (1995, 2000) identified: it promotes noticing of gaps and holes, which in turn pushes learners to revise their utterances; it can carry a metalinguistic function when learners negotiate forms, not only meaning, and reflect upon them; and it facilitates hypothesis testing when new forms are tried out in production and feedback is received from others as to their success and appropriacy.

In a rationale that resembles that of Gass and Varonis (1994) but included pre- and post-test measurement of gains, Van den Branden (1997) posited that the benefits of interaction would be most immediately evident in the quality of the subsequent output produced two hours later after the interaction. The participants were 16 11- and 12-year-old learners of Dutch, most of whom were home speakers of Berber as an L1 and all of whom had been schooled in Dutch since the age of three. They were asked to solve a murder case based on pictures. Eight of the L2 students were paired with a Dutch native-speaking friend from the same class. Another eight did the task one-on-one with the researcher, who systematically provided them with moves that were intended to push their output. A third group of eight students with Dutch as L1 acted as a comparison. The findings showed that all L2 learners extensively modified their output in response to negotiation moves. How they chose to do so depended not so much on whether the interlocutor was a peer or the adult researcher, but on the type of negotiation move they received. For example, a *yes/no* acknowledgement was more likely to be issued in response to a confirmation check (e.g. *you mean X?*), whereas more extensive modification was likely to ensue in response to clarification requests (e.g. *pardon me?*). Comparing the picture description task done for the pre-test with that of the post-test, Van den Branden found that the two interaction groups produced more language on the post-test (a productivity advantage) and provided more complete information (an information quality advantage). He concluded that negotiation indeed engenders pushed output.

The observation that different types of negotiation moves shape different kinds of interlanguage modifications was initially made by Pica (e.g. Pica et al., 1989). The same idea was later developed by Shehadeh (2001) into a careful taxonomy for the study of learner response to negotiation moves or output modification. For example, the learner may ignore the signal, fail to repair the problem, express difficulty (*I don't know how to say it in English*), repeat the previous utterance of the interlocutor without change, insert irrelevant information or branch into a new topic (pp. 455–6). The learner can also respond by modifying her utterance and revising it into a more target-like version, or what has been called **repair**, as shown in (7):

(7)   Learner 1: two small bottle
      Learner 2: two small what?
      Learner 1: bot (1.0) small bottles

$\qquad\qquad\qquad\qquad\qquad\qquad\qquad\qquad$ (Shehadeh, 2001, p. 456)

Shehadeh's work also drew attention to a type of modification of output that previous research had neglected: **self-initiated output modification**, or self-initiated repair, a concept that is borrowed from Conversation Analysis (Schegloff et al., 1977). As understood in cognitive-interactionist SLA work, the category refers to an attempt to self-correct that is not prompted by an interlocutor. It can be signalled by a silence, an overt comment like *I mean*, a cut-off or abandonment of an utterance, or the use of hesitation devices like *eh*, *emm* and *er* (pp. 456–7). For example:

(8)   NNS: yes because if the woman is (0.8) the wife always go out (0.6) goes out and left his his husband eh (1.0) her husband and her son in the home (0.7) at home it's it's not reasonable for for ...

$\qquad\qquad\qquad\qquad\qquad\qquad\qquad\qquad$ (Shehadeh, 2001, p. 437)

In his studies, Shehadeh has found robust evidence that output modification occurs more frequently as a result of self-initiated repair than as an outcome of other-initiated repair. In a 1999 study, he reports modifications at a higher rate of 2.5 per minute in response to self-initiation than other-initiation (only 1 per minute). In his 2001 study, he found 224 negotiation moves signalling the need for repair versus 535 self-initiated attempts at repair. Furthermore, the other-initiated repair resulted in output modification in 81 per cent of cases, whereas the self-initiated repair led to successful output modification (that is, to a more accurate revised form) in 93 per cent of the cases.

Izumi (2003) attempted to conceptualize the pushed output hypothesis within the psycholinguistic framework developed for the L1 by Levelt (1989). Izumi argued that meaningful productive use of the L2 during speaking or writing calls for grammatical encoding and monitoring processes (p. 190). During production, these two processes allow learners to 'assess the possibilities and limitations of what they can or cannot express in the [target language]' and in doing so they become 'an internal priming device for consciousness raising' that can promote language learning (p. 191). However, given that the psycholinguistic processes of grammatical encoding and monitoring can only be summoned during natural language use, he stipulates that pushed output cannot be expected to be involved in mechanical language use, only in meaningful language use. This claim has been substantiated in a later study by Izumi and Izumi (2004).

Perhaps because different output researchers have pursued different lines of interest and expanded the pushed output hypothesis into diverse directions, the available findings are less compact than the interaction findings reviewed in previous sections. Some years ago Shehadeh (2002) made a call for more research on output modification that directly looks at the link between output and acquisition. More recently, Toth (2006) noted that mounting evidence on 'the links among metalinguistic knowledge, output, and the L2 implicit system' (p. 373) is promising and warrants further research attention. To date, however, research on output appears to remain far from the goal of producing systematic accumulation of knowledge via a concerted research programme.

4.10 LEARNER-INITIATED NEGOTIATION OF FORM

Not only meaning, but also form can be negotiated. In these cases no communication difficulties are apparent, and instead it is a linguistic problem that attracts attention and results in language-mediated reflection during interaction. This focus on form is partly a natural consequence of formal instruction contexts. After all, students join language classes for the very concrete business of learning the L2. Excerpt (9) illustrates one such episode:

(9)   Student 1: He leaped. He freezed.
       Student 2: Freezed? Frozen?
       Student 1: Freeze, froze, frozen. Froze.
       Student 2: He froze?
       Student 1: F–R–O–Z–E. Froze.
       Student 2: Froze. OK.

(Jessica Williams, 1999, p. 601)

Excerpt (10) shows a more direct request for assistance from one learner to the other:

(10)   Learner 1: Los nombres en el mapa. ¿Es el mapa o la mapa?
[The names on the map. Is it the map masculine or the map-*feminine*?]
Learner 2: El mapa
[The map-*masculine*]

(Gass et al., 2005, p. 587)

Negotiations of form often involve use of the L1 when they occur in classrooms where students share the same mother tongue, as is typically the case in foreign language settings and also in language immersion education programmes. For example:

(11)   Student 1: *Et elle est tickelée.* How do you say 'tickled'?
[And she is tickelée. How do you say 'tickled'?]
Student 2: *Chatouillée.*
[Tickled]
Student 1: OK. *Chatouillée, chatouillée.* How do you say 'foot'?
[Ok. Tickled, tickled. How do you say 'foot'?]
Student 2: *Le pied.*
[The foot]
Student 1: Ah, *chatouillée les pieds.*
[Ah, tickled the feet]

(Swain and Lapkin, 2000, p. 259)

Such episodes need not lead to solutions that are always correct from the viewpoint of the target language, but the claim is that they engage meta-reflection and self-regulation processes that have the potential to foster L2 learning. Merrill Swain and her colleague Sharon Lapkin (1995) originally proposed the term **Language-Related Episode** (LRE) to refer to negotiation of form episodes that are learner-initiated, and which they noted are particularly fostered during collaborative writing activities. Others have studied similar occurrences, although more frequently focusing on purely oral interactions, under different labels. For instance, Rod Ellis and his colleagues at the University of Auckland (Ellis et al., 2001) have used the term **Learner-Initiated Focus on Form** and Jessica Williams (1999) at the University of Illinois in Chicago has redefined LREs as episodes containing negotiation of either form or meaning, as long as they are learner-initiated. However loosely called and defined, the research shows that learner-initiated negotiation of form can take many shapes, running the full gamut from implicit to explicit focalization on the language code, as shown in (9), (10) and (11) above.

Interestingly, more explicit negotiation of form episodes that involve the use of the L1 or metalanguage appear to be particularly beneficial for learning. Thus, Swain and Lapkin (2000) found that higher use of the L1 in LREs produced by French immersion eighth-graders during a jigsaw task was associated to higher-quality ratings on the collaborative narratives they subsequently wrote; and Basturkmen et al. (2002) reported that in the 165 learner-initiated and pre-emptive focus-on-form moves they studied, episodes were more likely to exhibit successful incorporation of the correct form when learners used some non-technical metalanguage (*how do you spell X? is it a noun? this sentence past or present?*) in them.

4.11 NEGATIVE FEEDBACK DURING MEANING AND FORM NEGOTIATION

A final benefit of the environment, not discussed so far, is that it may provide learners with information about the ungrammaticality of their utterances. When the interlocutor has the actual intention to provide such negative information, then we may want to speak of error correction. However, more often than not, it is impossible (for the researcher as much as for the parties involved in the interaction!) to decide whether the intention to correct was at work. Therefore, we will prefer the term **negative feedback** over *error correction* or the near-synonymous *corrective feedback* (both of which imply a clear pedagogical intention to correct) and also over *negative evidence* (which is used in formal linguistic discussions about what linguistic abstract information would be needed to reset certain values within the limits available in Universal Grammar; Beck et al., 1995).

Negative feedback can be provided in interactive discourse orally, but it also occurs very often in writing (both in classrooms and in non-school contexts for professional, technical and creative writing) and in the context of technology-mediated communication and study. For reasons of length, I will restrict the discussion in this section to oral negative feedback (I offer some suggestions for readings in the area of feedback on L2 writing and technology-mediated events at the end of the chapter). In Chapter 10, you will see how negative feedback can be conceptualized if we adopt a radically social perspective. Specifically, this has been done in distinct ways by SLA researchers guided by Vygotskian (section 10.6), conversation analytical (section 10.9) and systemic functional linguistic (section 10.12) perspectives.

From the perspective of cognitive-interactionist researchers, negative feedback may come about as part of negotiating meaning or form. For example, a **clarification request** (e.g. *sorry?*) is offered when intelligibility is low and meaning itself needs to be negotiated. Nevertheless, it may convey to the learner an indication, albeit a most implicit and indirect one, that some ungrammaticality is present:

(12) Learner: what happen for the boat?
      Interlocutor: what?
      Learner: what's wrong with the boat?

                                              (McDonough, 2005, p. 86)

At the other extreme, **explicit corrections** overtly focus on the form at fault and occur when a teacher clearly indicates to a student that some choice is non-target-like:

(13) Student: Ich empfehle den Beruf an
                [I recommend that profession + particle *an*]
      Teacher: Nein nein, empfehlen empfehlen ohne an, ich empfehle den Beruf
                [No, no, to recommend without the preposition *an*: 'I recommend
                that profession']

                                              (Lochtman, 2002, p. 276)

Somewhere in the middle are recasts and elicitations. **Recasts** occur when an interlocutor repeats the learner utterance, maintaining its meaning but offering a more conventional or mature rendition of the form. For example:

(14)   Greg: Nagai aida o-hanashi <u>shi-mashita</u> kara, benkyoo shi-nakatta
                          desu
                          [because I talk<u>ed</u> for a long time, I didn't study]
         Interlocutor: Nagai aida o-hanashi <u>shi-te i-ta</u> kara desu ka?
                          [because you were talk<u>ing</u> for a long time?]

(Ishida, 2004, p. 375)

Elicitations include moves such as asking *how do we say X?* or directly asking the interlocutor to try again. When they occur in classrooms, the teacher may initiate an other-repetition and pause in the middle of the utterance at fault to let the student complete it correctly, as in (15):

(15)   Teacher: Il vit où un animal domestique? Où est-ce que ça vit?
                    [Where does a pet live? Where does it live?]
         Student: Dans un maison
                    [In a-*masculine* house]
         Teacher: Dans… ? Attention
                    [In… ? Careful]
         Student: Dans une maison
                    [In a-*feminine* house]

(Lyster, 2004, p. 405)

Elicitations like the one in (15) are didactic and are therefore typically issued by the teacher. They would be rarely issued by interlocutors outside the classroom context.

Many language teachers and students believe the provision of negative feedback by the teacher in speaking and writing is a staple of good classroom instruction. And, at least logically, negative feedback would be the single most relevant way for L2 learners to figure out what is *not* possible in the target language. Among SLA researchers, however, there are dissenting voices who object that language is fundamentally learned without recourse to negative feedback information (Schwartz, 1993). Others maintain there is insufficient evidence to show conclusively that negative feedback works (Truscott, 1999). These sceptics discount the empirical evidence accumulated either because they feel it only reflects explicit, metalinguistic learning *about* the L2, or because they expect negative feedback should work across the board and universally in order to be pronounced useful, sometimes for both reasons. Most cognitive-interactionist researchers, on the other hand, argue that negative feedback is beneficial for learning (Long, 1996; Lyster et al., 1999; Russell and Spada, 2006).

How frequent is oral negative feedback? In non-classroom settings, early studies suggested that direct negative feedback is rare (Gaskill, 1980; Day et al., 1984). In essence, the same conversational principles that apply in natural L1 conversations and make other-repair deeply dispreferred (Schegloff et al., 1977) are powerful deterrents of other-correction in L2 conversations. Nevertheless, corrections may still happen, as Schmidt and Frota (1986) amply documented in both their recorded conversational data and their retrospective diary data. Their account suggests that whether corrections occur outside the classroom depends on the relationship between an L2 speaker and her interlocutors, and even on interlocutor personalities and how inclined towards didacticism they may be around L2 speakers.

In instructional settings, a good proportion of errors appear to be responded to. In classrooms, the lowest attested end of the range is feedback on 48 per cent of errors, reported by Panova and Lyster (2002) for ten hours of ESL lessons in Montreal with a majority of students who shared L1 Haitian Creole and French. The highest end is 90 per cent (or one negative feedback episode every 0.65 minutes), reported by Lochtman (2002) for ten hours of German as a foreign language lessons in Belgium with three high-school classrooms of 15- and 16-year-old speakers of Dutch as L1. In task-based dyadic interactions elicited in the laboratory with native-speaking interlocutors, somewhat lower rates of negative feedback are reported, probably because an instructional focus is not necessarily assumed by interlocutors. Between a half and a third of ungrammaticalities produced by learners appear to receive some kind of negative feedback in laboratory studies (e.g. Oliver, 1995; Iwashita, 2003; Mackey et al., 2003), but the proportion is sometimes lower (e.g. one-quarter of errors were responded to in Braidi, 2002).

How is negative feedback provided? Since the very beginnings of the field, SLA researchers have tried to identify and tally negative feedback after classifying it into a number of discrete move types: clarification requests, explicit corrections, recasts, elicitations and several more (other-repetition, prompts, translations, etc.). For the L2 classroom, the most influential of these taxonomies was developed by Roy Lyster at McGill University and his colleague Leila Ranta at Concordia University (Lyster and Ranta, 1997). They built on a complex coding system proposed 20 years earlier by Craig Chaudron (1977) in his dissertation at the University of Toronto. Yet, the caution is increasingly more frequently voiced that each of these 'types' can differ greatly in implementation and that any one of them can vary in, among other things, the degree of explicitness or implicitness it entails, which in turn often varies, as we will see, as a function of context.

A sobering illustration is provided by the burgeoning research on recasts. This type of negative feedback, shown earlier in (14), has attracted an unprecedented interest since the publication about a decade ago of the first classroom and laboratory recast studies, summarized in Table 4.1.

Spurred by the conflicting findings yielded in these and other studies, later discussions (e.g. Nicholas et al., 2001) have centred around the distinct nature of language classrooms and laboratories and the differences in implementation between rather implicit recasts, such as those documented by Lyster and Ranta (1997), and largely explicit recasts, such as those delivered quasi-experimentally by Doughty and Varela (1998). Indeed, even though recasts were proposed by Long (1996, 2006) to work precisely because they are reactive and implicit, and despite the fact that they are often considered to be potentially just a 'conversational

Table 4.1
Four early L2 recast studies

Oliver (1995)	Ortega and Long (1997)
Design: Descriptive, in the laboratory	*Design*: Quasi-experimental, in the laboratory
Context: 8- to 13-year-old ESL students in Perth, Australia	*Context*: Third-semester college Spanish FL in Hawai'i, USA
Who: 96 dyads (NS–NNS, NNS–NNS and NS–NS)	*Who*: 30 dyads (learner–researcher)
Task: Two-way communication tasks	*Task*: One-way communication tasks
Focus: Comparison of negotiation of meaning vs recasts after different error types	*Focus*: Comparison of recasts vs models vs control on two structures: object topicalization and adverb placement
Results: 61% of errors were responded to; opaque non-target-like utterances were negotiated, transparent non-target-like utterances were recast; L2 children were able to incorporate the recast in a third of instances when it was conversationally appropriate to do so	*Results*: No effects of either treatment on object topicalization; for adverb placement, there was clear evidence of learning for the recast condition and of no learning for the model condition
Lyster and Ranta (1997)	**Doughty and Varela (1998)**
Design: Descriptive, in the classroom	*Design*: Quasi-experimental, in the classroom
Context: French immersion in Montreal, Canada	*Context*: ESL science classroom in the East Coast, USA
Who: Fourth- and fourth-/fifth-graders (18.3 hours from four different classrooms and teachers)	*Who*: An intact class of 21 11- to 14-year-olds and their teacher–researcher
Task: Regular content-based lessons (science, social studies, maths, French language arts)	*Task*: Task-essential science reports embedded in the regular curriculum
Focus: Moves in negative feedback sequences: feedback moves (six types) and uptake moves (repair, with four types, and needs-repair, with six types)	*Focus*: Recasts on simple past tense *–ed* and conditional *would*
Results: Teachers corrected 62% of student error turns; only 27% of these led to repair; teachers preferred recasts (55% of all negative feedback); recasts resulted in the least repair (31%), metalinguistic feedback and elicitation moves led to the most repair (c. 46%)	*Results*: Compared to a no-feedback class, the recast class showed clear gains on oral task tests that were maintained two months later; gains on written task tests were less clear and less durable

lubricant' (Ellis and Sheen, 2006, p. 585), Nicholas et al. (2001) made the important point that they can largely vary in how implicit they really are. Conversely, Ellis et al. (2006) note that what Lyster (2004) calls prompts is a category that includes both explicit and implicit moves.

In the future, then, it would be more desirable to be able to classify and analyse negative feedback episodes by attributes or features that can cut across (and abstract out of) specific types. One of these features ought to be degree of *explicitness*, as proposed by Ellis and Sheen (2006; Sheen, 2006). Explicitness can be defined as the perceptual salience (e.g. intonation) and linguistic marking (e.g. by metalanguage) with which the negative information is delivered and thus the corrective intent is made clear to learners. Another promising feature would be *demand*, which refers to main arguments for the benefits of prompts put forth by Lyster (2004) and can be defined as the degree of conversational urgency exerted upon interlocutors to react to the negative feedback in some way, for instance, by incorporating it, modifying their output or self-correcting. While explicitness and demand have received the most attention to date, a third promising feature is *informativeness*, defined as how much information is provided about the blame of the ungrammaticality, for example, whether a model with the grammatical version of the utterance is included or withheld in a negative feedback event. We will see a very different attempt to categorize negative feedback episodes along a self-regulatory continuum in Chapter 10, section 10.6.

Just how effective has negative feedback proven to be? The accumulating evidence suggests that providing negative feedback in some form results in better post-test performance than ignoring errors (Russell and Spada, 2006). Much less agreement has been reached, however, with regard to when, how and why negative feedback works, when it does. In the last ten years, many studies have been designed to compare, descriptively or quasi-experimentally, different kinds of feedback. For example, a large number of studies have asked whether the learning potential of recasts is superior or inferior to negotiation for meaning (Oliver, 1995), models (Long et al., 1998; Iwashita, 2003; Leeman, 2003), prompts (Lyster and Ranta, 1997; Lyster, 1998, 2004; Ammar and Spada, 2006), or metalinguistic explanations (Ellis et al., 2006). Yet, the overall pattern of results indicates that when two or more implementations of negative feedback are compared, the more explicit one leads to larger gains, as observed by Suzanne Carroll and her Canadian colleagues in the early 1990s (see Carroll et al., 1992). This finding is hardly illuminating and comes as an extension of the same conclusion reached by Norris and Ortega (2000) in a meta-analysis of 49 instructional studies, featuring a range of instructional options that included grammar explanations, input manipulations, practice or output treatments and provision of various negative feedback regimes. At least as currently operationalized in treatments and measured in tests, explicit types of L2 instruction consistently result in more sizeable gains than implicit ones.

The research also tells us increasingly more clearly and loudly that instructional context helps predict and understand not so much what negative feedback types teachers will prefer (since study after study shows teachers' preferred strategy is recasts) but rather what degree of explicitness they will exert in their delivery of those types. Thus, in formal instructional settings that may be communicative but are not content- or meaning-based, negative feedback is delivered in a more explicit manner than in contexts where teacher and students are engaged in the business of learning content through the L2, such as immersion programmes (Sheen, 2004, 2006; Loewen and Philp, 2006). Moreover, within the same lesson, negative feedback may vary depending on the discourse and pedagogical context. Specifically, as Jessica Williams (1999) and Oliver and Mackey (2003) have shown for ESL classrooms with children and adults, respectively, more feedback is both provided and responded to in parts of a lesson that focus on language rather than content or management.

How students respond to teacher feedback on the fly (that is, as evinced in the immediate next turn or turns) also differs remarkably across contexts, even in classrooms which at first glance fit a 'same-context' profile. Lyster and Mori (2006) found this to be true for classes in two immersion contexts serving fourth- and fifth-graders, one (the same investigated by Lyster and Ranta, 1997, cf. Table 4.1) involving French in Quebec, a French-speaking province of Canada, and the other involving Japanese in the United States. The relative frequency of recasts and prompts was comparable in both contexts. However, in the French immersion programme, where an orientation to content and meaning making was prevalent and the second language was available outside the classroom, students repaired after prompts much more frequently than after recasts (53 per cent vs. 38 per cent). In the Japanese immersion programme, by way of contrast, the pattern was reversed. In this classroom culture, inserted in the climate of a foreign language setting, and where choral repetitions were a familiar script for students, students were less likely to repair after prompts (23 per cent) and much more likely to repair after recasts (68 per cent). To account for this asymmetry, Lyster and Mori proposed their Counterbalance Hypothesis. In a nutshell, they predict that in contexts that put a premium on meaning making and content, negative feedback may be more effective when the transient corrective episode is more overt and explicit, thus adding salience to the focus-on-form event against the overall communication-oriented culture of the classroom. Conversely, in contexts which put a premium on accuracy and the learning of language as an object, negative feedback may be more effective when it is implemented in a more implicit fashion that preserves and capitalizes on an unusual focus on meaning, making such episodes more salient against the overall form-oriented culture of the classroom.

In the end, as we have seen, the evidence suggests that any given type of negative feedback may vary widely in explicitness, and that findings will be different depending on the interplay between at least the explicitness with which feedback is implemented and the wider classroom and societal context in which negative feedback occurs. Given the importance of implementation of feedback types and wider curricular and social context, in the near future it will be necessary to reconceptualize the all-or-nothing comparative approach that has characterized L2 research on negative feedback to date.

4.12 THE LIMITS OF THE LINGUISTIC ENVIRONMENT

It is befitting to conclude our chapter on the environment by pausing to recognize voices that have warned all along that the ingredients of input, interaction, output and feedback are no magic bullet for L2 learning. Critiques offered all along by sociolinguistically and socioculturally minded researchers should help us temper our interpretations of cognitive-interactionist arguments about the benefits afforded by experience with the linguistic environment.

First, it is important to remember that, besides negotiations in the imminent face of communication failure, other more positive features of interaction can provide learners with potential linguistic benefits as well. Thus, Nakahama et al. (2001) showed that a conversational task engendered lower levels of negotiation than an information-gap task (a fact that is predicted by proponents of interaction, e.g. Pica et al., 1993), but that it also engendered more personal engagement and afforded many more opportunities to take risks, enabling these learners to produce longer turns and more complex language. Furthermore, Aston (1986) warned that interactional work is multifaceted and can accomplish things that have nothing to do with repairing communication problems. For instance, Foster and Ohta (2005) rightly note that not all other-repetitions are confirmation checks and that many are what they call a **continuer**, or a repetition that indicates rapport and has the function to encourage the speaker to say more, as in the case of (16):

(16)   M1:   I wasn't so fat before I came to England
         V2:   fat?
         M3:   yeah, but now I eat a lot of bread.

(Foster and Ohta, 2005, p. 421)

Second, the significance of negotiation work for the interlocutors may be deceptive. Hawkins (1985) showed that learners may feign understanding in order to avoid lengthy and cumbersome negotiations, and they may do so motivated by the very human need to be polite and save face. In her study, responses to comprehension checks (e.g. *uh-huh*, or an echoic repetition) were on the surface appropriate. When the two L2 participants were asked, it turned out that in fact about half of their investigated responses were issued as a polite way out. They were 'nothing more than repeating it because he [the interlocutor] was saying it', as one of Hawkins' participants put it (p. 173).

Furthermore, extremely low levels of negotiation may characterize some groups and settings, as discovered by Foster (1998) in a study with 21 part-time, intermediate-level English students in a college in the United Kingdom. In that classroom, and perhaps in many others, negotiation may be almost non-existent, perhaps once again out of politeness, or maybe disengagement. Alternatively, students may be engaged in the content being learned but produce minimal negotiation, presumably because comprehension problems do not arise and inaccuracies are forgiven, as both Musumeci (1996) and Pica (2002) have documented for college-level Italian and English content-based L2 instruction, respectively. In addition, negative and even confrontational interaction patterns can occur in learner–learner work as well, as shown in the work of Neomy Storch at the University of Melbourne (e.g. Storch, 2002). Conversely, a highly motivated partner may boost the other student's willingness to interact and engage with a given oral task (e.g. Dörnyei and Kormos, 2000). In general, then, unfavourable attitudinal and affective predispositions can make one interlocutor or the other uninterested in negotiation or they can make negotiation moves that do occur fruitless for comprehension, much more so for acquisition.

It should be clear that not all things that can go wrong in interactions can be blamed on the non-native speaker and their level of interest, engagement, politeness, cooperativeness or willingness to learn. Ehrlich et al. (1989) found that not all people who happen to have grown up with a language are equally skilful at using it to deliver the kinds of explanations required from the tasks that researchers typically use in cognitive-interactionist studies. A particular style of L1 speaker, who they called embroiderers, engaged in confusing excess of information, causing less successful communication.

Power and prejudice are also unexamined factors in cognitive-interactionist work about the environment. Lindemann (2002) was able to show experimentally that some native speakers hold pre-existing negative attitudes against non-native-speaking groups, and that these biased attitudes can affect the processes and outcomes of concrete interactions. In her study, attitudinally biased native-speaking interlocutors approached learner utterances as problematic by default. Some of them therefore avoided negotiating at all, even when they showed willingness to negotiate actively on a similar task with another native-speaking interlocutor. Actual comprehension problems affected task outcomes (the drawing of a map route) only for those dyads where such negotiation avoidance was observed. Nevertheless, when asked, all prejudiced interlocutors evaluated task outcomes as a failure rather than a success, even when their routes had been accurately charted.

Finally, and related to issues of power, a neglected consideration is that many people who use an L2 may take what we may call an equitable responsibility approach to communication. As Schmidt (1983) astutely points out, sometimes 'the nonnative may simply not accept the fairness of greatly disparate levels of effort by conversational partners' (p. 167). According to Schmidt, Wes was one of them. He 'expected native speakers to learn his interlanguage, … to consider it the native speaker's problem as much as his own' if mutual understanding was not achieved. More generally, and whatever language learning may come about as a result of interaction, interpersonal communication is never just about language, but it always involves interlocutors' sense of self as well as power differentials, as we will be able to see in Chapter 10.

While all the caveats raised in this section should temper utopian or deterministic views about what the linguistic environment has to contribute to language learning, they do not invalidate the claims made by cognitive-interactionists and documented across a large body of work reviewed in this chapter. Many of these insights have also been useful in the development of research on task-based language learning, an area that has continued to burgeon to this date (Ellis, 2003; Van den Branden, 2006; Samuda and Bygate, 2008). Nevertheless, the most important contribution (and the most important limitation) that we can remember as we leave this chapter is the realization that what matters in the linguistic environment is not simply 'what's out there' physically or even socially surrounding learners, but rather what learners make of it, how they process (or not) the linguistic data and how they live and experience that environment. In Chapter 5, we will examine how learner cognition exerts a powerful influence on what gets processed (or not) in the linguistic data. In Chapter 10, we will explore how social structures and individual agency also shape lived experience in a dialectic of tension and, in the process, help explain the learning (or not learning) of additional languages.

4.13 SUMMARY

A few generalizations that can be remembered from this chapter are:

- The five environmental ingredients that together contribute to (but do not guarantee) optimal L2 learning are: acculturated attitudes, comprehensible input, negotiated interaction, pushed output, and a capacity, natural or cultivated, to attend to the language code, not just the message. These five ingredients were likely present in a case like Julie (see Chapter 2, section 2.2), the first of several exceptionally successful learners discovered since the mid-1990s. The last ingredient, attention to the language code, was fundamentally missing from a case like Wes (see Chapter 4, section 4.1), who epitomizes the frequently attested phenomenon of mixed learning success.

- Neither positive attitudes towards the target language and its speakers nor abundant and meaningful comprehension of L2 messages are in and of themselves sufficient for second language learning to be successful, although both are certainly important ingredients in a highly complex environmental equation.

- For successful grammar acquisition, attention to form is probably necessary. This attentional focus on form can be externally achieved by instruction or internally sought by self-study and self-directed analysis of the linguistic material available in the environment.

- Negotiation for meaning, other- and self-initiated output modification, negotiation of form during collaboration, and negative feedback of varying degrees of explicitness all carry potential for learning, provided they occur under optimal conditions that recruit attention to the language code. They facilitate psycholinguistic and metalinguistic processes of segmenting the input, noticing gaps and holes, parsing messages syntactically, monitoring and hypothesis testing; these are in turn processes that help L2 learners crack the language code.

- In the process of collaboratively negotiating choices of the code, L2 users generate language-related episodes (LREs) or pre-emptive focus-on-form episodes which are potential sites for learning. Using the L1 or metalanguage during these events may aid learning.

- Cognitive-interactionist researchers agree that negative feedback (or the implicit or explicit indication that some part of an utterance is ungrammatical) is better overall than entirely ignoring errors. Much less agreement has been reached as to when, how and why negative feedback works, when it does.

- Recent evidence strongly suggests that the effectiveness of negative feedback is moderated by at least two factors: the degree of explicitness with which it is implemented, and the wider instructional orientation towards language as a meaning-making tool or as object for learning.

Three more subtle observations deserve some pondering:

- The value of comprehension versus production for acquisition is an ill-understood conundrum that causes disagreement among SLA researchers. Some view learning as driven by comprehension exclusively and assign production a role for fluency-building. Others claim that productive, meaningful language use is in itself a catalyst for learning.

- Grammatical competence appears to evolve in ways that are less amenable to incidental benefits from the environment than other aspects of the language to be learned, such as vocabulary, discourse competence, and so on. It also seems to hold a special status in language acquisition. Specifically, grammar (a) requires more interest, attention and hard work than other aspects of the language to be learned; (b) may even require more time to simmer and deploy than the learning of other aspects of an L2; and (c) can act as a gatekeeper to development in other areas of the L2 beyond formulaic repertoires, particularly sociolinguistic competence.

- What matters in the linguistic environment is not simply 'what's out there' physically or even socially surrounding learners, but rather what learners make of it, how they process (or not) the linguistic data and how they live and experience that environment.

4.14 ANNOTATED SUGGESTIONS FOR FURTHER READING

The amount of SLA literature that has been (and continues to be) published on the linguistic environment and L2 acquisition is daunting. For this reason, a selective combination of seminal and recent studies is perhaps the best approach to this area.

You can begin by reading some of the overviews of the topic that have been written by its three most seminal proponents: a comprehensive book by Gass (1997), an oft-cited review by Long (1996) or two analytically detailed and pedagogically relevant reviews by Pica (1992, 1994). Following that, you will be able to fully appreciate the three field-influential readings by Schmidt: Wes's case study (1983), R's learning of Portuguese (Schmidt and Frota, 1986) and his most accessible explanation of noticing (Schmidt, 1995). Finally, your theoretical journey of the environment cannot be complete without reading the empirical study that gave rise to the Pushed Output Hypothesis (Swain, 1985). If you also then read Swain (1995) and (2000) in chronological order, you will be in a better position to understand the nuanced intellectual distance between traditional and sociocultural views of the environment (which we will explore in Chapter 10).

The empirical studies that one could read are many. The classics that marked a turning point in the field can be a good place to start: Gass and Varonis (1994), Loschky (1994) and Mackey (1999). A few recent investigations are also particularly original and felicitous (although not always easy to read). The study of LREs by Jessica Williams (1999; see also Williams, 2001) is unique in its longitudinal focus on eight students whose LREs were documented over an entire semester of instruction and 65 hours of video-taped lessons. Some of the best exemplars of recent cutting-edge research on interaction are Iwashita (2003), who examined both negative feedback and positive evidence with regard to L2 Japanese structures in a unique product-plus-process design, and McDonough (2006), who was the first to consider the potential of syntactic priming (a psycholinguistic phenomenon well studied in the L1) as a source of implicit learning through negative feedback. By contrast to the highly literate populations of college students that are featured in most research programmes, Bigelow et al. (2006) replicated an ingenious study by Philp (2003) and sought to explore the validity of cognitive-interactionist theories when they are applied to semi-literate learners. A new collection by Mackey (2007) gathers forward-looking studies of interaction across several target languages, and another by DeKeyser (2007a) covers a wide range of cognitive-interactionist topics across several contexts.

For anyone interested in negative feedback, specifically, Chaudron (1977) and the four studies summarized in Table 4.1 are excellent starter reading. Sheen (2004) and Lyster and Mori (2006) provide interesting insights about the role of the context. Recent publications by Rod Ellis and his present and former colleagues at the University of Auckland provide a fruitful direction for future research in this area (e.g. Ellis et al., 2001, 2006). Finally, two articles by Ferris (2004) and Hyland and Hyland (2006) offer excellent overviews if you are interested in L2 writing and negative feedback, and Heift (2004) and Lai and Zhao (2006) provide good examples of technology-delivered feedback.

5

Cognition

Cognition refers to how information is processed and learned by the human mind (the term comes from the Latin verb *cognoscere*, 'to get to know'). SLA researchers interested in cognition study what it takes to 'get to know' an additional language well enough to use it fluently in comprehension and production. We are far from a satisfactory understanding of second language as a form of cognition, however. This is because our capacities to investigate the relevant questions are shaped by the pace at which new theories and methods to inspect the workings of human minds and brains become available (typically in neighbouring disciplines) and the rate at which SLA researchers become conversant in them. In this chapter, more than in any other, I will make frequent reference to relevant L1 research and point at areas where future attention by SLA researchers will be needed.

It is also important to realize that, in cognitive research, the relevant behavioural and neurobiological evidence falls in the order of a few hundred milliseconds to a few seconds, or it consists of larger-scope performance that nevertheless lasts a few minutes to a few hours at the most. This is in sharp contrast with many of the data on language learning SLA researchers normally consider, which involve stretches of discourse, multi-turn interactions with human interlocutors, extended texts, referential and social meaning, and even years of studying, using or living with an L2. Thus, the differences in grain size, temporal and ontological, of the various phenomena that are brought together into cognitive explorations of L2 learning are puzzling.

In this chapter you will learn about cognitive SLA theories and constructs that have been developed to explain the nature of second language as a form of cognition. The theories can be broadly classified into traditional information processing, which has dominated SLA theorizing and research since the mid-1980s, and emergentism, which is a development of the late 1990s that grew out from the former. A central preoccupation in SLA research on cognition is with memory and attention in L2 learning.

5.1 INFORMATION PROCESSING IN PSYCHOLOGY AND SLA

Information processing emerged in the field of psychology in the 1970s, out of the so-called cognitive revolution of the late 1950s. Initially a reaction against behaviourist theories that could only offer stimulus–response explanations for human learning, it became the dominant psychological paradigm of the last third of the twentieth century. In a nutshell, the human mind is viewed as a symbolic processor that constantly engages in mental processes. These mental processes operate on mental representations and intervene between input (whatever data get into the symbolic processor, the mind) and output (whatever the results of performance are). Performance, rather than behaviour, is a key word in information processing theories. This is because inferences about mental processes can only be made by inspecting what is observable during processing while performing tasks, rather than by inspecting external behaviour in response to stimuli, as behaviourists used to do.

Several key assumptions made by information processing psychologists have been embraced in current SLA research about cognition. First, the human cognitive architecture is made of representation and access. Second, mental processing is dual, comprised of two different kinds of computation: automatic or fluent (unconscious) and voluntary or controlled (conscious). Third, cognitive resources such as attention and memory are limited. Let us unpack each principle in some detail for a better understanding of what information processing stands for.

Information processing theories distinguish between **representation** (or knowledge) and **access** (or processing). Bialystok and Sharwood Smith (1985) used a library metaphor to explain this distinction to their SLA audience: 'knowing what is in the library, plus how the contents are classified and related to one another, must be distinguished from retrieving desired information from the books at a given time' (p. 105). Linguistic representation is comprised of three kinds of knowledge: grammatical, lexical and schematic or world-related. New L2 knowledge is stored in the mind and has to be accessed and retrieved every time it is needed for use in comprehension or production.

Access entails the activation or use of relevant knowledge via two different mechanisms known as **automatic** and **controlled processing**. Canadian language psychologist Norman Segalowitz (2003) compares the two modes of processing to the difference between an automatic and a standard shift car: 'an automatic shift car changes gears without deliberate intervention by the driver, in contrast to a standard shift car which requires the driver to perform a manual operation' (p. 383). Unlike cars, however, which are built by manufacturers to function as either automatic or standard shift from the outset, human cognition is supported by both automatic and controlled processing. Information processing psychologists believe that all human perception and action, as well as all thoughts and feelings, result from the interaction of these two kinds of processing.

Automatic processes require small effort and take up few cognitive resources, and therefore many automatic processing routines can run in parallel. During automatic processing, cognitive activation is triggered bottom up by exogenous sources in the environment (something outside the processor, that is, some aspect of the data in the input or environment). By contrast, controlled processing is activated by top-down, endogenous sources (by something inside the processor, that is, by voluntary, goal-directed motivation in the individual's mind), and it is handled by what we call the **central executive**. We summon controlled processing when we intentionally set out to control behaviour, for example, when no automatic routines have been learned yet because the problem is new (as in a new language) or in the face of some kind of problem encountered during automatic processing (as when surrounding noise makes us strive to understand the few disconnected sounds that we can gather from our interlocutor). In such cases, we let our central executive system intervene to 'control' the processing task.

Controlled processes therefore allow us self-regulation, but they require a lot more effort and cognitive resources than automatic processes, and thus cannot operate in parallel; they are serial. For this reason, controlled processing is subject to a bottleneck effect. When we voluntarily attend to one thing, we need to block out the rest. If several demands are competing for controlled processing, they will be prioritized and certain processes will wait in line, so to speak, while only one is being executed. This is what we call a **limited capacity model** of information processing. The model predicts that performance that draws on controlled processing is more variable and more vulnerable to stressors than performance that draws on automatic processing. Therefore, a widely employed method in the study of automaticity is the **dual-task** condition, where the researcher creates processing stress by asking participants to carry out two tasks simultaneously, a primary task and a distracting task. Under this dual-task pressure, because the distracting task consumes attention away from the primary task, performance on the main task may become variable and vulnerable. If this happens, it is taken as evidence that the participant is relying on more controlled processing and therefore has not yet reached automatization on the performance called by the primary task.

5.2 THE POWER OF PRACTICE: PROCEDURALIZATION AND AUTOMATICITY

A particular kind of information processing theory, called skill acquisition theory, has been fruitful in guiding SLA efforts since the mid-1980s (e.g. Bialystok and Sharwood Smith, 1985; McLaughlin, 1987). The most influential version has been adopted from the early formulations of cognitive psychologist John Anderson's Adaptive Control of Thought theory (Anderson, 1983), although his most recent version of the theory goes well beyond traditional information processing notions (Anderson, 2007).

Skill acquisition theory defines learning as the gradual transformation of performance from controlled to automatic. This transformation happens through relevant practice over many trials, which enables controlled processes gradually to be withdrawn during performance and automatic processes to take over the same performance. The process has been called **proceduralization** or **automatization** and entails the conversion of **declarative or explicit knowledge** (or 'knowledge that') into **procedural or implicit knowledge** (or 'knowledge how'). It is important to realize that the learning of skills is assumed to start with the explicit provision of relevant declarative knowledge. Thus, L2 learners (particularly instructed learners) begin with explanations explicitly presented by their teachers or in textbooks and, through practice, this knowledge can hopefully convert into ability for use, or implicit-procedural knowledge made up of automatic routines.

How does practice work? It helps proceduralization of new knowledge by allowing the establishment and strengthening of corresponding links in long-term memory. The more this knowledge is accessed via practice, the easier it will become to access it without effort and without the involvement of the central executive at a future time. However, the power of practice is not constant over time. There is a well-known **power law of learning**, by which practice will at some point yield no large returns in terms of improvement, because optimal performance has been reached (Ellis and Schmidt, 1998). In addition, proceduralization is skill-specific. Therefore, practice that focuses on L2 production should help automatize production and practice that focuses on L2 comprehension should help automatize comprehension (DeKeyser, 1997). The final outcome of the gradual process of proceduralization or automatization is **automaticity**, which is defined as automatic performance that draws on implicit-procedural knowledge and is reflected in fluent comprehension and production and in lower neural activation patterns (Segalowitz, 2003).

Two misinterpretations of skill acquisition tenets are common: (a) that automaticity is simply accelerated or speedy behaviour; and (b) that L2 learners simply accumulate rules that they practise until they can use them automatically. Much to the contrary, Segalowitz (2003) discusses in depth how skilled performance cannot be understood in terms of sheer speed alone, and that instead a qualitative change is reached once performance is automatized. Likewise, rather than simply accumulating rules, prolonged and repeated practice changes the knowledge representation itself by making the stored knowledge become more elaborated and well specified, or more analysed, as Canadian psychologist Ellen Bialystok (2001) has called it. This happens via processes of accretion, tuning and restructuring of knowledge (discussed by McLaughlin and Heredia, 1996; see also Chapter 6, section 6.4). In other words, by the time they become automatized, rules may be just different from the declarative rules that were initially committed to memory.

How would anyone be able to study all these abstract principles of skill acquisition theory, when it comes to L2 learning? In the next section, I will walk you through a study by DeKeyser (1997) that embodies all these principles. The study is an exemplary full-blown effort to document the time course of proceduralization during second language learning.

5.3 AN EXEMPLARY STUDY OF SKILL ACQUISITION THEORY IN SLA: DEKEYSER (1997)

Robert DeKeyser (1997) investigated many of the predictions of information processing and cognitive skill theory in a clever and complicated study. DeKeyser recruited 61 college student volunteers and taught them a **miniature language** that he called Autopractan. He did so over 11 weeks and 22 one-hour sessions, using picture-and-sentence exercises delivered through a computer program. Autopractan comprised a small set of 16 nouns and 16 verbs and was designed to behave like natural languages, with morphological markings for gender, number and case, and the possibility of omitting the subject and having flexible word order (that is, Autopractan was a null-subject language with rich morphology). One challenge in this kind of study is that participants may not see the benefits of trying hard to study a language that they know is artificial, and therefore of no use to them outside the experiment. In an effort to address this problem, the researcher told the volunteers their monetary compensation for participating in the study would vary depending on their scores during the experiment. The difference was a modest $8 per hour for top scores versus $6 per hour for bottom scores, but this ought to have been enough of an incentive for undergraduate students in the mid-1990s!

The first phase was provision of explicit, declarative knowledge. It involved presenting all vocabulary and grammar rules of Autopractan and having participants learn them well over the first six sessions (about three weeks). The second phase was practice. It was designed to support proceduralization, or the transformation of performance from controlled to automatic. It involved different things for different groups, but it always took 15 sessions (eight weeks) and exactly the same total number of exercises for everyone. Finally, the last session in the study (session number 22) was devoted to testing participants on four Autopractan rules via comprehension and production test items.

How did the practice phase vary across conditions? One group ($n = 21$) practised Autopractan rules 1 and 2 only through comprehension and rules 3 and 4 only through production. A second group ($n = 20$) also practised the same four rules, but they practised rules 3 and 4 through comprehension and rules 1 and 2 through production. A third group ($n = 20$) practised all four rules as well, but all of them through half comprehension and half production exercises. Thus, this third group engaged in mixed-modality practice of all rules, but they also got half the amount of practice for each modality. For all groups, comprehension practice was done by asking participants to match sentences they read on the computer with one out of four pictures. Production practice was done by asking them to type the sentence that would describe a given picture. Negative feedback on their answers to each item during practice was immediate and included explicit explanation of the error and showing the correct response.

All 15 practice sessions were divided into cycles of practice followed by testing. During the practice, all items were done half under normal single-task conditions and half under stressful dual-task conditions. In the latter dual-task condition, participants saw a number on the screen before an Autopractan practice item would appear; they then heard beeps at irregular intervals while doing the Autopractan practice item. After responding to the item, they had to subtract the number of beeps from the number that had appeared on the screen. The intention was to see whether the level of performance would substantially deteriorate initially (a sign that controlled processing was involved) and whether the stressor would become less obtrusive over time (a sign that automatic processing was taking over performance).

DeKeyser looked at evidence into both the process and the product of learning. In order to understand the learning process, reaction times and accuracy were plotted over the 15 testing events taken at the end of each practice session. He found that responses quickly became faster and more accurate over the first two sessions, and that by practice session four or five performance had stabilized, with the speed and accuracy of responses remaining practically constant from that point on until the last session of practice. This pattern is predicted by the power law of learning. However, performance was essentially the same for the single- and dual-task condition items across all 15 sessions, which suggested that the distracting task in the dual condition had failed to sufficiently tax cognitive resources.

In order to document the product of learning, scores on the post-tests administered in the final session of the study were also inspected. It turned out that gains were, as predicted, skill-specific. For a given rule, the participants in the first two groups outperformed each other only on the items that tested them in the same modality in which they had practised that rule. By the same token, the balanced regime of comprehension and production experienced by the third group appeared to be effective for both comprehension and practice, with gains comparable to those made by the other two groups under the same-modality conditions.

As you see, testing the predictions of cognitive skill acquisition theory for L2 learning is complicated. Few studies have been conducted using this paradigm, and even fewer exist that document automatization over a sustained period of practice like DeKeyser (1997) did.

You may have noticed that a construct that underpins all the tenets and predictions of information processing is memory. Any information that our mind entertains, whether for milliseconds or for years, goes through memory and involves some form of memory. In the next sections, we examine some basic memory concepts and selectively look at some of the SLA insights they have spurred. Two types of memory are crucial in all cognitive operations: long-term memory and working memory. As we will see, both are fundamentally involved in second language processing and learning.

5.4 LONG-TERM MEMORY

Long-term memory is about representation. It is virtually unlimited in its capacity and it is made of two kinds: explicit-declarative memory and implicit-procedural memory. Much of the knowledge encoded in long-term memory is **explicit-declarative**, that is, verbalizable and consciously recalled. Explicit-declarative memory supports recollection of facts or events, and it is served by the hippocampus in the human brain. As much knowledge, or probably more, is encoded in **implicit-procedural** memory. These are things that we know without knowing that we know them. Implicit-procedural memory supports skills and habit learning, and it is served by the neocortex in the human brain. About 35 years ago, Endel Tulving, an Estonian psychologist based in the United States, argued for the existence of another important difference in the kinds of knowledge stored in long-term memory and proposed a further distinction: semantic and episodic memory (see Tulving, 2002). **Semantic** memory pertains to relatively decontextualized knowledge of facts that 'everyone knows'. **Episodic** memory involves knowledge of the events in which people are personally involved or 'the events we've lived through'. Episodic memory corresponds to a more recent type of memory in evolution, believed to have evolved from semantic memory. It 'allows people to consciously re-experience past experiences' and also to think of their future (Tulving, 2002, p. 6).

Because vocabulary knowledge is one of the best-studied areas of long-term memory in SLA, we will look into it in order to exemplify the range of issues that arise regarding how new language knowledge is represented and stored.

5.5 LONG-TERM MEMORY AND L2 VOCABULARY KNOWLEDGE

What does it mean to remember a word? At a fundamental level, a word is established in long-term memory when the link between a form and its meaning is made. However, knowing a word means a lot more: it includes the strength, size and depth of the knowledge represented in memory.

Vocabulary knowledge **strength** concerns the relative ability to use a given known word productively or to recognize it passively. Thus, strength is a matter of degree of proceduralization in implicit memory. Vocabulary strength has been the object of extensive investigation by Sima Paribakht and Marjorie Wesche in Canada (e.g. Paribakht and Wesche, 1997) and by Batia Laufer in Israel (e.g. Laufer and Goldstein, 2004). It is typically found that learners know more words receptively than productively, particularly if they are infrequent or difficult words, and that this gap becomes smaller as proficiency develops. Within the purview of explicit-declarative memory, by contrast, is the **size** of the mental lexicon, which refers to the total number of words known and represented in long-term memory. Size is often related to the relative frequency with which words are encountered in the input that surrounds learners, since high-frequency words usually make it into long-term memory earlier in the learning process than low-frequency words. Paul Nation in New Zealand has uncovered many interesting findings about vocabulary size in L2 learning (e.g. Nation and Waring, 1997; Nation, 2006). For example, in L1 a five-year-old child begins school with an established vocabulary of about 5,000 word families, and a typical 30-year-old college-educated adult ends up knowing about 20,000 word families (Nation and Waring, 1997). For L2 users, new vocabulary presents a formidable challenge. They need to learn about 3,000 new words in order to minimally follow conversations in the L2, and about 9,000 new word families if they want to be able to read novels or newspapers in the L2 (Nation, 2006).

Vocabulary **depth** resides in the realm of both explicit and implicit memory and refers to how well the known words are really known, that is, how elaborated, well specified and structured (or how analysed, in Bialystok's 2001 sense) the lexical representations are. Among the most active contributors to the study of vocabulary depth are Paul Meara in Wales (e.g. Meara, 1996; Wilks and Meara, 2002) and

Norbert Schmitt in England (e.g. Schmitt, 1998, 2000). Depth of knowledge includes whether L2 learners know how a word sounds (/di-'zərt/ in a meal and /'de-zərt/ in a landscape), how it is spelled (*exude*, not *exhude*), how many other word parts it can appear with (*pre-, -ment, -er, -s, -ing*), what is likely to precede or follow a word (*make a decision, do exercise; mental state, state of affairs/mind*), how many meanings the word may have (*demonstrate* = to show and to protest), in what registers different synonyms may be preferred (*weather, climate*), or how frequently and in what contexts the word will occur (many *oaths* in court but not in hospitals, many *incisions* in hospitals but not in court). As Meara (2007) has argued for many years now, the notion of depth of vocabulary knowledge assumes the existence in implicit long-term memory of networks of meaning-based and form-based associations across the entire mental lexicon.

Other long-term memory-related questions in L2 vocabulary pertain to the content of the lexical representations encoded in memory for bilinguals. For example, Nan Jiang has initiated a research programme in which the long-term representation of L2 words is posited to be initially filled with the conceptual content from the L1 (e.g. Jiang, 2004). A different suggestion has been made by Finkbeiner et al. (2004), who raise the possibility that, until full competence is reached in both languages, L2 words have fewer meanings represented in their entries than L1 words, that is, L2 lexical representations are conceptually less elaborated and analysed. Focusing on episodic memory and conceptual development, Aneta Pavlenko (1999) has explored the hypothesis that L2 words learned in naturalistic contexts allow for the encoding of richer information in episodic memory than L2 words learned in classrooms, because the former are learned more experientially and the latter more declaratively. She therefore suggests that conceptual L2 development will be fostered in naturalistic (i.e. experiential) learning contexts but might be limited in foreign language contexts.

Finally, an important related question is how the L1 and L2 lexicons of the bilingual speaker interact, which is reflected in the mechanisms of access in long-term memory. Psycholinguists Judith Kroll (at Penn State University) and Annette de Groot (at the University of Amsterdam) have been prolific contributors in this area (Kroll and de Groot, 1997). In their work they have shown that when bilinguals recognize or produce words, information encoded for both languages, not just the one of current use, is initially activated. This phenomenon is known as **non-selectivity** and has been documented also for three languages in trilinguals by Lemhfer et al. (2004). There is an interesting asymmetry, however. What is simultaneously activated in recognition is the L1-plus-L2 form representations, whereas in production what gets simultaneously activated initially is the L1-plus-L2 meaning representations (Kroll et al., 2005).

5.6   WORKING MEMORY

By contrast to long-term memory, which is about representation and is unlimited, **working memory** is about access and is limited. A simple but useful definition of working memory in SLA is offered via an example by Nick Ellis (2005): 'If I ask you what 397×27 is, you do not look up the answer from long-term memory, you work it out' (p. 338). Peter Robinson (1995) describes it as 'the workspace where skill development begins … and where knowledge is encoded into (and retrieved from) long-term memory' (p. 304). In other words, we need working memory to hold information (a storage function) as well as to integrate new information with known information already encoded in long-term memory (a processing function). Working memory handles automatic and controlled processing. Importantly, thus, it is **the site for the executive control**, which supports controlled processing (Baddeley and Hitch, 1974), and also **the site of consciousness** (Baars and Franklin, 2003). As Nick Ellis (2005) explains, working memory 'is the home of explicit induction, hypothesis formation, analogical reasoning, prioritization, control, and decision-making. It is where we develop, apply, and hone our metalinguistic insights into an L2. Working memory is the system that concentrates across time, controlling attention in the face of distraction' (p. 337).

Two characteristics help define working memory. First, unlike long-term memory, working memory is of **limited capacity**. Specifically, under normal conditions information can be remembered in working memory for about two seconds only. After that brief span, the representation is rapidly forgotten, unless it can be rehearsed subvocally in what Alan Baddeley, memory authority in the United Kingdom, called the phonological loop, so it can eventually enter long-term memory (Baddeley, 2007). A second characteristic is temporary **activation**. Activation is so central to working memory that Nelson Cowan, another main authority on L1 memory from the US, has obliterated the traditional distinction between long-term and working memory and suggests instead that working memory is just the part of memory that becomes activated during a processing event (Cowan, 2005).

Working memory has received intense attention in SLA since the mid-1990s. Perhaps its clearest application to SLA has been in the area of individual differences. The suggestion is that, since memory is involved in information processing in pervasive ways, people who have better working memory capacities can learn an L2 more efficiently. Thus, working memory capacity is posited to help predict learning rate and ultimate levels of attainment in the L2. We will examine these issues in Chapter 7 (sections 7.7 and 7.8). In terms of universal facts about L2 memory capacity, two observations have attracted some attention.

First, it has been observed that working memory capacity is smaller in the L2, when compared to the L1. For example, in one of the first SLA studies of working memory, Harrington and Sawyer (1992) found that their 32 EFL participants' memory performance was consistently lower in the L2 than in the L1 across a battery of memory tasks. More recently, Towell and Dewaele (2005) also found an L2–L1 lag, when the shadowing of a continuous oral passage was carried out in L2 and L1 by 12 participants, all students of French enrolled in second- or third-year levels at a university in the United Kingdom. As Vivian Cook (1996, p. 68) speculated at an early point in the investigation of L2 working memory, several mutually compatible explanations may account for this L2–L1 lag in capacity, each potentially related to a different component of working memory. It could be that the central executive functions less efficiently, because it has to work on L2 rather than L1 material. Or a slowdown in the capacity of the phonological loop to rehearse material subvocally could be at work, because one can articulate sounds in the L2 with less speed than in the L1. Or perhaps the interface between short-term memory and long-term memory is less efficient because the rehearsed and remembered material is in the L2. Unfortunately, no research programme in SLA has attempted to tease out these possibilities thus far. Second, it has also been noted that, as L2 proficiency develops, this lag in working memory capacity between the L2 and L1 should become smaller. However, even less is known empirically about this widely held assumption. Without understanding better the first question of how L2 working memory functions and what constellation of forces initially makes it smaller in capacity than L1 working memory, it will be difficult to explore the second question of how L2 and L1 working memory capacity align together with increasing proficiency.

5.7 MEMORY AS STORAGE: PASSIVE WORKING MEMORY TASKS

With memory, the first thing that comes to mind is the simple notion of 'storage size', or just how much fleeting information people can remember. This is actually the original scope of memory research in the L1, as reflected in the term **short-term memory**, a near-synonym choice with working memory. Enormous amounts of memory research have been devoted to the question of storage capacity in the L1, leading to the establishment of appropriate experimental tasks and interesting, if generic, benchmarks. These are briefly presented in Table 5.1.

Although the limitation is understood traditionally in terms of sheer storage capacity, increasingly more L1 memory researchers have suggested alternative conceptualizations. In their influential model, Baddeley and Hitch (1974) explained limitations in terms of time passage, but more recently Cowan (2001) has proposed that the limits come from increasing confusion or interference with other similar material that enters the focus of attention. Yet other proposals by Ericsson and Kintsch (1995) and Logan (1988) have explained (from otherwise markedly different perspectives) limited capacity in terms of insufficient relevant knowledge to draw from in long-term memory. Even more recently, Neil Burgess and Graham Hitch (2006) in the United Kingdom have proposed that short-term memory capacity is made of two distinct processes, one that enables memory for the content of the items themselves and the other that allows memory of serial position information within the items. Such fine-grained explorations of the storage function of short-term memory have rarely been undertaken by SLA researchers (but see Speciale et al., 2004, for an exception). And yet, as Majerus et al. (2006) note, such explorations would be crucial to understand why memory capacity on tasks such as those listed in Table 5.1 are so good at predicting new L2 vocabulary learning, as we will see in Chapter 7 (section 7.8).

Table 5.1
Memory tasks and benchmarks in the study of storage memory capacity

Digit span recall tasks are one of the oldest methods used in psychological research to measure storage capacity. Put simply, participants are asked to repeat increasingly longer sequences of numbers, sometimes in backward order. Great care is taken to minimize opportunities for subvocal rehearsal, since this is a good strategy to 'stretch' memory capacity. As Miller (1956) concluded in a seminal paper, average-memory adults have a working memory span in their L1 of about seven digits, which means that they can remember sequences of about seven digits accurately at least 50% of the time

Word span tasks are also frequently used. Most people can repeat sequences of five to six unrelated words, but after that they experience increasing memory difficulties. Rather than thinking in terms of digits or words, however, it is more accurate to think of memory capacity in terms of chunks, or pieces of information that are already linked and stored together in long-term memory. For example, you will probably be able to remember equally well the string '*Nicole, Gary, Tom, Katherine, Penélope, Sean*' and the double-length string '*Nicole Kidman, Cary Grant, Tom Cruise, Katharine Hepburn, Penélope Cruz, Sean Connery*'... that is, if you know these actors' names well and have 'chunked' their first and family names together for each of them

Non-word repetition span tasks are preferred to word span tasks by some researchers, precisely to eliminate recall-enhancing strategies that draw on long-term memory, like grouping and chunking. Examples of non-words are *johmbe, zabide, wakime, migene, shosane, tisseke, chakume* and *nawase* (taken from an L2 study by Williams, 2005) and *lus, vip, kug, taysum, kepponen, woogalamic* and *reutterpation* (taken from an L1 study by Gathercole et al., 1999)

Sentence repetition tasks (also called elicited imitation tasks) are another way to measure working memory storage capacity. We know that the typical human memory span for sentences is about 16 words, a sequence much longer than the typical word span of five or six isolated words. This is because in sentences we perceive words as 'chunked' into phrases. Our knowledge of grammar (which is stored in long-term memory) helps us group words into phrases and remember sentences better than isolated sequences of digits or words

5.8 MEMORY AS DYNAMIC PROCESSING: ACTIVE WORKING MEMORY TASKS

Working memory not only stores information, but it is also responsible for processing it. For this reason, L1 researchers have developed so-called active measures of working memory capacity that capitalize on the idea of a trade-off between storing and processing. This idea has become influential among L2 memory researchers through the work of cognitive psychologist Meredyth Daneman in Canada and her colleagues Patricia Carpenter and Marcel Just at Carnegie Mellon University (see Daneman and Merikle, 1996). They devised an active measure of working memory capacity in the L1 called the **reading span task**. In these tasks, people are asked to read sentences presented on cue cards and to comprehend or evaluate what they are reading. Immediately after reading all sentences, they are asked to recall the last word appearing on each sentence or the few selected words that were underlined on each card. This kind of reading span task is assumed to reflect how well people can maintain information in short-term memory (the targeted words they are asked to recall out of the sentence stimuli) while another processing task is executed simultaneously (reading the sentences for comprehension).

An interesting question in SLA is whether passive or active measures of working memory are better suited for the investigation of memory limits and L2 learning. Harrington and Sawyer (1992) argued that the predictive validity of active working memory measures was higher than that of passive measures, at least in their study. They found that the active measure of reading span scores predicted about 30 per cent of the variance in scores on the grammar and reading subsections of the TOEFL, whereas the passive measures of memory they used (digit and word span scores) did not correlate with any of these L2 proficiency measures. To some extent, however, the tasks yielding the correlations shared a heavy reliance on reading skills, and the reading span task was administered in the participants' L2. A positive development is that more recent L2 research has employed measures of active working memory in the L1 (e.g. Sagarra, 2008).

In the end, there is no doubt that passive storage capacity alone is insufficient to capture the varied contributions of memory to the acquisition of a second language. Cognitive psychologist Randall Engle (2002) argues that '[working memory] capacity is not about individual differences in how many items can be stored per se but about differences in the ability to control attention to maintain information in an active, quickly retrievable state. [It] is not directly about memory – it is about using attention to maintain or suppress information. Greater [working memory] capacity does mean that more items can be maintained as active, but this is a result of greater ability to control attention, not a larger memory store' (p. 20). By conceptualizing memory as dynamic processing, such contemporary views of working memory have catapulted attention to the centre of cognition.

5.9 ATTENTION AND L2 LEARNING

And, indeed, together with memory, attention is another essential component of cognition. Remember that under normal conditions simple activation of a stimulus in working memory will last for a few seconds and then fade away. Here is where attention comes in; it heightens the activation level of input in working memory, allowing it to remain there for longer through rehearsal and thus making it available for further processing and for entering long-term memory.

One main characteristic of attention is that its capacity is **limited**. You will note that this attribute was also mentioned when discussing working memory. These are all same-family metaphors. Working memory is capacity limited, possibly because attention is (Cowan, 2001). Because focal attention is limited, it is also thought to be **selective**. Only one attention-demanding processing task can be handled at the same time. Reflecting these selectivity effects, cognitive psychologists since the 1970s have contemplated metaphors that represent controlled attention as a bottleneck, a filter or a flashlight. A third definitional feature is that attention can be **voluntary**, in the sense that it can be subject to cognitive, top-down control that is driven by goals and intentions of the individual. A fourth characteristic is that attention controls **access to consciousness**. Under normal conditions, participants can tell researchers about their conscious perceptions, thoughts or feelings while they attend to some aspect of a task, through the method of thinking out loud (Ericsson and Simon, 1993) or via some other retrospective method, as discussed in detail by Gass and Mackey (2000) in relation to SLA.

As we will see in the next five sections, the third and fourth definitional attributes of attention, voluntariness and consciousness, have driven SLA investigations into attention and L2 learning. How attention affects L2 learning has been examined by investigating the *quality* of attention that is necessary for L2 learning. The focus has been on processes and outcomes of learning under three attentional conditions, which can be summarized as: **incidental** (i.e. learning without intention, while doing something else), **implicit** (i.e. learning with no intervention of controlled attention, usually without providing rules and without asking to search for rules) and **explicit** (i.e. learning with the intervention of controlled attention, usually summoned by the provision of rules or by the requirement to search for rules). In a nutshell, SLA researchers have asked themselves whether L2 learning is possible without intention, without attention, without awareness and without rules.

5.10 LEARNING WITHOUT INTENTION

Because attention can be voluntary, intentionality needs to be examined when evaluating what quality of attention is necessary for L2 learning. This is what we call the question of **incidental** L2 learning, which asks: Is it possible to learn about the L2 incidentally, as a consequence of doing something else in the L2, or does all L2 learning have to be intentional? It is unanimously agreed in SLA that incidental L2 learning is possible indeed. The learning of L2 vocabulary during pleasure reading is an incidental type of learning that has been found to be possible in the L2 as well as in the L1. This is what Jan Hulstijn (2003) concludes in a seminal review. This is also what the research reviewed by Krashen (2004), as well as the more recent evidence gleaned by Marlise Horst (2005) and others (e.g. Pigada and Schmitt, 2006), shows.

Nevertheless, lack of a priori intentions to learn while doing something in the L2 does not rule out the possibility that, in the course of processing, attention may be deliberately turned to the input. For example, while reading for pleasure and without any particular intention to learn vocabulary, an L2 reader may on her own suddenly become intent on finding out what a word means or may make a mental note to remember it and look it up later. In other words, we cannot ignore the fact that intentions wax and wane and fluctuate during online processing and that, in the end, it is online attention that is at stake in a cognitive understanding of L2 learning. Furthermore, while learning without intention is possible, people learn faster, more and better when they deliberately apply themselves to learning. Thus, learning with intention remains of central importance in SLA because of its facilitative role, as Hulstijn and Laufer (2001) have argued with respect to vocabulary learning.

5.11 LEARNING WITHOUT ATTENTION

Perhaps the most contested matter is whether new L2 material can be learned without attention, that is, if just detected pre-attentively. The debate has to do with Schmidt's highly influential Noticing Hypothesis, which we introduced in Chapter 4, section 4.6. The question asked is: Is detection only sufficient for L2 learning or is noticing necessary? **Detection** is defined as registration outside focal or selective attention (Tomlin and Villa, 1994), whereas **noticing** is defined as detection plus controlled activation into the focus of conscious attention (Schmidt, 1995).

Robinson (1995) and Doughty (2001) have argued that Nelson Cowan's (1988, 2001, 2005) unified model of memory and attention offers a framework for envisioning this problem as one that depends on a continuum in the quality of attention (from low-level, automatic attention to high-level, controlled attention), rather than on an all-or-nothing dichotomy between unattended and attended processing. In Cowan's model, detection that involves registration outside focal or selective attention is the kind of low-level, minimal attention typically assumed during automatic processing in information processing theories. For example, imagine we are taking a walk and our sensory storage catches a patch of green for several hundred milliseconds (Cowan, 1988). Immediate activation in long-term memory of an already existing representation that shares some fundamental feature will make us recognize it meaningfully, but pre-attentively, as a tree. This will occur without subjective experience, that is, without reaching consciousness. Any instance of language use mandatorily involves this kind of automatic, low-attentional processing (Ellis, 2002a). On the other hand, detection that goes on to involve focal or selective attention via controlled activation summons the kind of high-level, focal attention assumed during controlled processing in information processing theories. This quality of attention is thought to be accompanied by subjective experience or awareness at the time of processing. For example, we are taking a walk, our eyes catch a patch of green, we see a tree, but we also experience rapid feelings of vague pleasantness – maybe we even intuit that fall has begun. These are typical fleeting consciousness effects that range according to US consciousness scholar Bernard Baars from fringe conscious (the vague pleasantness, the tacit memory of signs of fall around us) to more substantial and qualitative (visual imagery or inner speech) (Baars and Franklin, 2003). But we may immediately move on to something else and forget about having seeing any tree or having had this experience of fleeting consciousness. Much of language use can also involve this kind of conscious, subjective awareness, while automatic, low-attentional processing also goes on (N. Ellis, 2002a, 2005).

Which of the two extreme qualities of attention (low-level automatic detection or high-level, controlled activation) leads to learning? Or can both result in learning? Herein lies the point of disagreement in SLA. Tomlin and Villa (1994) suggested, contra Schmidt, that detection at the periphery of focal attention is all that is necessary for L2 learning, whereas detection plus controlled activation into focal attention is facilitative of learning, but not necessary. Gass (1997) also agrees that noticing facilitates L2 learning but cannot be considered necessary. By contrast, Schmidt (1994, 2001) has maintained that detection involving peripheral attention is not enough for L2 learning, on the grounds that *novel* material that is attended peripherally could never be encoded in long-term memory. Instead, detection plus controlled activation into the focus of attention is needed for L2 learning: 'what learners notice in input is what becomes intake for learning' (1995, p. 20). Schmidt also proposes that nothing is free in L2 learning: 'in order to acquire phonology, one must attend to phonology; in order to acquire pragmatics, one must attend to both linguistic forms and the relevant contextual features; and so forth' (1995, p. 17).

Drawing on Cowan's (1988) unified model of memory and attention, Robinson (1995) agreed with Schmidt that noticing is necessary for learning, but stipulated that noticing should be conceived as involving focal attention plus rehearsal, thus eschewing the vexing question of proving phenomenological awareness of the experience of noticing. Nick Ellis concedes that the Noticing Hypothesis may be right, but only if accompanied by an Implicit Tallying Hypothesis (2002a, p. 174), which imposes two provisos: (a) noticing is necessary only for new elements with certain properties that make low-attentional learning unlikely, but not for all aspects of language to be learned, and (b) noticing may be necessary only for the initial registration of such 'difficult' elements so as to make an initial representation in long-term memory possible, but not for subsequent encounters. This is because 'once a stimulus representation is firmly in existence, that stimulus … need never be noticed again; yet as long as it is attended to for use in the processing of future input for meaning, its strength will be incremented and its associations will be tallied and implicitly cataloged' (Ellis, 2002a, p. 174). Acknowledging that it may be impossible to demonstrate *zero noticing at the time of processing* empirically (see discussion in section 5.12), Schmidt did shy away from his initial claim that noticing is the 'necessary and sufficient condition for converting input to intake' (1990, p. 129), and since then his position has been that 'more noticing leads to more learning' (1994, p. 18). That is, noticing is facilitative of L2 learning (see also Schmidt, 2001).

In the end, then, the jury is still out on the question of whether learning without attention is possible. The real challenge for future research is to be able to specify empirically what investigating this question really entails in the context of processing for L2 learning.

5.12 LEARNING WITHOUT AWARENESS

In its weaker form that states noticing is facilitative of L2 learning, the Noticing Hypothesis has attracted compelling support. Particularly the research programme led by Ron Leow at Georgetown University has offered ample evidence that noticing with awareness, and even more so with understanding, is facilitative of L2 learning. In these studies (e.g. Leow, 1997, 2001; Rosa and O'Neill, 1999; Rosa and Leow, 2004), think-aloud protocols are used to classify learners by their comments into: **unaware**, if no trace of noticing can be found in the introspective data; **aware**, if simple mention is made of the subjective experience of paying attention to the targets; or **aware with understanding**, if more abstract comments are made involving partial formulation of rules or generalizations. The results have consistently revealed better post-test scores for participants that produced verbal reports showing awareness and, even to a higher degree, understanding.

By contrast, in other research programmes where researchers have employed more delayed or indirect measures of awareness than think-alouds, a robust relationship between noticing and learning has not always been found. Thus, several interaction researchers (see Chapter 4, sections 4.7, 4.8 and 4.11) have indirectly measured noticing via uptake, or the incorporation of the interlocutor's correction in the learner's own utterance, and they have reported no relationship between uptake and score gains (Mackey and Philp, 1998; Loewen and Philp, 2006; McDonough and Mackey, 2006). Likewise, note taking as an indirect measure of noticing was also unrelated to post-test performance in at least one study (Izumi, 2002). It is unclear whether this pattern of results tells us something about the relationship between noticing and learning or about the validity of using uptake and note taking as awareness measures.

5.13 DISENTANGLING ATTENTION FROM AWARENESS?

It should be emphasized that the Noticing Hypothesis posits that 'learning requires awareness *at the time of learning*' (Schmidt, 1995, p. 26, italics in the original). No claim is made that learners need to remain aware of what they noticed at any later point. Likewise, learner's noticing does not need to include understanding of the nature of what they noticed; subsequent processes of hypothesis formation or rule abstraction are possible, but not a part of the noticing itself. It is therefore somewhat surprising that to date most SLA researchers have investigated the predictions of the Noticing Hypothesis by probing the presence or absence of self-reported, retrospective awareness. In doing so, SLA studies of noticing conducted since the late 1990s have entangled the question of controlled attention – Can there be learning resulting from low-level attention that is allocated outside the focal object of attention? – with a sequel question of awareness and consciousness – Can new L2 material be learned without awareness? (That is, Can there be a dissociation between L2 learning and awareness?)

A problem that is amply acknowledged in SLA is that demonstrating conclusively whether awareness was present or absent at the time of learning is methodologically impossible, because introspective and retrospective self-reporting is always imperfect. An additional problem that is rarely discussed, and one that is much more important from a theoretical perspective, is that the

Table 5.2

How can awareness versus automatic attention be measured in SLA studies?

AWARENESS

Self-report measures

People differ in how good they are at verbalizing explicit knowledge and the products of their awareness. Hence, positive reports are strong evidence of awareness, but absence of reports cannot be taken as evidence of zero awareness. See Gass and Mackey (2000) for further discussion

Concurrent reports

Thinking aloud while performing a task is the best window we have into the objects of consciousness, both fringe conscious awareness and more qualitative awareness at the time of processing (Baars and Franklin, 2003). For an example, see Leow (1997)

Retrospective reports

Debriefing questionnaires, interviews, and stimulated recalls have also been used. In addition to the general problems of all verbal report measures, retrospection is ill-suited to capture fleeting phenomenological awareness. One cannot discard the possibility that something was subjectively consciously attended to but the memory of being aware quickly faded away and was not available for recall at the later time when participants were asked. For examples, see Robinson (1997; questionnaire at the end of the study), Williams (2005, debriefing interview at the end of the task), or Mackey et al. (2000; stimulated recall interviews after the task)

AUTOMATIC/IMPLICIT ATTENTION

Dual-task performance

As an alternative to self-report measures, near-zero-awareness states can be built into the experimental conditions themselves, via a dual competing or interference task paradigm. Shanks (2005) explains that if attention is consumed by a task and the learning targets are embedded in another task, it is assumed that any evinced learning of the targets falls outside focal attention and is without awareness. However, the doubt always remains of whether attention was actually entirely depleted by the demands of the competing task. Moreover, Shanks notes that this paradigm has generated conflicting results in psychology to date

Objective tests of memory after the training

This is another alternative to self-report, favoured by experimental psychology researchers. If targets processed outside focal awareness during training were learned, they should be more frequently recognized implicitly as 'previously seen' after the training. Objective memory tests, however, differ in sensitivity

Traditional direct memory tests

A set of items may be presented and participants are asked to recognize the ones that were involved in the training phase of the study, by selecting the 'old' items. For an example of this measure in SLA, see Shook (1994)

Indirect memory tests

Shanks (2005) suggests that indirect memory tests may offer improved alternatives to traditional recognition tests. Items are presented, one by one very briefly, and participants are asked to identify the ones that they 'prefer' or 'like'. Note that the experimenter's question is not to make a judgement about novel versus old, but about liking. While the jury is still out in terms of whether cases of indirect recognition on these tests can be interpreted as cases of true implicit (unattended) learning, the evidence that these indirect tests elicit does seem more fine-grained than that of traditional recognition tests. This kind of indirect memory test has not been used in SLA, although the logic of matched sentence tasks is similar. In these tasks, participants make decisions about whether sentences are similar, whereas the evidence that is inspected by the researcher is simply whether they take longer or shorter in making such judgements with grammatical or ungrammatical sentences (see Gass, 2001) strategies that allow us to measure the involvement of automatic vs controlled attention may be rather different from the strategies that help us measure awareness, and – if we accept Cowan's reformulation of qualities of attention (see section 5.11) – the study of the former is more urgent than a pursuit of the latter.

UK-based cognitive psychologist David Shanks (2005), a sceptic of implicit learning, usefully explains the range of strategies that allow cognitive psychologists to measure the involvement of automatic-implicit attention versus strategies that help them measure awareness. Table 5.2 offers a summary of the main kinds of measures employed to bear on the issue of awareness in L2 learning, complemented with the insights offered by Shanks (2005) about measures of automatic-implicit attention.

In the end, then, in their zeal to shed light on the difficult issue of awareness, SLA researchers have largely neglected the issue of the involvement of automatic vs controlled attention. Therefore, the various positions taken around the Noticing Hypothesis by Ellis (2002a), Robinson (1995), Schmidt (2001) and Tomlin and Villa (1994) remain empirically untested at their core.

5.14 LEARNING WITHOUT RULES

As explained in section 5.2, skill acquisition theorists would strongly argue against the wisdom of trying to begin the learning process without first securing explicit declarative information about whatever new aspect of the L2 someone is trying to learn. Other SLA researchers interested in cognition, however, have a persistent interest in exploring the viability of implicit learning, or learning without rules. This interest is understandable if we remember that, when it comes to language, implicit (intuitive, tacit) learning has a special appeal. After all, children learn their L1 without any rules whatsoever, and many students experience a painful dissociation between what they 'know' in terms of rules and what they can 'do' with the L2 in real situations of use (we will return to this issue in Chapter 6, when we discuss the question of the interface in section 6.14).

At the heart of the SLA research programme on learning without rules is a focus on the products of **implicit** L2 learning: Can grammar generalizations result from experiencing L2 data without explicit knowledge being provided at the outset of the learning process? Or even without the learner actively and consciously searching to discover generalizations behind the language data she experiences?

United States psychologist Arthur Reber was the first to expend sustained effort into the study of implicit learning, which he defined as learning without rules. He pioneered an artificial grammar research paradigm in the 1960s that has been pursued by many others to this date (see Reber, 1996). In this type of experiment, participants in the implicit learning condition are asked to memorize strings of letters. This is an incidental-implicit learning condition in that: (a) participants think they are doing something (memorizing strings) that is different from what the researcher hopes they will do (extract formal regularities or rules), and (b) they are not given any explicit declarative knowledge (no rules for the artificial grammar) or any orienting towards the possibility of rules underlying the stimuli (no instructions to search for rules). When they are later asked to judge new strings as grammatical or not, they perform above chance level. This is interpreted as proof that they learned something about the artificial grammar indeed. When requested to verbalize any rules at all, however, they are at a loss. This is interpreted as evidence that their learning has resulted in implicit (intuitive, non-verbalizable) knowledge of the artificial grammar.

An important point of contention in interpreting these results, however, is whether learning without rules is about symbolic or associative learning. For those who, with Reber, believe we can learn without rules or awareness of rules, the proposal is that implicit (unconscious) processing leads to the abstraction of rules that are symbolically represented in the mind, only that they happen to be inaccessible to consciousness. That is, their theories of implicit learning are abstractionist and symbolic. However, increasingly more psychologists are willing to reinterpret the evidence from implicit learning studies as showing learning of underlying statistical structure, rather than learning of underlying rules (Shanks, 2005). This radical proposal has been made possible by the appearance and burgeoning of connectionist and associative theories in psychology since the 1980s (to be discussed in the last section of this chapter).

Returning to L2 learning matters, what would happen if no explicit information were made available to L2 learners at the outset of training? Would automatization look different from learning that begins with declarative rules, as in the study by DeKeyser (1997) we examined in section 5.3? And what would the resulting representations be like, since there is no declarative rule to be proceduralized? Would L2 learners abstract their own rules from the input they work on? Or would they show evidence of associative memories only? Robinson (1997) set out to investigate just these questions.

5.15 AN EXEMPLARY STUDY OF SYMBOLIC VS. ASSOCIATIVE LEARNING: ROBINSON (1997)

Robinson (1997) investigated whether 60 Japanese college students would learn an English grammar rule better without or with rules, after 25 minutes of training. Robinson focused on the products of automatization, defined as the accuracy and speed of response on an immediate post-test after the 25-minute treatment.

The target rule chosen was the English **dative alternation**, or rather a small aspect of it, which was of reasonable difficulty for the Japanese college students in this study. Consider the two sentences:

(1)   John gave the cake to Mary
       John donated the piano to the church

The verbs *give* and *donate* have close meanings in the above two sentences. So, why is it that we can choose the alternative option *John gave Mary the cake* but not **John* *donated the church the piano*? Many speakers of English, including of course first language speakers, are surprised to learn that *give* can alternate between the two options because it is an Anglo-Saxon verb, whereas Latinate verbs (e.g. *donate*) do not allow this word order alternative (there are several other, more abstract ways in which the alternation is motivated, explained in Pinker, 1989). In pedagogical terms, if a rule of thumb were to be given, we would tell English students that one-syllable verbs can take both word orders, whereas bi- or multiple-syllable verbs (because Latinate verbs always have at least two syllables) can only be well formed with the '*to*-phrase'. Robinson decided to use invented verbs rather than real ones, to circumvent the possibility that some participants would benefit from their existing memory of how commonly encountered verbs (e.g. *give*) work. Some examples of multisyllabic verb items used in the training and tests were:

(2)   Nick menided some hot coffee to Sue
       *Sandy bivarded Patrick some Swiss cake

You see how challenging it must have been for the participants to work through these sentences and to end up with some kind of ability to judge the grammaticality of test items after 25 minutes. For the researcher the challenge was to answer the following question: Would the participants under the different conditions end up making grammaticality judgements by relying on knowledge of the monosyllabic versus disyllabic rule for when to use the *to*-phrase? Or would they make their judgements aided by a stock of memorized instances (the ones they encountered in the 25-minute session)?

For the **implicit** group, the task required that participants remember the position of words in sentences (a modification of the implicit learning condition to memorize artificial grammar strings used by Reber). The **incidental** group read the sentences for meaning and answered comprehension questions (a condition that resembles Krashen's comprehensible input; see Chapter 4, section 4.3). These two groups would encounter the verbs and the syntax of those sentences but likely process the items without any awareness of a 'rule' being embedded in them. Consequently, Robinson predicted they would learn a stock of instances rather than an abstract rule. That is, their responses would be fast, but accuracy would be possible only for sentences already encountered in the training, and not for novel sentences that were also included in the post-tests. Two other groups in the study experienced the items under explicit learning conditions of two kinds. The participants in the **less explicit** of the explicit groups saw the input typographically enhanced and were encouraged to find out the underlying rule. The participants in the **more explicit** of the explicit groups received an explanation of the monosyllabic versus multisyllabic rule, followed by practice. This condition, therefore, was closest to the ideal in skill acquisition theory (see sections 5.2 and 5.3). The prediction for these two explicit conditions was that training would lead to abstract generalizations, precisely because the instructions asked these participants to try to discover or to use rules, respectively. They would be able to apply rules, perhaps in a slower fashion, but they would be more accurate with new sentences during testing, because they would be able to 'generalize' what they learned beyond the specific items they worked with during training.

The study results supported these predictions for the most part. Interestingly, however, the instructed (skill-acquisition-like) group outperformed all other three groups, as they were faster and more accurate on both old and new sentences. But all four groups also showed the same effect regarding a relatively faster reaction for already encountered items, as if the memory of those actual instances encountered during training had also contributed to learning, not just the conceptual guide of a rule. Robinson interpreted this as evidence that effects coexist from conceptually driven abstraction and data-driven, memory-based learning, even in the instructed condition.

In the end, then, is L2 learning possible without rules? Robinson concludes that, in the absence of rules, low-level associative learning that draws on data-driven processes supported by memory is certainly possible. Learning without rules leads to the formation of memories of instances that can be accessed more easily, allowing for faster performance, but without knowledge that can be generalized to new instances. That is, without the initial provision of rules (without an explicit learning condition), learning is bottom-up (i.e. data and memory driven), and it does not lead to knowledge of a systematic rule of some kind. With rules, learning proceeds by drawing on high-level attention and conceptually driven processes supported by conscious attention, resulting in generalization with awareness.

Robinson (1997), as well as Nick Ellis (2005) and John Williams (1999), have argued that in the future debates about implicit learning must be recast in terms of the interaction between low-level associative learning that draws on data-driven processes supported by memory and high-level cognitive learning that draws on conceptually driven processes supported by conscious attention. Both types of processing for learning can occur and both can interact. A pending question for future research is whether all aspects of an L2 are equally learnable by implicit means or whether some particularly complex aspects of the L2 may require conceptually driven processing in order for associations and representations to be formed (Ellis, 2002a, p. 174).

The reconceptualization of implicit learning as statistical learning is just one of many consequences of a wider trend in cognitive psychology to reconceptualize information processing as an associative, probabilistic, rational, usage-based, grounded, dynamic and, in sum, *emergent* adaptation of the agent to the environment. We finish this chapter with a forward-looking bird's-eye view of this trend.

5.16 AN EMERGENTIST TURN IN SLA?

In the last few years, what can be characterized as an imminent emergentist turn has made inroads into several research programmes about cognition in SLA. Emergentism refers to a contemporary family of theories in cognitive science that have coalesced out of increasingly critical examinations of the tenets of information processing theories. Because they have evolved out of information processing, they share much common ground with it. However, because emergentism is critical of traditional cognitivist notions and goes well beyond them, it is sometimes characterized as a post-cognitivist paradigm (Potter, 2000; Wallace et al., 2007). In the field of SLA the pioneer of emergentism has been language psychologist Nick Ellis. For over a decade now, he has led other SLA scholars to think about the associative, probabilistic and usage-based nature of L2 acquisition, first from the University of Wales Bangor (e.g. Ellis, 1993, 1996) and currently from the University of Michigan (e.g. Ellis and Larsen-Freeman, 2006; Ellis, 2007; Robinson and Ellis, 2008b).

In a manifesto of emergentism in SLA, Ellis and Larsen-Freeman summarized the position as follows:

> Emergentists believe that simple learning mechanisms, operating in and across the human systems for perception, motor-action and cognition as they are exposed to language data as part of a communicatively-rich human social environment by an organism eager to exploit the functionality of language, suffice to drive the emergence of complex language representations.
>
> (2006, p. 577)

The emergentist family of explanations for L2 learning is built on several nested assumptions that borrow from diverse contemporary schools in cognitive science, all sharing a post-cognitivist bent. Three important tenets on which emergentist approaches build are associative learning, probabilistic learning and rational contingency (Ellis, 2006a). From these three principles derive the 'simple learning mechanisms' to which Ellis and Larsen-Freeman (2006) refer in the quote above.

Associative learning, as we saw in section 5.15, means that learning happens as we form memories of instances or exemplars we experience in the input, in a process of automatic extraction of statistical information about the frequency and sequential properties of such instances. Ellis (2006a) explains that the human architecture of the brain is neurobiologically programmed to be sensitive to the statistical properties of the input and to learn from them. When processing stimuli, the brain engages in a continuous and mandatory (as well as implicit, in the sense of automatic and certainly unconscious) tally of overall frequency of each form and likelihood of co-occurrence with other forms. This statistical tallying is supported by neural structures in the neocortex (Ellis, 2006b). **Probabilistic** learning posits that learning is not categorical but graded and stochastic, that is, it proceeds by (subconscious) guesswork and inferences in response to experience that always involves ambiguity and uncertainty (Chater and Manning, 2006). However, this kind of probabilistic calculation is not a slave of whatever is experienced by the human brain as a contiguous temporal or spatial surface pattern. Instead, the probability calculations of the human mind are guided by principles of **rational contingency**, or automatically computed expectations of outcomes on the basis of best possible evidence (Chater and Manning, 2006; Ellis, 2006b). Specifically, the processor makes best-evidence predictions about outcomes based upon (a) the overall statistics extracted by accumulated experience, (b) the most recent relevant evidence, (c) attention to cues detected to be present and (d) the clues provided by the context (Ellis, 2002a, 2006a, 2006b, 2007). Each time the outcome is confirmed or not in another relevant event, the processor adjusts to the new evidence and modifies its prediction so its predictive accuracy is better next time.

Additional important tenets in the emergentist family of theories are perhaps broader in scope. One is **usage-based** learning, or the position that language use and language knowledge are inseparable, because we come to know language from using it. Hence the specification in the earlier quote by Ellis and Larsen-Freeman (2006) that learning from exposure comes about 'as part of a communicatively-rich human social environment' and is experienced 'by an organism eager to exploit the functionality of language' (p. 577). Among others, US cognitive scientist Michael Tomasello, now at the Max Planck Institute in Germany, has been instrumental in advancing a view of language acquisition that is usage-based, where grammar concepts emerge out of communicative and social needs: 'people construct relational and semantic categories in order to make sense of the world and in order to communicate with one another' (Abbot-Smith and Tomasello, 2006, p. 282). Importantly, this commitment to usage-based learning means that two traditional distinctions in linguistics and information processing, respectively, are transcended: competence and performance, and representation and access. Furthermore, meaning (rather than rules) is held to be of primary importance in understanding the language faculty. For this reason, the linguistic schools that best suit the emergentist project are cognitive linguistics (Langacker, 2008) and corpus linguistics (Gries, 2008).

Another broad-scope tenet of emergentism is that cognition is **grounded**, and therefore language is too. By this, it is meant that our species' experience in the world and the knowledge that we abstract from such experience is always structured by human bodies and neurological functions (Evans et al., 2007; Barsalou, 2008). This is why Ellis and Larsen-Freeman (2006) described learning mechanisms as 'operating in and across the human systems for perception, motor-action and cognition' (p. 577). Perception and action, and not only abstract or symbolic information, are believed to shape cognition (Wilson, 2002). Hence, perceptual and sensory-motor functions of the brain must also be implicated in language acquisition. They contribute to the emergence of language abstractions and they also constrain and guide many of the simple learning mechanisms of associative, probabilistic and rational contingent learning.

The final tenet that is worth highlighting in this synoptic examination of emergentism is that language acquisition, like the acquisition of other forms of cognition, is a self-organizing **dynamical system**. This entails viewing the phenomenon to be explained (e.g. language learning) as a system (or ecology) composed of many interconnected parts that self-organize on the basis of multiple influences outside the system; these influences provide constraints that afford self-organization, but no single cause has priority over others, as explicated in developmental psychology by Linda Smith and the late Esther Thelen at Indiana University (Smith and Thelen,

2003) and by Paul van Geert (1998) at the University of Groningen. In addition, a change in any given part of the system will result in changes in other parts, but the two need not be commensurate in size or importance. As Smith and Thelen describe, 'Development can be envisioned, then, as a series of evolving and dissolving patterns of varying dynamic stability, rather than an inevitable march towards maturity' (p. 344). In SLA, an early call of attention to dynamical systems was made by Diane Larsen-Freeman (1997), and a recent research programme has been more explicitly proposed by Kees de Bot and his colleagues at the University of Groningen (de Bot et al., 2007; de Bot, 2008). Dynamicity in self-organizing systems also places variability at the heart of investigation (de Bot et al., 2007). Much of the theory behind the tenet of dynamic systems originated from insights in meteorology sciences (Larsen-Freeman, 1997). It is no wonder, then, that Ellis (2002a) comments: 'The multiplicity of interacting elements in any system that nontrivially represents language makes the prediction of the patterns that will eventually emerge as difficult as forecasting the weather, the evolution of an ecological system, or the outcome of any other complex system' (p. 178).

It would also be an uncertain weather forecast exercise to predict how long it will take for usage-based, dynamic systems, emergentist SLA to really come to fruition. Certainly, emergentist thinking about L2 learning has been vibrant, but the consequences have been less noticeable in terms of empirical activity. Thus, for instance, the implications of connectionism for L2 learning have been discussed frequently, beginning in the 1990s (Ellis, 1998; Gasser, 1990), but empirical applications of connectionism to SLA have been rare (e.g. Ellis and Schmidt, 1998). Full empirical deployment is gradually on the rise, however, and may become a reality in the not-so-distant future, judging from the impressive array of not only theoretical but also empirical knowledge around cognitive linguistics and emergentist SLA that Robinson and Ellis (2008a) have gathered. However long it takes, what is certain is that emergentism in SLA will flourish, as it has in a number of other fields.

Second language learning under an emergentist perspective has the potential to look less like development that proceeds teleologically towards the ultimate attainment of a so-called native grammar, and more like a complex deployment of human multi-language capacities as a function of experience in the world. The picture of L2 development they offer resonates with what we know about learner language, which we will discuss in the next chapter. The new approach, by redefining cognition as emergent, helps envision additional language acquisition less as a formal, deterministic and symbolic feat and more as an ecological phenomenon, 'a dynamic process in which regularities and system emerge from the interaction of people, their conscious selves, and their brains, using language in their societies, cultures, and world' (Ellis, 2007, p. 85).

5.17 SUMMARY

- Information processing theories assume that: (a) the human cognitive architecture is made of representation and access; (b) mental processing is comprised of automatic or fluent (unconscious) operations and voluntary or controlled (conscious) operations; (c) cognitive resources such as attention and memory are limited; and (d) performance is variable and vulnerable to stressors, as shown during dual-task performance.

- A particular kind of information processing theory called skill acquisition theory explains L2 learning as the process of gradual transformation of performance from controlled to automatic, via proceduralization, or meaningful practice that is sustained over time.

- Proceduralization leads to automatization, which is a quality of fluent, automatic performance that goes beyond sheer speed.

- The benefit of practice drops off at some point in the learning curve due to the power law of learning; the benefits of practice are skill-specific.

- Prolonged and repeated meaningful practice changes the knowledge representation itself; with repeated access, the stored knowledge becomes more elaborated, well specified and analysed.

- Memory is composed of two types, long-term memory and working memory, which interact.

- Long-term memory is about representations and it is unlimited; it can be explicit-declarative (the facts and events we know and can talk about) or implicit-procedural (knowledge we do not know we hold, but which affects our behaviour and supports our skills, habits and performance). Another distinction that has received less attention in SLA is between semantic memory (decontextualized knowledge) and episodic memory (knowledge encoded with information about the lived experiences in which we acquired it).

- How L2 vocabulary is encoded in long-term memory has resulted in research about the strength, size and depth of word knowledge, as well as various theories about the content of the entries in the mental bilingual lexicon and how the L1 and L2 lexicons interact during lexical access.

- Working memory is about access and it is limited; it controls what information can be stored momentarily (the issue of storage) and how well and how long it can be activated and integrated with already known information in long-term memory (the issue of processing); it is the site for controlled processing and consciousness.

- It is known that working memory capacity is smaller in the L2 than the L1, and it is assumed that this lag narrows with increasing proficiency; there is also debate as to whether passive or active measures of working memory are more suitable to investigate the relationship between working memory and L2 learning. SLA researchers have not investigated these issues systematically yet. More is known about working memory capacity and individual differences in L2 learning, which we will examine in Chapter 7 (sections 7.7 and 7.8).

- Attention is thought to be central to understanding L2 learning. Attention is limited and selective, and it can be voluntary and accessible to consciousness. Several questions have been investigated in SLA with regard to attention.

- Is L2 learning possible without intention? Yes, incidental learning, or learning without intention, is possible in L2 learning. The best-known example is the incidental learning of L2 vocabulary while reading for pleasure. However, people learn faster, more and better when they learn deliberately or with intention.

- Is L2 learning possible without attention? Examination of this question has taken the form of a debate over whether detection (registration outside focal attention) is sufficient for L2 learning or whether noticing (detection plus activation into the focus of attention) is also required. The jury is still out, but rather than investigating the qualities of attention that are necessary for learning, most studies have examined the issue of awareness.

- Is L2 learning possible without awareness? This question cannot be directly answered, because zero awareness may be methodologically impossible to establish. However, awareness (as measured through reports of noticing and understanding during think-aloud protocols) has been shown to be related to higher post-test scores, suggesting that noticing with awareness is facilitative of L2 learning.

- Is L2 learning possible without rules? In the absence of rules, low-level associative learning is certainly possible. This kind of learning draws on data-driven processes supported by memory. With rules, learning proceeds by drawing on controlled operations and conceptually driven processes supported by conscious attention. Both types of processing of new L2 material can lead to learning, and both can interact. A pending question for future research is whether all aspects of an L2 are equally learnable by implicit means or whether some particularly complex aspects of the L2 may require conceptually driven processing in order for associations and representations to be formed.

- An imminent emergentist turn has made inroads into several research programmes about cognition in SLA. Emergentism refers to a contemporary family of theories in cognitive science that reconceptualizes information processing as an associative, probabilistic, rational, usage-based, grounded, dynamic and, in sum, *emergent* adaptation of the agent to the environment.

- It is difficult to predict how long it will take for emergentist SLA to really come to fruition and so far the publications offer discussions and expositions more than they offer L2-specific empirical evidence. Emergentism will likely flourish in cognitive SLA in future years, however, judging from the pervasiveness of emergentist thought in many other areas of the cognitive sciences.

5.18 ANNOTATED SUGGESTIONS FOR FURTHER READING

If you are looking to read some more about information processing and emergentism in SLA, the best accessible choices are DeKeyser (2007b) and Ellis (2007), both in the same collection and following a similar and helpful approach to their topics. The best overviews of memory and attention in SLA remain Robinson (1995) and Schmidt (2001).

   If you are interested in deeper readings, here are some recommendations. To delve deep into information processing, I recommend beginning by reading the chapters in DeKeyser (2007a) that examine skill acquisition theory and notions surrounding L2 practice, including DeKeyser's own. Following that, you can tackle Segalowitz (2003) and McLaughlin and Heredia (1996) in order to develop a better sense for what proceduralization, automaticity and restructuring are or are not. The emergentist range of positions can nicely be reviewed in a special issue of the *Modern Language Journal* guest-edited by de Bot (2008) and the seminal collection by Robinson and Ellis (2008a).

   If you are interested in concrete empirical applications, you can read DeKeyser (1997) and Robinson (1997), already discussed in depth in this chapter, and three more related influential studies by Ellis (1993) and John Williams (1999, 2005). If you want to delve into this empirical area even more deeply, you can read the studies gathered in two special issues of the journal *Studies in Second Language Acquisition* in 1997 (issue 2) and 2005 (issue 2). They will make good sense now!

   An alternative route to developing expertise in cognition and SLA is to read foundational L1 articles, and only then embark on the SLA-specific readings that I outlined above. You would probably get a lot more mileage out of your readings in this way. If you want to take this mini-journey, I strongly recommend you begin with an interview with K. Anders Ericsson (Schraw and Ericsson, 2005), in which he describes in personable terms his development, with Herbert Simon, of the think-aloud method, his research on expertise through deliberate practice (a concept that is very relevant to L2 learning but has not made it into SLA yet!), and the ideas about memory and knowledge that he developed with Walter Kintsch. It is also particularly useful to consult a few journals whose mission is to disseminate advances to a generalist audience in psychology and cognitive sciences. In *Annual Review of Psychology* you will find the accessible and fascinating recount of episodic memory by Endel Tulving (2002) and the informative and readable introduction to grounding in the study of cognition by Barsalou (2008). Both articles make for a good case not to shy away from investigating meaning, consciousness and experience in cognition (as well as in cognitively oriented SLA). In *Current Directions in Psychological Science* you can read Randall Engle's (2002) eloquent discussion about working memory and attention. In *TRENDS in Cognitive Sciences*, you will find an introduction to dynamical systems theory by Smith and Thelen (2003) that is lucid and engaging and can be a good way to lead into de Bot et al. (2007) for an SLA-specific treatment. Also in *TRENDS* is the technical but brief and worthwhile introduction to probabilistic learning by Chater and Manning (2006), which makes for good reading to pave the way into Ellis (2006a, 2006b).

Finally, if anything mentioned in this chapter about vocabulary piqued your interest, accessible and enjoyable are any readings by Paul Nation (e.g. his recent 2006 article about vocabulary size), Norbert Schmitt (e.g. the longitudinal study he conducted in 1998; or the case study of extensive reading reported in Pigada and Schmitt, 2006) and Batia Laufer (e.g. Hulstijn and Laufer, 2001).

6

Development of learner language

SLA scholars who investigate learner language seek to explain L2 competence and L2 development. **Competence** is defined as the nature of the mental representations comprising the internal grammar of learners and **development** refers to the processes and mechanisms by which those representations and the ability to use them change over time. The focus is typically on grammar, and more narrowly on morphology and syntax. In order to understand what it means to become a competent user of an additional language, many other dimensions of the target language system must be learned, including vocabulary, phonology, pragmatics and discourse. However, thus far SLA efforts have been most persistent and most fruitful in the L2 areas of morphology and syntax. This will be our focus in this chapter, too. In the study of learner language there are two traditions: interlanguage studies and formal linguistic studies of L2 acquisition. Even though ultimately both share the same goal of understanding learner language, each has its own constructs, tenets and preferred methodologies. In this chapter, I will familiarize you with insights about learner language gleaned by the study of interlanguage from the general cognitive learning position and I will emphasize development over competence. Throughout the chapter, I will illustrate findings and arguments with oral and written discourse data. Whenever possible, I have drawn on a variety of attested examples from a number of target languages.

Before we delve into the wealth of knowledge about the development of learner language that the interlanguage research tradition has generated, let us briefly consider the major differences between the approach we will explore in this chapter and the SLA tradition that investigates L2 acquisition from a formal linguistic perspective.

6.1 TWO APPROACHES TO THE STUDY OF LEARNER LANGUAGE: GENERAL COGNITIVE AND FORMAL LINGUISTIC

The awakenings of the first tradition in the study of learner language can be situated in the coinage of the technical term **interlanguage** (Selinker, 1972), which refers to the language system that each learner constructs at any given point in development. The emergence of this construct was a watershed point that marked the beginnings of SLA as an autonomous field, and it was influenced by findings that had begun to accumulate about child L1 acquisition (e.g. Roger Brown's seminal 1973 study of three children acquiring English as a mother tongue). As we briefly mentioned in Chapter 3, section 3.1, it initially represented a shift away from the older school of Contrastive Analysis. Researchers abandoned the contrastive cataloguing of linguistic differences favoured by that school and, instead, they began analysing the actual language samples that learners produced when they attempted to use their L2. The second tradition began thriving in the early 1980s, at another watershed point in the field, when the school of Chomskyan linguistics finally made substantive inroads into SLA. As a result, researchers began to take seriously the possibility that an innate **Universal Grammar** (UG) would constrain L2 acquisition, as it was believed to constrain L1 acquisition. Since then, SLA researchers with training in formal linguistics have also pursued the study of the mental representations of grammar that learners build, with the aim to describe the universal and innate bounds of such knowledge (White, 2003).

The formalist approach is driven by two tenets that are often summarized by the characterization of domain-specific nativism. The tenet of **nativism** holds that humans as a species are biologically endowed with the basics of grammar knowledge prior to any experience with language. The tenet of domain-specificity or **modularity** posits that the human mind has a language-dedicated module (i.e. separate from other mind functions), where language learning and language use are handled. The approach emphasizes competence over development. It favours evidence about learner language gleaned via experimental elicitation, particularly the methodology of grammaticality judgements, where participants are asked to judge how grammatical or acceptable sentences are, in their estimation. This is because these researchers value evidence about learners' tacit intuitions of language, especially when the intuitions speak to abstract UG phenomena that are unlikely to be known from exposure to L2 input alone, from knowledge of the L1 or from explicit instruction (Schwartz and Sprouse, 2000). From this formalist perspective, it is thought that grammaticality judgements and experimental data offer a better window into underlying linguistic competence than discourse data do.

By contrast, interlanguage researchers believe that the same general cognitive learning mechanisms that help humans learn and process any other type of information help them extract regularities and rules from the linguistic data available in the surrounding environment. They draw on functional linguistic schools and language psychology, including information processing (cf. Chapter 5, section 5.1) and usage-based emergentism (cf. Chapter 5, section 5.16), and they emphasize development over competence. They also rely equally on experimental elicitation of evidence and on free production data. The latter type of data is valued because the evidence that learners generate when they speak, write or sign in an additional language offers a window into ability for use in real time and across communicative contexts, and such a focus is particularly useful when investigating development.

You should be aware that many of the findings and facts gleaned from interlanguage studies and discussed in this chapter have also been examined in the formal linguistic SLA tradition. However, because they are vested with specialized theoretical significance that requires highly technical knowledge, they are beyond the scope of this book. If you are interested in the formalist lines of SLA work on learner language, you should consult the excellent specialized treatments offered by Hawkins (2001) and White (2003).

6.2 INTERLANGUAGES: MORE THAN THE SUM OF TARGET INPUT AND FIRST LANGUAGE

Since the 1970s, close attention to the language that learners produce has enabled important insights about the nature of interlanguage. Consider the sentences in (1) and (2), the first one produced orally by an L1 Japanese speaker (from my unpublished data archive) and the second one produced in an essay by a L1 Korean user of English (from Oshita, 2000, p. 313):

  (1)   she … runned away
  (2)   … he falls a piece of note into dough by mistake

In (1), the English simple past morpheme *–ed* has been applied to a verb that is irregular in the past (*run, ran*). In (2), a verb that is intransitive (*fall*) has been made into a causative verb with a transitive meaning ('drop'). Both solutions are combined in (3), from an essay written by an L1 Spanish speaker (also from Oshita, 2000, p. 313):

  (3)   It [a wall] was falled down in order to get a bigger green house

We may wonder what kinds of mental representation of English past tense and causative verbs these learners held when they produced the solutions in (1), (2) and (3). Most certainly, they did not pick them up from their surrounding input (e.g. textbooks or L1 English friends). Furthermore, nothing in Japanese, Korean or Spanish would necessarily explain these innovations. This illustrates two important generalizations about interlanguage: L2 learners end up building mental representations that are different from what the target input in their surrounding environment (be it the classroom or the wider society) looks like, and also different from the grammar representations available in their first language.

Moreover, and this is a third generalization about interlanguage, many of the same developmental solutions are attested in the speech of young children who are learning their mother tongue (and who therefore do not have any L1 knowledge on which to rely, for good or bad!). For example, many children learning L1 English are seen to overregularize the past tense of irregular verbs (*comed* instead of *came*) at around two and a half to three years of age (Maratsos, 2000). Likewise, young children are fond of overextending causation to intransitive verbs in their early L1 production, as in example (4), reported by Sharwood Smith and Kellerman (1989, p. 223), who credit it to child language acquisition researcher Melissa Bowerman:

  (4)   I'm going to fall this on her

If interlanguage solutions are often shared by first and second language acquirers, and if neither the target input nor the L1 influence can entirely explain them, then what can?

6.3 COGNITIVIST EXPLANATIONS FOR THE DEVELOPMENT OF LEARNER LANGUAGE

In first language acquisition, the idea that children are guided by universal **Operating Principles** in their processing of the input for learning was first proposed by Slobin (1973), who offered a list of 40 statements that described what children seemed to 'look for' in the input data in order to learn the L1 grammar. These statements included maxims such as 'Pay Attention to the End of Words' (which helps explain why children learn suffixes earlier than prefixes in words) and 'Avoid Exceptions' (which is consistent with many overregularization phenomena in L1 and L2 acquisition). In the 1980s, Roger Andersen applied Slobin's framework to SLA with relative success. His One to One Principle (Andersen, 1984a), for example, has met with ample support in the L2 (see section 6.5). A similar effort at compiling psycholinguistic principles is Bill VanPatten's (2002) **Input Processing theory**. He posited that (a) learners will process content words before anything else (a strategy we exploit naturally when we compose telegrams or read newspaper headlines); (b) they will also process lexical encodings before synonymous grammatical encodings (*yesterday* before *–ed*) as well as semantic or non-redundant encodings before formal or redundant ones (the pronoun *he* before the third person singular marking *–s* in *he works here*); and (c) they will interpret first nouns in sentences as subjects (*the eraser hits the cat*, 'eraser = doer'; see discussion in MacWhinney, 2001, pp. 75–6). From this view, the process of L2 acquisition is one of overcoming these psycholinguistic strategies and preferences and forging new ones that will work better in the L2. In the end, however, Operating Principles, Input Processing Strategies and other such inventories are excessively metaphorical in nature to take a research programme far enough into actual explanations.

A powerful family of cognitivist explanations for how L2 development works is provided by usage-based emergentist theories, which we introduced in Chapter 5 (section 5.16). These theories are far from unified. Robinson and Ellis (2008b), for example, list not only emergentism and dynamic systems theory but also cognitive linguistics, corpus linguistics, probabilistic and frequency-based theories, and connectionist and rational models of language. However, they all share some tenets. First, they hold that grammar learning is not rule-based or deductive, but driven by experience or inductive (Robinson and Ellis, 2008a). In addition, they take frequency and salience *in the input*, and cognitive processes of attention and categorization *in the learner*, as explanatory cornerstones of language learning (Ellis, 2006a, 2006b). Third, the contemporary cognitivist-emergentist perspectives afford variability an unprecedented importance, as variability is thought to be a major property of systems and a manifestation of development (Verspoor et al.,

2008). Finally, they also hold that learner language development cannot be explained by recourse to isolated causes or back to a single force (Larsen-Freeman and Cameron, 2008). Instead, explanations must account for the simultaneous interaction of multiple forces. As we will see in section after section of this chapter, much evidence supports this contention and suggests that multiple factors simultaneously conspire to shape learner language and its development.

6.4 FORMULA-BASED LEARNING: THE STUFF OF ACQUISITION

It is clear that learners make ample use of memorized bits and pieces of language. These memorized formulas, which can be found in many learner transcripts, have been seen under different theoretical lights over the history of interlanguage studies. In the 1970s and 1980s, L2 users' initial reliance on memorized formulas was thought to be spurred by communicative and strategic motives that happened to promote learning. This was Lily Wong Fillmore's (1979) conclusion in her study of five Mexican children whose families had just emigrated to California for farm work. She recorded the children weekly over a year as they interacted in the playroom of their school and, in doing so, she documented their gradual transformation from no English at all to being relatively functional in their daily dealings with English-speaking peers. All five children were driven by social needs and adopted a general 'speak now, learn later' approach (p. 215). They soon began using memorized material which 'was learnable and memorable by virtue of being embedded in current, interest-holding activities over which the learners had already acquired some mastery, and from which they had already received social rewards' (p. 211). These bits and pieces of language were used in an unanalysed fashion at first: *Wait a minute, You know what?, Knock it off, It's time to clean up, No fair!, Gotcha.* Among the children, six-year-old Nora proved to be a 'spectacular success as a language learner' (p. 221) because she exhibited the fastest learning pace by far. Wong Fillmore discovered part of the reason was Nora's formula-based analysis of the input, which she intently sought through abundant social interactions. Table 6.1 summarizes the attested history of Nora's use of *how do you do dese* ('how do you do this') over the school year. As can be seen, the formula began to be combined with increasingly more varied slots and was successively analysed and broken down into grammar-like constituents. By the end of the study, *how*-questions had emerged in Nora's interlanguage, even though they still 'lacked the detailed refinements which required further analysis' (p. 215).

More contemporary usage-based theories of L2 learning posit that the process of formula-based analysis is not only a springboard to communication and grammatical analysis at beginning stages, but the stuff of acquisition, in that it guides the majority of the acquisitional task (N. Ellis, 2008). In this view, language acquisition proceeds bottom up, from formulas to low-scope patterns, to constructions, in an implicit and inductive process that is only peripherally intentional or strategic. Ellis (2002a, 2002b) explicates the process as follows. The first step is the registration of **formulas** (also called *items* or *exemplars*), defined as

Table 6.1
Nora's use of *How do you do dese* over a school year

Time	Formulaic part ...	... Slot variation part
Second school quarter	*How do you do dese*	
Third school quarter	*How do you do dese* ...	... *September por la mañana*
		... *flower power*
		... *little tortillas*
		... *in English*
Fourth school quarter	*How do you* ...	... *like to be a cookie cutter*
		... *make the flower*
	How ...	... *did dese work*
		... *do cut it*
		... *does this color is*

Note: Data reported and discussed in Wong Fillmore (1979, pp. 212–15).

the pairing of a form and a meaning that is experienced in a particular language use event. As part of the processing of meaningful input, all experienced material is mandatorily tallied, and information about the frequencies, distributions and contexts of exemplars is implicitly encoded in memory upon each new encounter. Learners will encounter some items repeatedly and in contexts of meaning that are relevant to them; if the form–meaning pairings are frequent enough, and the formal and functional cues to how they work salient enough, they will extract information that cumulatively leads to generalizations from such experiences. In other words, repeated experience of the same formulas enables the abstracting of **low-scope patterns**, the second step of usage-based language learning. As Lieven and Tomasello (2008) explain with respect to L1 acquisition, low-scope patterns are often extracted around a single high-frequency word or chunk that is prototypical of the pattern, or an 'island' that helps learners get a quick fix on some generalization at first (e.g. Nora's *how do you do dese*). Mechanisms of bootstrapping, or induction by categorization and generalization, enable the third step of gradual abstraction of the pattern into a **construction or schema**. As Lieven and Tomasello put it, 'distributional analysis based on the relation between a form and (child-identified [or learner-identified]) functions, leads to linguistic representations developing internal structure' and makes the inductive analysis progressively 'less item-based and more schematic' (p. 169).

It is important to note that L2 learners vary widely in their relative ability to make successful use of these processes. For example, we saw in Chapter 4 (section 4.1) that Wes was extremely adept at memorizing language and using it to great communicative effectiveness, but he never showed evidence of unpacking formulas (Schmidt, 1983). The same individual variation has been found in formal classroom learning. For example, in a study of *wh*-questions in French as a foreign language conducted in the United Kingdom, Myles et al. (1999) documented how 11-year-old school students diligently memorized the question *comment t'appelles-tu?* ('what's your name?') from their teachers and materials. Many began using it as a chunk when asking questions about a third entity: *Comment t'appelles-tu le garçon?* (with the intended meaning 'what's the boy's name?'). Gradually, other versions appeared in their oral production that suggested some analysis, for example, without the post-verbal clitic *tu*: *Comment t'appelles la fille?* (meaning 'what's the girl's name?'). Finally, the third person form of the verb with its pre-verbal clitic also emerged: *comment s'appelle le garçon?* However, only ten of the 16 students they investigated underwent this full process of analysis. At the end of their first two years of French in school, the remaining six had not gone far enough beyond the initial formula.

It would also be misguided to think that once formulas are analysed and give way to abstract constructions and schemata, they 'disappear' or dissolve themselves into this generalized knowledge. Instead, all levels of knowledge (formulas, low-scope patterns and constructions or schemata) 'remain in the inventory ... that speakers have created, to be drawn upon at various levels of abstraction' (Lieven and Tomasello, 2008, p. 175). In fact, many language researchers are interested in describing the end result of such multi-layered repertoire of creative plus memorized language (e.g. Wray, 2002; Schmitt, 2004; Meunier and Granger, 2008). In addition, interesting efforts are beginning to be directed to support the L2 learning of formulas through instruction (Cortes, 2006; Fitzpatrick and Wray, 2006; Taguchi, 2007). These studies help us appreciate the central role that knowledge of formulas plays in the making of idiomatic and fluent L1 and L2 speakers.

6.5 FOUR INTERLANGUAGE PROCESSES

Aided by memory of formulas and experience-based induction of abstract generalizations, learners' internal knowledge systems continually engage in processes of building, revising, expanding and refining L2 representations, as the new grammar develops. Four important ways in which they do so are simplification, overgeneralization, restructuring and U-shaped behaviour.

Simplification reflects a process that is called upon when messages must be conveyed with little language. It is particularly pervasive at very early stages of L2 development and among naturalistic learners, as we will see in section 6.8. In later development too, simplification may be seen in early representations of L2 morphology, when a one-meaning-one-form mapping is initially assumed by learners, as predicted by Andersen's (1984a) One to One Principle. For example, Sugaya and Shirai (2007) found that even though the Japanese marker *te i-ru* can have a progressive meaning (*Ken-ga utat-te i-ru*, 'Ken is singing') and a resultative meaning (e.g. *Booru-ga oti-te i-ru,* 'The ball has fallen'), L2 Japanese learners at first use it to express progressive meaning only. Likewise, Andersen (1984b) found that Anthony, a 12-year-old L1 English learner of Spanish he investigated, used two invariant forms of the Spanish article – one devoted to mark definiteness (*la*, 'the' in feminine singular form) and one to mark indefiniteness (*un*, 'a' in masculine singular form). This was despite the full choice of eight forms that are available in the Spanish target input.

Overgeneralization is the application of a form or rule not only to contexts where it applies, but also to other contexts where it does not apply. Overgeneralization has been particularly well documented with morphology. For example, learners begin using *–ing* from very early on, but they also overgeneralize it to many non-target-like contexts, sometimes for substantially long periods. Thus, Schmidt (1983, p. 147) reported that over three years Wes produced many instances of *–ing* that were appropriate in terms of meaning, as in (5), but also many instances of oversuppliance, as in (6):

(5)   I don't know why people always talking me
(6)   so yesterday I didn't painting

You will remember that Wes learned English naturalistically (see Chapter 4, section 4.1). In instructional contexts, too, classroom students have been seen to overgeneralize *–ing* frequently, even during the same period when they may not provide it in other required contexts, as in (7) and (8), produced by L1 Spanish learners of English as a foreign language and reported by Pica (1985, p. 143):

(7)   I like to studying English
(8)   I was study languages all last year

Overgeneralization can be apparently random, as in examples (6) through (7) above, or it can be systematic. An important case of systematic overgeneralization in morphology involves overregularization, or the attempt to make irregular forms fit regular patterns. The overapplication of *–ed* to irregular verbs, shown earlier in illustrations (1) and (3), is a well-known case of overregularization, whose important theoretical consequences have been discussed by many researchers (e.g. see Clahsen, 2006, for L1; and Leung, 2006, for L2). Overgeneralization does not need to be interpreted negatively. Indeed, this process typically manifests itself after a certain level of development has been reached, in that it presupposes that learners have at least partially figured out some regularity. After systematically overgeneralizing, the learning task is to retreat from the overgeneralization and to adjust the application of the form or rule to increasingly more relevant contexts.

Restructuring is the process of self-reorganization of grammar knowledge representations. In their review of this concept for an SLA audience, McLaughlin and Heredia (1996) explained that restructuring covers a range of processes by which existing knowledge schemata may be quite radically modified, or a new organization may be imposed on already stored knowledge structures so as to accommodate smaller-scale knowledge changes that may have occurred previously. It is therefore assumed that restructuring involves knowledge changes that can be large or small, abrupt or gradual, but always qualitative and related to development or progress. However, the kind of progress that is implied in the notion of restructuring should not be equated with increased accuracy.

That progress does not always translate into accuracy is clear in the notion of **U-shaped behaviour**, which typically manifests itself as part of restructuring. The process is defined by Sharwood Smith and Kellerman (1989) as 'the appearance of correct, or nativelike, forms at an early stage of development which then undergo a process of attrition, only to be reestablished at a later stage' (p. 220). That is, in U-shaped learning curves, the linguistic products of the final phase cannot be distinguished from those of the first phase, as both are seemingly error-free. However, the underlying representations at the two times are qualitatively different. In the first phase, accuracy is purely coincidental, because it lacks the full representation of target-like functions and meanings that underlies the final phase. We saw a case of U-shaped behaviour in Chapter 3 (section 3.6), when we discussed Kellerman's research with three groups of Dutch L1 students of English. The group at the intermediate level of proficiency appeared to worsen in their intuitions about the L1–L2 meaning correspondences of *breken/break*. Another oft-cited L2 illustration of restructuring accompanied by U-shaped behaviour can be found in Huebner's (1983) study of Ge, a naturalistic learner of English in his early twenties who also spoke Hmong as an L1 and Lao as an additional language. In fact, Ge's learning of the English article *the* provides a good illustration of the interrelationship of all four interlanguage processes we have examined in this section.

6.6 INTERLANGUAGE PROCESSES AT WORK: GE'S *DA*

Huebner (1983) described how Ge initially used *the* (or *da*, as he pronounced it) to mark nouns as specific and known to the hearer but not the current topic, to use a non-technical description. Notice, for example, how in (9) below no article is used when the referent is a specific entity known to the hearer and also the topic of the utterance. By contrast, in (10) *da* is used when the referent, although also specific and known to the hearer, is not the topic ('we' is) (both examples are taken from Huebner, 1979, p. 27):

(9)   chainis tertii-tertii fai. bat jaepanii isa twentii eit
        [literally: Chinese thirty, thirty-five, but Japanese is twenty-eight]
        [The Chinese man is thirty-five, but the Japanese is twenty-eight]
(10)   gow howm, isa plei da gerl
        [literally: go home, is play the girl]
        [When we went home, we would visit with the girls]

Ge's initial analysis of the functions of *da* was felicitous because it resulted in high levels of accuracy, since a large proportion of nouns are used with *the* in English precisely when they are specific and known to the hearer (e.g. *The book that you lent me is great*). A month and a half into the study, Ge suddenly began using *da* to mark between 80 and 90 per cent of all noun contexts he produced, mostly where the referent was specific, regardless of assumed hearer knowledge. This level of overgeneralization was so pervasive that Huebner used the term **flooding** to describe it. At this point, Ge's system may have been exploring the range of contexts that apply to *the*, a necessary step on the way to restructuring *da* from an information status marker (which signals known or new and topical or non-topical information) to the more encompassing grammatical category of 'article' (which in English signals referentiality, a combined property of specificity and hearer knowledge, but not topicality). While this was great progress in the building of an internal grammar of English, it of course resulted in much lower levels of accuracy than before. However, a little over five months into the study, oversuppliance of *da* disappeared from first-mention contexts (which are 'unknown to hearer' albeit specific and require the indefinite article *a*, as in *a woman is walking down the street*) and shortly before reaching month seven of the study, *da* began to retreat from other non-target-like indefinite contexts, giving way to a restructured rule that yielded stable target-like suppliance of *da* at 80 to 90 per cent levels for the rest of the observation period.

Ge's case shows that interlanguage development is not haphazard but instead changes in predictable, systematic ways (a matter of development). At the same time, and just as all natural languages are, so is interlanguage simultaneously characterized by systematicity and variability. In other words, albeit systematic, interlanguage change is always non-linear (a matter of accuracy) and unevenly paced (a matter of rate). The next six sections of the chapter are devoted to an examination of seminal interlanguage findings that attest to the complex relationship among development, accuracy and rate of learning.

6.7 DEVELOPMENT AS VARIABILITY-IN-SYSTEMATICITY: THE CASE OF JORGE'S NEGATION

In the SLA literature, the study of English negation offers a good example of systematic, non-linear and unevenly paced development along predictable stages. I will illustrate the stages here with longitudinal data from Jorge, a young English L2 user investigated by Cancino et al. (1978) and also by Stauble (1978). The ten-month developmental pathway towards his acquisition of English negation is depicted in Table 6.2.

Jorge was born in Bogotá, Colombia, in an upper-middle-class family. At the age of 12, he and his family moved to Boston, where he attended regular school. He had had only three months of private tutoring in English prior to his arrival in Boston and subsequently received only minimal ESL instruction in his school, where he attended regular classes and studied regular school subject matters in English. He spoke Spanish at home and English in school. Over ten months, his knowledge of negation went along a process that involved the restructuring of his representation of negation in English from pre-verbal to post-verbal position (stage 3 in Table 6.2). As we mentioned in Chapter 3 (section 3.4), pre-verbal negation is the first stage

Table 6.2
Jorge's development of English negation

Stage	Time (recording)	Attested L2 examples	Developmental description
1. Pre-verbal negation with *no/not*	Months 1–2 (tapes 1–4)	No *saw* him [I didn't see him]	Pre-verbal negation; preferred negation functor is non-target-like *no*
2. Pre-verbal negation with *don't*	Month 3 (tapes 5–6)	I don't *saw* him [I didn't see him]	Pre-verbal negation; use of unanalysed but more target-like negation functor *don't* intensifies
3. Post-verbal negation in restricted contexts (COP/AUX + *not/don't*)	Month 4 (tapes 7–8)	I *will* don't *see you tomorrow* [I will not see you tomorrow]	Onset of post-verbal negation; by the beginning of month 4 (tape 7) *no* declines; *don't* begins to be applied post-verbally but only in copula/auxiliary contexts
4. Post-verbal negation in all contexts	Months 5–6 (tapes 9–12)	I *didn't went to Costa Rica* [I didn't go to Costa Rica] Not at the ranch	Evidence of incipient analysis of *don't*, which consolidates over time; consolidation of target-like negation with copula/auxiliary; by month 6 (tape 12), *no* completely disappears and negation of phrases is done with target-like functor *not*
	Months 7–10 (tapes 13–20)	They *didn't see nobody* [They didn't see anybody]	Post-verbal negation is complete; analysis of *don't* into carrier of tense and negation is complete; however, instances of unanalysed *don't* still co-exist with analysed *don't/didn't* in production

Note: All illustrations are reported in Stauble (1978). The verb which the negation functor modifies is underlined in each example.

regardless of the learners' L1 background, although speakers of L1s where pre-verbal negation is the grammatical norm may remain in the first stage in English longer than speakers whose L1s require post-verbal negation. (Incidentally, Jorge's L1 is a pre-verbal negation language, but it only took him three or four months to restructure into post-verbal negation in L2 English.) Hyltenstam (1987) suggests that the first pre-verbal stage may be motivated by some typological basic influence, since across languages of the world pre-verbal negation is a more common grammar configuration than post-verbal negation.

Jorge's traversing of the four stages was unevenly paced. The early stages were brief and lasted only one or two months each, whereas the rest of the development was much slower and lasted six months. Restructuring into post-verbal negation (at stage 3) was also gradual, first applied to restricted contexts only (after copula and auxiliary verbs) and only later (at stage 4, in month five or six) to the remaining relevant contexts. This kind of gradual application of a rule that spreads from a subset of simpler contexts to increasingly more relevant and complex contexts is often seen in interlanguage development (e.g. in the development of tense and aspect; see section 6.10 and Table 6.6).

Moreover, Jorge's development of negation did not proceed linearly from error-full to error-less solutions. Instead, and as shown in Table 6.2, only the final fourth stage is target-like. Nevertheless, each new stage reflects a more advanced solution to the developmental problem of negation. Thus, *I didn't went to Costa Rica* is a better, more advanced 'error' than *I will don't see you tomorrow*, which in turn is a better and more advanced non-target-like interlanguage innovation than *I don't saw you*. We must note here, then, that not all 'errors' are equal, and that interlanguage solutions which may look like 'errors' can nevertheless be good news.

Finally, it is worth pointing out that Jorge's development also involved overgeneralization (see section 6.5) of a given form as the preferred negation functor. Initially, this was *no* but it soon became *don't* (at stage 2, three months into the study). Towards the middle of the study, his knowledge representation of *don't* also underwent analysis from a memorized formula to a construction that carries not only negation but also tense (as evinced in Jorge's attested utterance *I didn't went to Costa Rica*) and person (i.e. *doesn't*).

Jorge was lucky enough to reach the last stage of negation after ten months of immersion in the L2 environment. However, neither eventual attainment of the highest stage in a given developmental sequence nor convergence with the target grammar or even ultimate high levels of accurate use is a necessary outcome of L2 development. This is particularly true of naturalistic adult learners, as we will see in the next section.

6.8   INTERLANGUAGE BEFORE GRAMMATICALIZATION: THE BASIC VARIETY OF NATURALISTIC LEARNERS

We know much about the acquisition of an L2 when learners begin from zero L2 knowledge and without the aid of instruction, that is, when interlanguage development must proceed solely under naturalistic circumstances. A main contribution to this knowledge comes from a large-scale investigation conducted in the 1980s under the auspices of the European Science Foundation (ESF) and led by Wolfgang Klein and Clive Perdue (Perdue, 1982; Klein and Perdue, 1997). The ESF project had two remarkable strengths: it was longitudinal and also crosslinguistic.

Forty adults who were immigrants in five different European countries were studied over two and a half years, as they acquired one of five L2s: Dutch, English, French, German and Swedish. The resulting data amounted to a dense and longitudinal corpus of 15,000 pages of L2 oral transcriptions, spanning 30 months of study (Klein and Perdue, 1997). The combinations of L1 and L2 investigated were determined in part by the political realities of immigration in European countries at the time, which explains the narrow range of L2s included. This was more than compensated, however, by the purposeful 'two L2s by two L1s' design, shown in Figure 6.1. You can see how the crosslinguistic insights about interlanguage development yielded by such a design can be deep. In the end, however, the ESF study uncovered strong universal patterns rather than large crosslinguistic particularities.

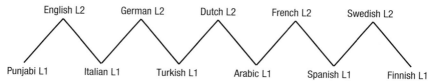

Figure 6.1
The two L2s by two L1s design of the ESF project (adapted from Perdue, 1982, p. 47)

Over the two and a half years, all learners in the project showed evidence of developing a rudimentary but systematic and fully communicative interlanguage system that was called the **Basic Variety** by Klein and Perdue (1997). Its main characteristics are summarized in Table 6.3. In a nutshell, the Basic Variety can be described by recourse to a few simple principles for how utterances must be structured (i.e. phrasal constraints) and how constituents must be ordered and information organized along pragmatic and lexical resources (i.e. semantic and pragmatic constraints). The Basic Variety shows no evidence of grammaticalization of resources, that is, it makes little use of morphology or subordination. A good case in point is the expression of temporality, which in the absence of morphology needs to rely on pragmatic and lexical resources, as summarized in Table 6.3 (see also Table 6.5).

We may wonder what, if anything, may make naturalistic learners move beyond the Basic Variety, that is, beyond the reliance on pragmatic and lexical principles and towards the grammaticalization of language resources. Klein and Perdue (1997) posited that it may be the increasingly more pressing need to express complex thoughts and the challenge of putting ideas into words when the concepts

Table 6.3
The Basic Variety summarized (Perdue, 1982; based on Klein and Perdue, 1997)

Area of analysis	Main findings
Lexicon	• Mostly noun-like and verb-like words, plus a few adjective-like and some adverb-like words • There is no inflection, words occur in an invariant form • Closed words (demonstratives, pronouns) are only a few and mostly with lexical rather than grammatical meaning • Other closed words (articles, conjunctions and pronouns) are rare if at all present
Phrasal constraints on utterance structure	• There are no complex structures, no syntactic movement • Utterances can be verbless or with a non-finite (non-conjugated) verb; utterances with finite or conjugated verbs never occur • Verbless utterances are made up of a noun phrase followed by another constituent • Non-finite utterances can appear in three basic forms: (1) Noun phrase plus verb (plus optional noun phrase); (2) Noun phrase plus copula plus another element; (3) Verb or copula plus noun phrase • With verbs of saying and giving, three arguments can appear (e.g. the sayer, the hearer and the said); the Basic Variety does not have four-argument utterances
Semantic constraints on case role assignment	• 'Controller first': The noun phrase with the highest degree of control (more agentivity, depending on the semantics of the verb) comes first (there is no real concept of 'subject' in the Basic Variety)
Pragmatic constraints on the organization of information in connected text	• 'Focus last': The Basic Variety structures information mostly through word order; topic comes first, focus comes last • Maintained information can be marked by zero anaphor (or rarely a pronoun) but only if the entity maintained is highest in control and no other agentive entity is in the same utterance; otherwise full noun phrases are used
Temporality	• Tense and aspect are marked pragmatically and lexically, not grammatically (an invariant form or 'base form' of each verb is used: the bare stem, an infinitive, sometimes *–ing* form for English) • The pragmatic marking is realized through the principle of chronological order: 'recount events in the order they occur' (e.g. *I went home and had dinner* versus *I had dinner and went home*) • The lexical marking is realized through a rich repertoire of adverbs • Calendric (*Sunday*) and anaphoric (*after, before*) adverbials are abundant • Anaphoric (*yesterday*), frequency (*always*) and durational (*two hours*) adverbs are less developed • Adverbs denoting two reference points (*again*) are absent

involve conflicting semantic and pragmatic conditions. This meaning-making pressure apparently worked for two-thirds of the 40 naturalistic learners investigated in the ESF project. However, it did not seem to be enough for the remaining third, who were seen to reach a plateau after a year and a half, sometimes earlier, and had not progressed beyond the Basic Variety by month 30, at the conclusion of the study.

6.9 PATTERNED ATTAINMENT OF MORPHOLOGICAL ACCURACY: THE CASE OF L2 ENGLISH MORPHEMES

The results of the ESF project clearly show that not all L2 users will go beyond pragmatic and lexical resources. However, many (both naturalistic and instructed) will indeed do so. For them, morphology, particularly inflectional morphology associated with verbs and nouns, will deploy slowly and non-linearly, but surely. One of the earliest SLA discoveries, made in the 1970s, is that a set of English inflectional morphemes is mastered by L2 English users in a certain order, which is shown in Table 6.4. This order represents the point at which learners across studies reached a conventional level of accurate suppliance of these forms, usually set at 80 or 90 per cent, depending on the particular researcher. The original evidence is nicely reviewed in depth by Heidi Dulay, Marina Burt and Stephen Krashen (1982, chapter 8), the researchers who conducted the initial studies, and more recently by Goldschneider and DeKeyser (2001). The accuracy order has been shown to be relatively similar for both young and adult L2 learners, for both naturalistic and instructed learners, and regardless of L1 background or whether the data are collected orally or via writing.

Three qualifications are in order. Obviously, in paper and pencil grammar tests, instructed learners may be able to supply all morphemes with relative accuracy, but that would not show their ability for real-time use of the L2, only their capacity to study language rules. In addition, as is true of all interlanguage systematicity, this patterned attainment of accuracy should not be equated with linear progression from inaccurate to accurate use of the L2 in a form-by-form, piecemeal fashion. Before reaching the 80 or 90 per cent accuracy benchmark for any of these morphemes, L2 users undergo non-linear increases and decreases in accuracy (remember, for instance, Ge's development of *da/the* in section 6.6), and some of them may never progress all the way to full target-like morphological accuracy when they speak, write or sign.

The third qualification is that, on occasion, some studies have reported slightly different ranks for structures within a given box in Table 6.4. For example, in a five-year longitudinal study, Jia and Fuse (2007) reported that ten Mandarin-speaking participants who had arrived in the United States between the ages of five and 16 found past tense *–ed* more challenging than third person *–s* (possessive *–'s* was not investigated). Three among the youngest starters were seen to master third person *–s* to 80 per cent accuracy after a year and a half or later in the United States, but none of the ten participants had yet mastered *–ed* at the end of the five-year study

Table 6.4
Morpheme accuracy order, from earliest to latest mastery

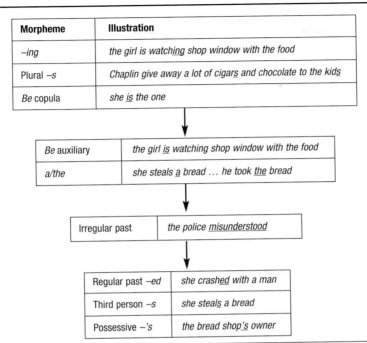

Morpheme	Illustration
–ing	*the girl is watching shop window with the food*
Plural *–s*	*Chaplin give away a lot of cigars and chocolate to the kids*
Be copula	*she is the one*

Be auxiliary	*the girl is watching shop window with the food*
a/the	*she steals a bread … he took the bread*

Irregular past	*the police misunderstood*

Regular past *–ed*	*she crashed with a man*
Third person *–s*	*she steals a bread*
Possessive *–'s*	*the bread shop's owner*

Note: Illustrations are from L2 oral narratives produced by college-level learners of English in Japan after watching *Alone and Hungry*, a short video clip from Charlie Chaplin's *Modern Times*; unpublished author data © Ortega, Iwashita, Rabie and Norris.

period. (Incidentally, these findings give you a clear sense for just how very slow L2 development can be!) However, the rank of structures is never violated across the boxes in Table 6.4.

In a meta-analysis of 12 previous studies, Goldschneider and DeKeyser (2001) devised five ways of operationalizing frequency and salience and showed that each operationalization on its own predicted the pooled results across studies reasonably well (in the range of 16 per cent to 36 per cent shared variance), and that when combined they could explain a great amount (71 per cent) of the variance in the data (for some help with how to interpret shared variance, see Chapter 7, section 7.1). These findings support the usage-based contention that input frequency and input salience can go a long way in predicting how difficult it is for learners to acquire certain aspects of the L2 grammar (Robinson and Ellis, 2008b).

6.10 MORE ON THE DEVELOPMENT OF L2 MORPHOLOGY: CONCEPT-DRIVEN EMERGENCE OF TENSE AND ASPECT

The development of L2 morphology has also been studied from a functional perspective that is known as the **concept-oriented** approach to language development. This approach places meaning making at the heart of language acquisition and posits that 'an L2 system can more adequately be described if the content to be expressed is taken as the starting point of the analysis' (von Stutterheim, 1991, p. 141). The expression of temporality has been well studied from this perspective.

There is consensus that learners of a second language (as well as children learning their first language) undergo three broad phases, each characterized by reliance on a different set of resources that help them express temporality: pragmatic means, lexical means and morphological means (see review in Bardovi-Harlig, 2000). The three phases are represented schematically in Table 6.5. In the first phase, pragmatic devices are used exclusively. For example, learners narrate in the natural chronological order of events (von Stutterheim and Klein, 1987) and they recruit the help of interlocutors in order to fill in temporal reference during interaction (Sato, 1990). In the second phase, lexical devices are added; for example, a range of adverbial expressions of time is used (see illustrations for the Basic Variety in Table 6.3). In this section, we examine development that happens during the third phase, at the point when temporality begins to be expressed via grammatical resources, that is, by means of verbal morphology.

Table 6.5
Three broad developmental phases in the expression of temporality

Phase 1	**Pragmatic means:** *she steal bread / and run away from the shop*

Phase 2	**Lexical means added:** *then the car of police come / so he ride on this car / next the woman ride too*

Phase 3	**Morphological means added:** *and suddenly she cried / and later she tried to run away*

Note: Illustrations are from L2 oral narratives produced by college-level learners of English in Japan after watching *Alone and Hungry*; unpublished author data © Ortega, Iwashita, Rabie and Norris.

It is known that, when morphology emerges in interlanguage to express grammatical tense and aspect, not all forms emerge at once. Moreover, only one function or meaning is expressed by a given form initially, as posited by Andersen (1984a) in the One to One Principle (see also our discussion of simplification in section 6.5). It is also known that some form–meaning pairings are more basic or earlier acquired than others. For example, in English, L2 users learn to use the present and past contrasts in the following progression: present progressive > simple past > past progressive > present perfect > past perfect (Bardovi-Harlig, 2000). Finally, it is a well-established fact that the patterned development of tense and aspect during the phase of morphological deployment is guided by the inherent aspect or lexical semantics of each verb to which morphology is attached. This is the prediction, in a nutshell, of the **Aspect Hypothesis** formulated by Andersen and Shirai (1996). More specifically, the Aspect Hypothesis predicts that the developmental pathway of emergence of tense and aspect will reflect prototypical pairings, that is, combinations where the semantics of the verb morphology is congruent with the semantics of the meaning of the verb to which the morphology is attached.

To illustrate, in L2 English the first functionally appropriate uses of the imperfective marking *–ing*, which carries a prototypical durative meaning, emerge in interlanguage in combination with verbs depicting events that imply duration, such as *run, walk, sing* or *watch* (such verbal meanings are called 'activities' in linguistic theories of tense and aspect). Conversely, the English simple past tense carries a prototypical punctual meaning, and it begins to be used appropriately first in combination with verbs that imply an action with a beginning and end, such as *meet someone, catch something, see someone/something, recognize, find* or *bump into* (called 'achievements'). Achievements and also verbal contexts denoting actions with an outcome, such as *paint a picture* or *steal a bread* (called 'accomplishments') also tend to invite new morphology involving perfective markers (*have/had*+participle). Gradually, tense and aspect markers will pair with non-prototypical verbal meanings, as well. For example, *–ing* will spread to mark non-prototypical situations where the inherent meaning of the verb phrase is an 'accomplishment' but the action is viewed from a durative perspective (e.g. *I can't believe she is stealing some bread*).

A good number of L2 studies across different languages has lent support to the predictions of the Aspect Hypothesis. Table 6.6 summarizes the attested emergence of perfective and imperfective aspect in L2 Spanish, which is expressed by the morphology of *pretérito* and *imperfecto*. As can be seen, development unfolds in a gradual form–function mapping process that is guided by prototypical pairings of verbal morphology with verb semantics. As Roger Andersen (1993) acknowledged, it is unclear whether this semantically constrained emergence of tense and aspect morphology is a case of the frequency in the input shaping acquisition (assuming that prototypical pairings are more frequent in the input than non-prototypical ones, something that awaits empirical confirmation with sufficiently large L1 corpora), or a case of the human perceptual and conceptual architecture shaping both how we use language and how we acquire it. Usage-based SLA researchers (for example, most of the authors in Robinson and Ellis, 2008a) would say it is probably both.

Stages of development that are similar to those depicted in Table 6.6 have been found for other L2s that have the perfective–imperfective distinction as well (e.g. French *passé composé* and *imparfait*; Italian *passato prossimo* and *imperfetto*; see review in Bardovi-Harlig, 2000). Although the tense and aspect systems of other languages may be rather different, they too have been found to exhibit similar

Table 6.6

Stages in the development of perfective (*pretérito*) and imperfective (*imperfecto*) aspect in L2 Spanish

Form–function development	Stages	Verb semantics (inherent lexical aspect)			
		Achievements + Punctuality + Telicity + Dynamicity	**Accomplishments** − Punctuality + Telicity + Dynamicity	**Activities** − Punctuality − Telicity + Dynamicity	**States** − Punctuality − Telicity − Dynamicity
Emergence of one form in one context	**1.**	PRETERITE			
		Preterite in achievements: *por fin los dos líderes de la parroquia <u>cambiaron</u> su actitud hacia mí* [finally, the two leaders of the parish changed their attitudes towards me]			
	2.	Preterite			IMPERFECT
		Imperfect in states: *cuando <u>era</u> pequeña* [when I was young]			
Spread to additional contexts	**3.**	Preterite	PRETERITE	IMPERFECT	Imperfect
		Imperfect in activities: *me <u>dolía</u> la cabeza mucho por la altitud* [my head hurt a lot because of the altitude]			
		Preterite in accomplishments: *en las navidades pasadas <u>vení</u> a casa de mis padres* [last Christmas I comed to my parents' house]			
	4.	Preterite	Preterite IMPERFECT	Imperfect	Imperfect
		Imperfect in accomplishments: *cada navidad <u>venía</u> a casa de mis padres* [every Christmas I would come to my parents' house]			
	5.	Preterite	Preterite Imperfect	Imperfect PRETERITE	Imperfect
		Preterite in activities: *no sé por qué, pero ayer me <u>dolió</u> la cabeza toda la tarde* [I don't know why, but my head hurt all afternoon yesterday]			
Full form–function mapping	**6.**	Preterite IMPERFECT	Preterite Imperfect	Imperfect Preterite	Imperfect PRETERITE
		Preterit in states: *aquel día … <u>fue</u> fatal* [that day … was terrible]			
		Imperfect in achievements: *se fue … porque no <u>encontraba</u> trabajo aquí en Dinamarca* [he left … because he couldn't find a job here in Denmark]			

Note: Capitalized labels indicate first emergence of a form with a given semantic verb type. Illustrations show cutting edge of interlanguage (i.e. new attested form–function pairings) at each successive stage. All illustrations are from Cadierno (2000) and were produced in essays by ten advanced college-level learners of Spanish in Denmark, except for illustrations for stages 4 and 5, which are invented examples that have been added here.

prototype influences (see Sugaya and Shirai, 2007, for L2 Japanese; and Lee and Kim, 2007, for L2 Korean). That these principles of form–function mapping should be relevant across such a range of L2s attests to the centrality of meaning and the pervasiveness of systematicity in interlanguage development.

6.11 DEVELOPMENT OF SYNTAX: MARKEDNESS AND THE ACQUISITION OF L2 RELATIVIZATION

SLA researchers have uncovered developmental systematicity not only in many areas of morphology but also with respect to various domains of syntax. The concept of markedness, discussed in Chapter 3 (see section 3.5) in connection with phonology, has also been applied with remarkable success to the description of how L2 learners will acquire one area of syntax in the target language: relative clauses.

Ever since the first pioneering studies by Schachter (1974; see section 3.7) and later Eckman et al. (1988), this prolific line of work has drawn on Keenan and Comrie's (1977) proposal of a Noun Phrase Accessibility Hierarchy that describes relativization options across all human languages. The hierarchy is illustrated with

Table 6.7
Relative clauses in L2 German following Keenan and Comrie's (1977) Noun Phrase Accessibility Hierarchy

Clause type	L2 illustration	English equivalent translations
Subject	*Aber eine Frau, die auch daneben stand, hat ihn das gesagt*	'But a woman <u>who was also there</u> said that to him'
Direct Object	*Und geniessen sie zusammen die Freiheit, die sie sich gewonnen haben*	'And together they enjoy the freedom <u>that they have won for themselves</u>'
Indirect Object	*Charlie liebt das Mädchen, dem er seinen Hut gegeben hat*[a]	'Charlie loves the young woman <u>to whom he gave his hat</u>'
Object of Preposition	*Und der Mann, gegen den das Mädchen gestoßen hat, läßt sich von Polizisten verhaften*	'And the man <u>whom the young woman bumped into</u> gets himself arrested'
Genitive	*Aber eine Zuschauerin sagt dem Bäcker, dessen Wagen das war, woraus das Brot geklaut wurde 'nee, das ist eigentlich nicht Charlie, das ist die Frau gewesen'*	'But a bystander tells the baker <u>whose truck was the one</u> from which the bread was stolen "no, that is actually not Charlie, that was the woman"'
Object of Comparison	n.a.[b]	'The police arrested a suspect <u>who the woman is more guilty than</u>'[c]

[a] This example is invented here for the purposes of illustration, as no cases of Indirect Object relative clause were found in the corpus.
[b] n.a. = not attested in the L2 data and not allowed in German L1.
[c] The English example for Object of Comparison is invented.

Note: Illustrations are from German L2 oral narratives of Charlie Chaplin's *Alone and Hungry* clip, produced by Australian L1 English college students; unpublished author data © Ortega, Iwashita, Rabie and Norris.

L2 data in Table 6.7. At the highest position of the hierarchy (that is to say, the most frequent and least marked) are subject relative clauses; at the lowest (i.e. the least frequent and most marked) are object of comparison relative clauses. Crosslinguistically, these six possible types of relative clause are in a markedness relationship which is hierarchical and implicational. That is, each lower (more marked) type is seen to be possible in a given language only if all other preceding (less marked) types are also possible. No matter how few or how many possibilities for relativization a given language allows, it will do so following the pattern from highest to lowest in the hierarchy, without gaps.

The same implicationally related markedness hierarchy has been observed within learner grammars in studies that have examined not only L2 English (e.g. Pavesi, 1986) but other target languages as varied as Chinese (Hu and Liu, 2007), German (Byrnes and Sinicrope, 2008), Swedish (Hyltenstam, 1984) and several other L2s (Tarallo and Myhill, 1983; Shirai and Ozeki, 2007). The evidence is particularly robust for subject, direct object and object of preposition types, whereas evidence on the other three types is more scarce and difficult to interpret (see Tarallo and Myhill, 1983, for discussion). Specifically, when a given learner is able to produce more marked types (particularly the in English conspicuous object of preposition), she or he will also likely be able to produce the highest (least marked) positions of subject and direct object, and not the other way around. The L2 findings are largely in accord with the facts reported for the development of relativization in L1 acquisition (Diessel and Tomasello, 2005).

In fact, both L2 and L1 findings about relativization concur not only for acquisitional patterns but also for patterns regarding use and processing (e.g. Fox and Thompson, 2007; Reali and Christiansen, 2007). Thus, as in L1 production, in L2 production the types in the higher positions of the hierarchy are more frequent, and the types in the lower, more marked positions tend to exhibit less accuracy and attract more non-target-like solutions, such as resumptive pronouns in L2 English (*The teacher who you introduced me to _her_ works for me now*) (see Hu and Liu, 2007, and Hyltenstam, 1984, for more discussion). As Reali and Christiansen (2007) note, the explanations for these universal patterns in L1 and L2 relativization phenomena are likely to be related to a number of syntactic, semantic-discoursal, cognitive and statistical influences.

6.12 A LAST EXAMPLE OF SYSTEMATICITY: CUMULATIVE SEQUENCES OF WORD ORDER

Let us finish this overview of findings about interlanguage systematicity with an examination of a large-scale study conducted by Jürgen Meisel, Harald Clahsen and Manfred Pienemann in the late 1970s, known as the ZISA project (the acronym for *Zweitspracherwerb Italienischer, Portugiesischer und Spanischer Arbeiter* or 'The Second Language Acquisition of Italian, Portuguese and Spanish Workers'; see Meisel et al., 1981). The project culminated with the discovery of a developmental pattern for the emergence of word order in German L2 among 45 informants, all migrant workers from Romance language backgrounds living in Germany. The pattern consists of five stages, summarized in Table 6.8. At the time, two processing strategies were hypothesized by Meisel et al. to be relevant in order to explain the findings: a canonical word order strategy (COS) and an initialization/finalization strategy (IFS). The strategy of COS posited that producing subject–verb–object word order is easier than other word orders. The strategy of IFS was predicted on the assumption that initial and final edges of strings are perceptually more salient to learners and therefore moving material to the initial or final position of a syntactic string is easier than moving material from or to positions inside the same string.

In order to appreciate the observed stages illustrated in Table 6.8, it is important to stress that the findings are based on **emergence**, or the first productive use of a given word order. The benchmark of emergence indicates what level of processing (operationalized as COS and IFS) a learner is capable of handling – even if only part

Table 6.8
The emergence of word order in L2 German according to Meisel et al. (1981)

Stage	Strategies	Description	Illustration
1	[+COS] [–IFS]	Canonical word order	Subject–Verb–X: *ein junges Mädchen geht durch die Straße* [a young woman walks along the street]
2	[–COS] [+IFS]	Adverb preposing	*X–Subject–Verb: *und dann die Mädchen kommt* [and then the girl comes]
3	[–COS] [+IFS]	Particle separation	Verb .... AUX/COMP and Particle: *Ich hab sie gesehen* [I have her seen] *der arme Mann wollte ihr helfen* [The poor man wanted her to help] *sie sieht sehr hungrig aus* [she looks very hungry like]
4	[–COS] [–IFS]	Inversion	X–Verb–Subject: *Und am Ende seiner Mahlzeit will er nicht dafür bezahlen* [and at the end of his meal, doesn't he want for it to pay]
5	[–COS] [–IFS]	Verb-end	Clause-final verbs in subordinate clauses: *die Frau, die das Brot gestohlen hat* [the woman who the bread stole]

Note: COS = Canonical Word Order Strategy; IFS = Initialization/Finalization Strategy. Illustrations are from German L2 oral narratives of Charlie Chaplin's *Alone and Hungry* clip, produced by Australian L1 English college students; unpublished author data © Ortega, Iwashita, Rabie and Norris. Close English translations reflect German word order; underlined parts show the scope of the IFS movement.

of the time – in spontaneous production. In addition, the developmental stages in Table 6.8 are implicationally constrained in an upward direction, meaning that learners tend to traverse this developmental progression without skipping stages. This implicational systematicity is unlike the systematicity discovered for the negation stages (see section 6.7 and Table 6.2), which learners also traverse without skipping. With negation, each lower stage is gradually 'outgrown' and eventually abandoned (in the case of learners who converge towards the target language). By contrast, the word order development is cumulative, as each attained stage adds another possibility to the full repertoire of German word order.

All stages of German word order are grammatical, with the only exception of stage 2, which, while more advanced than stage 1, happens to result in an ungrammatical solution. This is because, in German, placing an element other than the subject in the beginning of a sentence (see Table 6.8, 'then + the girl comes') triggers inversion of the subject–verb sequence: *dann kommt das Mädchen*, 'then comes the girl' (German is a V2 language, where the verb in a main clause always needs to take the second position). Only after separation has emerged at stage 3 are learners finally able to cope with movement inside the string and hence with the subject–verb inversion rule, thus producing at least some adverb-initial sentences that are grammatical in German. Remember, however, that these developmental sequences are about emergence and not accuracy. Therefore, a learner could apply the inversion rule to only one or two relevant cases and miss its application to another ten cases, which therefore are cases of stage 2 ungrammatical adverb preposing without inversion, and we would still consider her to be at stage 4, not 2 (some researchers use a conventional safety minimum of three successful applications out of at least four attempted cases). The non-target-like stage 2 may or may not eventually fade away from learners' interlanguage, depending on how accurate they become, but all other stages are cumulative, as already noted.

The same rationale for the initial developmental sequences uncovered for German L2 word order was later applied by Manfred Pienemann and colleagues in Australia to explain the developmental order of emergence of word order in English questions (Pienemann et al., 1988), which was briefly introduced in Chapter 3 (section 3.4). Table 6.9 summarizes and illustrates the stages. Once again, one stage typically results in ungrammatical solutions (stage 3) and thus may be phased away (in the case of learners who become accurate), but all other stages result in grammatical solutions and are cumulatively added to the repertoire of how to ask questions in English.

In the late 1990s, Pienemann's thinking evolved into a processing-sensitive but largely linguistic framework that he called Processability theory (Pienemann, 1998). In a nutshell, he proposed that in the beginning L2 learners are limited in their capacity for what syntactic information they can hold in memory during processing (hence the term 'processability' in the name of the theory). They need to gradually develop the psycholinguistic capacity to match grammatical information contained within and across units in the linguistic material they encounter, and they are capable to do so gradually with more distant elements in linguistic units. This matching presents a hierarchical and increasingly more difficult processing

Table 6.9
The emergence of questions in L2 English according to Pienemann et al. (1988)

Stage	Description	Illustration
1	Words and fragments with rising intonation	*A ball or a shoe?*
2	Canonical word order with rising intonation	*He have two house in the front?* *The boy threw a shoes?*
3	Fronting of a questioning element (*wh*-word, *do*, something else)	*Where the little children are?* *What the boy with the black short throw?* *Do the boy is beside the bus?* *Is the boy is beside the bus?*
4	Inversion in two restricted contexts: (1) in *wh*-questions with copula (2) in *yes/no* questions with auxiliaries other than *do*	(1) *Where is the sun?* (2) *The ball is it in the grass or in the sky?* *Is there a dog on the house?*
5	Inversion expands to the full range of target-like contexts	*How many astronauts do you have?* *What is the boy throwing?*
6	Negative questions Question tags Questions in embedded clauses	*Doesn't your wife speak English?* *You live here, don't you?* *Can you tell me where the station is?*

Note: All illustrations are from Spada and Lightbown (1993, 1999); questions for stages 1 through 5 were produced by Francophone 10- to 12-year-olds in intensive English programmes in Canadian schools during task-based oral interactions with a researcher. Questions for stage 6 are unattested examples invented by Spada and Lightbown.

problem: within categories (e.g. *walk* + *ed* = pastness), then noun phrases (e.g. *two girl* + *s* = plural agreement), then verb phrases (e.g. *John walk* + *s* = person agreement), then sentences (e.g. it is raining / *is it* raining? = question inversion) and finally subordinate clauses (e.g. he will come / *he said* he *would* come = reported speech). Remarkably, the current formulation of Processability theory has offered explanations for a variety of word order phenomena across several target languages, including morphosyntactic aspects of typologically distant languages such as Arabic, Chinese and Japanese (Pienemann, 2005).

6.13 FOSSILIZATION, OR WHEN L2 DEVELOPMENT COMES TO A STOP (BUT DOES IT?)

There is no guarantee that all learners will converge with the target grammar system along the pathways we have described in the preceding six sections. Much to the contrary, many L2 users may continue developing without aligning with the target representations, while many may stop along the way, perhaps permanently. The term **fossilization** was coined by Selinker (1972) and is used to characterize cases of 'permanent lack of mastery of a target language (TL) despite continuous exposure to the TL input, adequate motivation to improve, and sufficient opportunity for practice' (Han, 2004, p. 4). There are several well-studied cases of adult learners whose development appears to fit the fossilization diagnosis, at least at first blush.

One is Alberto, the 33-year-old immigrant worker from Costa Rica whose naturalistic acquisition of English was studied by Schumann (1976; see Chapter 4, section 4.2). He appeared to be unable to move beyond basic English. After ten months in Boston, Schumann noted that, in terms of morpheme accuracy (cf. Table 6.4), his suppliance of *–ing* and copula was relatively accurate but below conventional mastery levels of 80 per cent while his suppliance of *–ed* was virtually zero. In terms of questions (cf. Table 6.9), he only produced uninverted ones and thus remained at stage 3. With regard to negation (cf. Table 6.2), he remained at the pre-verbal first stage for the entire ten months of the study. Hoping he could destabilize what seemed to be an unusual lack of growth, Schumann delivered an intensive regime of one-on-one instruction about English negation to Alberto over seven additional months. This was to no avail. After 17 months in the L2 environment, of which seven months also included instruction, Schumann reports that Alberto remained in the pre-verbal stage of negation, at 20 per cent overall accuracy in this area, the same level he had exhibited before instruction.

Not all learners who allegedly fossilize are naturalistic, and not all fossilization occurs at only incipient levels of development. The study of Patty by Lardiere (2007) is a well-known case of an instructed learner who achieved a very high level of competence in the L2 but nevertheless seems to have ceased developing in one specific area of the L2: bound verbal morphology, particularly *–ed* and third person singular *–s* (cf. Table 6.4). Patty, an L1 speaker of Hokkien and Mandarin, moved to the United States at age 22 and was 31 years old when Lardiere first interviewed her, nine years after that move. About nine years later, at age 40, she was interviewed again, and once again two months later. Over two decades of being surrounded by English in graduate school and later in her workplace, Patty developed advanced English abilities, including rather high levels of accurate article usage (84 per cent accuracy for *the* and 75.5 per cent for *a*), despite this being an area of great difficulty for many L2 users from no-article language backgrounds (as Mandarin and Hokkien are). But in interview data after a decade, and later, two decades, of residence in the L2 environment, Patty continued to supply two of the morphemes that are typically mastered last (cf. Table 6.4) at extremely low rates: about 35 per cent for regular past *–ed* and about five per cent for third person singular *–s*.

Fossilization, particularly among very advanced learners, does not always need to involve basic syntax or morphology, but can also affect subtle areas where syntax and semantics interface. This was shown in a seven-year study by Han (2000, 2006) of Geng and Fong, two male adults from Chinese L1 backgrounds who were otherwise extremely advanced users and had enjoyed optimal learning circumstances. Geng and Fong had had formal English instruction for six years in their country, China, and had scored over 600 on the TOEFL before they moved to the United Kingdom to obtain their doctoral degrees. Upon receipt of their degrees, each continued living in English-speaking environments, and both actively published in English in international journals in their fields. In her analyses of grammaticality judgements as well as free writing over the seven-year span, Han found that both Geng and Fong consistently failed to supply passive in some cases where English requires it, as illustrated in (11), and they oversupplied it in other contexts where the active voice would be pragmatically and discoursally preferred in English, as shown in (12):

(11) I do not know whether these problems have solved in the newest release
      (written by Fong in 1996; Han, 2000, p. 89)
(12) What I can do for you is to give you a list of professors … The list will be sent to you later
      (written by Fong in 1996; Han, 2000, p. 94)

In addition, both L2 users showed indeterminacy in their knowledge of English unaccusativity, or the use of certain verbs in the active voice with a quasi-passive meaning (e.g. *These doors will close at midnight*). Specifically, on occasion Geng and Fong ungrammatically overgeneralized the passive voice by applying it to verbs with unaccusative meanings, as illustrated in (13), while other times they used unaccusatives grammatically, as shown in (14):

(13) Thanks to John's blocking the event were stopped after 3/7/03
      (written by Geng in 2003; Han, 2006, p. 69)
(14) The action already stopped on 1/6 probably after receiving our mail
      (written by Geng in 2003; Han, 2006, p. 69)

The persistence of both the non-native-like and native-like solutions over the seven years is indeed suggestive of likely permanent cessation of learning in this one area of the L2.

In the end, the notion of fossilization, while strongly intuitive, has proved to be extremely problematic to pin down. Three are the most serious caveats raised by the experts (see reviews in Long, 2003; Han, 2004). One, complete and permanent cessation of learning cannot be conclusively demonstrated unless learners are followed over their lifetime, or at least over a very long period of time. Two, the studies rarely document in depth whether the so-called fossilized learners enjoyed truly optimal learning conditions, including: (a) sufficiently rich opportunities for exposure and practice; (b) positive attitudes towards the target language and society; and (c) the aid of (high-quality) instruction. Three, even if it could be demonstrated that fossilization exists, the reasons behind it have resisted any consensus thus far. For example, Schumann offered negative attitudes towards the target language and culture as the culprit (see Chapter 4, section 4.2); Han, Lardiere, and also Sorace (1993), proposed that fossilization is caused by a subtle ceiling that the L1 imposes on L2 development for even the most advanced learners;

Long (2003), reviewing a variety of studies, suggested that sensitivity to the input (or lack thereof) may be the best explanation for fossilization in general (cf. the discussion of noticing in Chapter 4, section 4.6); and Selinker and Lakshmanan (1992) stipulated that it is all of these causes in various combination that can lead to fossilization.

Perhaps the biggest challenge when trying to understand fossilization is that there are two different meanings confounded in the concept. Some researchers discuss fossilization as an *inevitable* universal characteristic of all L2 learning. Under this perspective, fossilization ultimately means that L2 grammars cannot reach an isomorphic state with the grammars of native speakers. All learners are expected to fossilize, and the fact that some do sooner and others do later is of peripheral interest (e.g. Coppieters, 1987; Sorace, 1993; see the discussion about ultimate attainment and age in Chapter 2, section 2.4). In the name of fossilization, other researchers investigate the *premature* cessation of learning, as manifested, for instance, in the radically different outcomes reported after just three years of naturalistic learning in the cases of Julie (Chapter 2, section 2.2) and Wes (Chapter 4, section 4.1). For SLA researchers who have begun to examine L2 learning through a bilingual prism (Chapter 2, section 2.8), inevitable fossilization is problematic because it rests on a tautological and intractable assumption, namely that bilingual grammars will never become monolingual grammars. For language teachers, premature fossilization is of utmost interest. Yet, contemporary research on fossilization has favoured the first notion and neglected the second one. This is not to say that individual variation in L2 learning has not received research attention. As we will see in the next three chapters, the study of cognitive, conative and affective sources of individual differences has a long history in SLA. However, differential learning rate, rather than the possibility of permanent cessation of learning, has been a central concern in the study of individual differences. Thus, until our understanding of rate and cessation of learning phenomena is better, a cautious attitude towards fossilization is advisable.

6.14 WHAT IS THE VALUE OF GRAMMAR INSTRUCTION? THE QUESTION OF THE INTERFACE

The phenomena about interlanguage development that we have examined in this chapter have been documented across diverse contexts and thus are relevant for instructed as well as naturalistic learners. However, we should ask ourselves: What is the value of grammar instruction, if any, in the face of what we know about L2 development? This question has met with diverse answers in the field of SLA.

Some experts question the value of instruction, based on the widely felt gap between the classroom and the outside world. If you have ever learned or taught a foreign language in the classroom, you too will no doubt remember many times when what was learned through grammar explanations and conscious effort did not transfer well to spontaneous, idiomatic usage in real-world situations. This was Krashen's (1985) position when he distinguished between **learning**, or conscious knowledge obtained through grammar study, and **acquisition,** or the incidentally developed ability to use an L2 fluently and naturally. He claimed that learning cannot become acquisition. Yet, the SLA scholarly community soon deemed it impossible to investigate these constructs and the related prediction, for a number of reasons that Barry McLaughlin (1987) authoritatively summarized a few years later (see particularly pp. 55–8).

Nevertheless, rather than disappearing, the issue has metamorphosed into the question of whether implicit and explicit knowledge can interface in long-term memory (see Chapter 5, section 5.4). Because many formal linguistic SLA researchers subscribe to the modularity hypothesis that we briefly introduced in section 6.1, they argue that implicit (subconscious) and explicit (conscious) learning are supported by separate knowledge systems which are neurophysiologically distinct and thus cannot communicate. Schwartz (1993) explains this no interface position with the allegory of an electric shaver (instruction) and a plug (the language module):

> Take a bearded man who moves to a foreign place. Unbeknownst to him, all men must be clean shaven in this culture. He soon discovers this custom, and he is the type that tries to fit in as best he can in other cultures. Luckily for him, he has the solution: He (coincidentally) brought an electric shaver along, so logically the shaver is what is necessary to solve his problem. He goes to his hotel and plugs it in, but nothing happens. The current is different. It turns out that a transformer is needed to make the shaver work. Even though the shaver is necessary, it cannot be used.
>
> (p. 153)

Although the possibility of a transformer remains open in this allegory, many Universal Grammar researchers are sceptical of any interface. Cognitively oriented SLA researchers, by way of contrast, endorse the position of two systems with an interface, at least for adults. Skill acquisition researchers have been particularly firm on this point, as they view deliberate and systematic practice as an optimal 'transformer', to build on Schwartz's allegory above (see Chapter 5, sections 5.2 and 5.3; DeKeyser, 2007b). Usage-based and emergentist theories of L2 learning reject most dichotomies in traditional thinking about language and psychology and therefore find the metaphor of two separate systems with an interface 'an unfortunate appellation' (Ellis and Larsen-Freeman, 2006, p. 569). They also accord explicit knowledge a smaller role in the overall task of acquisition (see sections 6.3 and 6.4) than skill acquisition theorists do. Nevertheless, they agree that L2 instruction has value. If instruction targets implicit processes, they argue, it can boost bottom-up induction of constructions by making exemplars in teaching materials more frequent, salient and consistent (Robinson and Ellis, 2008b). If instruction targets explicit processes, on the other hand, it can help summon conscious attention in ways needed to optimize the learning of particularly challenging generalizations, such as those that involve low salience or high complexity, and those that depart from what learners expect based on their L1 (N.

Ellis, 2005). In a meta-analysis of 49 L2 studies reflective of the research of the 1990s, Norris and Ortega (2000) were able to show that, indeed, instruction targeting various kinds of implicit and explicit learning processes had sizeable effects. As Rod Ellis (2005) has pointed out, if both implicit and explicit knowledge are likely to be implicated in the learning of an L2, it will be important to investigate their respective contributions to L2 acquisition in much more detail in the future.

6.15 INSTRUCTION, DEVELOPMENT AND LEARNER READINESS

Most SLA researchers who believe in the value of grammar instruction also qualify their position with the proviso that instruction is constrained by development (just as the influence of the L1 is; cf. Chapter 3, sections 3.3 through 3.5). In other words, teachers can only hope to teach successfully what learners are developmentally ready to learn. This idea was formalized in the Teachability Hypothesis, also known as the issue of **learner readiness**, which Pienemann (1984, 1989) proposed in response to results he obtained in two quasi-experimental studies of German word order (see section 6.12 and Table 6.8). In them, he taught stage 4 (inversion) to ten seven- to nine-year-old Italian children in Germany and three adult classroom learners of German in Australia, respectively. On both occasions, those who bene-fited from the instruction were 'ready' learners who exhibited evidence of stage 3 (verb separation) at the time of the teaching, but nothing was gained for the 'unready' learners who had begun the study at stage 2 (adverb preposing). In fact, Teresa, one of the unready young learners, began avoiding the use of adverb prepos-ing (stage 2), presumably to avoid making errors. She may have been the type of accuracy-oriented learner who is concerned with perfectionism, as we will discuss in Chapter 9 (sections 9.3 and 9.4). In any case, error avoidance was an unwanted consequence that may have slowed her development of word order, since no stages, not even the ungrammatical stage 2, can be skipped. (As I have insistently reiterated in this book, an important lesson to be learned is that making fewer 'errors' is not always a good thing for language learning.) Later findings by Mackey (1999) and Spada and Lightbown (1999) suggest that some unready learners may benefit from instruction on word order (of English question formation, in their studies; see Table 6.9), but that the effects are only modest enough to help them advance to the next stage *prior to* the one taught, not to skip stages. Thus, language teachers should care-fully consider what their students are developmentally ready to learn.

Although there is much merit in the principle of learner readiness, it should not be followed slavishly, because not all interlanguage systematicity presents equal challenges for instruction. True, for some developmental areas, such as sequences for word order (Tables 6.8 and 6.9) and tense and aspect morphology (Table 6.6), learners appear psycholinguistically unable to skip stages. But for other areas of the grammar, instruction above the cutting edge of a given interlanguage may accelerate development. Thus far, this has been shown to be possible only with language subsystems that exhibit crosslinguistic markedness relations, such as the development along the relative clause hierarchy in Table 6.7. Specifically, a good number of small-scale studies (e.g. Eckmann et al., 1988; Doughty, 1991) have reported that teaching object of preposition relative clauses to students who are already able to handle relativization, but only of the simplest subject type, can result in gains not only in the taught type but also in all the less marked intervening types in the hierarchy. For yet other grammar areas, instruction may be essentially unconstrained by readiness. This appears particularly plausible in matters of accuracy rather than emergence, for example, with the morpheme accuracy orders depicted in Table 6.4. In sum, developmental constraints on what can be taught are likely to play out differently across different areas of L2 development, and more research is needed to shed light that is of use in making instructional decisions.

6.16 ADVANTAGES OF GRAMMAR INSTRUCTION: ACCURACY AND RATE OF LEARNING

While the value of language instruction regularly becomes the object of heated debates in scholarly and public policy circles, supporters and sceptics often fail to pay sufficient attention to the fact that the accumulated evidence clearly shows accuracy and rate advantages for instruction. Simply put, instructed learners progress at a faster rate, they are likely to develop more elaborate language repertoires and they typically become more accurate than uninstructed learners.

Several compelling examples are available in the area of syntax. Thus, while many naturalistic L2 German learners may not reach the particle separation stage (stage 3) even after several years of living in the L2 environment (Meisel et al., 1981), in the foreign language classroom most students will have reached that stage (and some may even have traversed the entire developmental sequence!) by the end of the second semester, judging from the findings reported by Rod Ellis (1989) with 39 students of German in the United Kingdom and by Jansen (2008) with 21 students of German in Australia. For relativization, too, Pavesi (1986) found that only about 25 per cent of 38 naturalistic learners with six years on average of living in the L2 environment were capable of producing object of preposition relative clauses in English, whereas the same stage had been reached by about 40 per cent of 48 high-school students in Italy with an average of only four years of foreign language instruction. Likewise, Byrnes and Sinicrope (2008) found evidence of the object of preposition stage at just the end of the second year of study for about one-quarter of 23 college students of German in the United States that they investigated longitudinally. In addition, as mentioned in the previous section, the acquisition of relative clauses can be greatly accelerated when (more marked) object of preposition relative clause exemplars are presented or otherwise focused on in instructional materials, because the (less marked) direct object relative clause construction is learned for free, as it were (e.g. Doughty, 1991).

Evidence of clear rate and accuracy advantages of instruction is also available for L2 morphology. After daily use of English but without specific instruction, many naturalistic learners do not produce –*ed* or produce it with extremely low levels of accuracy. This has been documented for late starters (e.g. Alberto, as discussed in section 6.13; but also Wes, as briefly noted in Chapter 4, section 4.1). It is also true of learners who had the advantage of a relatively early start when they were first surrounded by the L2, as was the case for the two 10- and 12-year- old Vietnamese boys studied by Sato (1990) for ten months or the ten young Chinese children and adolescents studied by Jia and Fuse (2007) for five years. By comparison, Bardovi-Harlig (1995) found that 135 instructed English learners enrolled in a college English programme exhibited levels of accuracy in the use of –*ed* that averaged about 70 per cent for the lowest curricular level and 90 per cent for the highest. In addition, numerous quasi-experimental instructional studies have shown that providing any form of corrective feedback on the use of –*ed* to learners who already are using the simple past tense but at low levels of accuracy can foster more target-like performance (e.g. Doughty and Varela, 1998; Ellis et al., 2006).

6.17 THE FUTURE OF INTERLANGUAGE?

Many questions remain regarding how and why L2 learners develop (or not) sufficiently detailed and idiomatic representations across various fundamental areas of grammar, and what roles various kinds of context and type of instruction can play in supporting or weakening success along the way. In the end, despite our incomplete knowledge, the study of interlanguage offers a valuable window into the recognition that the emergent competence of L2 users is shaped by the same systematicity and variability that shape all other forms of human language learning. Such recognition can help us combat deep-held views of learner language as a defective version of the target language and of errors as the sign of dangerous habits that need to be eradicated.

And, indeed, SLA has a distinguished lineage of empowering statements by interlanguage researchers to this effect. Since the inception of the field, some have argued that language learners' errors are a source of insights about the processes of second language learning (Corder, 1967; Selinker, 1972), others have called for the study of L2 development in its own right (Huebner, 1979, 1983), and yet others have warned against the fallacy of taking native speakers as an interpretive benchmark of learner language (Bley-Vroman, 1983). Yet, these good intentions and signs of enlightenment have not been enough, and many if not most of the studies we have reviewed in this chapter suffer from what can be described as a 'teleological' view of interlanguage (Ortega and Byrnes, 2008, p. 287). That is, wittingly or unwittingly, SLA researchers often portray development as a transitional state that is (or should be) ever changing *towards* the target. Implied in this construal is also an idealized monolingual native speaker, who is held to be the ultimate yardstick of linguistic success. Harsh critiques have been levelled against this state of affairs. From a sociolinguistic prism, Sridhar (1994) suggested that SLA researchers need 'a reality check' in their silence about postcolonial and multilingual contexts for L2 learning all over the world, where the norm and model of nativeness makes no sense. From an educational stance, Seidlhofer (2001) lamented the conceptual gap between, on the one hand, the recognition that the native speaker is not the point of reference for L2 learning in many contexts of international communication, which is carried out almost exclusively among non-native speakers and, on the other hand, the inability to let that recognition permeate research programmes.

From within SLA, criticisms are also slowly mounting. From a psycholinguistic perspective, Cook (1991, 2008) has long argued that the emergent competence of bilinguals can hardly be expected to become isomorphic with the competence of monolinguals. From a concept-oriented perspective, Klein (1998) has accused researchers of treating 'learners' utterances as deviations from a certain target, instead of genuine manifestations of underlying language capacity' (p. 527) and he has identified this deficit orientation as the culprit for lack of disciplinary impact. From an emergentist and complexity theory perspective, Larsen-Freeman (2006) has expressed doubts on the value of past interlanguage findings because they are based on the metaphor of 'a developmental ladder' (p. 594). She sees a solution forward in her proposed view of languages (whether L2 or L1) as dynamic and self-organizing systems, ever adapting to changing contexts.

In an ethics-centred reflection about the value of instructed SLA research, I predicted that 'the content of SLA constructs of high currency, such as *interlanguage, target language*, and *fossilization*, will undoubtedly need to be revised once the monolingual native speaker is no longer held as the legitimate model for L2 learning' (Ortega, 2005, p. 433). It is yet to be seen if sufficient future developments, whether in the emergentist direction envisioned in recent calls, or in other innovative directions, will help make it possible to study learner language in its own right and to overcome the analytical and conceptual pitfalls that arise when we equate L2 development with monolingual development.

6.18 SUMMARY

- This chapter focuses on the study of learner language from the perspective of interlanguage studies, a tradition that emphasizes general cognitive explanations for the development of L2 morphology and syntax and draws on evidence from both experimental and free production data.

- 'Interlanguage', a term coined by Selinker in 1972, is the language system that each learner constructs at any given point in development; it is a natural language characterized by systematicity and variability; and it is more than the sum of the target input and the L1 influence.

- A family of usage-based and emergentist theories offers promising explanations for language learning and posits that: (a) language learning is driven by experience and induction of generalizations; (b) important influences on development arise from frequency and salience *in the input* and from attention and categorization processes *in the learner*; (c) variability is central to development; and (d) language learning must be explained by the simultaneous interaction of multiple forces.

- According to usage-based accounts, rules emerge from experience as follows. Learners register frequently encountered form–meaning pairings and implicitly tally their frequencies, distributions and contexts; upon repeated encounters, memorized formulas eventually give way to the abstracting of low-scope patterns; given sufficient experience and favourable conditions, low-scope patterns can give rise to abstract constructions.

- Aided by memory and experience, four interlanguage processes are at work as the internal grammar develops: simplification, overgeneralization, restructuring and U-shaped behaviour. Ge's acquisition of the English article *the* (Huebner, 1983) offers a good illustration of all four processes.

- Interlanguage change is always systematic (a matter of development), but also non-linear (a matter of accuracy) and unevenly paced (a matter of rate). All three dimensions of development, accuracy and rate are necessary to jointly characterize interlanguage change over time. Jorge's acquisition of English negation (Cancino et al., 1978; Stauble, 1978) illustrates the three dimensions at work.

- Within a year and a half of immersion in the L2 environment, most naturalistic adult learners will develop a rudimentary but systematic and fully communicative system, called the Basic Variety by Klein and Perdue (1997). After some more time, and probably pushed by the need to communicate complex messages, many but not all of them will grammaticalize resources and develop morphology and subordination.

- We know that a set of English morphemes is mastered at 80 per cent or 90 per cent accuracy levels in a predictable order, which is at least in good part explained by the combined frequency and salience of these morphemes in the input.

- We know that in English, Spanish and many other target languages, the emergence of tense and aspect morphology is patterned and strongly shaped by the semantics of the verb. The details of how this happens have been spelled out in the Aspect Hypothesis (Andersen and Shirai, 1996) and supported in many studies and across many L2s.

- Relativization is another area in which development has proved to be systematic rather than random. Learners of a wide number of target languages are seen to be able to relativize in more frequent and less marked positions (e.g. subject, direct object) before they can do so in less frequent and more marked positions (e.g. object of preposition).

- Several word order phenomena across target languages, including German and English, have been mapped along cumulative developmental sequences that describe how the full repertoire of word order possibilities in a language emerges in a systematic but gradual and non-linear fashion.

- Fossilization is a technical term used to refer to cases when L2 development comes to a seemingly permanent stop. For some researchers, fossilization is the inevitable end result of all L2 learning; for other researchers, fossilization is a premature cessation of learning that affects some learners but not others. There are several studies of learners who allegedly fossilized (e.g. Alberto, Patty, Geng and Fong, and quite a few others not mentioned in this chapter). However, conceptual and methodological difficulties make fossilization a contested construct that must be regarded with caution.

- The value of instruction is doubted by researchers who endorse a nativist and modular view of language learning, but it is supported by researchers who endorse a general cognitive view of language learning, and who believe in the possibility of an interface between explicit and implicit knowledge.

- Instruction cannot override development, but it has been shown to result in clear benefits in the areas of accuracy and rate of learning for both syntax and morphology.

- A great challenge will be to find ways of studying learner language in its own right, rather than as an imperfect version of the target grammar; it is yet to be seen if future innovations will help overcome teleological notions of development as convergence towards the representations assumed of an ideal monolingual native speaker.

6.19 ANNOTATED SUGGESTIONS FOR FURTHER READING

To gain a historical understanding of learner language research, it is worth reading the seminal articles by Corder (1967) and Selinker (1972), and the more methodologically oriented but incisive overview by Long and Sato (1984). A number of edited collections are also standard citations and contain great historical wisdom in the individual studies they feature: Davies et al. (1984), Eisenstein (1989) and Eubank et al. (1995). It is also important to read about the ESF and the ZISA project, because both have made a profound impact on the study of learner language (see the references cited in sections 6.8 and 6.12). If you are interested in how the notion of interlanguage has been applied to other areas of language besides morphology and syntax, you can read some of the papers in Ioup and Weinberger (1987) for phonology; and the reviews by Kasper and Schmidt (1996) and Bardovi-Harlig (1999) for pragmatics. You can avail yourself of a short cut to the present day in the study of learner language if you read the contributions in two 2008 special issues in the *Modern Language Journal* and *Lingua*, guest-edited by Kees de Bot and Roger Hawkins, respectively.

One of the most powerful ways of understanding learner language is to read qualitative case studies of linguistic development across a variety of learners and contexts. For this reason, I strongly recommend you read some of the classic primary studies. If your interest lies with school-aged children acquiring an additional language, much can be learned from reading about the acquisition of English by Nora (Wong Fillmore, 1979), Jorge and some other children and adults studied by Cancino et al. (1978), Tai and Thanh (Sato, 1990), or the ten Mandarin L1 children studied by Jia and Fuse (2007, complemented by the very interesting demographic and social information reported in Jia and Aaronson, 2003). You can also read about Anthony (Andersen, 1984b) acquiring gender in Spanish and about efforts to teach German word order to Teresa and other children (Pienemann, 1989). For adult acquisition, the gallery of learners investigated is also highly informative. Some adult learners appear to struggle with going beyond basic competencies, such as Alberto (Schumann, 1976), Wes (Schmidt, 1983), Ge (Huebner, 1983) and also JDB, whom we mentioned in section 3.10 of Chapter 3 (Duff, 1993; and you can read the interesting additional information about JDB in Duff, 2008, pp. 2–17). Other adults retain some non-target-like solutions in their interlanguages amidst very high levels of competence, such as Patty (Lardier, 2007) and Geng and Fong (Han, 2000, 2006). Lest you forget some cases of amazing success, remember to read again about Julie (Ioup et al., 1994; see Chapter 2, section 2.2).

Finally, if you are interested in getting some research experience with interlanguage, two excellent books that can guide you in your efforts are Ellis and Barkhuizen (2005) and Gass and Mackey (2007). For an advanced discussion of conceptual issues surrounding the collection, analysis and interpretation of evidence about learner language, you can read Norris and Ortega (2003).

7

Foreign language aptitude

People greatly differ in how fast, how well and by what means they learn an additional language. The variability in rates, outcomes and processes can be strikingly large, particularly for people who begin learning an L2 later in life. For example, in Chapter 2 you read about Julie (Ioup et al., 1994), who was remembered by friends and family to be as good as native speakers after only two and a half years of 'picking up' Arabic from living immersed in the L2 environment; but you also read about Wes (Schmidt, 1983) in Chapter 4, who appeared to make only slow progress in his acquisition of English even after three years of positive engagement in the L2 environment. In light of this evidence, SLA researchers ask themselves: Is there something in learners' cognitive abilities, their motivations and their personal predispositions that could help explain such a wide variation? This question guides the study of what is known as individual differences in L2 learning, an area of SLA that draws on theories and methods from the neighbouring fields of cognitive, social and crosscultural psychology.

In this chapter we will examine aptitude, a construct that is mostly cognitive. In Chapter 8, we will discuss motivation, a conative construct. Aptitude and motivation alone are the two best-researched sources of individual differences in L2 learning. However, a number of other sources of variability in L2 learning have attracted considerable attention as well, and they are associated to affective dimensions, such as temperament, emotions and preferences for how to process new information. We will complete our treatment of individual differences with an examination of these other aspects in Chapter 9. You will find the topics across the three chapters are often interconnected. You will also notice that much of what we know about individual differences pertains mostly to formal learning by (highly literate) adolescents and adults in schools and universities. We simply lag behind in knowledge about individual differences as they play out under conditions of naturalistic learning and by children and adults from a wider range of socioeconomic and educational backgrounds.

Throughout the three chapters devoted to individual differences in L2 learning, you will see that the psychology of learners is difficult to extract away from their learning contexts and lived experiences. As you read on, some questions may linger in your mind: Are many or even most of these individual differences immutable? To what extent do context and life experience contribute to shaping and even changing such abilities, motivations and predispositions? In these three chapters the answers you will find to these questions are framed by a psychological framing of both learner and context, which is theoretically congruent with an individual differences framework. You will encounter social accounts of why people may vary in their L2 learning processes and outcomes in Chapter 10.

7.1 THE CORRELATIONAL APPROACH TO COGNITION, CONATION AND AFFECT IN PSYCHOLOGY AND SLA

Psychologists interested in individual differences have traditionally made a distinction among three concepts. **Cognition** refers to how information is processed and learned by the human mind; **conation** addresses how humans use will and freedom to make choices that result in new behaviours; and **affect** encompasses issues of temperament, emotions and how humans feel towards information, people, objects, actions and thoughts. However, contemporary psychologists recognize one must consider cognitive, conative and affective explanations in a symbiotic fashion in order to fully understand individual differences. Likewise, SLA researchers are increasingly more willing to examine aptitude, motivation and other sources of individual differences in L2 learning in the context of complex interrelationships among cognition, conation and affect.

Given the psychological roots of this topic, it should not be a surprise to see that correlations are widely used by individual differences researchers. I will often mention correlation coefficients (called r) and shared variance (called r^2) when referring to study results in Chapters 7 through 9. Correlation coefficients indicate the degree to which two sets of scores co-vary together, from 0 to 1 in either a positive or a negative pattern. It is important to keep in mind the positive or negative sign of the correlation as well as the size of it. For example, a positive-sign (and large) correlation between introversion and lexical diversity would indicate that *the more* introverted a person, *the higher* their lexical diversity scores are likely to be (and that this relationship is strong); but a negative-sign (and large) correlation between the same two variables would mean that *the more* introverted a person is, *the lower* their lexical diversity scores are (and that this relationship is strong). In fact, the closer to a perfect 1, positive or negative, the stronger the relationship; the closer to 0, whether in the positive or negative direction, the weaker the relationship. Shared variance or r^2 is another index that provides an intuitive estimate of the magnitude of the relationship between two sets of scores. It simply tells us the percentage of overlap between two observed sets of scores, or what percentage of variance can be explained by the two variables. It is reported by many psychology authors, but even if it is not reported it can be easily calculated by the attentive reader if correlation values are given, just by squaring them (hence the name r^2).

The prevailing power of correlational survey methods and the emphasis on group tendencies can sometimes make research on individual differences dangerously faceless. To ameliorate this, I would like to open our discussion with a qualitative comparison of two fascinating book-length autobiographical accounts: *French Lessons* by Alice Kaplan (1993) and *The Philosopher's Demise: Learning French* by

Richard Watson (1995). I first had notice of them thanks to SLA researcher John Schumann, who studied these two and other cases in Schumann (1997). The books are written by academics who are not linguists. Their stories and self-chronicled L2 experiences will offer a tangible way to frame our understanding of individual differences in L2 learning in this chapter and the next two.

7.2   LEARNING AND NOT LEARNING FRENCH: KAPLAN VS. WATSON

Alice Kaplan grew up in Minnesota in the 1960s. In her 1993 book, she tells the story of the development of her unconditional, life-long affiliation with French. Her memoirs begin at the age of eight, when her father, a Jewish lawyer who prosecuted Nazi war criminals at Nuremberg, died. Kaplan explains that she felt a deep connection between feeling the loss of her father and feeling different from others in her pursuit of French: 'Learning French was connected to my father, because French made me absent the way he was absent, and it made me an expert the way he was an expert' (pp. 203–4). She began studying French in grade 5, and at the age of 14 attended a French immersion summer programme in Maine. The two formative experiences, however, were a year abroad in a French-medium school in Switzerland at the age of 15, while still in high school, and another academic year abroad in Bordeaux three years later, while she was a French literature undergraduate. Her interest was always as intense for French culture as it was for the French language: 'even in beginning French classes, you knew there was a French beyond the everyday, a France of hard talk and intellect' (p. 138). By the end of the two full-year study abroad experiences, a complete self-identification with the new community and culture had taken place. She later became a French language teacher and eventually completed a doctorate in French. To this day, Kaplan is committed to a life in which both French and English play prominent roles.

Richard Watson grew up in Iowa in the 1930s. In his 1995 book, he describes his strenuous and anxiety-driven attempts at learning to speak French at age 55. As a college philosophy major, at the age of 19, he had successfully completed a French course that involved ten weekly hours of intensive reading-only instruction over an academic year. He went on to do a Master's and a doctorate in philosophy in the early 1960s. His speciality being in Cartesian philosophy, over the next 25 years of his successful academic career he regularly read and translated complex philosophy texts in French and he also frequently travelled to Paris and other locations in France, spending much time in French libraries. In 1986, at the age of 55, a serendipitous life event made him want to learn how to speak (not just read and translate) French. He was invited to deliver a paper in French at an important Cartesian conference in Paris. This propelled an intense desire in him: 'All those years of guilt and embarrassment at being a Cartesian scholar who could not speak French … I would learn to speak French, whatever it took, however long' (p. 65). He took French tutorials for three hours a week during six months prior to his travel and then decided to take more French classes at the Alliance Française after the conference, while he was spending his summer in Paris. Despite all these efforts, he failed his final examination ('the first course and the only examination I had ever failed in my life', p. 122) and could not move on to the next curricular level at the Alliance. The book ends with a painful dialogue during a dinner conversation towards the end of Watson's three-month stay in Paris. He is curtly informed by a famous French Cartesian specialist: 'Don't try to speak French. Your French is terrible' (p. 133). With this ending, readers cannot but conclude that Watson will never achieve his dream to 'sit at a table in a restaurant in Paris with a group of French Cartesian scholars, and ... talk' (p. 65). Almost inexplicably, he had been defeated in his pursuit to learn to speak French.

How can the very different cases of Kaplan and Watson be explained? One might note the differing ages at which each began learning the L2 (see Chapter 2). Nevertheless, why was Kaplan so intensely attracted to French as a child? Does her love for everything French at a young age suffice to explain her amazing success in learning the language and her life-long commitment to it? How can we explain that this love only grew with time and experiences, rather than, say, wane and leave room for other important life quests? And, conversely, what are the roots for the 'French failure' in Watson's case? Why were his determination and desire to speak French well (and his energetic efforts at getting there) not enough? How can we explain that such a highly educated, creative and risk-taking individual – someone who had excelled in life not only as a philosopher, but also as a bestselling author, aerial photographer and amateur field archaeologist! – could not master spoken French?

The cases of Kaplan and Watson are not the rare figment of literary embellishment. Neither are they typical only of people who try to learn a foreign language in the formal setting of a classroom, as similar differences have been attested by research with naturalistic learners as well, for example, in the cases of Julie and Wes. How can we explain such radical variability across individuals who, due to various elective or circumstantial reasons, attempt to learn an L2?

7.3 LANGUAGE APTITUDE, ALL MIGHTY?

An intuitive reaction to cases of amazing success like those of Alice Kaplan and Julie is that they may have had a special gift for learning foreign languages. We all have admired someone who seemed to have 'an ear' for foreign languages, 'a knack' for language learning. It must be a matter of abilities, we assume, and abilities we are born with, at that. At first blush, this intuition is supported by the research findings. When employing any of the various language aptitude tests available and correlating the resulting scores with proficiency levels, final course grades, or teacher ratings, researchers typically find correlations that fall in the range between $r = 0.40$ and $r = 0.60$. That is, study after study, aptitude and achievement explain each other or overlap with each other by 16 to 36 per cent. For some, this is a remarkable amount of patterned variation in a phenomenon as multivariate as second language learning.

Should we then conclude that language aptitude is an omnipotent force in language learning? Not quite. Once we go beyond a strict prediction of achievement, the almighty quality of the construct breaks down into a handful of more humble questions. For one, what does it mean to say that someone has a special gift for foreign languages? Do we mean ease for learning it *fast* (a posited advantage in L2 learning rate) or do we mean ability for learning it *extremely well* (a posited advantage in absolute capacity for very advanced attainment)? Could it be that individuals who are talented foreign language learners are simply highly intelligent, or perhaps particularly verbally gifted in their first language? Does aptitude matter across ages and conditions of learning? And what is language aptitude made of, in the first place? Some of these difficult questions have engaged L2 aptitude researchers for nearly a century now. Yet, as will become clear in subsequent sections, our success in understanding L2 aptitude has been limited. This is partly because much less effort has been invested in explaining the construct than in developing tests that measure it, and partly because until recently the relevant research has attempted in vain to isolate cognitive abilities from the other conative, affective and contextual affordances of the various environments in which L2 learning happens.

7.4   APTITUDE AS PREDICTION OF FORMAL L2 LEARNING RATE: THE MLAT

Psychological work on foreign language aptitude began in the 1920s but did not witness a first renaissance until post-World War II times. The true peak occurred in 1953, when late Harvard psychologist and founder of language aptitude research John Carroll secured a five-year grant from the Carnegie Corporation of New York that allowed him to develop his Modern Language Aptitude Test (MLAT) (*Modern Language Aptitude Test*, 2000–2001; Carroll, 1981). The MLAT turned out to be extremely successful as a predictive test of language learning rate in formal instruction settings, and it remains the aptitude instrument most widely used in the United States and (in translation) in other countries. It comprises five subtests designed to tap three cognitive abilities: grammatical sensitivity, phonetic coding ability and memory capacity. The test content and design is shown in Table 7.1. There is a long and a short form. The long form contains a total of 146 items and the typical average performance reported across studies falls between 100 and 135 points (e.g. Wesche, 1981; Ehrman, 1998). Thus, if you ever take the long form of the MLAT and you score above 100, or perhaps above 135 points, you know your foreign language aptitude is definitely above average.

The high predictive validity of the MLAT (as mentioned, between 16 per cent and 36 per cent of shared variance with achievement) is coupled with high content and face validity as well. For example, as you can see in Table 7.1, a good part of the MLAT stimuli are 'linguistic material that would be novel to the examinees' (Carroll, 1981, p. 89), just like any new language would be novel to zero-beginning learners. Likewise, two of the subtests are aurally delivered, reflecting the primarily

Table 7.1
Design of the MLAT

Components	Subtests	Item illustration
Grammatical sensitivity Special facility with recognizing the functions of linguistic parts in linguistic wholes	Part 4. Words in Sentences Task: Look at underlined word in sentence and find the word in a new sentence that has a matching function	Match: <u>JOHN</u> took a long walk in the woods <u>Children</u> in blue <u>jeans</u> A B were <u>singing</u> and C <u>dancing</u> in the <u>park</u>. D E
Phonetic coding ability Special ability with identifying sounds, connecting them to graphic symbols, remembering sound–symbol connections	Part 1. Number Learning (aural) Task: Listen to invented number names, learn them, and then write out the numbers one hears (up to 3-digit numbers)	Learn: 'ba' is 'one'… 'tu' is 'twenty'… Write down the number you hear: 'tu-ba' (= 21)
	Part 2. Phonetic Script (aural) Task: Learn the orthographic symbols for a number of speech sounds, then listen and match syllables with symbols	Learn: 'bot' 'but' 'bok' 'buk' Listen: 'buk' Match: which syllable did you hear?
	Part 3. Spelling Clues Task: Read words that are written as pronounced and choose synonyms	Match: prezns A. kings B. explanations C. dates D. gifts E. forecasts
Memory capacity Good capacity for rote, decontextualized learning of sound–meaning associations	Part 5. Paired Associates Task: Memorize 24 Mayan words in two minutes, then show how well one has learned them	Learn: bat = axe Match: bat A. animal B. stick C. jump D. axe E. stone

Note: For more details on the MLAT and other L2 aptitude tests, see http://www.2lti.com/htm/Test_mlat.htm.

oral nature of much language learning in the beginning stages. Nevertheless, the construct validity of the MLAT has been the target of critiques which have cast doubt on whether it measures aptitude per se, as it purports to do. For one, the five subtests reflect only three of the four components that Carroll thought made up language aptitude. The fourth component, inductive language learning ability, was left out (cf. Table 7.1) for reasons that were never fully discussed. Perhaps the most serious criticisms are the following two. One, as SLA individual differences authority Peter Skehan (2002) points out, the conceptualization of the three constructs that the test does address is outdated, and this is particularly evident in the memory capacity component, which is conceptualized as rote memory in the MLAT. This is in contrast to the centrality of dynamic memory models in contemporary cognitive psychology (see Chapter 5, section 5.8). Two, as also prominent SLA aptitude specialist Peter Robinson (2005a) notes, present-day L2 aptitude researchers are not so much interested in understanding differential potential for L2 learning rate in formal classroom contexts. Instead, two other issues are considered more pressing and theoretically interesting today: adult learners' differential potential to achieve the highest levels possible of ultimate attainment, and the relevance of aptitude across various learning conditions, including people's differential ability to learn from implicit versus explicit and from naturalistic versus more decontextualized language experiences.

Despite the increasingly critical appraisal of the test and the availability of alternative aptitude instruments, the MLAT remains extremely popular among SLA researchers even today. In the end, however, no test administration or correlational prediction can tell us whether language aptitude really exists, and if so, what it is made of.

7.5 IS L2 APTITUDE DIFFERENT FROM INTELLIGENCE AND FIRST LANGUAGE ABILITY?

In an oft-cited aptitude study, Marjorie Wesche (1981) reported that out of 455 Canadian Public Service French language trainees she investigated, the 165 participants with the highest MLAT scores also had statistically significantly higher intelligence scores. In other aptitude studies too, the MLAT Words in Sentences subtest (see Table 7.1) was repeatedly found to correlate with intelligence. Thus, it is legitimate to ask whether L2 aptitude may not simply be a spin-off of intelligence. After reviewing the available evidence, however, Skehan (1998) concluded that intelligence partially overlaps with foreign language aptitude for grammatical sensitivity (as in Words in Sentences) and other tests of analytical ability, but not for other components of the construct. Intelligence psychologist Robert Sternberg (2002) finds the overlap rather unsurprising, since some of the same narrow academic abilities implicated in traditional intelligence measures (e.g. IQ tests) are also implicated in the construct of grammatical sensitivity that is measured in traditional language aptitude tests like the MLAT. Sternberg calls for future research programmes that explore less conventional dimensions of both constructs.

There has also always been concern with the real possibility that foreign language aptitude may just be a residue or by-product of differential mother tongue ability. The most striking evidence comes from Skehan (1986), who conducted a ten-year retrospective longitudinal follow-up to the Bristol Language Project (Wells, 1985). Wells' study was a seminal investigation of the first language acquisition of two cohorts of 128 children, who were recorded every three months for about two years, starting at ages between one and three and ending at ages between three and five, respectively. Ten years later, Skehan was able to test a subsample of these children (now 13 to 15 years old) for foreign language aptitude and for attained proficiency after their first year of French or German study in school. He found, as expected, that the scores on a battery of L2 aptitude measures correlated with the concurrent L2 proficiency measures. More unexpectedly, however, several aptitude measures (precisely those tapping analytical and grammatical abilities) correlated in the range of $r = 0.40$ with some of the L1 ability measures drawn from the language samples collected a full ten years earlier! On the other hand, none of the L1 measures was associated directly with current L2 proficiency scores. This Skehan (1998) interprets as firm indication that first language ability and the grammatical sensitivity component of foreign language aptitude are related, but that first language ability and overall aptitude are distinct factors.

In the end, then, the conclusion reached by L2 aptitude scholars is that intelligence, first language ability and foreign language aptitude partially overlap because they all seem to share a substrate in which academic skills and grammatical sensitivity are implicated. However, the three constructs are sufficiently different from one another to be considered distinct and worthy of investigation, each on its own.

7.6   LACK OF L2 APTITUDE, OR GENERAL LANGUAGE-RELATED DIFFICULTIES?

When one thinks of the relationship between foreign language aptitude and first language ability, a related line of reasoning is that difficulties in learning an L2 may be related to difficulties experienced during the most challenging aspect of L1 learning: literacy. This hypothesis has been investigated by learning disabilities experts Richard Sparks and Leonore Ganschow (see Sparks, 2006). In work they developed with other colleagues over the 1990s, they took as their point of departure what they call the Linguistic Coding Differences Hypothesis. The hypothesis posits that people differ in their ability to handle phonological–orthographic processing operations, in their L1 as much as in their L2. Difficulties in the mother tongue may become apparent in the early school years. Indeed, as many as 15 to 20 per cent of all schoolchildren will experience difficulties associated with specific literacy tasks in the critical months when they begin learning how to read (International Dyslexia Association, 1998). Many will be diagnosed with some language-based learning disability. Diagnosed children are usually treated. In other cases, difficulties remain undiagnosed and are overcome on their own; and yet other times they persist undetected.

Individuals who experienced (diagnosed or undetected) language-based learning difficulties during early schooling may try to learn a foreign language later in school or even in college, and then the difficulties may resurface.

These general-language coding and processing difficulties emerge most clearly in the areas of **phonological awareness**, which is defined by Snow et al. (1998) as 'a general appreciation of the sounds of speech as distinct from their meaning' (p. 51). Within phonological awareness, critical areas of difficulty are **phonemic awareness**, which is defined as the ability to segment sounds (e.g. k-æ-t in cat) and 'hidden' parts in spoken words and put them back together (e.g. transformation = trans + form + ation), and **phonological decoding**, which refers to the fluent ability to access spelling cues and automatically integrate them to identify words and retrieve associated meanings. These abilities make it possible to read fluently in our L1 and they can be measured via a variety of experimental tasks like syllable deletion, pseudoword repetition, speeded word naming or word recognition. As you can easily see if you inspect the sample items for Parts 1 and 3 of the MLAT in Table 7.1, these abilities are similar to the skills implicated in the phonetic coding component of L2 aptitude.

In sustained longitudinal work, Finnish researcher Mia Dufva and several Dutch colleagues have investigated deep and complex relationships between phonological awareness and foreign language aptitude, tracing the relationship of these two and several other variables to phonological memory, which many consider the underlying substrate that helps explain differential language and literacy capacities in the L1 and L2 alike (Dufva and Voeten, 1999; Dufva et al., 2001). The team investigated Finnish children in preschool up to the end of the third grade. It appears that **phonological memory** exerted a direct and stable influence on the levels of **L1 phonological awareness** developed by the children at about age six, and an indirect influence (via this differential phonological awareness) on the levels of **L1 word recognition** and **listening comprehension** that they went on to achieve by about age seven or eight. By age eight or nine, in turn, the latter two variables predicted a large proportion of children's **L1 reading comprehension** levels (60 per cent of the shared variance in the sample of 222 children in Dufva et al., 2001). Finally, after the first year of studying English as a foreign language in school, at about age nine, native language literacy levels (measured via word recognition and reading comprehension), together with phonological memory (measured through an English-sounding non-word repetition task), helped explain a large proportion of the individual variation in **attained communicative English proficiency** (58 per cent of the shared variance in the sample of 160 children in Dufva and Voeten, 1999). Thus, the quality of automaticity and fluency when handling literacy in the L1 appears to be related to, and to be largely predictive of, the facility exhibited by schoolchildren in learning a foreign language.

At this juncture it is informative to return to our less successful French learner, Watson (1995). Consider the recollection he offers in the following excerpt (pp. 102–3):

(1)   I have always thought my bad spelling [in English] was due to inattention as to whether words end, say, with 'an' or 'on' and the like. Would not

impatient inattention also explain how I can look up the spelling of a word, clamp the dictionary shut, and then turn to my writing and still not know how to spell it? I had gone to the procedure of looking it up; did I have to remember it, too? And doesn't everyone now and then reverse letters and numbers – '57' for '75' and even 'Nood Gight'? Just today I asked for the 'palt and sepper' at lunch, and as long as I can remember I have made that kind of exchange of initial letters perhaps once a week. Is that a kind of dyslexia? It really is not a serious problem in speaking and spelling. What is serious is my inability to listen to sounds and repeat them back. I was poor at memorizing poems and piano pieces in my youth.

Watson's description strikingly resonates with the claims of Sparks and Gaschow's Linguistic Coding Differences Hypothesis and with the picture of complex differential L1 and L2 development that Dufva and her colleagues paint of Finnish children. It is also consistent with many of the symptoms associated with the kinds of general language coding and processing difficulties described in the specialized literature. These are the symptoms experienced by individuals who perform low on phonetic coding ability tasks such as those contained in Parts 1 through 3 of the MLAT. For example, Wesche (1981) observed that they show more disfluent L2 spoken production. Similarly, Carroll and others hypothesized that they may have difficulties with mimicking foreign sounds and remembering new words.

In her review of the evidence, Yale psychologist Elena Grigorenko (2002) concludes that 'there is a nonrandom association between failure to master [a foreign language] and difficulties in acquiring [the native language] in both its oral and its written formats' (p. 100). Ultimately, and in agreement with the findings reported by Dufva and her colleagues, she attributes linguistic coding difficulties to differential memory capacity. And, indeed, memory has always occupied a privileged place in conceptualizations of L2 aptitude.

7.7   MEMORY CAPACITY AS A PRIVILEGED COMPONENT OF L2 APTITUDE

Perhaps the first signs of interest in exceptional memory capacities are those of neuropsychologists, rather than SLA researchers, who during the 1970s and 1980s discovered individuals with colossal foreign language talents and studied their brain functioning in depth (e.g. Schneiderman and Desmarais, 1988; Obler, 1989; Smith and Tsimpli, 1995). A notable example is CJ, described by Obler (1989) as a 29-year-old Caucasian male who from the age of 15 managed to learn very well five languages through a mixture of instruction and naturalistic exposure. He learned French, German, Latin and Spanish by studying them in high school and later through further study and living abroad. And he later learned Moroccan Arabic after college, through a mixture of instruction and naturalistic immersion while holding a government post in the country.

As Obler and Hannigan (1996) explain, exceptional verbal memory abilities consistently emerged as the distinguishing trait in all these case studies, in association with talented L1 verbal performance and with a cognitive style that favours successful performance on tasks that call for implicit and memory-based processing. At the same time, the talent was said to be symptomatic of some abnormality in these individuals' brain functioning, possibly due to hormonal 'accidents' during foetal development of the brain. It was commented that such exceptional verbal abilities and foreign language feats appear in people who exhibit some genetically inherited characteristics, including left-handedness, occurrence of twins in the family and propensity to allergies. Thus, a danger in this early line of research was that a colossal talent for foreign languages was easily reconstrued as a freakish one.

Contemporary SLA researchers who investigate aptitude and memory capacity appear to have little interest in pursuing case studies of individuals who are exceptional (with or without a pathological profile) and concentrate instead on studying within-normal ranges of individual differences in group performances. In this more recent line of research, good memory capacity, including verbal memory and memory as a substrate of both L1 and L2 skills, remains a prime candidate in explanations of differential levels of L2 achievement.

It has been shown that short-term memory capacity measured by span task performance (see Table 5.1) can predict individual differences in the ability to learn new vocabulary in a foreign language, with correlations that fall typically between $r = 0.30$ and 0.40. For example, Helsinki-based researcher Elisabet Service (1992; Service and Kohonen, 1995) found that Finnish elementary schoolchildren who were good at repeating random non-word lists also learned vocabulary in English as a foreign language with greater facility than other children with lower span scores. Likewise, adults with low short-term memory capacities have difficulty remembering new words. For example, Chun and Payne (2004) tracked the look-up behaviour exhibited by 13 second-year L2 German college students as they worked through reading materials on a computer program. They found that the individuals who performed poorly on a non-word repetition task looked up vocabulary three times more often than those with high memory span scores.

Memory capacity has also been related to differential achievement in L2 listening ability and overall L2 proficiency by Mary Lee Scott, who conducted two early studies investigating these issues. In the first study (published under her maiden name: Call, 1985) the listening proficiency scores of 41 ESL students from Arabic and Spanish L1 backgrounds correlated the strongest with recall of L2 words in passages ($r = 0.57$) and repetition of exact sentences ($r = 0.65$). The participants in the second study (Scott, 1994) were 112 male and female missionaries sampled by age into younger (in their early twenties) and older (between 50 and 79 years old) and by language learning experience into monolingual (who had served in English-speaking missions) and bilingual (who had served in Spanish-speaking missions). As it turned out, the younger bilingual group had achieved consistently higher L2 proficiency levels than the older bilingual group after the same period of approximately a year and a half of living abroad. The gap was substantial. For example, on the L2 listening test, the younger bilingual group attained a 90 per cent performance level on average, whereas the older bilingual group's average was 42 per cent. Contrary to Scott's expectations, however, once proficiency was controlled for statistically, no relationship between short-term memory performance and proficiency scores was observed on a rich battery of eight memory tests. Nevertheless, a closer look at other reported results is revealing. Scott compared ten participants in the younger bilingual group with four participants in the older bilingual group, all matched for listening proficiency at about 80 per cent scoring level. If you inspect the descriptive data she offers there, you will notice that the four older bilingual participants' memory performance was remarkably higher than that typical for their age group and much closer to the means obtained for the younger bilingual group. This makes for suggestive, if tentative, evidence that above average short-term memory capacities may have been a requisite for the older learners in this sample to attain levels of L2 listening proficiency that were uncharacteristic of their own age group and comparable to the high levels achieved by many younger learners.

Interest in aptitude and memory research has recently been shifting towards active working memory capacity, in accord with contemporary developments in the study of human memory (see Chapter 5, sections 5.6 through 5.8). The first SLA investigation in this line of research was an oft-cited study by Michael Harrington and Mark Sawyer (1992), who found that individuals with longer reading spans achieved higher scores on the grammar and reading subsections of the TOEFL, with 30 per cent co-variance between the two measures. However, when Alan Juffs (2004) used very similar working memory measures to investigate individual differences in online processing of ambiguous L2 sentences (rather than attained global proficiency) the evidence he found for a role of working memory in such L2 performance was extremely weak.

7.8 THE CONTRIBUTIONS OF MEMORY TO APTITUDE, COMPLEXIFIED

Current enthusiasm for the study of individual differences in working memory and L2 learning needs to be tempered by the realization that the ways in which memory facilitates differential rate and success of L2 learning may be more complex than a simple correlation between memory tasks and proficiency measures can capture. For example, clear evidence shows that the much talked about power of memory span tasks to predict L2 vocabulary learning rate is strongest at very early stages of development but weakens as proficiency in the L2 increases. Thus, Masoura and Gathercole (2005) found that the ability to repeat non-words in the L1 (Greek) and the L2 (English) was associated with the L2 vocabulary levels achieved by 75 8- to 13-year-old Greek children after three years of formal EFL study. Yet, the facility in adding new English words to the lexicon already in place after three years was greater for a subset of students with higher than average L2 vocabulary knowledge but not for a subset of students with higher than average non-word repetition abilities. The authors conclude that once a threshold size of vocabulary knowledge is established in the L2, further vocabulary learning is boosted by a better developed and larger-sized L2 mental lexicon rather than by superior memory capacity.

In fact, rather than remaining constant, the predictive power of phonological memory capacity may well shift to different aspects of learning as individuals traverse their L2 developmental pathways. That is, perhaps memory helps explain differential success at early stages better in some areas and at later stages better in other areas. This is precisely what O'Brien et al. (2006) suggest in their study of L2 changes observed over a semester among 43 L2 Spanish learners. They found that among the lower proficiency learners better phonological memory was associated with greater gains in lexical areas of L2 performance (narrative skills and content word use). Among the higher proficiency learners, by contrast, higher memory capacity was associated with greater gains in grammatical areas (subordination and function word use). If these findings withstand the test of time and replication, we may eventually need to revise the intuitive dictum that 'good memory helps foreign language learning', and replace it with a more nuanced formulation, such as 'good memory helps vocabulary learning in the beginning and grammar learning later on'.

Even within the same area of L2 learning, short-term memory capacity may predict individual differences for some specific L2 phenomena better than for others. John Williams (2005) raises this possibility in the area of L2 grammar, based on the findings he obtained across several investigations of implicit L2 learning (that is, learning without the benefit of rule explanation; see Chapter 5, section 5.14). In some experiments he found that differential performance on non-word repetition span tasks was clearly correlated with the participants' ability to learn certain rules that involve surface form–form co-occurrence (e.g. gender agreement in *la musica moderna*, where each word ends in –*a*; Williams, 1999; Williams and Lovatt, 2003). However, in other experiments, such as Williams (2005), which we briefly mentioned in Chapter 3 (section 3.9), it turned out to be unrelated to the ability to learn semantically motivated artificial grammar rules, such as: '*gi* and *ro* both mean "the-near"; we say *gi cow* because "cow" is a living thing but *ro cushion* because "cushion" is a nonliving object'.

Finally, interesting is the suggestion put forth by Alison Mackey and colleagues (Mackey et al., 2002) that for certain areas of learning, such as learning from interactions (see Chapter 4, sections 4.4 and 4.7), high memory capacities may accrue an advantage that is measurable only after a certain time lag. In their study these researchers found that, as predicted, ten high-memory speakers were superior to ten low-memory speakers at noticing the corrections they received during interactions with more proficient interlocutors. In terms of actual L2 gains, however, a trend on the post-tests indicated that low-memory speakers outperformed the high-memory ones on the immediate test, whereas the high-memory speakers showed lagged gains on a delayed post-test two weeks later. The researchers comment: 'Although speculative, it may be that these learners had gleaned more data to process [during the interactional treatment] and consolidated this over time, compared to low WM capacity learners who could not "hold on" to data with great accuracy' (p. 204). As can be appreciated, research on the relationship between memory and differential L2 achievement has only begun to scratch the surface.

7.9 APTITUDE AND AGE

Many SLA researchers believe that children learn their first language so well because they have the cognitive and linguistic endowment to learn it entirely implicitly. Conversely, they posit that adolescents and adults will rarely if ever attain complete success in learning an L2 because they try to learn the language via analysis and analogy (that is, explicitly) and in doing so they are using the 'wrong' route, as it were (although for good reason, these researchers say, since for adults analysis may be the only route left available for language learning). This is, in a nutshell, the Fundamental Difference Hypothesis first formulated by Bley-Vroman (1990). It is because of the involvement of the less adept explicit learning route, the contention goes, that late-starting learners will vary greatly in their facility and relative success with the task, depending on how naturally good their analytical capacities (for explicit learning) and their memory (for implicit learning) are. Children, by way of contrast, will uniformly develop their L1 competence because they rely on implicit (tacit, intuitive) types of innate language learning mechanisms. One corollary of such a position is that aptitude (as well as other individual differences) should matter only or mostly when learning the L2 after a certain age. Do individual differences matter even for young L2 learners?

DeKeyser (2000) found support for the claim that aptitude only matters for adults and adolescents, but not for young learners, in his partial replication of Johnson and Newport (1989) with 57 Hungarian US immigrants (see our discussion in Chapter 2, section 2.4). Performance on the Words in Sentences subtest of the MLAT correlated with the grammaticality judgements for only the subset of participants whose age of arrival in the L2 environment was above 16. For arrivals below 15 years of age, no relationship between aptitude and ultimate attainment was found, as predicted. These findings are difficult to interpret, however. This is because all but one of the participants who had arrived before the age of 16 answered correctly at least 180 of the 200 items on the grammaticality judgement task. With so little variation in their linguistic performance, correlations are unlikely. This stems from the psychometric reality that low variability in either set of two given scores will attenuate or eliminate any possibility of correlation (whether we have good theoretical reasons to posit a relationship between the two variables or not).

Other researchers have taken a slightly different approach to investigating the relationship between age and aptitude. Harley and Hart (1997) predicted that individual differences will be found at all ages (provided the situation is one of L2, as opposed to L1, learning), but that different dimensions of aptitude will matter more at different ages. Harley and Hart reasoned that, since memory is heavily involved in general implicit learning processes and analytical processing of information in general explicit learning processes, memory may be more predictive of differential outcomes with young learners, whereas analytical ability might play a much larger role in explaining differential success among older learners. They found some evidence in support of this hypothesis in the context of French school immersion education in Canada. Proficiency differences in a group of early-starting students (who began immersion in grade 1 and had been schooled in the L2 for 12 years) correlated to individual differences in memory ability, whereas in a group of late-starting students (who began immersion in grade 7 and had been schooled in the L2 for four years), proficiency differences were more related to individual differences in analytical ability. As the authors warn, however, the reason for this pattern of results may in part be a consequence of how young and old starters had grown accustomed to approach French in their classroom instruction. Namely, the curriculum in French immersion education is age-appropriate, and therefore it capitalizes on memory-related activities at younger ages only to gradually move on, in older grades, to more 'school-like' activities that pose higher analytical processing demands. Thus, it is a challenge to separate age and learning context when investigating these questions. Harley and Hart (2002) followed up on these issues with a second study, conducted with Canadian students of similar age (tenth- and eleventh-graders) but enrolled in non-immersion French instruction and hence similar in learning history to the previous group of late starters. The 27 participants took part in a three-month bilingual exchange programme in a Francophone environment which afforded them their first immersion-like experience, after about seven years of formal French classroom instruction. An association between analytical kinds of aptitude and proficiency scores was observed despite the three months of immersion, but the researchers caution that this pattern of results for late starters was less clear than it had been in the earlier study.

Ross et al. (2002) concur with DeKeyser in reporting findings that support his claim that the importance of aptitude emerges only after puberty (in their study, around the age of 12). In their discussion, however, they offer useful insights that bring the position closer to that of Harley and Hart. Specifically, Ross et al. suggest that aptitude will matter gradually more as starting age is older. This will happen as a result not only of biological maturation (older age) but in conjunction with the learning context. Specifically, many older-starting learners typically obtain less abundant exposure to natural input, because they tend to learn the L2 through formal classroom instruction. Therefore, both age and reliance on formal instruction will conspire to make aptitude differences matter much more for such late starters.

7.10 DOES L2 APTITUDE MATTER UNDER EXPLICIT AND IMPLICIT LEARNING CONDITIONS?

An extension of the question of whether aptitude matters across all ages is the problem of whether aptitude matters across all learning conditions, particularly learning with or without intention, attention, awareness and rules, as we discussed in Chapter 5 (see sections 5.9 through 5.15). During the 1970s and 1980s, Stephen Krashen in the United States and Helmut Zobl in Canada reasoned that aptitude differences would be only relevant when learning with rules, that is, with explicit instruction, because such learning involves conceptually driven processing that depends heavily on overall intelligence and academic abilities. Aptitude would probably not matter in conditions of implicit learning (by which they meant incidental learning, or learning language while doing something else; see section 5.10) because there all humans are endowed with the same universal capacity to implicitly (by which they meant tacitly or intuitively) learn language. Their logic was based on a broadly Chomskyan position of continuous availability of implicit (Universal Grammar based) learning even for adults (see Schwartz, 1998; and our discussions in Chapter 6, sections 6.1 and 6.14).

Robinson (2002) makes a counterproposal, claiming that for adults aptitude will matter equally across all conditions of learning because the same basic cognitive abilities are involved in any kind of language learning. This hypothesis stems from the position of SLA researchers who do not commit to a Chomskyan view of language learning and instead posit that language learning is a general cognitive phenomenon, like learning history, mathematical operations, music or cooking (e.g. DeKeyser, 1997; Segalowitz, 2003; see discussion in Chapter 5, sections 5.1 through 5.3). They would predict that individual differences matter across explicit and implicit conditions of learning because humans draw from both implicit and explicit general learning processes in order to learn additional languages beyond their mother tongue.

Of course, still under a general cognition theory of L2 learning (rather than a Chomskyan one), it is also reasonable to expect that aptitude will make the most important contribution to success precisely under implicit learning conditions, when people receive no external help and are left to rely on their own devices and strengths (i.e. their differential analytical or memory-driven capacities) to extract, make sense of, retain and structure the relevant information to be learned. In contrast, most learners may benefit from external help via explanations and guided practice, provided these are well designed. Or at least this may be true of literate adult learners who are used to formal language learning anyway. If this third line of reasoning were correct, then it would mean that in fact individual differences across (adult, highly literate) learners emerge more strongly under implicit than under explicit learning conditions.

The empirical evidence regarding this problem is mixed. There is no firm pattern in favour of aptitude mattering more in implicit or explicit conditions consistently. Some studies have shown effects in relation to implicit learning (J. N. Williams, 1999). Of the studies that directly compared an implicit and an explicit condition, some have found that aptitude mattered across the board (de Graaff, 1997), while in others individual differences across learners emerged more strongly under implicit than under explicit learning conditions (Nation and McLaughlin, 1986). Robinson's research programme in this area has yielded mixed evidence as well, in that comparisons of three or four types of learning conditions have yielded effects for aptitude that are not always consistent with the theoretical predictions he had put forth (for example, Robinson, 1997 versus 2005b).

Classroom investigations of this issue are rare, but have begun to appear. Rosemary Erlam (2005) examined whether aptitude scores on three different dimensions (analytical ability, phonemic coding and working memory) would correlate with the amount of learning accrued from three different instructional approaches (traditional explicit grammar teaching and practice, collaborative consciousness-raising inductive rule discovery, and explicit explanation plus meaningful comprehension practice only), all focusing on French direct object pronouns and all delivered via three 45-minute lessons. The participants were 14-year-old students of French at a high school in New Zealand, and the aptitude measures were administered retrospectively, six months after the instructional treatments were delivered. She found several significant correlations between analytical ability (measured by the Words in Sentences subtest of the MLAT, see Table 7.1) and working memory and better performance on the written delayed post-tests among the participants who received either the inductive or the comprehension-only practice instructional treatments, but no noteworthy correlations between any of the aptitude measures and the learning exhibited by the participants in the explicit instructional treatment. Erlam interprets this evidence as suggestive of a levelling off of aptitude-treatment interactions for explicit instruction, which seem to benefit learners regardless of their aptitude profiles and strengths. However, Younghee Sheen (2007) obtained a dissimilar pattern of results, when she provided error correction on the English article to learners in six intact classrooms at a community college in the United States, who were asked to read and then retell in writing two stories. She found a stronger relationship between aptitude measures and gains on immediate and delayed post-tests among participants who had received metalinguistic corrections on their article usage in the story than among those who received similarly explicit corrections but without metalinguistic explanations.

In the end, then, before the interaction between L2 aptitude and learning conditions can be understood, we will need more studies involving comparisons of short- versus long-lasting explicit and implicit treatments. It will be also important to employ different paradigms, triangulating the artificial and semi-artificial language paradigms favoured to date with more classroom studies, such as those by Erlam and Sheen. The latter line of research, in particular, can shed light on the ecological conditions under which aptitude makes different instructional approaches more or less successful or appropriate, thus helping advance knowledge for how to orchestrate successful aptitude-treatment interactions, as we will discuss in section 7.12.

7.11 MOST RECENT DEVELOPMENTS: MULTIDIMENSIONAL APTITUDE

In a widely read collection on individual differences published in 2002, Peter Robinson and Peter Skehan, the two SLA researchers that have probably contributed the most to recent theorizing of aptitude, each offered new directions for future foreign language aptitude research.

Robinson (2002) builds on the seminal work of the late educational psychologist Richard Snow and proposes what he calls the Aptitude Complex Hypothesis. In Snow's work, three principles are highlighted: (a) human aptitude is made up of a complex of abilities, interrelated in a hierarchical fashion rather than a simple or direct fashion; (b) differential cognitive processing abilities are intertwined with the contexts and affordances of the environment; and (c) differential aptitude cannot be fully explained unless motivational and affective influences are taken into account as well (see Ackerman, 2003, for a good overview of Snow's work in this area). Robinson (2002, 2005a) capitalizes on these three premises, emphasizing the first two: 'abilities ... have their effects in combination of "complexes" ... which jointly facilitate processing and learning in a specific instructional context' (Robinson, 2005a, p. 51). He then applies them to L2 learning issues specifically.

To illustrate, let us assume that different learners are better or worse at learning from recasts (see Chapter 4, section 4.11). How would Robinson set out to explain this aptitude difference? Regarding Snow's first premise, two **aptitude complexes** would be involved in explaining specifically why some learners are better than others at benefiting from recasts: 'noticing the gap' when the learner compares their own utterance to the one they heard back from the interlocutor and 'memory for contingent speech' when the learner actually remembers the utterance offered by the interlocutor well enough to rehearse it in memory or to recognize it later on, when it occurs again. In turn, each of the two complexes would be made up of a number of more **basic cognitive abilities.** The complex to 'notice the gap' probably involves pattern recognition and processing speed, whereas the complex of 'memory for contingent speech' would involve phonological working memory. There is some initial evidence that this latter basic cognitive ability is important for recasts in a study conducted by Jenefer Philp (2003), which showed that longer recasts (defined as strings with more than five morphemes) were repeated back less accurately than shorter recasts by most learners. That being so, learners with better phonological working memory will be less limited by recast length. This may be true at least of highly literate learners, since learners whose literacy skills are low (because they come from predominantly oral language backgrounds) may be less affected by length constraints and therefore less amenable to working memory differences, as Bigelow et al. (2006) suggested in a replication of Philp's study. It may even be that in the study by Mackey et al. (2002) (mentioned in section 7.8) weaker 'memory for contingent speech' may have worked against the low-memory students being able to 'hold on to data' offered during the interactions (p. 204) and expand on their initial gains on the immediate post-test over two weeks, like the high-memory students did. However, they may not have necessarily been weaker in their ability to 'notice the gap,' since they were able to show they benefited from recasts on the immediate test.

The second premise relates to the **specific instructional context,** and in this case would include the range of contextual considerations we discussed in section 4.11 about how explicit or implicit recasts are delivered by teachers in a given setting and even during a given part of a lesson, with various balances of communication and attention to the code. In agreement with Snow's third premise, Robinson

(2005a) recognizes that **motivational and affective forces** will also influence how well the hierarchical web of basic cognitive abilities and aptitude complexes is put to use under real-world conditions. One may suspect, for example, that the benefits of recasts may be reaped more easily by individuals who are highly motivated (see Chapter 8) because they may take every encounter in the L2 as an opportunity for learning; or for individuals who score high on personality traits such as openness to experience or extraversion (see Chapter 9), because they might be more attuned to positive and negative evidence that is delivered via interpersonal communication. Clearly, in order to take this third dimension of the theory to its full consequences, in future studies researchers of L2 aptitude will need to more vigorously incorporate conative and affective variables of the kinds we will examine in Chapters 8 and 9.

Skehan (2002) proposes a different but largely compatible model of aptitude for future consideration. His main concern is with linking aptitude components to the processes that SLA theory tells us are involved in L2 grammar learning. Skehan chooses to work with information processing theory (see Chapter 5, section 5.1) and identifies noticing, patterning, controlling and lexicalizing as the four macro-processes involved in learning any new aspect of the L2. Because during **noticing** attention is placed on a to-be-learned aspect of the L2, Skehan reasons the kinds of aptitude components that may matter for differential noticing advantages include things like attention management, working memory and phonemic coding ability. During **patterning**, hypotheses about what has been noticed are implicitly or explicitly made, tried out, revised, extended to relevant cases and eventually a final resulting generalization (that is, a new 'rule') is integrated into the existing knowledge of the L2, which thereby undergoes restructuring. The aptitude components involved in doing this patterning less or more successfully probably include grammatical sensitivity and inductive language learning ability. The next learning process is **controlling**. Since this involves effortful attempts to use the newly noticed and patterned knowledge to levels that are accurate, Skehan proposes that differential retrieval and proceduralization abilities must underlie aptitude differences in this area. Finally, **lexicalization** (also called chunking and dual coding) is the process of making the now acquired new aspect of the L2 into a fluent and automatic commodity that can be retrieved for use via a memory representation as much as via the application of a rule (lexicalization is related to our discussion in Chapter 6, section 6.4). Therefore, individuals who are adept at cognitive processes such as memory and chunking are likely to have aptitude strengths in the lexicalization stage of L2 learning. The resulting picture is one suggestive of aptitude complexes and profiles, as with Robinson (2002).

7.12 PLAYING IT TO ONE'S STRENGTHS: THE FUTURE OF L2 APTITUDE?

A tantalizing possibility that stems from these recent proposals formulated by Robinson (2002) and Skehan (2002) is that instruction that plays to the strengths and preferences of certain profiles in students will bring about the most learning for them. This is an old hope in educational psychology investigated in what is known as **aptitude-treatment interactions** research. Can language instruction be matched so as to play it to the relative strengths of different L2 aptitude profiles?

Wesche (1981) evaluated this question by looking at 'streaming' practices for Canadian public servants who have to learn French for their job. As a regular practice during the 1970s, they would be placed on the basis of their MLAT scores into types of course that best matched their aptitudinal strengths. Thus, French was taught audiovisually as an option. Since audiolingualism/audiovisualism as a method involves mostly aural and visual input and quick repetition and expansion drills, students had to score at a certain high level on the phonetic coding ability parts of the MLAT (cf. Table 7.1) in order to be placed into such courses. Another instructional option was analytical teaching. The course enrolled students who had a certain high score on the grammatical sensitivity part of the MLAT (the Words in Sentences; see Table 7.1) and seemed to enjoy and be good at what we would call traditional grammar explanation and practice. In 1975 a group of students who exhibited a profile most apt for analytical instruction were either matched into an analytical class or mismatched into an audiovisual class. After three months of six daily hours of instruction, the matched students scored statistically significantly higher on three of four achievement tests. In other words, the streaming seemed to be an effective practice in bringing the best out of each individual's strengths with language, whereas the aptitude-treatment mismatch appeared to put students at a disadvantage.

The old question of whether L2 aptitude can be profiled and then matched with responsive instructional approaches has great value but is difficult to investigate. The aptitude profiles that Skehan (2002) and Robinson (2002) have put forth have the advantage of making predictions of aptitude-treatment interactions much more amenable to empirical investigation, because they unpack the early suggestions of aptitude profiles, which were mostly binary ones (i.e. memory-based and analytical profiles), into more theoretically viable and specifically researchable terms. For example, Robinson's (2002) model makes it possible to postulate that an L2 learner is high on some basic abilities and low on others (HL), or high on all (HH) or low on all (LL), thus making up for a range of strong, weak or mixed ability on each of several aptitude complexes. Likewise, it follows from Skehan's (2002) model that some people may be very good at one or more of the processing stages of learning (e.g. noticing or lexicalizing) but average or poor at the remaining ones (e.g. patterning or controlling). In other words, both models allow for mixed profiles and both point at the potential to diagnose specific areas where individuals will need external help (and can benefit from it) in order to boost their L2 learning success.

7.13 SUMMARY

- Language aptitude is the psychological formulation behind the intuition that some people have a gift for additional language learning while others seem to struggle.

- At a practical level, it can be measured by existing tests that predict how well someone is likely to do when embarking on the formal study of an additional language. The best known and most widely employed test of language aptitude is the MLAT, although several other tests also exist.

- Scores on the MLAT and other aptitude tests correlate with proficiency levels, final course grades, or teacher ratings in the order of $r = 0.40$ to $r = 0.60$. This is a considerable shared variance between 16 per cent and 36 per cent.

- Two challenges have importantly limited our ability to understand L2 aptitude in the past: the investment of much less effort in explaining the construct than in developing tests that measure it; and the difficulty of extracting the cognitive abilities from the conative, affective and contextual affordances of the environments in which L2 learning happens.

- Language aptitude partially overlaps with traditional intelligence and with early first language ability. Language aptitude and traditional intelligence may share a subset of academic abilities implicated in both types of test; language aptitude and early first language ability may share a common substrate of grammatical sensitivity and analytical kinds of abilities. Despite the partial overlaps, each of the three constructs is also distinct enough to be worthy of study in its own right.

- Language aptitude is also related to differential abilities implicated in the development of literacy during the early school years. That is, language-related learning difficulties when learning to read in the L1 may resurface later on when studying another language. The common substrate resides in abilities to handle phonological–orthographic processing operations and include the constructs of phonological awareness, phonemic awareness and phonological decoding.

- Differential memory capacities are thought to play a central part in creating differential likelihoods of success when learning a foreign language. Memory alone is thought to help predict how well people will learn new vocabulary, what levels of comprehension they will achieve in listening or reading, how much they may benefit from recasts or how easily they will learn a grammar rule.

- However, a complex picture of memory and differential L2 facility and success emerges in the available evidence. For example, good short-term memory facilitates vocabulary learning at beginning stages, but this predictive power wanes for more advanced learners. Good memory may boost learning of vocabulary first, and confer an advantage in the learning of surface grammatical phenomena (but perhaps not all rules alike) later in the course of L2 study.

- We do not know for sure (a) whether language aptitude matters only (or mostly) for late L2 starters and (b) whether equally strong differences in language aptitude emerge when the learning conditions call for memory-driven, implicit ways versus analytical, explicit ways of processing the new material. These two questions are of extreme theoretical and practical importance, but have been insufficiently studied to date.

- At a theoretical level, language aptitude as a construct is thought to be made up of various cognitive abilities, some better understood than others, but all related to two broad types: analytical abilities and memory abilities.

- Recent efforts to reconceptualize language aptitude beyond the two kinds of broad ability have been made by Skehan and Robinson. The strength of both proposals is that they make it possible to study L2 aptitude as a well-motivated, textured set of cognitive capacities that correspond to theoretically postulated processing demands that are specific to L2 learning.

- In the future, the two proposals may also help to understand better how instructional approaches can be designed to boost L2 learning success for a greater variety of individual needs.

7.14 ANNOTATED SUGGESTIONS FOR FURTHER READING

The literature on language aptitude is not easy to read, but if you strategize on sequencing the readings appropriately, you can benefit from direct knowledge of the primary sources. To begin with, it may help to read about the full story of the development of the MLAT, which is interestingly narrated by Carroll (1981) himself or in an interview with Stansfield and Reed (2004). The initial reading of one of these two articles can then be followed by Spolsky (1995), who offers a sobering historical view on language aptitude research and its tests. Returning to the same seminal collection where Carroll (1981) was published, Wesche (1981) offers a good handle on the theoretical as well as practical implications of measuring language aptitude. Ehrman (1998) nicely complements it (this journal is available online at no charge). After that, you will be ready to benefit from the more comprehensive but also more contemporary overview offered by Skehan (1998) in an excellent chapter devoted to the topic, followed by the helpful treatment of aptitude as it pertains to instruction offered by Sawyer and Ranta (2001). You can end your journey through the general L2 aptitude literature by reading the most current proposals that open new possibilities for future research programmes: Skehan (2002), then Robinson (2005a), followed by Robinson (2002).

If you are intrigued by any of the details about memory research, aptitude and language-related difficulties, aptitude and age, or aptitude and learning conditions, you can read the studies cited in those sections. You should do so with the awareness that they are all quite advanced readings. They should probably be tackled only after you have covered the basic journey of L2 aptitude literature I sketched in this section, from Carroll to Skehan and Robinson.

Finally, here is a bonus reading tip. If you have ever wondered whether musical ability can help with learning foreign languages (or you have been asked that question by colleagues or students, as I regularly am), you can read Slevc and Miyake (2006), who were able to provide some evidence that indeed musical ability helps with developing good pronunciation, and Patel and Iversen (2007), who offer a brief overview of the topic.

8

Motivation

In Chapter 7 we examined aptitude, a construct that is comprised of many cognitive abilities and helps explain why people differ so greatly in how fast and how well they are likely to learn a second language. Contemporary psychologists working in the general area of human cognition agree that cognitive abilities alone cannot tell the whole story of individual differences. Since humans are conscious and volitional creatures, in explaining perception, behaviour and learning we also need to account for human intentions, goals, plans and commitments. These are conative influences that at the broadest level include volition and motivation, and they can make language learners succeed or fail. In this chapter we turn to the best researched L2 factor in the general area of conation, foreign language motivation. As you will see, SLA work on motivation draws heavily on theories and methods from social psychology. The specific case of additional language learning requires that motivation be conceptualized as a complex set of constructs that subsume social–psychological perceptions and attitudes.

8.1 THE TRADITIONAL APPROACH: THE AMTB AND MOTIVATIONAL QUANTITY

Motivation is usually understood to refer to the desire to initiate L2 learning and the effort employed to sustain it, and in lay terms we all understand it to be a matter of quantity, as in the everyday observation that some learners are highly motivated and others have little or no motivation. In the late 1950s, Canadian researchers Robert Gardner and Wallace Lambert developed what would become the dominant model of L2 learning motivation, which they framed within a wider model of foreign language learning known as the socio-educational model (Gardner and Lambert, 1972; Gardner, 1985). Over four decades, Gardner and associates furthered their definition of motivation via large survey studies mostly carried out in Canada. However, in the 1990s the model underwent serious criticisms for being too restrictive and unresponsive to wider developments in psychology (e.g. Crookes and Schmidt, 1991; Dörnyei, 1994; Oxford and Shearin, 1994).

Most of the studies used the same instrument, the Attitude/Motivation Test Battery (AMTB; Gardner, 1985). Therefore, all illustrations in this section and the following ones come from items in the AMTB, unless differently indicated. In the

Table 8.1
Watson vs Kaplan on three dimensions of motivation

	Richard Watson (1995)	Alice Kaplan (1993)
Effort	HIGH: But now I was trying. I was practicing. I was listening and repeating back. I read Georges Simenon's mystery novels out loud in French, trying to accumulate an auditory vocabulary. But time and again when I wanted to use a French word that I knew I knew, a word I would recognize instantly if I either read it or hear it, it would not come up. I could not hear nor see it in my mind (p. 103)	HIGH: That was what woke me up: absorbing a new reality, repeating it, appreciating it. I felt a pull toward learning I hadn't felt since the fifth grade: quiet mastery of a subject. Knowing I knew the material, that I had it down. Knowing how to find out more. Inventing methods for listening and making them habits. Feeling a kind of tickle in my ear at the pleasure of understanding. Then the pleasure of writing down what I had heard and getting every detail, every accent mark right (pp. 55–6)
Enjoyment	LOW: … what made me realize how much I dislike the sound of French was the continual, unctuous, caressing repetition of 'l'oiseau' ('the bird'). It is a word the French believe to be one of the most beautiful in their language. It is a word that cannot be pronounced without simpering, a word whose use should be restricted to children under five. I did not want to speak French because it gave me the bird (p. 53)	HIGH: I went into the village in search of French. I went to the train station. I bought tickets to Geneva, 'aller et retour à Genève' – that is what you had to say to get a round trip ticket. I loved to let it roll off my tongue, 'alleret-retour' in one drum roll, 'to go and return.' I bought tickets just to say it. Most of what I did, in town, I did in order to speak. Complicated conversations at the Tabac, the newsstand, the grocery (p. 53)
Investment	HIGH: All those years of guilt and embarrassment at being a Cartesian scholar who could not speak French … I would learn to speak French, whatever it took, however long. One day, by God, I would sit at a table in a restaurant in Paris with a group of French Cartesian scholars and we would talk! (p. 65)	HIGH: Learning French and learning to think, learning to desire, is all mixed up in my head, until I can't tell the difference … French demands my obedience, gives me permission to try too hard, to squinch up my face to make the words sound right (pp. 140–1)

socio-educational model overall amount of motivation is quantified via three dimensions, each reflected in a separate scale in the AMTB:

- Motivational intensity, which we can explain as how much **effort** people reportedly expend in learning the language (as in 'I keep up to date with

French by working on it almost every day' and 'I don't pay much attention to the feedback I receive in my French class').

- Attitudes towards learning the L2, which we can see as probing how much **enjoyment** people report feeling when they learn the language (as in 'I love learning French' and 'I hate French').

- Desire to learn, which can be generally understood as how much personal **investment** in succeeding in the language people claim for themselves (as in 'I want to learn French so well that it will become second nature to me' and 'To be honest, I really have little desire to learn French').

For any given statement, what is known as a Likert scale (Likert, 1932) is offered and respondents choose on a seven-point continuum from 'strongly agree' (which gets scored as a seven) to 'strongly disagree' (which gets scored as a one). The three scales above contain each ten statements and the scores derived from them contribute to a single, strict quantification of motivation. The 'truly motivated individual' scores high on all three dimensions, according to Gardner (2001, p. 6). In order to appreciate more concretely the significance of these three dimensions, let us return to the comparison of Richard Watson and Alice Kaplan that we initiated in Chapter 7 (see section 7.2). Table 8.1 shows excerpts comparing the two French learners on the three dimensions of effort, enjoyment and investment. It would seem as if enjoyment is where the only difference between the two learners lies. It is on this dimension only that Watson would be rated extremely low (to the point of aversion!), whereas Kaplan would be rated extremely high. If we accept Gardner's stipulation of what constitutes a 'truly motivated individual', then Kaplan, but not Watson, is truly motivated – and, indeed, she learns French more successfully.

8.2   INTEGRATIVENESS AS AN ANTECEDENT OF MOTIVATION

A goal of early motivation research was to be able to reliably measure the amount of motivation an individual will feel towards learning the L2 and to determine whether this measured quantity can predict a reasonable proportion of his or her L2 achievement level. Equally or more important in understanding language learning motivation, however, is to explain what variables contribute to increases or decreases in motivational quantity. In motivation jargon, these variables are called **antecedents** or 'motivational substrates' that give form to the structure of motivation.

Of all antecedents, **integrativeness** is the one that has played the most central role in the development of a theory of foreign language motivation. Unfortunately, this construct has also often misinterpreted (see discussion in Dörnyei, 2005, p. 69) and since the 1990s has attracted harsh criticism, to the point that most contemporary scholars of L2 motivation have turned their backs to the construct. According to Gardner (2001), integrativeness is an attitude defined as 'a genuine interest in learning the second language in order to come closer to the other language community' (p. 5). It involves three dimensions:

- Favourable attitudes towards L2 speakers ('if Canada should lose the French culture of Quebec, it would indeed be a great loss').

- General interest in foreign languages and low ethnocentrism ('I would really like to learn a lot of foreign languages').

- Endorsement of reasons for learning the L2 related to interaction with L2 members or, in Gardner's terms, an **integrative orientation** ('studying French is important to me because it will allow me to meet and converse with more and varied people'; we will examine this and other orientations in section 8.3).

For learners who score very high on integrativeness (i.e. on the three dimensions above combined), complete identification with the L2 community may be observed. For example, learners may express desires to think and behave like a person from the L2 community, at times to the point of detachment from the L1 community. Some signs of this extreme case of integrativeness can indeed be found in Kaplan's (1993) account, when she writes: 'Why do people want to adopt another culture? Because there's something in their own they don't like, that doesn't *name them*' (p. 209, italics in the original).

Gardner (2001) believed the highest and most facilitative form of motivation is what he called *the* **integrative motivation**, which is attained only when three conditions are met: (1) the antecedent of integrativeness itself is high, (2) motivation quantity (that is, the combined amount of effort, enjoyment, and investment) is also high, and (3) attitudes towards the learning situation (teachers, curriculum) are positive. Indeed, Gardner (2001) asserted that exceptionally successful learners who attain native-like competence are likely to be integratively motivated individuals. This is something that is anecdotally supported in Kaplan's case but has never been systematically studied in the exceptional adult learner studies of the kind illustrated in Table 2.3 in Chapter 2. In any case, in the sociocultural model integrative motivation evolved to signify the epitome of optimal and highest motivation.

As we will see later in this chapter, the emphasis on identification with the other language community as a precondition for optimal L2 learning motivation eventually attracted criticisms for being too narrow. In addition, the disregard for contexts for language learning other than Canada limits the usefulness of Gardner's notion of integrativeness and of the socio-educational model in general. Thus, since the mid-1990s the construct of integrativeness has undergone tremendous conceptual renovation as part of an effort to make it more researchable as well as more applicable across L2 learning contexts (Csizér and Dörnyei, 2005b).

8.3 OTHER ANTECEDENTS: ORIENTATIONS AND ATTITUDES

Table 8.2 presents a synopsis of most antecedents of motivation that have been identified over the years. They comprise at a minimum three central ones:

Table 8.2
Main antecedents investigated in L2 motivation research

Antecedent	Comments
Attitudes towards the L2 community and its speakers	They are grounded in the sociocultural milieu of the learners, with its shared values, beliefs, norms and practices; oftentimes researchers also include questionnaire items about socially based attitudes towards a number of interrelated dimensions, for example, attitudes towards French Canadians, European French people, the learning of foreign languages in general and bilingualism as a societal value
Integrativeness	It refers to an attitudinal complex globally defined as 'a genuine interest in learning the second language in order to come closer to the other language community' (Gardner, 2001, p. 5) and it subsumes many of the attitudes above
Attitudes towards instructional setting	They include attitudes towards teachers and curriculum, where a good part of the learning takes place; more recently attitudes towards peers and group dynamics have also been explored
Orientations	These are reasons for learning the L2, which in turn may influence the intensity and quality of motivation of learner's experience
Social support	Support from significant others (including parents, siblings, peers and teachers), since believing that they want one to learn the language creates rewards and reinforcements that may be important in boosting motivation
Inter-group contact	It includes potential and actual contact as well as how those experiences are remembered as positive or negative by the learners (e.g. Noels, 2005)
Ethnovitality	It refers to the 'sociopolitical presence of the language in the community' (Masgoret and Gardner, 2003, p. 132); it can include more generally other geopolitical factors such as globalization and tourism (e.g. Dörnyei and Csizér, 2005)
Self-confidence when using the language	It includes communicative anxiety and self-perception of communicative competence (see Chapter 9, section 9.5 on willingness to communicate (WTC) and the work of Richard Clément)

integrativeness (which we just examined in section 8.2), orientations (that is, reasons for learning the L2) and attitudes (both towards the L2 community and its speakers and towards teachers and curriculum in the instructional setting). The affective variables of foreign language anxiety and communicative self-confidence are also considered key in predicting motivation, but we will examine them separately when we look at affective sources of individual differences in Chapter 9 (see particularly sections 9.3 and 9.4).

Orientation refers to reasons for learning the L2, because they contribute to the setting of goals that will propel and sustain motivation of varying intensities and qualities. Of course, reasons are not antithetical or mutually exclusive, and therefore a given individual may exhibit several orientations at once. There are five orientations for learning a language that L2 learners most commonly report across contexts:

- **instrumental** when pragmatic and utilitarian reasons are important, such as getting a better job or pursuing a higher level of education in the L2

- for **knowledge** or enlightened understanding of one's own identity, language or culture and to become a more knowledgeable person

- to facilitate **travel** to other countries or parts of a country

- for fostering general **friendship** with members of the target language

- for **integrative** reasons related to identification with the target culture and a genuine desire to become more like members of the L2 group (as a reminder, in the socio-educational model this integrative orientation is only one of three components of integrativeness, which in turn is only one of several components of the integrative motivation; see section 8.2).

In an influential study, Clément and Kruidenier (1983) added several other important reasons for learning the L2 that contribute to shaping motivation beyond these five. Even more importantly, they showed that orientations for L2 learning are not context free but arise from forces related to 'who learns what in what milieu' (p. 288). For example, they found that in their sample of 871 grade 11 students, Canadian Anglophones, who can be considered to be members of the linguistic majority in Canada, often reported learning a minority language like French or Spanish because they sought the prestige and respect they felt they stood to gain by attaining familiarity with those increasingly important minority groups (a **dominance-recognition** orientation, as in 'It will permit me to become an influential member of my community'), or to maintain control over the wealth and influence they enjoy as a dominant group (a **pragmatic control** orientation, as in 'It will allow me to gain influence over French Canadians'). By way of contrast, Clément and Kruidenier also found that genuine integrative motives can indeed thrive among individuals from the dominant group who may have a **familiarity-involvement** orientation and want to learn the language for reasons that include empathy and desire to become familiar with the other (as in 'It will help me to appreciate the problems that French people have in a predominantly English-speaking country') or even to become an involved participant in the other's community and fulfil a true integrative identification in Gardner's sense (as in 'I want to become a member of the French Canadian community'). These researchers also found evidence, however, that this familiarity-involvement orientation is more common in dominant-group individuals who live in multilingual settings and who therefore meet two conditions: they 'are assured of their first language and culture and have immediate access to the target language group' (1983, p. 287). In unilingual settings, by contrast, where contact with L2 members is not frequent, the researchers found that an interest may emerge in the culture of the L2 group as an object of distant study and celebration (a **sociocultural** or what we could also call a belletristic orientation, as in 'It will enable me to better understand and appreciate French Canadian art and literature').

In addition to the reasons that cause people to want to learn an L2, **attitudes** towards the L2 and its speakers will contribute to increased or diminished L2 motivation. These attitudes come from the collective values, beliefs, attitudes and even behaviours that are rewarded and modelled for the learner in the communities in which he or she participates, be it a classroom, the family or the wider environment of neighbourhoods and institutions. These influences constitute what social psychologists call the sociocultural milieu. Several attitudes grounded in the sociocultural milieu have been investigated over the years in the SLA literature on individual differences (see Table 8.2).

Gardner et al. (1999) investigated the relationship between motivation and attitudes in a sample of 109 undergraduate students enrolled in an English-speaking university in Canada who had taken at least one year of high-school French in the past. The respondents were asked to react to five scales with items that were worded to prompt their recollections of feelings and attitudes back when they were taking French in high school. For example, items included 'I really looked forward to the time I spent in French class' and 'My parents stressed the importance French would have for me when I left school'. Another number of scales probed their motivation, not during high school, but at the time the study was conducted (e.g. 'I wish I were fluent in French') as well as their attitudes towards bilingualism (e.g. 'Both English and French are important to Canada'), and their self-evaluation of communicative competence (rating their estimated difficulty to use the four language skills across situations like 'ordering a simple meal in a restaurant' or 'understanding newspaper headlines'). Also completed by all students was a matched-guise task, a technique commonly used by sociolinguists to study language attitudes and stereotypes. In this task, the participants had to choose evaluative adjectives (insincere–sincere, impolite–polite, and so on) best describing each speaker whose voice they heard in six recordings (three in English, the students' L1; and three in French, the students' L2), blind to the fact that the same three bilingual individuals had produced each pair.

The findings of this study revealed that attitudes back in high school were directly associated with current motivation, with integrativeness, and (to a lesser extent) with French anxiety during college. Gardner et al. (1999) also found indirect associations between past high-school attitudes and current attitudes towards bilingualism and self-perceptions of communicative competence. The findings supported the theoretical relationships posited in the socioeducational model and led Gardner et al. (1999) to conclude that past experiences and attitudes that emerge in a given sociocultural milieu play a causal role in shaping L2 learning motivation.

8.4 FIRST SIGNS OF RENEWAL: SELF-DETERMINATION THEORY AND INTRINSIC MOTIVATION

If the first renaissance of L2 motivation research took place in the 1960s with the consolidation of the socio-educational model, a second burgeoning period began in the mid-1990s after three well-known critical reviews by Crookes and Schmidt (1991), Dörnyei (1994) and Oxford and Shearin (1994) summoned L2 motivation scholars to search for theoretical renewal. The more contemporary motivation research generated since those critiques has distanced itself from the emphasis on *quantity* of motivation and the antecedent of integrativeness, and instead has turned to an exploration of various *qualities* of motivation. Another reason for dissatisfaction was that, despite the inclusion of both social milieu and instructional context in the motivation theory of Gardner and colleagues, their interest in the Canadian context led them to emphasize attitudes rooted in the social milieu at the expense of the impact that the micro-context of the classroom environment (e.g. teacher, curriculum, instructional quality) can play in boosting or depleting motivation to learn an additional language. Many of these shortcomings were addressed in explorations of language learning motivation from the vantage point of self-determination theory, an influential 'macro-theory' of human motivation developed in the late 1970s by Edward Deci and Richard Ryan, both psychologists and the University of Rochester in the United States. This framework takes the lens away from motivational quantity and on to the nature and quality of L2 learning motivation, while it also accommodates important sources of motivational influence that stem from the instructional micro-context of the classroom.

As Vansteenkiste et al. (2006) explain, self-determination theory construes humans as volitional beings who are growth-oriented, that is, predisposed to life-long learning and development. Essential in meeting a few basic fundamental human needs is a sense of choice and personal causation in everything we humans do. Thus, human behaviour in this theory is posited to be guided by the drive to self-determine our actions and activities. A few years ago, Canadian researchers Richard Clément and Kimberly Noels took it upon themselves to apply the theory to the study of L2 motivation and to compare it with the Gardnerian model, to which both have also contributed much important work over the years. To this end, they teamed up with Canadian self-determination experts Robert Vallerand and Luc Pelletier and developed an instrument to measure the constructs of self-determination theory, the Language Learning Orientation Scale (LLOS; Noels et al.,

2000). In what follows, I draw from LLOS items in order to illustrate the model and its constructs.

When individuals engage in behaviour that they understand as self-initiated by choice and largely sustained by inherent enjoyment in the activity (that is, as an end in itself, for the sheer sake of learning), they are said to be **intrinsically motivated**. This quality of motivation is considered optimal because it has been experimentally shown to be consistently associated to higher levels of achievement (Vansteenkiste et al., 2006). An L2 learner would be intrinsically motivated, according to the LLOS, if she said she studied the L2 for the 'high' she feels when hearing/speaking the foreign language (stimulation), for the pleasure of 'surpassing oneself' and 'grasping a difficult language concept' (self-accomplishment), or for the sheer satisfaction to know more (knowledge). Note that the characteristic feature in all three cases is enjoyment. If you now reread the quotes pertaining to enjoyment from our French learners shown in Table 8.1, you will appreciate just how intrinsically motivated Kaplan is ... and the extent to which Watson is not!

Naturally, choice and personal causation cannot always be possible. For example, threats or even simply controlling language, rewards, deadlines, surveillance and exams can divest people from a sense of choice and take the pleasure away from almost any activity (Vansteenkiste et al., 2006). When individuals construe their behaviour as structured by a means–end, pragmatic–instrumental causation that is imposed from the outside, their sense of self-causation and autonomy is low, if present at all, and they are said to be **extrinsically motivated**. This is a less ideal quality of motivation that is associated with externally regulated actions. Learners who are extrinsically motivated may say, for example, that they are learning the L2 for ulterior goals that have little to do with the L2 itself, such as a better salary, a more prestigious job, or simply because it is expected of them (all three possibilities comprise the three-item scale for external regulation in the LLOS).

However, this simple binary picture is further complicated by the human desire to feel we belong to a community, that is, to feel relatedness. Because of the need for relatedness, certain external values, beliefs and behaviours may be gradually adopted and internalized, thus allowing individuals to function more successfully. Extrinsic regulation, then, can undergo a process of internalization, resulting in two intermediate states between absolute external regulation and complete self-regula-tion. **Introjected regulation** happens when people 'buy into' the external pressure, by developing feelings of guilt or shame that then can only be avoided via compli-ance with the expected behaviour (as in 'I would feel ashamed if I couldn't speak to my friends from the second language community in their native tongue'). It would seem as if this was the case with Watson, whose intense desire to learn the L2 at a later point in his career was rooted in 'years of guilt and embarrassment at being a Cartesian scholar who could not speak French' (1995, p. 65). **Identified regulation**, by the same token, is closer to the intrinsic pole. It happens when external values are accepted and adopted as one's own and an individual comes to see the relevance and meaningfulness of an activity that in principle was not self-determined. In the LLOS instrument, for example, an item tapping identified regulation is 'I choose to be the kind of person who can speak more than one language'.

Finally, in extreme dysfunctional cases, individuals may fail to see any internal or external value to their actions. This happens, for example, when some students in compulsory foreign language courses say they do not know why they are studying the L2 or they express resentment at what feels like a waste of their time. These learners suffer from **amotivation**, and their performance in formal learning settings is predicted to suffer from it too.

Noels and her colleagues have found robust empirical support for self-determination principles in L2 motivation. For example, in a surveyed sample of 159 psychology volunteers who were enrolled at the University of Ottawa (a French–English bilingual institution) and had studied L2 French for varying periods ranging from as little as a few months up to as long as 34 years, Noels et al. (2000) found that freedom of choice ('I experience a lot of freedom in learning a second language') and intention to continue ('I want to continue to learn a second language') were clearly associated to each other as well as positively associated to the most self-regulated forms of motivation (intrinsic and identified) and negatively associated to amotivation. Three reasons for learning the L2 (for travel, friendship or knowledge) were associated to the two most self-regulated motivational types as well, whereas instrumental reasons (e.g. a better job) patterned very strongly with extrinsic motivation.

In several other studies, Noels and her colleagues have found further convergent validity for self-determination theory in that instructional environments that are perceived to be controlling and thwarting self-regulation and autonomy erode levels of intrinsic motivation. Specifically, students who perceived their teachers to be controlling showed noticeably less intrinsic motivation (e.g. Noels et al., 1999; Noels, 2001). This finding is fully predicted by self-determination theory and has indeed been consistently observed in other non-language academic subject matters (see Vansteenkiste et al., 2006). As you can see, evidence yielded by L2 research on the self-regulation model of motivation is not only theoretically promising but potentially useful to language teachers as well. Or at least this should be true of Western education contexts such as Canada, the United States and Europe, where autonomy and independence are valued by many students and teachers and is generally rewarded by the social and educational milieux.

How does intrinsic motivation in self-determination theory relate to integrative motivation, the optimal type of motivation posited by Gardner? Noels (2001) set out to investigate precisely this question, by measuring the correlational strength between integrative orientation (which, you should remember, is only one of the three dimensions that make up the antecedent of integrativeness in the socio-educational model) and the intrinsic–extrinsic continuum of motivation proposed by self-determination theory. She examined the answers to a battery of questionnaires administered to a sample of 322 L1 English students who were enrolled in L2 Spanish courses at a university in California and had studied the L2 for no time at all and up to 38 years. She concluded that integrative and intrinsic motivation were reciprocally related in the California sample: 'the more individuals wish to learn a language because it is interesting and enjoyable, and because the activity has value to them personally, the more they are likely to learn the language because they wish to have interactions with members' of the L2 community (p. 137). On the other hand, only integrative orientation, but not intrinsic motivation, helped explain inter-group dimensions of motivation, such as frequency of contact with L2 speakers, in this Spanish sample.

Thus, while pointing out that a strength of the self-determination model of L2 motivation is its focus on broad human motives underlying motivational states, Noels (2001, p. 114) also recognized that a weakness is that it lacks the theoretical apparatus to accommodate societal attitudes towards the L2 and its speakers, the influence of the sociocultural milieu, and issues of ethnic vitality and identification. In these L2-specific areas the socio-educational model continues to provide important insights for understanding L2 motivation.

So far the theories and studies introduced in this chapter engage with the learning of languages that are widely salient and present in North American contexts, such as English, French and Spanish. We may want to ask ourselves: Just how useful is this knowledge, if we want to understand L2 motivation beyond those few contexts? Hungarian researcher Zoltán Dörnyei was among the first SLA scholars to suggest that motivation research as the field of SLA knew it since the 1960s probably needed modification if it was to explain L2 motivation beyond the Canadian context where most studies had been conducted. In doing so, he unchained a profound series of explorations for renewal and innovation that have provided the foundations for contemporary and future understandings of language learning motivation.

8.5 MOTIVATION FROM A DISTANCE: EFL LEARNERS' ORIENTATIONS AND ATTITUDES

Dörnyei's critique began in 1988 with his dissertation research, completed at Eotvös University in Budapest, and has been sustained ever since through a systematic research programme at the University of Nottingham (see Dörnyei, 2001). His main concern initially was with probing the explanatory power of the main antecedents that the socio-educational model had identified as the bedrock of L2 motivation (that is, orientations and attitudes). Specifically, he suggested that integrativeness might have less explanatory power for learners in foreign language contexts, such as his native Hungary, because they rarely come into personal contact with L2 members. Without contact, they cannot form strong attitudes towards L2 speakers or harbour intense desires of integrating or being 'like them'. He reasoned that, at least in the beginning stages of L2 learning, instrumental types of orientation (wanting a good grade, passing university entrance exams, and so on) and classroom attitudes (towards the teacher, curriculum, materials, and so on) may influence the motivation of foreign language learners more heavily.

Other researchers have joined since then in these efforts to reconceptualize the antecedents of motivation so as to make L2 motivation models more relevant to foreign language contexts. Particularly, motivation in EFL contexts has attracted considerable attention in recent years.

For one, orientations (i.e. the reasons for learning an L2) can be quite different in foreign as opposed to second language contexts. Clément et al. (1994) investigated orientations in a sample of 301 17- and 18-year-old Hungarian students learning English. They discovered that the orientations reported in previous Canadian studies required a few interesting modifications. First, the friendship and travel orientations were blended, probably because the main means for making friends with foreigners in a context like Hungary is when travelling abroad. Furthermore, because the desire to make friends was expressed with regard to foreigners in general, rather than specifically with members of the L2 group, the term **xenophilic orientation** was suggested as more appropriate in such cases than a 'friendship' orientation. Third, the instrumental and knowledge orientations were also intertwined, and the researchers suggest this is because in the context of post-communist Hungary 'being more educated and knowledgeable [in English] is related to success in work and studies' (p. 431) and thus 'English as knowledge is perceived to have pragmatic consequences' (p. 432). Finally, Clément et al. discovered a new orientation, the English media orientation, which refers to learning English to watch TV and listen to music, above all. This media orientation has been more recently renamed as indirect contact (Csizér and Dörnyei, 2005b) or cultural interest orientation (Csizér and Dörnyei, 2005a) because it broadly 'reflects the appreciation of cultural products associated with the particular L2 and conveyed by the media [and] ... cultural products and artifacts' (Csizér and Dörnyei, 2005a, p. 21). It is related to the special status of English as a world language that evokes positive as well as negative symbolic images of globalization and economic prowess. Clément and his associates summarize the orientations that are likely to be important in EFL contexts like Hungary in the following manner:

> The absence of Anglophones from the immediate environment would appear to sustain distal friendships (through travel), an interest in English culture as a foreign phenomenon, and an instrumental orientation based on the acquisition of knowledge and media usage rather than on achievement of pragmatic outcomes.
>
> (1994, pp. 433–4)

Not only orientations but also attitudes towards the L2 and its speakers may be quite different when characterizing motivation in EFL learning contexts. Japanese researcher Tomoko Yashima and her colleagues (Yashima et al., 2004) proposed the notion of **international posture**, a positive international attitude made up of at least three dimensions successfully measured by this research team:

- interest in international vocation or activities ('I want to work in an international organization such as the United Nations')

- tendency to approach rather than avoid dissimilar others, such as non-Japanese in Japan ('I would share an apartment with international students')

- interest in foreign affairs ('I often talk about situations and events in foreign countries with my family and/or friends').

It is interesting to note that the construct of international posture resonates with one of Gardner's three conditions that support integrativeness in general, namely openness to other groups or lack of ethnocentricism (see section 8.2). Yashima and colleagues were able to establish strong associations between international posture and L2 learning motivation in two studies with college and high-school samples of Japanese EFL students ($n = 297$ and 160, respectively; see Yashima et al., 2004).

Lamb (2004) also uncovered support for a shared set of orientations and attitudes that characterize EFL learning in a sample of 219 11- and 12-year-old students in a very different context, an elite junior high school in Sumatra, Indonesia. These young adolescents had exposure to English mostly through TV and music and rarely through direct contact with any English speakers, a pattern which is consistent with the English media or cultural interest orientation discovered by Clément et al. (1994). They also appeared to hold a xenophilic orientation, in the terms of Clément et al., as they envisioned needs and desires for L2 communication with regard to 'foreigners' and 'foreign countries' in general rather than with respect to particular target groups and cultures. In close connection with Yashima's notion of international posture, Lamb uncovered clear evidence that these students had been exposed to the collective discourse of globalization through media, school and family and they viewed English as a resource of 'citizens of the world'. He argues that this international predisposition also involved an identification process that nurtured 'a vision of an English-speaking, globally-involved but nationally-responsible future self' (2004, p. 16).

Whether methodologies are quantitative as in Clément et el. (1994) and Yashima et al. (2004) or qualitative as in Lamb (2004), and whether the so-called foreign language contexts are countries as different as Hungary, Japan or Indonesia, the similarity of findings and themes is clear. It would be naive, however, to imagine that a positive international attitude is all there is to EFL learners' motivation towards learning English as an international language and the language of globalization. For example, in the largest scale motivation study to date, Dörnyei and Csizér (2005; see also Dörnyei et al., 2006) investigated attitudes towards five L2s (including English and German, the most studied in that context) among more than 8,500 13- and 14-year-olds studying foreign languages in schools in Hungary. Their findings suggest that respondents who were residents of regions with relatively small volumes of tourism but reported high frequency of personal encounters turned out to exhibit the most positive attitudes. By contrast, respondents who resided in top touristic areas (e.g. Budapest) and reported similar frequency of contact entertained more negative attitudes than the former group. Dörnyei and Csizér speculate that at some point, if the presence of foreigners is very large in a particular foreign language setting, a deterioration in attitudes is observed, possibly because students of the target language come to entertain more realistic perceptions of the benefits and drawbacks of tourism and globalization (for more on L2 contact, see also Chapter 9, section 9.5).

Taking a more critical perspective, Lamb (2004) also notes that some of the Indonesian students' comments suggested 'not so much [... a sense] of language learners reaching out to integrate with the foreign culture or community, but of knowing they must embrace the changes already sweeping their own culture' (p. 13) and a sense of learned urgency to become functional English users in order 'not to be pushed away' (p. 11). Thus, some foreign language learners will develop positive attitudes towards the somewhat distant image of English speakers or even 'foreigners' in general and will entertain a positive international posture, but other learners may grow disappointed after sufficient actual contact or they may contest such positive international attitudes and even subvert them, depending on complex and dynamic forces of identity formation that may change over the life span.

8.6 LANGUAGE LEARNING MOTIVATION: POSSIBLE IN SITUATIONS OF CONFLICT?

Clément and Kruidenier's (1983) dictum that motivation and the orientations that underlie it greatly depend on 'who learns what in what milieu' (p. 288) is highly relevant when applied to yet other contexts, particularly to settings where language learning happens despite the speakers of the target and the first languages being directly in conflict. This is the case of the study of Arabic in Israel. Is high motivation for learning another language even possible when the context is characterized by serious conflict between the L1 and L2 group?

We have some good insights into this difficult question thanks to a team of researchers at Tel Aviv University who investigated the motivation of Hebrew speaking school-aged children in Israel (Inbar et al., 2001; Donitsa-Schmidt et al., 2004). The researchers describe this national context in the following terms. The Hebrew speaking school population in Israel is required to study a foreign language besides English (that is, an L3) from grades seven through nine. In 70 per cent of the schools, students have no choice but to enrol in Modern Standard Arabic, either because no other alternative L3 is provided by the school or because for resource efficiency reasons the school randomly decides which students will be assigned to study Arabic or another language (typically French). By contrast, in 30 per cent of Israeli schools students do have a choice to enrol in either Arabic or French during these three compulsory years of an L3 in junior high school. In addition, during the mid-1990s the Tel Aviv Municipality initiated an experimental introduction of Spoken (as opposed to Modern Standard) Arabic in grade four, at age nine or three years earlier than is the national norm, in 65 per cent of the Jewish elementary schools in the city (that is, 38 schools).

Donitsa-Schmidt et al. (2004) studied a representative sample of 539 fourth-, fifth- and sixth-graders in nine schools in Tel Aviv who had begun studying Spoken Arabic experimentally at age nine; these children's attitudes and motivation were compared to those of a representative sample of 153 same-age students in five other schools who, following the national norm, would not begin studying Arabic until the seventh grade or age 12. When the researchers gave all these middle-school children the opportunity to provide open-ended comments about why the study of Spoken Arabic should be given priority as an L3 in schools in Israel, the most frequently mentioned reasons were:

(a) the Arabs surround us; (b) we need to communicate with the Arabs; (c) we need to learn about their culture and make peace with them; (d) it is instrumental for finding a job, university studies, watching TV, and so on; and (e) we need to fight the enemy.

(2004, p. 223)

Fortunately, the subset of 539 students who were already studying Spoken Arabic at the time answered the question by consistently emphasizing mostly reasons (c) and (d) above, when compared to the other students who would not begin learning Arabic until seventh grade. Specifically, they mentioned peace oriented (e.g. 'to promote peace between Jews and Arabs') and pragmatically oriented (e.g. 'so I can become Prime Minister once I grow up') reasons for the study of Arabic in Israel more frequently. The researchers also found that the youngsters who had begun studying Arabic at age nine thought more frequently this language was important to study in school. This patterned difference in opinions gives hope that actually studying a language can make people hold more positive orientations and attitudes towards both the L2 and its speakers, even in conflictual contexts.

In an earlier study Inbar et al. (2001) investigated the same population of Hebrew-speaking Israeli children, but this time focusing on older students (seventh-graders, or 12-year-olds) at the school juncture when the study of an L3 becomes obligatory for three years. A major focus in the 2001 study was whether having a choice to study Arabic or to opt for some other L3 would make a difference in motivation. The researchers found that it did not: The 12-year-old children who were studying Arabic had higher motivation and more positive attitudes towards the L2 and its speakers than students who were studying another language (French, typically), and this was true regardless of whether they had enrolled in Arabic or the other L3 voluntarily or forced by the institutional circumstances. As in the 2004 study, actually studying the language seemed to make the real positive difference, this time on motivational intensity in addition to attitude or orientation.

The findings of the 2004 and 2001 studies are largely in agreement with respect to most other areas investigated as well. First, for both the younger total sample of 692 students (in the 2004 study) and the older total sample of 1,690 students (in the 2001 study), factors that associated strongly with the likelihood of children being more motivated towards studying Arabic (at the time or in the future) were attitudes towards the L2, its speakers and its culture and also whether they perceived their parents to want them to study Arabic.

More disappointingly, in the 2001 sample there was no difference in motivation for the students who, within each group (with or without a choice), had enjoyed prior exposure to communicative instruction in the Spoken Arabic dialect in the fourth to sixth grade (at ages nine through 12) (that is, for students who had been enrolled in the early-start experimental programme investigated in the 2004 study). It appears, therefore, that the higher motivation and better attitudes documented for early starters in the 2004 study are not likely to grow exponentially with age, or at least in this sample they did not confer them any special motivational advantage later, when compared to late starters. The positive finding remains, however, that in this Israeli context what matters most, regardless of starting age or L3 choice, is the fact that children are actually exposed to Arabic in school. This first-hand study of Arabic is what affects both their motivation and attitudes positively.

The single most important finding from the two Tel Aviv studies may have been that motivation was best predicted by student satisfaction with the quality of Arabic instruction. That is, among the students who were studying Arabic (539 9- to 11-year-olds in the 2004 study and 1,132 12-year-olds in the 2001 study), those who expressed more satisfaction towards their teacher and curriculum tended to be those who also reported higher motivation. It is a pity that the 2001 group who was currently studying French rather than Arabic in junior high were not asked about this issue, as it would be interesting to know if students place the same kind of importance on the quality of L2 instruction when learning a more politically 'neutral' language in a given context, such as French in Israel. Be that as it may, the researchers conclude that 'learning a foreign language in a school context enhances students' motivations towards the culture and the language being studied' (Inbar et al., 2001, p. 307). That this was the case with young children studying a target language in a national milieu of social and political conflict is all the more hopeful and places tremendous responsibility on teachers and curriculum developers (Donitsa-Schmidt et al., 2004, pp. 226–7). Thus, as McGroarty (2001) also notes, this finding sheds an extremely hopeful light on the role that good language teachers can play in motivating their students.

These two studies also make it clear that new orientations need to be considered in situations of conflict between languages and speakers: a peace orientation and a conflict–dominance or national security orientation. Indeed, much of the post-9/11 public rhetoric in the United States in favour of learning certain (so-called critical) foreign languages has been dominated by the latter conflict–dominance orientation and driven by national security concerns (for a useful commentary on this issue, see Edwards, 2004). And yet, despite the largely positive findings reported by Inbar et al. (2001) and Donitsa-Schmidt et al. (2004), the reality of Arabic enrolments in the Israeli school system should give us little reason for optimism about long-term motivation for studying another language out of conflict–dominance-related orientations. Namely, the authors report that once students who take Arabic starting at age nine or 12 move on beyond grade nine and into high school, where English is the only requirement, Arabic enrolments suffer a serious dropout rate of 96 per cent! More in-depth study of the motivation of language learners across a larger variety of conflictual settings, and including not only orientations, attitudes and motivational intensity, but also behavioural evidence of actual long-term commitment and persistence to learn the L2, would make a real contribution to motivation theory as well as to promoting world peace.

8.7 DYNAMIC MOTIVATION: TIME, CONTEXT, BEHAVIOUR

Since the turn of the new century, L2 motivation researchers have ventured into increasingly new territory and have begun exploring novel directions that may help us hone our understanding of motivation as a central source of individual differences in L2 learning. The times are now ripe for such changes, after the legacy accrued from four decades of systematic development, validation and critique of several previous models. These newer perspectives are related to an emphasis on the dynamic nature of L2 motivation and were fuelled by Dörnyei and Ottó (1998), who for the first time argued that L2 motivation was mostly portrayed as static in the extant research, whereas in reality we all know that motivational changes over time are to be expected. They also warned that the dual focus on antecedents and 'whys' of L2 motivation, on the one hand, and on L2 achievement as the only criterion to establish that motivation mattered, on the other, meant that there was almost a complete disregard among L2 researchers for explicating the consequences of high or low motivation on actual behaviour. They therefore proposed the Process Model of L2 Motivation, which is partly based on Heckhausen and Kuhl's (1985) Action Control theory, and conceived of motivation in relation to specific contexts, activities and situations. McGroarty (2001) characterizes well what this theoretical move is to mean for future L2 motivation research:

> The motivational tenor of any classroom, including its constructive social relations, can probably only be gauged over time. It is likely that the motivational level of a social unit, whether an entire classroom or a small group or pair working within the class, waxes and wanes somewhat depending on both the variety of activities and tasks occurring ... and on the social interactions framing the activity.
>
> (2001, p. 86)

Now SLA researchers feel compelled to investigate L2 motivation not only as a generalized trait, but also as a state trait (as Gardner et al., 2004 call it) or a set of goal-directed predispositions to act (or not to act) in a certain way (as Dörnyei and Ottó, 1998, prefer to describe it) that is subject to **change over time**. That being so, the need is also felt to study L2 motivation longitudinally. At a macro level, for example, small declines in attitudes towards speakers of an L2 can happen out of historical shifts, as seems to have been the case in Hungary, where Dörnyei and Csizér (2005) found a small but noticeable motivational decline following the disillusionment with the promise of tourism and globalization that appears to have taken place in Hungary between 1993 and 1999, during a decade marked by changes towards the privatization of the economy after the end of the Communist rule in 1989. At a more local but still institutional level, it is not unusual to observe some decline in overall motivation for a given group of students from beginning to end of the curricular life of a semester or year of study, as Inbar et al. (2001) and Gardner et al. (2004) reported for very different contexts. Gardner et al. (2004) also report smaller sized changes in anxiety and teacher evaluation that emerged only towards the end of the semester, when final exams were approaching. Looking at motivation at a more individual level and more qualitatively, Ushioda (2001) captured how the nature of the motivation experienced by 14 undergraduates learning French in Dublin changed over the course of about 15 months. They went from more intrinsic kinds of motivation related to academic interest and sheer enjoyment, in the beginning of study, to a heightened awareness of the pragmatic rewards and usefulness to be accrued, towards the end. Ushioda calls the former causal motivational thinking, perhaps evoking a retrospective view at the beginning of the course of study that was rooted in the 'why's' of studying French based on past positive learning histories; the latter type Ushioda terms teleological motivational thinking, as it suggests a prospective view directed to future goals and returns. She speculates teleological motivational thought evolves only gradually over time but eventually may 'assume motivational importance and clarity' (p. 117) as learners progress in their instructional efforts.

Contemporary work on L2 motivation is also beginning to consider how motivated behaviour is a property that emerges out of the situated activity of a social unit of the classroom or group. That is, motivation is considered in its **micro context** with the aid of explanations from group dynamics and situated cognition. To illustrate, Dörnyei (2002) found that students with high integrativeness and positive course attitudes were more likely to hold positive attitudes towards doing a specific oral argumentative L2 task than peers scoring low on these dimensions. In turn, positive task attitudes (as well as positive course attitudes) resulted in more L2 output being produced while doing the task. Even more importantly, the oral participation of students who were low in attitude towards the task was improved and resulted in relatively more language being produced whenever such a low task-motivation student nevertheless held positive attitudes towards the course in general, or whenever a student with less positive attitudes towards the specific task was paired with a highly motivated peers. These findings, although from a single study, suggest the need to probe the relationship between motivation, tasks and the collective motivational state of peers.

Another recent change is the recognition that beyond L2 achievement we need to see what changes in **behaviour** motivation can cause. As Csizér and Dörnyei (2005a) bluntly put it, 'motivation is a concept that explains why people behave as they do rather than how successful their behavior will be' (p. 20). At a minimum, behavioural estimation points like self-projected language choice ('if you could choose, which foreign languages would you choose to learn next year at school (or work)?') and self-reported intended learning effort ('how much effort are you prepared to expend in learning these languages?') can be considered (see Appendix 1 in Dörnyei et al., 2006). Besides looking into motivation and L2 achievement, we now have to take into account (directly observed or at least self-reported) behaviour.

8.8 LOOKING FORWARD: THE L2 MOTIVATIONAL SELF SYSTEM

Perhaps the most significant change in how we may understand motivation in future years is the L2 Motivational Self System, formulated by Dörnyei (2005; Csizér and Dörnyei, 2005b). This proposal synthesizes previous models into one macro model of language-specific motivation, but building on the general social psychological theory of regulatory focus and the notion that humans make decisions as to how to act motivated by references to an ideal self.

The theory of regulatory focus was developed by affect and motivation psychologist from Columbia University E. Tory Higgins (2000, 2005). He posits that humans self-regulate their behaviour motivated by the need to balance a promotion focus, in which we are able to anticipate gain or pleasure from an action, and a prevention focus, in which we are able to anticipate pain or shame from the same action. According to Higgins, a promotion focus entails a reference to an 'ideal self' (the kind of person we would like to be) and the accomplishments and aspirations we have attached to it. It also relates to a more intrinsic kind of motivation and to asking ourselves the question: Is it worthwhile to do X? By contrast, a prevention focus entails a reference to an 'ought-to self' (the kind of person we think we should be) and the safety and responsibility values we have attached to it. It also relates to more extrinsic or only partially internalized motives and to posing ourselves the question: Is it worth it to do X?

In applying these ideas to L2 motivation, Dörnyei proposes the construct of the L2 Motivational Self System, which is made up of three main components:

1. 'Ideal L2 Self', referring to the L2-specific facet of one's 'ideal self' – if the person we would like to become speaks an L2, the ideal L2 self is a powerful motivator to learn the particular language because we would like to reduce the discrepancy between our actual and ideal selves.

2. 'Ought-to L2 Self', referring to the attributes that we believe we ought to possess to avoid possible negative outcomes – this motivational dimension may therefore bear little resemblance to our own desires or wishes.

3 'L2 Learning Experience', which concerns executive motives related to the immediate learning environment and experience [...].

(Dörnyei et al., 2006, p. 145)

He further proposes that integrativeness be redefined not as a drive to identify with members of the target language (something that his work and that of others has shown to be of low relevance in many foreign language contexts), but as a drive to close the gap or discrepancy between the actual self and the ideal self, who in highly L2 motivated individuals happens to have been conceived as an L2-speaking self. That is, the highly motivated individual will score high in integrativeness while simultaneously being intrinsically as well as instrumentally motivated to learn the L2 because of a formed L2 speaking ideal self that she or he can anticipate as a reference point and that links L2 success with a promotion focus. Under this proposed reconceptualization, integrativeness is indeed the major and most immediate antecedent of L2 motivation across contexts, but only if relabelled as **ideal L2 self** (Csizér and Dörnyei, 2005a, 2005b), which is in turn directly affected by the antecedents of **instrumentality** and **attitudes towards L2 speakers**. Given these antecedents of motivation, at least four motivational profiles can then be

Table 8.3
The L2 Motivational Self System according to Csizér and Dörnyei (2005b)

Antecedents	Motivation profiles			
	Most motivated	**Less motivated**	**Not very motivated**	**Demotivated/ amotivated**
Self-reference (reconceptualized integrativeness)	ideal L2 self	ought-to self	neither	neither
Perceived Instrumentality	high	high	low	low
Attitudes towards L2 and FLs in general	high	low	high	low

distinguished in the L2 Motivational Self model. The model is schematically represented in Table 8.3.

The four profiles have been empirically supported in the findings reported by Csizér and Dörnyei (2005b; and Chapter 6 of Dörnyei et al., 2006). The most motivated individuals will develop high motivation (correlated to a self-reported strong intention to invest effort to learn the L2) and high levels of all motivational antecedents, including high instrumentality, positive attitudes towards the L2 speakers and culture, and general high interest in learning foreign languages. These motivated individuals exhibit this pattern because of a well-developed ideal L2 self. The highly motivated individual will be also instrumentally or more extrinsically motivated by anticipated pragmatic rewards and utility that we see in learning an L2. After all, '[i]n our idealized image of ourselves we want to appear personally agreeable (associated with positive attitudes towards the L2 community and culture) and also professionally successful (associated with instrumental motives)' (Csizér and Dörnyei, 2005b, pp. 637–8).

Individuals with a lesser quality of motivation to learn an L2, however, will be of three kinds. Some have high instrumentality scores, but have less positive attitudes, cultural interest, and so on; that is, they exhibit less powerful motivation that is nourished by reference to the ought-to self rather than the ideal L2 self. They are still fuelled by motivation, but of an extrinsic kind. Other learners score high on attitudes but low on instrumentality, meaning that they do not see personal relevance or usefulness to being able to know or use the L2. These types of learner are typically even less motivated because, without a sense of instrumentality (by reference to the ought-to self) or integrativeness (by reference to the ideal L2 self), positive attitudes alone cannot sufficiently boost motivational intensity. Finally, the least motivated profile comprises individuals who score low on motivation because they are not moved to exert effort to learn the L2 by either the ideal or the ought-to selves; they simply do not experience sufficient levels of integrativeness, instrumentality, or positive attitudes to L2 speakers and hence are demotivated or amotivated.

The importance placed in the L2 Motivational Self model on the self-concept when explaining the nature of motivation in L2 learning opens the horizon to research on individual differences where cognitive, conative and affective dimensions can be blended and studied as interrelated. We will examine some of such additional influences in Chapter 9.

8.9 BEHOLD THE POWER OF MOTIVATION

We end this chapter on motivation with what is perhaps the most important question that teachers and learners of languages ask themselves: How central is motivation in explaining the relative degree of success that different people encounter when they attempt to learn an additional language? That is, how much can motivation buy us in predicting successful L2 learning?

Based on a meta-analysis of studies produced by Gardner's laboratory, Masgoret and Gardner (2003) concluded that scores on the three AMTB subscales of effort, enjoyment and investment combined consistently explain on average between nine per cent ($r = 0.30$) and 16 per cent ($r = 0.40$) of the variation shared between motivational quantity and L2 achievement, which in their line of work is always defined as course grades, self-reported competence or proficiency test scores, depending on the studies. Although nine to 16 per cent may be thought of as a modest effect size, the finding is nevertheless impressive, because it is based on over 50 independent samples comprising a total of over 8,000 students and it pertains to only one component (motivational quantity) of a multi-construct model. By the same token, we must avoid overinterpreting this finding, as the relationship uncovered by Gardner and associates is a strictly quantitative one, measured via the narrow framework of the AMTB.

Considering more contemporary theories of motivation, Dörnyei (2007) reports unpublished results that suggest the association is much higher, in the range between $r = 0.38$ and 0.78, with an average of $r = 0.59$, which amounts to 35 per cent explained variance. This other evidence draws on contextualized and personality-related views of L2 learning of the new family of motivation theories reviewed in sections 8.7 and 8.8. It comprises scores extracted from more theory-relevant criterion measures than holistic reactions to AMTB statements. For example, more contemporary motivation surveys, such as the one developed by Dörnyei et al. (2006), may include statements and questions about reported intended effort ('how much effort are you prepared to expend in learning X language?' 5 = very much, 1 = not at all) and reported behaviours ('I often watch satellite programmes on TV' 5 = absolutely true, 1 = not true at all). Other researchers have begun to actually measure behaviours, such as amount of participation in L2 activities (Dörnyei, 2002; Dörnyei and Kormos, 2000).

A caution worth keeping in mind, however, is that the association between motivation and behaviour changes as well as L2 learning success has always been viewed as reciprocal, not causal: being motivated nurtures more successful L2 learning, but, conversely, experiencing L2 learning success also boosts motivation to even higher levels, in a reinforcing cycle. Thus, motivation is indeed central in explaining L2 learning, but it cannot be reduced to a few variables, nor can it be exhausted with just a few questionnaires and group data. The challenge that has opened up with the innovations since the late 1990s, and particularly since the turn of the new century, resides in implementing studies that do justice to the complexity and dynamicity of motivation to learn additional languages. Such future studies will have to take into consideration the ebbs and flows of time, the fluctuations that come with changing contexts and the many reciprocal influences that fuel and sustain behaviours and desires needed to learn an additional language.

8.10 SUMMARY

- Motivation is usually understood to refer to the desire to initiate L2 learning and the effort employed to sustain it. We can measure different aspects and dimensions of motivation reliably through questionnaires, by focusing on motivational quantity (e.g. Gardner's AMTB), motivational quality (e.g. Noels and colleagues' LLOS) and antecedents of motivation such as orientations and attitudes.

- Integrativeness is defined as 'a genuine interest in learning the second language in order to come closer to the other language community' (Gardner, 2001, p. 5). While this construct has often been misunderstood and its relevance to foreign language settings was for some time doubted, the centrality of integrativeness seems rather resilient (Csizér and Dörnyei, 2005b). What seems obsolete is the narrow focus on identification with the L2 speakers and culture; integrativeness, however, can be more productively redefined as a drive to close the gap or discrepancy between the actual self and an ideal self, who in highly L2 motivated individuals happens to have been conceived as an L2-speaking self.

- Many antecedents of motivation have been investigated, but broad motives to learn (or orientations) and social perceptions towards the target L2 and community (or attitudes) have been most extensively explicated. Orientations and attitudes vary across contexts for L2 learning, including second versus foreign language contexts, but also unilingual versus multilingual contexts, and contexts where the L2 has attached symbolic values related to globalization or to immediate political conflict.

- A healthy crisis during the mid-1990s called into question the hegemony of Gardner's motivation model and caused the L2 motivation community to turn to a variety of theories of motivation available in wider social psychological research. Particularly useful has been the adaptation of theories that focused on motivational quality rather than quantity, such as self-determination theory.

- Another positive outcome of the crisis was the push for expanding motivation research beyond just a few contexts (and particularly the French–English Canadian context). Many important insights have been possible only after researchers have opened up to investigating diverse contexts.

- Attitudes towards the formal learning context have been shown to exert a lasting and important influence on motivation. In particular, positive attitudes towards the learning context as well as the L2 community and culture (developed through prior positive learning experiences) and current satisfaction with teachers and instruction can boost motivation considerably. It follows that motivational changes, including changes for the better that can be planned and orchestrated in the curriculum, are at the reach of teachers and educators (Dörnyei, 1994).

- Even newer perspectives have been a most recent but also most natural addition to this vibrant landscape of change. The main thrust for these changes is the recognition that L2 motivation is dynamic rather than static, which in turn has resulted in increased attention to time, context and behaviour. These themes are likely to be integrated in future research with what is an important new concept: the ideal L2-speaking self.

8.11 ANNOTATED SUGGESTIONS FOR FURTHER READING

Reading motivation studies demands two things from readers: attention to the detail of questionnaire prompts and correlational results, and imagination to put the theoretical predictions and the quantitative results in a contextual perspective. I hope this chapter has oriented you towards developing both reading instincts. If you are interested in motivation mostly from the practical perspective of teaching ('how do I enhance and nurture my students' motivation?'), I would recommend that you read Dörnyei (1994), followed by the chapter in Dörnyei (2005) devoted to L2 motivation. You can then end with Csizér and Dörnyei (2005b), which will be easier to understand at that point. A complete report of the same large-scale research project is presented by Dörnyei et al. (2006).

If you want to understand motivation in its research context, the two collections by Dörnyei and Schmidt (2001) and Dörnyei and Ushioda (2008) offer an unmatched and truly remarkable variety of quantitative and qualitative studies across diverse contexts plus seminal position papers. Of the many empirical studies cited in this chapter, in my opinion the ones that make for most enjoyable reading are: Clément and Kruidenier (1983), Clément et al. (1994), Ushioda (2001), Lamb (2004) and Donitsa-Schmidt et al. (2004) (which is nicely complemented with the reflection offered by Edwards, 2004, particularly for readers in the United States).

Any of these studies alone, or each read in this proposed sequence, may spark useful insights.

Finally, if your goal is to keep up with the newest L2 motivation research, the best strategy is to regularly search the contents of recent issues of the following key journals: *Language Learning, Modern Language Journal* and *System* (in applied linguistics) and *Journal of Language and Social Psychology* and *Learning and Individual Differences* (in psychology).

9

Affect and other individual differences

Our understanding of why people differ so greatly in how fast, how well and by what means they learn a second language would be incomplete if we did not consider affect and the multiple roles it plays in L2 learning. Let us return briefly to our French learners from Chapter 7. The most pervasive and startling difference in the two experiences recounted in their books resides with the affective relationship Watson and Kaplan appear to have developed towards the L2. As Table 9.1 illustrates, for Watson learning French felt like an assault to his own self ('alien influences seeping down from above'), whereas for Kaplan French felt like nourishing and welcome transformation of the self ('I was full of French, it was holding me up, running through me').

Learning and using a foreign language poses a threat to one's ego. It makes people vulnerable – particularly grown-ups who are accustomed to function perfectly well in their own language. For example, many beginning L2 learners resentfully report feeling 'infantilized' when they use the L2 (Spielmann and Radnofsky, 2001). At least until high levels of proficiency have been reached, someone who is trying out a new language cannot have good control over what they say in the L2, how they say it and what image of self they are able to project for their interlocutors. Similarly, they may be embarrassed and frustrated by the realization that they are unable to understand interlocutors fully and cannot respond appropriately. Perhaps some

Table 9.1
Affect and L2 learning

Richard Watson (1995)	Alice Kaplan (1993)
… I was appalled to find myself using French forms when I was writing English. French was undermining my very being! My personality was in danger of disintegrating! A great clanging of alarm bells was set off in my deep unconscious, irritated by these alien influences seeping down from above (p. 57)	In June I took the plane home. I could feel the French sticking in my throat, the new muscles in my mouth. I had my ear open, on the plane, for the sounds of anyone speaking French because these were my sounds now. I was full of French, it was holding me up, running through me, a voice in my head, a tickle in my ear, likely to be set off at any moment. A counter language. When I got off the plane the American English sounded loud and thudding – like an insult or lapse of faith (p. 70)

individuals (like Alice Kaplan) are better equipped for coping with these self-threatening experiences. By contrast, other individuals (like Richard Watson) suffer under such circumstances, sometimes with disastrous consequences for ultimately learning or not learning the L2. But where do these differences reside? What can psychologically oriented investigations of affect and L2 learning tell us about such differences?

We will examine these questions in this chapter. Before entering our discussion of affect and L2 learning, you should be warned that, although traditionally affect was thought of as encompassing temperamental and emotional aspects of personality (and perhaps some aspects of volition), psychologists nowadays believe that affect both influences and is influenced by cognition as well. Thus, it is difficult to separate affect from cognition and from conation, and the range of dimensions we will examine in this chapter attests to this challenge.

9.1 PERSONALITY AND L2 LEARNING

Can the personality of L2 learners be implicated in the different affective reactions to learning a new language that they experience? We are not in a position to know, because SLA researchers have only begun to investigate this factor, despite the fact that general psychological research on personality has a long history.

Personality can be conceived of as stable traits or qualities in a person, as more dynamic moods that are related to the cognitive processing of emotions, or even as predispositions that have been learned through social experience. In SLA research, trait personality models have been privileged so far, and three main such models and their concomitant instruments have been used. These are shown in Table 9.2. The first is Eysenck's model of personality, which is perhaps the best well-known and most traditional model. It focuses on temperament and is comprised of three traits: Psychoticism, Extraversion and Neuroticism (this is why it is also known as the PEN model). The three traits have a biological basis. Psychoticism is related to aggressivity and is reflected in testosterone levels. Extraversion is related to cortical arousal measured by sweating, skin conductance and brain waves. Neuroticism is related to reactions in the presence of danger and is reflected in activation thresholds in certain parts of the brain, and measured through heart rate, blood pressure, cold hands, sweating and muscular tension. The model and its instrument (Eysenck and Eysenck, 1964) have been empirically widely validated and theoretically supported, but PEN is by now outdated.

A second well-known model of personality was developed by daughter and mother Myers and Briggs. In a telling reminder that affect and cognition are difficult to separate, this model of personality has a strong focus on cognitive style, or preferred ways of processing information (which we will examine in depth in sections 9.5 and 9.6). Myers and Briggs proposed four traits with two opposite poles: extraversion/introversion, feeling/thinking, perceiving/judging and intuiting/sensing. The Myers-Briggs Type Indicator (MBTI) (Myers and McCaulley, 1985) is a well-known survey instrument, widely used despite important

Table 9.2
Three models of personality employed in SLA research

	Eysenck PEN model	Myers-Briggs Personality Type model	Big Five model
Description		**Personality traits**	
Propensity to be calm or nervous under pressure; inclination towards embarrassment, pessimism, guilt, low self-esteem	Stability – Neuroticism		Emotional stability
Social interest, energized by social activities; inward interest, energized by solitary activities	Extraversion – Introversion	Extraversion – Introversion	Extraversion
Propensity to tolerance, aggression, Machiavellian behaviour; propensity to be logic, analytical and objective or to focus on values, warmth and relations	Psychoticism	Feeling – Thinking	Agreeableness
Orientation towards or away from goals, closure, plans, organization, norms		Perceiving – Judging	Conscientiousness
Holistic and meaning-driven vs. realistic and detail-driven perception of stimuli, interest in innovation, tolerance for ambiguity		Intuiting – Sensing	Openness to experience
Focus	Temperament	Cognitive style	Personality
Instrument manual	Eysenck and Eysenck (1964)	Myers and McCaulley (1985)	Costa and McCrae (1992)
SLA sample study	Dewaele (2002)	Moody (1988)	Verhoeven and Vermeer (2002)

reservations that have led to researchers using it less over recent years (see Sternberg and Grigorenko, 1997). The MBTI classifies people into 16 personalities, combining the four positive and four negative poles of preferred ways of responding to the world.

Finally, the five-factor model of personality (FFM, also known as 'the Big Five') emerged out of converging empirical research during the 1990s and has become the dominant contemporary model of personality in psychology, in part because it has succeeded in combining well all preceding ones. Specifically, it accommodates

Eysenck's and Myers-Briggs' models well, as shown in Table 9.2. The Big Five personality model is commonly measured by the NEO Five-Factor Inventory (NEOFFI) (Costa and McCrae, 1992).

Could it be that certain personality types are more attracted than others into the study of foreign languages? In order to address precisely this question, Moody (1988) administered the Myers-Briggs Type Indicator to 491 students who had chosen voluntarily to enrol in first- and second-year European foreign language classes at the University of Hawai'i, and he compared his results to the patterns obtained for a large normative sample of close to 20,000 general college students published by the developers of the MBTI (Myers and McCaulley, 1985). Moody found that in his sample there was a strikingly large proportion of intuiting and thinking personalities, namely, people who tend to rely on memory and associations, visualize relations, look for the big picture and read between the lines (intuiting) but who also are strong at being analytical and logical (thinking). Why would 'intuitive thinkers' be particularly attracted to studying foreign languages? Moody suggested that these are people who like working with language words and symbols (intuitive) as well as applying grammatical analysis and rules (thinking). Interestingly, Ehrman (1990) also found that intuitive thinkers were the most common personality combination type among 79 students and teachers of non-European languages in the US Foreign Service Institute. Ehrman's finding lends important support to Moody's, because her study involved high-aptitude learners studying so-called hard languages (language students in the US Foreign Service Institute typically have to meet a cut-off score of high aptitude of about 130 score on the MLAT to be able to study so-called 'hard' languages like Japanese, Korean, Thai and Turkish). Perhaps somewhat surprisingly, both Moody (1988) and Ehrman (1990) also found that their participants were equally divided between extraverted and introverted types. Considering that the norm established for the US population on the MBTI gives an imbalance in favour of extraverts (75 per cent versus only 25 per cent introverts), we can suspect that, quite surprisingly, disproportionate numbers of introverts are attracted to the study of a foreign language.

Of course, it would be interesting to find out not only what personality types are attracted to learning foreign languages, but also whether certain personality profiles are associated with higher levels of success in learning those foreign languages. Precisely this direct relationship between personality and attained L2 communicative competence was investigated by Ludo Verhoeven and Anne Vermeer (2002) in a study conducted with 69 sixth-graders enrolled in 12 different schools in the Netherlands. They were second-generation immigrant boys and girls between the age of 11 and 13, who came from working-class families where a language other than Dutch was spoken. They had all been schooled in Dutch since kindergarten. Personality in this more contemporary study was defined in terms of the Big Five model. In this kind of research it is typical to administer a questionnaire like the NEOFFI. In this particular study, however, the teachers were asked to observe closely their pupils and rate them on 30 pairs of judgements on a five-point Likert scale. This strategy appears to have worked well for this study, judging from the reported high reliability of the instrument and the fact that upon a principal components analysis, the distributions of scores responded neatly to five components of factors that reflected well the five personality traits and explained 73 per cent of the total variance in the 69 children's personality scores. Communicative competence was defined, following the widely accepted model proposed by Bachman and Palmer (1996), as composed of three dimensions: organizational, pragmatic and strategic competence. Each dimension was measured carefully via eight sets of scores derived from six instruments. The researchers conclude that this battery was a successful operationalization of this complex construct, because when they submitted the scores to principal components analysis they patterned rather clearly around the three theoretically posited dimensions.

What did Verhoeven and Vermeer (2002) show, regarding the relationship between personality and ultimate L2 attainment? In essence, for this sample of sixth-graders schooled in L2 Dutch, the personality factor that was most strongly associated with most measures of attained communicative competence turned out to be openness to experience, which accounted for about 15 to 25 per cent of the shared variance. Extraversion was strongly associated only to two sets of scores (monitoring and strategic competence) and conscientiousness was related to the scores on planning of communicative behaviour. Agreeableness and stability, by contrast, appeared to bear no relationship with attained communicative competence.

Findings such as those reported by Verhoeven and Vermeer (2002), if replicated in future research, would indicate that having curiosity in and feeling stimulated by new experiences, and to a lesser extent being gregarious and sociable, may be valuable personality assets in people who want or need to learn a second language. The study also points at the potential importance of openness to experience for the study of individual differences in L2 learning. Interestingly, this component of personality in the Big Five model resonates with lack of ethnocentrism (Gardner, 2001) and with international posture (Yashima et al., 2004). It is, however, a much wider construct that relates to predispositions that allegedly have a range of consequences for cultural innovation, interpersonal relations and social attitudes (McCrae, 1996). It has also been found to be related to sophisticated play behaviour at preschool age and self-confidence during adolescence (Abe, 2005). In adults, Sternberg and Grigorenko (1997) note that openness to experience is also related to the construct of intelligence, and Albert and Kormos (2004) remark that it is also related to measured creativity. Openness to experience, therefore, emerges as a fruitful site for future personality research in SLA, particularly in view of Verhoeven and Vermeer's intriguing and convincing findings.

9.2 EXTRAVERSION AND SPEAKING STYLES

The personality trait of extraversion has always attracted the imagination of L2 researchers, but the results were initially so mixed that they led to disillusionment and avoidance of research in this area, making extraversion an 'unloved variable' in the L2 field (Dewaele and Furnham, 1999). In the late 1990s, however, SLA researcher Jean-Marc Dewaele and psychologist Adrian Furnham joined forces to champion a revival of L2 work on this variable, arguing for its importance at the crossroads between affect and cognition. They synthesized convincing evidence from L1 studies showing that extraversion and speaking styles are related. Dewaele and Furnham (1999) point at three robust L1 findings in psychology: (a) extraverts have better short-term memory, (b) they are more impervious to stress and anxiety than introverts and (c) they speak more fluently than introverts. How do these predictions connect personality to ultimate L2 learning success? They argue that at least the first two assets should logically translate into a critical advantage when it comes to L2 speech production, namely more available and more efficiently allocated cognitive resources, which alone may explain the third asset of an oral fluency advantage. If extraversion were shown to be conducive to more self-confidence and less anxiety about using the L2, one would expect to find that extraverted people are better able to maintain higher degrees of fluency when speaking in an L2, even under stressful conditions. By implication, one might also expect that extraverts would seek and obtain more frequent and richer opportunities to use the L2 than introverts. All this in turn may lead extraverts to obtain higher grades in second language classrooms and to achieve better learning outcomes in the long run. Dewaele and Furnham furnished evidence supporting their hypotheses in two studies.

Dewaele (2002) administered the Eysenck Personality Inventory to 100 last-year high-school students, approximately half of whom were male and half female, in Belgium. He also measured their reported self-confidence and anxiety levels as well as their recorded class grades. The study is unique in that all participants were multilingual individuals, and thus the relationship between personality and confidence levels in their L2 versus their L3 could be compared. Most of the participants were L1 Dutch speakers, and all had studied French since the age of ten and English since the age of 12 (and about half of them had also studied an L4, German or Spanish). Dewaele found that psychoticism and (to a weaker extent) extraversion and neuroticism were predictors of anxiety for L3 English. The relationships were similar in magnitude for L2 French anxiety, but statistically not significant. (Curiously, overall levels of anxiety were higher for L2 French than for L3 English, which Dewaele interprets to be a function of sociopolitical historical attitudes towards French in Belgium.) This pattern of results should be evaluated with caution because it is not supported in another study by MacIntyre and Charos (1996), who found no evidence for a link between personality and anxiety.

More firm evidence was gleaned in Dewaele and Furnham (2000), who investigated the relationship between extraversion and fluent speech production among 25 L2 French learners in Belgium. They were all Flemish (Dutch L1) university students between the ages of 18 and 21, and they had studied French as a foreign language in high school for six to eight years (for about 1,200 hours). They were rated on their extraversion via the Eysenck Personality Inventory. The researchers then examined seven linguistic qualities manifested in 30 minutes of speech per learner. They found reasonably sized correlations (in the $r = 0.40$ to 0.55 range) between extraversion and six of the seven variables, and particularly a clear effect for the fluency measure of speech rate. Across the board, the more extraverted a speaker was, the faster speech rate he or she was likely to display. The speech had been elicited under two conditions, a high-stress ten-minute oral exam situation and a more relaxed untimed conversation with the researchers. It turned out that the stress of the situation made a noticeable impact on introverted, but not extraverted, speakers. Specifically, there was suggestive evidence that, under stressful conditions, the introverted participants achieved higher lexical richness and more explicit language but at the expense of engaging in more hesitation-marked lexical searches and in more disfluency. Overall, then, an advantage in fluency for extraverts was counterbalanced by an advantage in complexity and lexical richness for introverts. By comparison, morphological accuracy was the only variable examined by Dewaele and Furnham (2000) that did not yield any correlations with either extraversion or introversion.

9.3 LEARNER ORIENTATION TO COMMUNICATION AND ACCURACY

Related to the findings we have just discussed, Dewaele and Furnham (1999) also make an interesting theoretical link between the personality trait of extraversion/introversion and concern for accuracy versus communication. They summarize the point in the following way:

> It is also possible that extraverts and introverts make, consciously or unconsciously, different choices in what has been called the speed–accuracy trade-off … , especially when they are under pressure. The extraverts, being risk takers … may opt for more speed in the speech production, whereas the greater cautiousness and fear of punishment of the introverts may cause them to slow down, taking more heed of the maxim 'be sure brain is engaged before putting mouth into gear'.
>
> (p. 536)

This is an old concern in the field that dates back to the 1970s, when such individual tendencies were first noted and Krashen (1978) coined the labels of 'monitor underuser' and 'monitor overuser' to characterize them. Monitor underusers tend to be overly focused on communication to the point of miscalculated risk-taking L2 behaviour, whereas monitor overusers tend to be overly mindful of accuracy to the point of anxiety or reticence. Nevertheless, the matter has rarely been pursued systematically and whether the antecedents of such predispositions are indirectly related to personality traits such as extraversion is unknown.

Hungarian researcher Judit Kormos (1999) investigated whether differences in speaking predispositions towards communication or accuracy would be reflected in differences in speech production, and particularly in self-correction moves. Rather than looking at extraversion or some other general personality trait, Kormos devised a questionnaire to get at each speaker's concern for communicating their message either fluently or accurately and for avoiding mistakes. She recruited 30 L2 English user participants from Hungary, almost all of them females. Of them, ten were secondary-school students aged 16 to 18 with pre-intermediate proficiency, ten were college first-year English majors aged 18 to 22 with minimal exposure to second language contexts but with advanced or upper-intermediate proficiency, and the last ten were elementary-school teachers who formerly taught Russian and were in the process of being retrained to teach English, and whose proficiency and ages ranged widely. After taking a proficiency test and completing the brief questionnaire, the participants were asked to do a five-minute role-play activity with the researcher, the task being to reserve a private room in a restaurant. Following the recording of this activity, each participant did a retrospective interview in which they explained choices and perceptions as they listened to their speech, which later helped the researcher identify instances of self-correction.

Based on their responses on the questionnaire, Kormos assigned the 30 speakers to the category of: monitor underusers, who seemed strongly oriented towards communication; monitor overusers, who were strongly concerned with accuracy; and average monitor users, who did not seem to hold strong attitudes towards either communication or accuracy. After accounting for proficiency differences, speaking styles were found to matter only in terms of fluency and one of seven measures of self-correction. Specifically, monitor overusers clearly spoke less fluently and rephrased themselves more frequently, looking for a better way to express themselves. However, they did not self-correct lexical or grammatical mistakes more frequently overall than the other groups. This observation resonates with the results presented by Dewaele and Furnham (2000). Although Kormos's findings were somewhat disappointing, given that only two of eight measures yielded the theoretically posited connections, it is possible that a relationship between personality and speaking style, on the one hand, and monitoring behaviour during speech production, on the other, would indeed emerge in larger-scale studies. That said, neither Kormos (1999) nor Dewaele and Furnham (2000) reported effects for personality factors in terms of accuracy. Thus, another plausible prediction is that personality and learners' concern for either communication or accuracy may have an impact on speaking style by triggering trade-offs between fluency and complexity, rather than fluency and accuracy. The latter, however, is the possibility usually favoured in information-processing theoretical predictions, as in the earlier quote by Dewaele and Furnham (1999) and in the work of Skehan (see, for example, Skehan and Foster, 2001).

Relationships between personality and L2 learning are intriguing and have only begun to be explored by SLA researchers. In the end, however, it would be misguided to imagine that some mysterious inherent property of people's predispositions affects how fast and how well they can learn languages. Rather, personality traits such as openness to experience, extraversion, concern towards communication or accuracy, and so on, influence goals and actions, and it is then these goals and actions that have an impact on eventual achievement. For example, intellectually curious and interpersonally inclined people are likely to seek and have added exposure to (and interaction in) the L2, which in turn may enhance their chances to develop faster and better towards full L2 communicative competence. That is, personality is related to L2 achievement in as much as it shapes the types of experience people seek or avoid.

9.4 FOREIGN LANGUAGE ANXIETY

The variable of anxiety has been mostly studied in SLA in its own right, rather than in connection with personality. Simply put, some individuals report experiencing intense feelings of apprehension, tension, and even fear, when they think of foreign languages. As MacIntyre and Gardner (1994) note, this propensity to feel anxious is specific to foreign language learning, like the consistent apprehension some college students report in relation to situations that call upon the use of mathematics, statistics or public speaking. High-anxiety foreign language students exhibit many symptoms, but the most common ones are two: freezing up when asked to say something in the L2 in front of the class, and blanking on the right answers during a language test despite having studied hard and even knowing the answers.

The two researchers that have been most central in advancing our knowledge about language anxiety are Elaine Horwitz in the United States and Peter MacIntyre in Canada. Although both research programmes are compatible and have produced convergent results, it is useful to highlight some differences. Horwitz has focused on classroom-related types of anxiety experienced by foreign language learners who may not have many opportunities to use the L2 outside the instructional setting, and her explorations have concentrated on psychological states and self-beliefs. By way of contrast, MacIntyre has emphasized communicative anxiety as rooted in direct contact with L2 speakers in second language settings, and he has pursued explanations that emphasize social attitudes and behavioural communication correlates. As we will see in section 9.5, these latter emphases have eventually given rise to the investigation of willingness to communicate (WTC) as the main construct, to which anxiety is only a contributing force or antecedent.

The best well-known measure of anxiety is the Foreign Language Classroom Anxiety Scale (FLCAS), developed by Horwitz and colleagues (Horwitz et al., 1986). It comprises 33 five-point Likert scale items, mostly statements about anxiety when speaking or producing the language and more general apprehensive attitudes towards foreign language learning. Examples of these items are: 'Even if I am well prepared for language class, I feel anxious about it' and 'I always feel that the other students speak the foreign language better than I do'. Another instrument is the Input, Processing and Output Anxiety Scales (IPOAS), developed by MacIntyre and Gardner (1994). It includes 18 five-point Likert scale items specifically related to anxiety caused at the input stage of encountering aural or written input ('I get flustered unless French is spoken very slowly and deliberately'), the processing stage of comprehending messages and figuring out words and meanings ('I am anxious with French because, no matter how hard I try, I have trouble understanding it') and the output stage of producing evidence of what one has learned and can do in speaking or writing ('I may know the proper French expression but when I am nervous it just won't come out'). Based on the findings reported by MacIntyre and Gardner (1994) and the validation study conducted by Bailey et al. (2000), the two instruments correlate with each other acceptably and are two equally good alternatives to measure foreign language anxiety.

Scores on the FLCAS and the IPOAS have been found to be moderately associated with course grades, suggesting that high-anxiety students expect and do indeed receive lower grades in their foreign language courses than do low-anxiety students. In addition, substantial negative correlations in the order of $r = -0.45$ to $r = -0.65$ (that is, 20 to 40 per cent explained shared variance) have been obtained across studies between anxiety scores and scores on direct measures of L2 proficiency, whether global grammar tests or tasks requiring speaking, listening, writing and vocabulary learning. This is a robust indication that high, debilitating levels of anxiety do interfere with academic achievement in foreign language classes. Besides lower achievement, several other more subtle effects experienced by overly anxious students have been uncovered. These include slower speed in their learning and processing of L2 materials, a tendency to underestimate their true L2 competence and a propensity to engage in risk-avoiding behaviours, such as speaking less and attempting less complex messages (Steinberg and Horwitz, 1986; MacIntyre and Gardner, 1994; MacIntyre et al., 1997).

Where does foreign language anxiety originate? Recent studies underscore the importance of self-perception and self-concept. For example, Onwuegbuzie et al. (1999) found that among 210 university students enrolled in foreign language courses in the US, anxiety levels were associated to low sense of self-worth and low perceptions of their own general academic ability. For people who may have low self-esteem to begin with, feelings of vulnerability in L2 learning situations may be particularly intense. If the threat is unmanageable and anxiety rises, it will contribute to these students' poor performance in situations where they feel evaluated and anticipate failure.

Counterproductive beliefs about language learning (nicely explicated in Horwitz, 1988) can also contribute to foreign language anxiety in a different way, namely by leading to high levels of disappointment and intense sense of failure. Misguided myths about language learning include that one should be able to study vocabulary and grammar and then speak or write without mistakes, that learning a foreign language well means being able to pronounce it like a native speaker, or that a foreign language can be learned in two years of college. In one of the rare published anxiety studies carried out outside North America, Gregersen and Horwitz (2002) found that these perfectionist attitudes and unforgiving expectations strongly characterized the four most anxious students in a sample of 78 EFL second-year students in a Chilean university. For example, one of these high-anxiety students said (p. 567):

(1)   I am bothered a little [about my errors] because I get nervous, and I think that the other person thinks that I don't know how to speak. It happens a lot. I try to pronounce the best I can, and when I try to pronounce better, my

pronunciation gets worse, because I get flustered. That is, I get flustered because I sometimes pronounce words badly. I try so hard to pronounce perfectly.

These concerns for accuracy resonate with Kormos's (1999) investigation of accuracy- versus communication-oriented learners examined in section 9.3. It is important to note, however, that perfectionism does not always need to have a negative effect. Thus, for example, Purcell and Suter (1980) found that concern for having an excellent pronunciation among their sample of 61 international students learning English, all post-pubertal learners, was one among the four best predictors of ratings of L2 pronunciation (the other three factors were the L1 background, aptitude for oral mimicry, and length of L2 residence). Elliott (1995) found that the same concern to develop a native-like accent was the most significant variable positively correlating with L2 pronunciation among college-level L2 Spanish students. Similarly, the exceptional learners whose outstanding pronunciation made them pass for native speakers of English in Bongaerts (1999) and of German in Moyer (1999) reported that they were highly motivated to sound like native speakers (and, notably, they had also received high-quality instruction specifically on pronunciation issues). These findings remind us that some degree of tension can help people invest extra effort and push themselves to perform better. This is what we would call facilitating anxiety. As MacIntyre and Gardner (1994) note, anxiety feelings reach debilitating levels only when anxious students engage in self-deprecatory and negative thoughts that detract from concentration and disperse mental effort that should normally be invested in the foreign language learning task at hand.

9.5 WILLINGNESS TO COMMUNICATE AND L2 CONTACT

Adopting a more recent social psychological tradition, anxiety has begun to be studied under the wider construct of willingness to communicate (WTC), which was developed in the field of communication in the 1980s and was imported into SLA a decade later by Canadian researchers Richard Clément, Peter MacIntyre and their associates. In the first language, WTC is associated to a complex of personality sub-traits such as introversion, shyness, apprehension of communication and reticence. WTC in the L1 is thought to systematically predict how inclined people are to initiate communication, when they have a free choice to do so, across situations and interlocutors (e.g. face-to-face, in writing and in technology-mediated environments). In the L2 literature WTC has been called 'the most immediate determinant of L2 use' (Clément et al., 2003, p. 191), and its independence from WTC in the L1 has been firmly established by Baker and MacIntyre (2000). What are then the antecedents of L2 WTC, if not L1 WTC? It turns out that WTC in the L2 is predicted to a large extent by L2 communicative confidence and to a lesser extent by L2 attitudes.

An individual's **communicative confidence** in the L2 greatly contributes to her or his WTC in the L2. Across studies, the correlations observed between these two variables have been in the range of upper 0.60s all the way to high 0.80s. The initial work of Clément, in particular, was instrumental in showing that L2 communicative confidence can be best measured by eliciting learner responses tapping two distinct affective responses when they use the L2: how relaxed or nervous they are (**anxiety**, an affective variable) and how competent or incompetent they feel (**self-perceived competence**, a cognitive self-evaluation variable). In turn, Clément et al. (2003) have shown that these positive or negative feelings of anxiety and competence will be related to the frequency and (even to a greater extent) to the perceived quality of past L2 contact (e.g. in the family, neighbourhood, workplace or school), in a pattern where frequency and quality influence each other. In other words, the two traits of communicative anxiety and self-perceived competence, while stable, are shaped by past experiences through contacts with L2 speakers, and both contribute to the degree of L2 communicative confidence.

In addition, it appears that the two antecedents of L2 communicative confidence take a different weight in explaining WTC depending on the learning context. Namely, anxiety will be more predictive of L2 confidence in settings where use of the L2 is high, such as second language and immersions contexts, whereas in settings where use of L2 is low, such as foreign language contexts, it is perceived communicative competence that will be more related to L2 confidence. WTC work carried out in such different settings as Canada (Baker and MacIntyre, 2000) and Japan (Yashima, 2002) converges to this same conclusion. Baker and MacIntyre (2000) offer the following explanation. Speakers in a high-use L2 environment have typically developed higher communicative competence and are relatively accustomed to successful experiences. Therefore, any salient negative experience is more intensely lived and remembered. In addition, the communication demands they face are more complex and entail higher stakes than in low-use L2 environments. All this leads to anxiety contributing more strongly to their formed L2 communicative confidence. On the other hand, speakers in a low-use L2 environment are still developing their communicative competence, their contact with L2 interlocutors is rare and the communicative demands placed on them are less complex and less consequential to their daily lives. Thus, they are likely to worry more intensely about how well they believe they will be able to function in the L2 with their incipient abilities and less about seldom lived experiences of contact (positive or negative) with speakers of the L2. All this explains why their perception of current communicative competence contributes more strongly to their formed communicative confidence than anxiety.

Although WTC is about intentions, the point of understanding intentions is to help predict behaviours. Yet, the link between WTC in the L2 and frequency of communicative behaviour has been difficult to establish. No SLA study has attempted to study WTC responses vis-à-vis actual observation of communicative behaviour, but the few studies that have attempted to look at the relationship of WTC with self-reported frequency of L2 communication have yielded only tenuous correlations in the $r = 0.20$ order. This association appears small by comparison to the correlation values in the range between $r = 0.45$ and $r = 0.60$ which are typically found in psychology studies that investigate the link between strength of intention and goal achievement (see Sheeran, 2002; Gollwitzer and Sheeran, 2006).

Despite the weak quantitative results, **self-reported contact** with L2 speakers appears to be an important factor in WTC because it plays reciprocal roles as antecedent and consequence of WTC. Contact is also mediated by L2 attitudes formed in particular learning contexts and sociocultural milieus. Thus, Clément et al. (2001) suggest that in contexts of low L2 use (e.g. unilingual contexts in Canada or foreign language contexts elsewhere), actual L2 competence and L2 self-confidence are weak (and therefore WTC levels are low as well) because opportunities to use the L2 are low. These researchers predict that under such premises empathy and affinity for the minority L2 group may help encourage learners to seek more L2 contact, which in turn may boost their confidence. And indeed in the data produced by Clément et al. (2001), stronger identification levels went hand in hand with higher self-reported frequencies of L2 contact among such low-L2-use speakers. By contrast, identification with the L2 group ceased to be important in explaining reported frequency of L2 use for high-L2-use speakers (who had also developed advanced levels of competence and were more generally confident).

There is other evidence of the reciprocal relationship between contact, self-confidence and attitudes, even in foreign language settings, where L2 use is low and is likely to involve more distant activities such as meeting tourists, watching TV channels in the L2, and so on. For example, Dörnyei and Csizér (2005) found that the more frequent the L2 contact reported by their Hungarian respondents, the more generally self-confident of their communicative competence the students were likely to be. In the low-L2-use context of learning English as a foreign language in Japan, the construct of international posture developed by Tomoko Yashima and her colleagues is the closest equivalent to 'identification' or empathy for L2 members (see section 8.5). Yashima et al. (2004) found that students with a high score on the international posture were somewhat more willing to engage in communication in the L2, although the direct contribution of international posture to WTC was small ($r = 0.27$).

In sum, it has been well established that WTC in the L2 is largely predicted by L2 communicative confidence (which itself is predicted by anxiety and self-perceived competence) and to a lesser but nevertheless considerable extent by L2 attitudes. Such attitudes are shaped by the frequency and quality of past L2 contact but they also help shape willingness to seek and engage in future L2 contact. Whether WTC develops in second or foreign language contexts also influences the relative importance of antecedents and consequences. In light of theses findings, change in WTC becomes a theoretical necessity, a function of increased proficiency and wider communication experiences accrued through participation across different contexts that foster diverse circumstances for L2 use. For example, the shape of WTC may change as learners move from one learning context to another, as they gain substantial competence as a result of myriad voluntary or involuntary changes in their life circumstances that are related to work, immigration, marriage, and so on, or as they learn yet another language that alters the stability of WTC-related factors previously associated with the first learned L2. Future studies will hopefully elucidate how WTC and its related antecedents and consequences can change as a function of context and time. (You can compare this social psychological view of contact and willingness to communicate with the sociocultural view of access and participation that will be presented in Chapter 10, section 10.14.)

9.6 COGNITIVE STYLES, FIELD INDEPENDENCE AND FIELD SENSITIVITY

In Chapter 7 we examined the notion that cognitive abilities (that is, people's aptitude profiles and complexes) influence their capacity for learning languages with ease. But people do not only differ in their cognitive abilities. It is a well-known fact in psychology that they also differ in the ways they prefer to put their cognitive abilities to use. For example, different people hold different 'typically preferred modes of processing information' (Sternberg and Grigorenko, 1997, p. 700) or ways in which they feel comfortable when perceiving, remembering and using information for problem solving and for learning. Such preferences are known under the terms 'cognitive styles' or 'learning styles'. Cognitive and learning styles are neither good nor bad, but simply bipolar dimensions (e.g. holistic vs analytic; reflective vs impulsive; field-dependent vs. field-independent), with potential strengths and weaknesses on both extremes, and sometimes with mixed characteristics on sub-dimensions along multiple style continua. In this section we will examine field dependence and independence (FDI), which is the cognitive style with the longest research tradition in SLA. In section 9.7 we will look at more encompassing models that attempt to explain cognitive style profiles involved in L2 learning.

Field dependence/independence is a construct imported to SLA from psychology. It is usually measured via the Embedded Figures Test (Gottschaldt, 1926), in which simple forms are hidden in larger figures and the mean time it takes to discover those forms yields a score. The higher the score (i.e. the less time spent), the more field independent a person is. In an oft-cited L2 study, Chapelle and Green (1992) examined 32 correlations between the embedded figures test and various measures of L2 proficiency yielded across ten studies published in the 1970s and 1980s. They found that only a few of those correlations were statistically significant in the subset of primary studies where some other cognitive ability (often mathematic ability and language aptitude) had been measured and partialled out. Thus, they noted that a considerable challenge in researching FDI is to tease out ability on the Embedded Figures Test from other non-verbal abilities. Nevertheless, an inspection of the data provided by Chapelle and Green in their Table 1 shows relatively consistent findings. The median of statistically significant correlations is about $r = 0.35$, whether or not other factors are partialled out. This points at a modest but non-spurious relationship between FDI and L2 proficiency.

Another challenge resulting from measuring FDI via the Embedded Figures Test alone, as noted by Sternberg and Grigorenko (1997), is that the performance elicited is more readily interpretable as an ability than as a cognitive style, yielding as it does a score that reflects a 'higher is better' evaluative assumption (as when we look at an IQ score of 100 or an MLAT score of 135). The valuation, furthermore, is clearly biased in favour of the field-independent pole in both psychology and SLA. The theoretical ammunition for a truly bipolar interpretation is nevertheless obvious: The ability to cognitively restructure spatial information (e.g. by spotting simple forms while ignoring the larger figures which hide them) is predicted to be high for field-independent profiles but low for field-dependent ones, whereas an interpersonal orientation is predicted to be low for field-independent, but high for field-dependent profiles. Consequently, as Canadian psychologists Johnson et al. (2000) argued, in the context of L2 learning field independence may be related to better success with detecting patterns in the L2 input, dealing with grammatical rules and being able to self-monitor during L2 production, whereas field dependence may facilitate learning holistically from input via memorization as well as learning through communication with others by picking up pragmatic and social cues. When they inspected oral performance data elicited from 28 L1 English students and 29 ESL students at a Canadian university, they did find evidence that field dependence was associated with higher communicative abilities. They speculated that field dependence may foster the holistic learning of patterned formulas and expressions that contribute to fluent communicative expression.

Ehrman and Leaver (2003) have addressed the challenge of investigating FDI as a truly bipolar cognitive style in a different way. They have proposed two separate labels that help unpack the two poles of the FDI construct as two distinct constructs: field independence and field sensitivity. They define field independence as the ability to see the trees in the forest, as it were, and to detect important information and separate it out from its context, whereas they reserve the term 'field sensitivity' to denote the ability to employ 'a floodlight to maintain awareness of the entire forest, registering the presence of all the flora, fauna, and moment-to-moment changes in the environment' (p. 397). According to Ehrman and Leaver, the best language learners can learn new material well both in and out of context and therefore can be expected to score high on field independence as well as on field sensitivity.

9.7 LEARNING STYLE PROFILES

A plethora of other learning styles has been researched in SLA with varying degrees of small success. In Australia, Ken Willing (1988) first interviewed 40 teachers and 25 adult ESL learners and later surveyed 517 more learners, using learning styles models and scales developed in psychology and made up of four learning profiles: convergers, divergers, accommodators and assimilators. The findings led to a number of rich recommendations for immigrant education policy and for programme, staff and materials development. Because of the practical nature of the project, however, this study has regrettably had little theoretical impact on other SLA efforts. In the United States, Joy Reid (1995) created an instrument designed to tap the preferred sensory learning styles of ESL and EFL learners, such as visual, auditory, kinaesthetic/tactile and group/individualistic orientation towards learning. However, subsequent attempts by other researchers to validate the instrument psychometrically have failed.

The most promising model of language learning style has been developed by Ehrman and Leaver (2003), based on years of field pilots with adult language students in the US Foreign Service Institute (see Ehrman, 1990, 1998, cited in Chapter 7, section 7.14 and in 9.1). It consists of a binary continuum, the **synopsis–ectasis** dimension. According to these researchers, 'the distinction ... addresses the degree of conscious control of learning desired or needed' (p. 395). Synopsis refers to the preference to rely on holistic, at-a-glance perception of information. Synoptic learners thrive with subconscious learning approaches because they are intuitive learners. 'Ectasis' is a neologism coined by the researchers from the Greek word *ectasis*, meaning 'stretching out'. It refers to the preference to rely on detail and system when processing new information. Ectenic learners thrive when they can exercise conscious control over their learning, because they are methodic learners. Ehrman and Leaver note that synopsis is related to right-hemisphere-dominant learners and ectasis to left-hemisphere-dominant learners. The continuum is measured via ten subscales (for a total of 30 items – three per scale), most of which are well grounded in previous literature. Particularly interesting in the proposed model is the rich characterization of ways in which information may be processed. In particular the six scales outlined in Table 9.3 are interesting because, arguably, they might be related to the differential ability to notice new features of the L2 (Schmidt, 1995; see Chapter 5), an ability that is also posited to matter a great deal in new conceptualizations of aptitude (see Chapter 7, section 7.11).

Table 9.3
Six of the ten dimensions in the Ehrman and Leaver (2003) Learning Style Model

Learning style	Definition
random–sequential	How information is structured (by internal or systematic and planned criteria)
holistic–specific	The level of attention paid to detail during processing
gestalt–analytic	The level of analysis done on information during processing
global–particular	The top-down or bottom-up preferences in attentional direction while processing new material
levelling–sharpening	Whether learners prefer to store and recall information in memory by relying on loosely merged episodic memory and looking for commonalities, or by relying on highly detailed and differentiated, factual long-term memory encodings
impulsive–reflective	The speed of processing

In his authoritative evaluation of this and other SLA work on cognitive and learning styles, Dörnyei (2005) notes that Ehrman and Leaver's (2003) framework holds great promise, but he also warns that it will need to be tested and modified across a range of contexts and learner populations.

9.8   LEARNING STRATEGIES

If styles are preferred ways of processing information, strategies are conscious mental and behavioural procedures that people engage in with the aim to gain control over their learning process. Kaplan (1993), our successful French learner, provides a good illustration in the following excerpt, where she remembers using an intricate web of vocabulary learning strategies while in boarding school in Switzerland, at age 15 (p. 48):

> (2)   I always had five or six new words on a personal in-progress-list. Each time I heard one of the words on my list, I would notice the context and try to figure out the meaning. When I thought I had the meaning I would wait for the word to come up again, so I could check if my meaning was still right. Finally, I'd try the word out to see if a strange look came over the face of the person I was talking to. If it didn't, I knew I was home free. I had a new word.

It is worth reiterating that with learning strategies, as with other individual difference variables, the boundaries between cognition and affect blur. This is particularly true because when humans want to exert better control over their thoughts and actions they strategize about their emotions as much as about their cognitive and conative processes.

The first empirical studies of L2 learning strategies appeared in the mid-1970s, in a line of work that soon became known as 'the good language learner' research. Among the most classic citations from these initial years is a monograph by that title, written by a team of Canadian researchers (Naiman et al., 1978). The team's goal was to understand any and all factors that might help explain why some people are particularly successful in their quest to master an L2, whereas many are not. These early findings quickly indicated that beyond natural language ability (i.e. aptitude) and personal commitment to learning (i.e. motivation), these 'good' learners were also characterized by a high degree of active involvement in their own learning processes. Joan Rubin (1975) summarized the first-generation findings in six key attributes of good learners, all related to strategic behaviour:

- they are good guessers
- they pay analytical attention to form but also attend to meaning
- they try out their new knowledge
- they monitor their production and that of others

- they constantly practise
- they cope well with feelings of vulnerability for the sake of putting themselves in situations where they communicate and learn.

You will notice that all six attributes of strategic behaviour are nested in Kaplan's description of her vocabulary learning strategy use in (2).

Building on the success of these initial efforts, many SLA researchers continued to invest great energy into studying L2 learning strategies in the 1980s. These efforts gave way to two separate but essentially compatible traditions in the United States (Chaudron, 2006): the observation-based research programme conducted by Anna Chamot and colleagues, and the questionnaire-based research on learning strategies developed by Rebecca Oxford and colleagues.

A series of descriptive studies conducted by O'Malley, Chamot and colleagues in the mid-1980s were the first ones to attempt to document the use of learning strategies observationally and behaviourally and in connection with specific language task types. The research methodology rested on the use of structured interviews in which small groups of three to five students were asked to recall or imagine strategies they would use in the context of hypothetical L2 tasks and situations. In some of the studies, think-aloud verbal accounts while performing actual L2 tasks were also used. The studies encompassed ESL as well as foreign language learning and they included students of beginning, as well as intermediate, levels of proficiency enrolled in both high-school and college settings.

The most important of the studies was a three-year project involving three successive phases and summarized in O'Malley and Chamot (1990). The cross-sectional phase confirmed previous strategy findings but also revealed some differences between the high-school foreign language Spanish and the college foreign language Russian samples, apparently related to the tasks that were typical of the respective curricula in each setting. The longitudinal phase focused on documenting the development of strategy use over a school year by 13 high-school students of Spanish and six college students of Russian. The findings confirmed and expanded those of previous studies and led to the generation of an exhaustive list of learning strategies, classified into the three categories of cognitive, metacognitive and social-affective strategies (see O'Malley and Chamot, 1990, pp. 137–9). However, no clear patterns were found in terms of longitudinal change per se. During the third, strategy training phase, three Russian instructors and one Spanish teacher were observed teaching strategies on nine occasions over two semesters. The training results were largely disappointing. Overall, the research programme contributed by Chamot and her colleagues offers the following sobering insight: the types of strategy used by L2 learners can be determined to a great extent by course objectives and course syllabus, by students' motivation for learning the language and by the task itself.

Oxford's prolific strategy work is based on a long inventory and an accompanying instrument, the Strategy Inventory for Language Learning (SILL) (Oxford, 1990). The SILL elicits levels of reported strategy frequency via five-point Likert scales. Six types of strategy are posited in the model: affective (e.g. 'encouraging oneself when afraid to speak'), social (e.g. 'practising the L2 with other people'), metacognitive (e.g. 'having clear goals for improving one's own skills', 'noticing one's own mistakes'), cognitive (e.g. 'guessing from context', 'writing notes'), memory-related (e.g. 'connecting word sounds with a mental image or picture') and compensatory (e.g. 'using circumlocutions'). This classification is essentially compatible with the three types proposed by O'Malley and Chamot (1990), a conclusion supported by the findings reported by Hsiao and Oxford (2002) in their factor analysis of SILL responses from 517 Taiwanese college-level EFL students. Oxford's survey approach to L2 learning strategies has been frequently used. This popularity may be in part explained by the convenience of a questionnaire with good psychometric properties that makes it easy for other researchers to adopt the framework. For example, Peacock and Ho (2003) used the SILL in a large-scale study in Hong Kong. By surveying 1,006 university students and further interviewing 48 of them, they were able to uncover some differences in the L2 learning strategy use related to academic discipline, age and gender.

Two concerns have been repeatedly raised regarding the value of studying L2 learning strategies as a potential source of differential L2 success: contextualization and theorization. The need for a more contextualized understanding of strategies became particularly clear in the early 1990s, when a few researchers turned to the in-depth case study of 'unsuccessful' learners (e.g. Vann and Abraham, 1990) and found that these students often used as many strategies as so-called 'good' language learners, just not quite in a manner that could be considered sophisticated or appropriate to the tasks and goals at hand. Furthermore, when Oxford and Nyikos (1989) surveyed 1,200 foreign language learners in US universities, they corroborated the warning by Chamot and colleagues that many reported strategies are linked to the pressures of courses and curricula, for example, driven by tests and grammatical discrete-point learning goals that still dominate much foreign language college instruction. In light of such findings, the importance of taking into account the curricular context when investigating L2 learning strategies has been underscored by other researchers. It may also be important, as MacIntyre and Noel (1996) tried to do, to explore empirically learner perceptions of difficulty and usefulness of particular strategies across specific contexts of use.

Other important but less heeded observations regarding context were contributed by Politzer and McGroarty (1985), who investigated the reported learning behaviours of 18 Asian and 19 Hispanic ESL graduate students vis-à-vis their proficiency gains over an eight-week intensive course in California. They found consistently lower self-reported levels of strategy use in the Asian sample by comparison to the Hispanic sample, but no relationship between strategies and actual proficiency gains across the two groups. They noted that many of the strategies in their questionnaire referred to behaviours that may be culturally inappropriate for non-Western students, such as asking the teacher or other interlocutors to repeat when something is not understood, or correcting fellow students when they make mistakes. Politzer and McGroarty conclude their study by suggesting that what researchers classify as 'good' or 'successful' L2 learning behaviours may actually suffer from rather ethnocentric assumptions (p. 119). From a sociocultural perspective (see Chapter 10), the appellation of 'good' language learner has other shortcomings that are eloquently exposed by Norton and Toohey (2001).

The need to theorize the construct of 'strategic behaviour' has been voiced particularly insistently from a social psychological perspective by both Peter Skehan and Zoltán Dörnyei over the years (see, for example, Dörnyei and Skehan, 2003). They have noted that, in the end, L2 learning strategic behaviour cannot and should not be reduced to a taxonomy of observed heuristics and reported mental processes (O'Malley and Chamot, 1990) or an inventory of self-reported frequencies of strategy use (Oxford, 1990). The solution to theorizing learning strategies may have been found by Dörnyei (2005), who has pointed at self-regulation theory as a framework that offers SLA researchers a theoretically principled way to reconceptualize their thinking about strategic behaviour during L2 learning. We conclude our chapter with a brief examination of this promising direction.

9.9 THE FUTURE PROMISE OF AN ALL-ENCOMPASSING FRAMEWORK: SELF-REGULATION THEORY

The starting point of self-regulation theory is that human endeavours are always goal-directed, intentional, effortful and voluntary (Boekaerts et al., 2006). In the face of multiple (often competing and almost always hierarchically interconnected) goals and ensuing environmental challenges, humans are capable of achieving the ends they choose to pursue because they are able to self-regulate their behaviour. Self-regulation involves *creative* and *conscious* efforts that address many facets of action control, including 'selfdirected problem analysis, commitment building, progress evaluation, and long-term maintenance' (Karoly et al., 2005, p. 302). Moreover, it is not only actions and thoughts but also feelings that are self-regulated, since coping with emotions and negative affect is crucial when goals become difficult or even unattainable. Thus, one novel advantage of self-regulation theory is that cognition and affect can be studied together in principled ways. Another strength is that multiple methods are used, and the traditional questionnaire data are triangulated with more qualitative data elicited via interviews, observation, diaries and even real-time computer-based task simulations (Karoly et al., 2005). The relevance of self-regulation theory to SLA and individual differences is clear: learning another language poses a high-anxiety and complex challenge that demands cognitive as well as affective self-regulation, and individuals differ in their capacity to self-regulate.

Focusing on the area of volitional action control, Tseng et al. (2006) have developed the Self-Regulatory Capacity in Vocabulary Learning Scale (SRCvoc), an instrument with 20 six-point Likert scale statements that denote greater or lesser creative effort to control one's own actions in vocabulary learning. Note that this

Table 9.4
Self-Regulatory Capacity in Vocabulary Learning Scale illustrated (Tseng et al., 2006)

Dimensions of volitional action control	Item illustration
Commitment control: Keeping goals in focus	'When learning vocabulary, I persist until I reach the goals I make for myself'
Metacognitive control: Minimizing procrastination or distraction and maximizing concentration	'When learning vocabulary, I think my methods for controlling my concentration are effective'
Satiation control: Avoiding boredom or impatience and enhancing interest	'During the process of learning vocabulary, I am confident that I can overcome any sense of boredom'
Emotion control: Overcoming negative moods and affirming emotional stability	'When I feel stressed about vocabulary learning, I know how to reduce this stress'
Environmental control: Eliminating negative environment elements and maximizing positive ones	'When I am studying vocabulary and the learning environment becomes unsuitable, I try to sort out the problem'

emphasis is quite different from the emphasis on sheer frequency of strategy use in much past research. The SRCvoc instrument consists of five subscales comprising four items each, as illustrated in Table 9.4.

Based on the responses from a sample of 172 Taiwanese students in their last year of EFL in high school, the researchers evaluated the SRCvoc favourably. They noted that its reliability is acceptable and the outputs of confirmatory factor analysis support the five-subscale structure, although the last subscale of environmental control was somewhat less clearly useful.

Because this line of research has just begun to unfold in SLA, it remains to be seen if it will reach the sophistication and wealth of insights that self-regulation theory has attained in other fields (see Baumeister and Vohs, 2004). It certainly is a welcome change of direction in social psychologically oriented SLA research, in that the self-regulatory approach allows for the combined study of motivation and strategic behaviour, and of cognition and affect, under a single theoretical framework.

9.10 SUMMARY

- Learning and using an L2 poses a threat to one's ego and makes people vulnerable. Under such conditions, the affective reactions developed by individuals towards the L2 and their own L2 speaking and L2 learning self can vary. Some people may be psychologically better equipped than others for managing affective reactions during L2 learning.

- Certain personality traits may favour interest in the study of an L2 and increase the likelihood of success. It appears that intuitive thinkers are likely to be attracted to the study of foreign languages, perhaps because they enjoy the intuiting or holistic demands of working with words and meaning symbols as well as the thinking or analytical demands of grammatical analysis. Rather unexpectedly, many introverts are also attracted to the study of foreign languages.

- Openness to experience has emerged in recent research as a potentially important personality variable that may be auspicious for achieving high levels of success in L2 learning. This personality trait may be related to lack of ethnocentrism, self-confidence and creativity, among other qualities that may be important for L2 learning.

- Some personality traits (extraversion) and speaking predispositions (concern for communication versus accuracy) appear to be related to speaking styles that are most directly measurable via fluency effects. Introverts and L2 speakers concerned for accuracy produce less fluent speech, searching for better lexical terms and rephrasing themselves more. These speaking styles are traditionally explained as fluency–accuracy trade-offs, but the lack of actual accuracy or self-correction effects in the available studies suggests that they may in fact be better conceived of as fluency–complexity trade-offs instead.

- Foreign language anxiety is a measurable, L2 specific affective variable that is associated with a number of symptoms, including lower grades, lower proficiency performances, difficulty with processing and learning new L2 material, reticence and L2 risk-avoiding behaviours. Its roots can be found in overall low self-concept regarding general academic abilities and in unrealistic beliefs about language learning. The consequences of anxiety are difficult to predict, however, because anxiety can have facilitative as well as debilitating effects for different individuals.

- Willingness to communicate (WTC) is defined as the self-reported likelihood for an L2 learner to want to initiate communication in the L2 when given the choice to engage in or to avoid such action. The antecedents of L2 WTC are L2 communicative confidence (which itself is predicted by anxiety and self-perceived competence) and to a lesser but nevertheless considerable extent by L2 attitudes. Such attitudes are shaped by the frequency and quality of past L2 contact but they also help shape willingness to seek and engage in future L2 contact. Context matters a good deal in understanding the relative importance of WTC antecedents and consequences. Two important areas for pending research are how WTC may be related to actual increases in L2 contact-seeking behaviours, and how it can change across time and contexts.

- Cognitive or learning styles are ways in which individuals prefer to put their general cognitive abilities to use. They are neither good nor bad, but simply bipolar dimensions, with potential strengths and weaknesses on both extremes. A cognitive style investigated in SLA is field independence. Individuals who are high on the field-independence pole of this construct may be better at detecting patterns in the L2 input, dealing with grammatical rules and being able to self-monitor during L2 production. Individuals who are high on the field-dependence pole (also called field sensitivity by Ehrman and Leaver, 2003) may be better at learning holistically from input via memorization as well as learning through communication with others.

- An encompassing mega-model of synoptic–ectenic learning styles has been proposed by Ehrman and Leaver (2003). Synopsis is related to the preference to rely on holistic, at-a-glance perception of information, whereas ectasis refers to the preference to rely on detail and system when processing new information.

- Learning strategies are conscious mental and behavioural procedures that people engage in with the aim to gain control over their learning process. Strategies can be cognitive (among which memory-related and compensatory strategies are important), metacognitive, social and affective. Strategy use appears to be greatly shaped by the curricular context and the specific tasks at hand.

- It has been relatively easy to describe how L2 learners use strategies. More difficult has been to establish a link between strategic behaviour and actual learning gains, to demonstrate that strategies are not culturally biased, or to explain why poor strategy users differ from good strategy users only in how they use strategies in context but not in the kinds or frequency of strategy they use.

- A recent alternative to the study of strategic behaviour is self-regulation, a theory of how humans take control over their actions, thoughts and feelings in order to achieve their complex goals. A promising innovation in this framework is that the traditional emphasis on sheer frequency of strategy use is being replaced by an emphasis on the creativity of efforts employed to control one's learning processes.

9.11 ANNOTATED SUGGESTIONS FOR FURTHER READING

As Dörnyei and Skehan (2003) and Dörnyei (2005) lament, the area of affect and L2 learning is fraught with theoretical, conceptual and methodological challenges. If you prefer to think more holistically and qualitatively about individual differences at the crossroads between cognition and affect, I recommend you read Bailey (1991) and Carson and Longhini (2002), which afford global insights into affect for L2 learning in naturalistic and classroom contexts, respectively. In addition, although perhaps idiosyncratic and one-sided, the book by Ehrman (1996) is unsurpassed in its fascinating, holistic treatment of cognitive and temperamental individual differences at the crossroads of cognition and affect.

An alternative, more methodical reading plan is the following. You can first go to Dörnyei (2005), which offers the best current treatment of affective individual differences. As a next step, you can read the chapters by Anna Chamot, Diane Larsen-Freeman and Anita Wenden in Breen (2001), as they offer useful overviews of various related areas.

If you would like to pursue selected areas of individual differences, I recommend reading Dewaele and Furnham (1999) and Verhoeven and Vermeer (2002) on personality and L2 learning; Horwitz (1988) and MacIntyre and Gardner (1994) on anxiety; and Baker and MacIntyre (2000) and Yashima (2002) on willingness to communicate. A comprehensive theoretical discussion of WTC, although somewhat outdated by now, can be found in MacIntyre et al. (1998). When it comes to cognitive and learning styles, I recommend you read the proposal by Ehrman and Leaver (2003). To learn more about learning strategies, an interesting (because varied) collection of empirical studies is Oxford (1996). The recent study by Tseng et al. (2006) is a must-read for anyone wanting to know where L2 learning strategy research may be headed in coming years.

10

Social dimensions of L2 learning

As we noted at the beginning of Chapter 4, the field of SLA during the 1980s and 1990s was largely driven by the quest to understand the interaction of learner-internal and learner-external variables, guided by the cognitive-interactionist framework that has its roots in Piagetian developmental psychology. The goal of this research is to identify universal patterns that should be largely true of any human who learns an additional language and the underlying belief is that universal patterns can help us explain L2 learning as a general phenomenon. Beginning in the mid-1990s, however, several SLA researchers felt dissatisfied with this state of affairs and opened up new venues for SLA thought (Hall, 1993; van Lier, 1994; Block, 1996; Lantolf, 1996; Firth and Wagner, 1997). Attuning to the spirit of the times, which in many other human and social sciences had for some time been shaped by a social turn, these critics suggested that the nature of reality was social and fundamentally unknowable and that a pursuit of the particular, and not the general, would be a better disciplinary strategy to illuminate complex human problems, such as additional language learning. Other scholars from the wider field of applied linguistics also pointed at the paucity of social theorizing that characterized SLA work (Rampton, 1990; Sridhar, 1994; Norton Peirce, 1995). This increasing disciplinary awareness set forth a process of intellectual crises and reconceptualization that has yet to be completed, but that was characterized in the early twenty-first century as 'the social turn in SLA' (Block, 2003). By now, diverse lines of work in the field have begun to harvest a social understanding of the very same L2 learning phenomena that others have been trying to explain through universal principles and psychological–individual constructs.

This chapter, which is also the final one in the book, offers a bird's-eye view of the efforts associated with the social turn in SLA and reflects on what we know about social dimensions of L2 learning thus far. We will see how five constructs – cognition, interaction, grammar, learning and sense of self – can be respecified as fundamentally social, if L2 learning is investigated with the aid of five concomitant theories: Vygotskian sociocultural theory, Conversation Analysis, Systemic Functional Linguistics, language socialization theory and identity theory. We will also survey some findings about the role of technology in supporting socially rich L2 learning. The discussion will be selective by necessity. My intention is to pinpoint major ways in which social dimensions of L2 learning have begun to be illuminated.

10.1 THE UNBEARABLE INELUCTABILITY OF THE SOCIAL CONTEXT

Under the new social perspectives, the study of additional language learning is not only shaped by the social context in which it happens; it is bound inextricably to such context. The metaphor of the chameleon is helpful in appreciating the full importance of this point. Richard Tucker drew from an undated attribution to Hamayan, cited by Donato (1998), when he noted that capturing L2 proficiency 'is in many ways similar to painting a chameleon. Because the animal's colors depend on its physical surroundings, any one representation becomes inaccurate as soon as that background changes' (Tucker, 1999, pp. 208–9).

The metaphor can be applied to the study of not only L2 proficiency but the entirety of L2 learning. It rests on the widely held belief that chameleons change the colour patterns of their skin so they can camouflage themselves. These colours change when specialized cells (called chromatophores, or carriers of colour) respond to hormonal discharges, which are thought to be triggered by the surrounding physical context. In fact, biologists (e.g. Stuart-Fox and Moussalli, 2008) have persuasively shown that, even though sometimes the purpose of disguise does motivate these colour changes, most often they are a manifestation of social mood swings when interacting with other fellow chameleons, for example during male contests and courtships! Thus, the chameleon metaphor is a doubly meaningful reminder of the inseparability of agent and environment as well as of the centrality of the social in understanding all living agents.

The radical reorientation towards the fundamental role of social processes in SLA draws inspiration from social-constructivist, sociocultural and poststructuralist theories which, since the 1960s, have been in ascendancy in the neighbouring fields of anthropology, sociology, education, philosophy of science, cultural studies and literary criticism. How does the new conceptual apparatus help us study the social in L2 learning? **Social constructivism** tells us that reality is not given naturally; it does not lie out there, to be apprehended by the individual mind. Instead, reality is created by human agents and social groups. **Socioculturalism** goes beyond social constructivism by positing that reality is not only a matter of interpretive construction but that it is also radically collective and social, appropriated and transformed through relational knowledge. In other words, the individual mind finds the source of learning in social communities; learning is available in historical and social processes and emerges among agents in a given context. Only processes, events and activities are real, whereas structures and patterns are epiphenomenal to those processes. Thus, reality is always processual and social and emerges anew each time and again, out of specific interactions with the world, the word and others, always in situated contexts. **Poststructuralism** goes yet even further than socioculturalism by telling us that the structures of human meaning and human social activity that were proposed by structuralist thinkers (notably, Freud, Marx and Saussure) are insufficient to explain the human condition, and that there is nothing that can be known or understood independently from the discourse that names and creates that knowledge. Furthermore, power is enmeshed in knowledges and discourses. That is, reality is not only socially constructed and socially distributed; it is irreducibly multiple, intersubjective, discursively constituted and the site of struggle over conflicting power interests.

It should be clear, then, that social inquiry into L2 learning must value social experience not as externally documented, fixed environmental encounters, as perhaps suggested by the camouflage theory of the chameleon's change of pigmentation in the metaphor above, and as certainly assumed in much of the research presented in all other chapters in this book. Instead, as suggested by the theory of a social motivation for chameleonic colour repertoires, experience must be understood as radically social. It must be theorized as lived and contested experience, always unfinished and never fully predictable, and always contingent on the situated context of human relational activity. Ineluctably, in order to understand L2 learning from a radically social perspective, one must focus on experience that is lived, made sense of, negotiated, contested and claimed by learners in their physical, interpersonal, social, cultural and historical context. In other words, nothing can be known if it is not known in a given social context – and out of the social, nothing can be known.

10.2 COGNITION IS SOCIAL: VYGOTSKIAN SOCIOCULTURAL THEORY IN SLA

Socioculturalism encompasses not one but many theories. However, without a doubt, the sociocultural approach that has made the strongest contribution to SLA thus far is Vygotskian sociocultural theory of mind. Lev Vygotsky was a Russian psychologist who in the first quarter of the twentieth century developed an influential theory of cultural-historical psychology. It was designed in reaction against behaviourism and its exclusive focus on lower-level mental operations and also against mentalism and the duality of mind and environment that characterized Piaget's psychology. Its main goal was to enable the study of consciousness, defined as higher-level mental operations involved in language, literacy, numeracy, categorization, rationality and logic (Lantolf and Thorne, 2007, p. 202). It reconceptualized cognition as fundamentally social. Others in the Soviet Union expanded on Vygotsky's work in the following decades, notably Alexander Luria and Aleksei Leont'ev, the founder of Activity Theory.

In the context of L2 learning, already in the 1980s James Lantolf began applying Vygotsky's insights to SLA concerns, and he has made the theory and its variations well known to SLA audiences (e.g. Lantolf and Appel, 1994; Lantolf and Thorne, 2006, 2007; Lantolf, 2006b). Beginning in the mid-1990s, Merrill Swain reworked output and interaction – main concepts in cognitive-interactionist SLA, as we saw in Chapter 4 – into new sociocultural meanings (Swain, 2000, 2006). These two SLA researchers have opened the way for many others to reconceptualize L2 learning through a Vygotskian prism, leading to a steady and vibrant growth in the current size and scope of Vygotskian SLA research. Indeed, this is the only social approach to L2 learning that has begun to enjoy full acceptance as an SLA theory. For example, it has already been reviewed in a state-of-the-art paper commissioned by a flagship SLA journal (Lantolf, 2006b) and a special issue of the same journal has been devoted to work within this framework (McCafferty, 2008). Furthermore, it has become a must-include chapter in SLA textbooks (e.g. Lantolf and Thorne, 2007).

Vygotskian sociocultural theory posits that consciousness has its basis in the human capacity to use symbols as tools. Lantolf and Thorne (2007) offer a useful allegory between a spider and an architect to explain this point. Spiders spin their webs out of instinct, without a prior plan or a will to change its shape or size. The web is spun always in the same way, depending on the arachnid species, and always for the same function – to trap food. The architect, by contrast:

> plans a building on paper in the form of a blueprint before actually constructing it in objective physical space. The blueprint is the ideal form of the building, which of course no one can inhabit, but at the same time, it must be sensitive to the physics that operate in the concrete world. The blueprint, then, is a culturally constructed symbolic artifact that represents the actual building and also serves to mediate the construction of the real building. It allows the architect to make changes ideally without ever having to act on the objective physical world.
>
> (p. 205)

Mental activity is always mediated by tools, physical and symbolic; through the use of tools humans can change their reality, but the use of tools also changes them. In addition, no matter whether activity is solitary or with others, cognition and consciousness are always social, and so are the tools that mediate both. For example, a professional body of collective knowledge, a client who wants a house built and a construction crew who can actualize the blueprint in physical space are all part of the architect's activity of designing a blueprint of a building. Indeed, without the social legitimacy of a professional licence, which is sanctioned by a collective group, an architect would not be an architect and her drawing of a building plan would not be recognized as such by others. Importantly, consciousness exists only as a process that emerges out of (past, present and future) activity with others and with tools, physical and symbolic, each with their historical and cultural genealogies. Language is also a process, rather than a product, and it is the most important of all symbolic tools. As all tools, language is used to create thought but it also transforms thought and is the source of learning.

The next four sections are devoted to a discussion of some of the main insights about L2 learning that Vygotskian SLA has contributed to this date.

10.3 SELF-REGULATION AND LANGUAGE MEDIATION

Consciousness helps humans regulate problem solving and achieve their *goals* (what they want to do and anticipate doing) in light of their *motives* (why they want to do it) and their chosen *operations* or means (how they want to do it) (Lantolf and Appel, 1994, pp. 17–21). Regulation can be of three kinds: object, other- and self-regulation. When people have yet to learn how to control their world and themselves in the context of carrying out a given activity, they orient towards objects. That is, they are initially **object regulated**. Object regulation can be both negative, as when an object in the way of another distracts a child's attention and makes her forget what toy she was told to fetch, and positive, as when a child uses blocks or fingers to solve an addition problem (Lantolf and Thorne, 2007, p. 204). People can also orient during an event towards other people and thus they can be **other-regulated**. This happens characteristically when they participate in new, complex activities with the aid of other co-participants. For example, initial cooking-together sessions between a child and a parent may involve the parent assisting the child to break down the steps of cooking into more manageable actions, many instruction-giving events, some modelling and even some intermittently taking over for parts of the activity where the child is estimated to need help, such as when chopping vegetables with a sharp knife. At the highest level of regulation, people orient to their own mental activity. That is, they are **self-regulated**, if they are capable of carrying out an activity largely independently.

Because language mediates all mental activity, it also mediates all three kinds of regulation. To continue with the example of a cooking session, someone who wants to learn how to cook a new meal, for example the Greek ground meat and eggplant dish called moussaka, may seek object regulation by following a recipe that she has printed from the web. In this case, during the cooking event, there may be many instances of abbreviated but audible speech essentially directed to the self, for example, reading parts of the recipe out loud, verbalizing actions as they are performed, or even proffering expressions of self-encouragement (*OK, good, the béchamel sauce is ready! Well done … Now, next!*). This is what Vygotsky called egocentric speech (following Piaget, but giving it a very different interpretation) and what contemporary Vygotskian theorists prefer to call **private speech**. It is abbreviated but audible speech mostly directed to the self. It emerges most often in the face of some challenge, when people are attempting to self-regulate. Our inexperienced moussaka cook might look for other-regulation by asking a friend – perhaps, but not necessarily, someone who has cooked the dish before – to assist her with the preparation of the meal. In this case, **social speech** will also occur (in addition to private speech) if the friends can support each other and jointly cook the meal, as they other-regulate. By way of contrast, a professional chef may need to 'talk' to the self or to others very little during the moussaka-cooking activity (even in a restaurant's kitchen shared by many other people) and might do most of her meditational thinking in the form of **inner speech**, or subvocally articulated speech that cannot be observed by others.

Vygotskian SLA researchers see the learning of an additional language as a process that involves gradually appropriating the L2 to make it into our own tool for self-regulation and thinking, just as once we learned to do the same with our L1 as children. Therefore, they have great interest in understanding regulation during L2 activity through the study of social, private and inner speech. They focus on the degree to which regulation of the three kinds can happen, and whether each happens in L2 and L1, while doing activities in the L2. Lantolf and Thorne (2006, pp. 83, 110–11) noted that the ultimate accomplishment of self-regulation in the L2 is if mediation can be performed via L2 (as opposed to L1), for example, when either private speech, inner speech, or both, are carried out in the L2 incarnating appropriate L2 forms and meanings.

10.4 SOME FINDINGS ABOUT INNER, PRIVATE AND SOCIAL SPEECH IN L2 LEARNING

We all are aware of inner speech when we feel we can listen to ourselves thinking, as it were. And, in fact, brain imaging studies have captured brain activity in the left inferior frontal gyrus during inner speech, an area which is associated with self-awareness (Morin and Michaud, 2007). Inner speech, which is typically sustainable during self-regulated mental activity, can be studied only indirectly. In a book treatment of the concept, María de Guerrero (2005) reviews brain imaging methodologies as well as introspective methodologies involving questionnaire and interview responses about mental rehearsal. The latter methods have been employed in SLA studies, beginning with de Guerrero's (1994) pioneering study, where she documented many mental strategies employed by L2 learners of English in Puerto Rico. For example, one of them, Amarilis, reported memorizing material for an English oral activity, going blank, being disappointed because she only got 44 points out of 50 on the assignment, and later using inner speech to regain affective control over the situation (p. 112):

(1)   On the bus … I did it all over again [the activity dialogue] to see if I was so stupid that I would forget everything. And I gave myself a 50.

Most research, however, has concentrated on private and social speech during L2 activity, both of which are more readily amenable to study than inner speech.

Private speech, in particular, is central to the study of mental functioning because it constitutes a link between inner speech, to which it may convert during completely self-regulated activity, and social speech, from which it takes its source. Lantolf and Thorne (2006, pp. 83–94) reviewed the main findings gleaned from seven studies that inspected private speech during L2 task performance. At higher levels of L2 competence, learners were more able to self-regulate, as reflected in generally less pervasive use of private speech during L2 narrative retellings. Instances of private speech (e.g. affective markers such as *oh boy, oh no, oh my god, OK, oh well, now I get it, alright let me see*, which can occur in the L2 or the L1) were attested much more frequently among lower-level proficiency learners in many of the studies. More proficient learners also generally exhibited fewer traces of object regulation and more evidence of self-regulation as indexed in some of their language choices during L2 activity. For example, compare the following three L2 renditions of the same ice cream story task employed by Frawley and Lantolf (1985):

(2)   This is a boy who is standing in the street. This is a boy and a man who is selling ice cream. The man is selling ice cream for 50 cents. The boy is telling the man 'Thank you' (p. 32)

(3)   This man, he took the ice cream from the boy, and the boy became angry because his father took the ice cream and he left (p. 32)

(4)   … And an ice cream man comes, meets him … And the little boy looks … The first boy gets … So the little boy says … (p. 35)

The choice of present progressive in (2) appeared more frequently, across studies, in the language of narratives created by many lower-proficiency speakers. The interpretation proposed is that it indexes regulation difficulties. That is, the use of the progressive aspect may suggest that speakers are object regulated by the task because they describe the events in the story as immediate; these speakers are discovering a story as they speak rather than narrating a story. The use of the simple past, shown in (3), however, is interpreted in some studies, although not all, as attempts by more advanced L2 learners to self-regulate in the face of difficulty. As Lantolf and Thorne (2006) explain, this is because simple past tense helps speakers gain a sense of unified, distant gaze towards the story that allows for a better story-telling effect than the progressive form. Yet, this choice is perhaps less self-regulated than the historical present, shown in (4). Advanced learners and L1 speakers were more often able to maintain a consistent use of the historical present across the seven studies reviewed, and Lantolf and Thorne argue there is evidence that this choice shows self-regulation 'in the narrative task because the meaning it carries in this case is simultaneously distance and immediacy' (p. 87). It is important to appreciate just how different these analyses and conceptualizations are from the traditional ways in which learner language is analysed by cognitive-interactionists. Thus, under the interlanguage development view of tense and aspect that we examined in Chapter 6 (section 6.10), the goal was to describe language as an objective system that encodes meaning through different form choices. In the Vygotskian perspective, these tense and aspect choices are studied for what they can help us discover about processes of mediation in the development of regulated L2 mental activity.

Taking a slightly different but still fully Vygotskian perspective, Swain has also investigated the mediating role of language in L2 learning, often concentrating on the study of social speech. She is guided by the tenet that 'verbalization changes thought, leading to development and learning' (2006, p. 110) and she focuses on what she calls 'languaging' to convey the Vygotskian view of language as process in flight (Tocalli-Beller and Swain, 2007, p. 145), rather than as product, which is typically conjured in the cognitive-interactionist notions of pushed output during language production (see Chapter 4, sections 4.5 and 4.9).

Languaging is illustrated in a study by Tocalli-Beller and Swain (2007). They captured the joint learning that occurred between Lisa and Helen, two ESL students in a North American college programme, during a pair-work discussion of the following pun:

Waiter, I'd like a corned beef sandwich, and make it lean.
Yes, sir! In which direction?

Each of the learners knew only one meaning of the word *lean*, and both learned the other meaning from each other during this dialogue (p. 160):

(5)   Helen: I don't understand what is lean.
         Lisa: Uh ... lean can mean uh not fat, not fatty.
         Helen: Oh. And also uh ... you lean on something. That direction or that direction.

The dialogue continued when each learner unpacked the one meaning that was new to them and had been offered by the other partner:

      Lisa: Oh, lean against the wall?
      Helen: Yeah. And lean is not fat?
      Lisa: Yeah.
      Helen: There is no fat in the meat.

They then checked with the dictionary, thus using object regulation productively after having achieved other-regulation, and they ended with a mutual acknowledgement of the new meaning each had learned. Both learners remembered the two meanings of the word *lean* seven weeks later, when they were asked to supply it on a post-test.

In another study, Richard Donato (1994) captured three speakers collaboratively learning the past compound reflexive form of the verb 'to remember' in French, while jointly planning for an oral activity for their French class (p. 44):

(6)   S1:   ... and then I'll say ... *tu as souvenu notre anniversaire de mariage* ... or should I say *mon anniversaire?*
       S2:   *tu as ...*
       S3:   *tu as ...*
       S1:   *tu as souvenu ...* 'you remembered?'
       S3:   yes, but isn't that reflexive? *tu t'as ...*
       S1:   ah, *tu t'as souvenu*
       S2:   oh, it's *tu es*
       S1:   *tu es*
       S3:   *tu es, tu es, tu ...*
       S1:   *t'es, tu t'es*
       S3:   *tu t'es*
       S1:   *tu t'es souvenu*

Donato notes that each participant in this activity contributed one piece of knowledge that they already had control over. Speaker 1 controlled the past participle form (*souvenu*), speaker 3 knew the verb is reflexive (*tu t'as*), and speaker

2 controlled the choice of the auxiliary compound form: *être*, not *avoir* (*es*, not *as*). By thinking together in joint activity, and mediated by the tool of social speech, they came up with the new, complete solution: *tu t'es souvenu*.

Activity that is mediated by social speech should not be equated with the cognitive-interactionist notion of learner-initiated negotiation of form (see Chapter 4, section 4.10). While much of the same analysis and evidence would fit both approaches, the differences of interpretation are also deep. The cognitive-interactionist prism would conceive of events such as the ones illustrated in (5) and (6) as linguistic exchanges that facilitate individual learning. The sociocultural perspective, instead, conceptualizes them as captured instances of the process of 'the collective acquisition of the second language' (Donato, 1994, p. 53), which is driven by 'the construction of co-knowledge' (p. 39). Learners strive to self-regulate in their social world and, in the process, they mediate action – and as a consequence, both intended and unintended, they learn – through social, private and inner speech.

10.5 SOCIAL LEARNING IN THE ZONE OF PROXIMAL DEVELOPMENT

As already noted, Vygotskians view learning as social: 'the source of development resides in the environment rather than in the individual' (Lantolf, 2006a, p. 726). That is, any knowledge and any capacity to engage in regulated activity appears always first at the social, interpersonal level during activity with others and only later can be seen to operate also at the psychological, intrapersonal level. What must be studied is therefore not the individual but joint social activity, because, as Poehner and Lantolf (2005) explain:

> The individual and the environment form an inseparable dialectical unity that cannot be understood if the unity is broken. As Vygotsky often said, if we want to understand the property of water that allows it to extinguish fire, we cannot reduce it to its component elements – oxygen and hydrogen.
>
> (p. 239)

Not only must the unit of analysis be joint social activity, but this joint activity must be investigated as it unfolds in real time, a methodology that Vygotskians call the **microgenetic method** and which refers to the study of situated change in real time. The analysis of examples (5) and (6) in the previous section illustrates microgenesis. Learning or development is encapsulated in the important Vygotskian construct of the **Zone of Proximal Development** (ZPD), defined as the distance between what a learner can do in the L2 if assisted by others (in joint activity that is other-regulated) versus what she or he can accomplish alone (in independent activity that is, hopefully, self-regulated). To distinguish this novel conceptualization from traditional previous definitions, it is helpful to think that the traditional view of learning provides a *retrospective* account of whatever development has been achieved, whereas the Vygotskian view entails a *prospective* account of development that can be anticipated in the near future (Aljaafreh and Lantolf, 1994, p. 468; Poehner and Lantolf, 2005). Wells (1999) notes that the ZPD is not a fixed property of an individual, but instead 'constitutes a potential for learning that is created in the interaction between participants in particular settings' and therefore must be seen as 'emergent', because the ongoing interaction during joint activity can open up unforeseen new potential for learning (p. 249). The ZPD potential emerges among peers, not only with an expert, and it does not imply an intention to teach or an overt focus on learning, although it can entail both, particularly in instructional formal settings.

10.6 NEGATIVE FEEDBACK RECONCEPTUALIZED

An area of L2 study where the notion of the ZPD has been fruitfully applied is that of error correction. The proposal was initiated in a pioneering study by Aljaafreh and Lantolf (1994; Lantolf and Aljaafreh, 1995) which involved seven weekly L2 writing tutorials between each of three female ESL learners and Aljaafreh as the writing tutor. The tutorials focused on affording the L2 writers optimal negative feedback on articles, tenses, prepositions and modals. However, feedback was not conceived as transfer of linguistic information from a tutor to a tutee, as is often conceptualized in the cognitive interactionist approaches described in Chapter 4 (see section 4.11). Rather, it was defined as 'help that is jointly negotiated between experts and novices' (Aljaafreh and Lantolf, p. 480). Ultimately, the purpose was to investigate negative feedback as other-regulation that is finely tuned to provide assistance within the ZPD of a given learner and encourages the emergence of self-regulation. This can be illustrated with a brief and successful exchange (p. 479):

(7) Tutor: Is there anything wrong here in this sentence? 'I took only Ani because I couldn't took both' ... do you see anything wrong? ... Particularly here 'because I couldn't took both'
Tutee: Or Maki?
Tutor: What the verb verb ... something wrong with the verb ...
Tutee: Ah, yes ...
Tutor: that you used. Okay, where? Do you see it?
Tutee: (points to the verb)
Tutor: Took? Okay
Tutee: Take
Tutor: Alright, take
Tutee: (laughs)

Optimal negative feedback, exemplified in (7), is thus defined by Aljaafreh and Lantolf as *graduated* and *contingent*. Graduated, rather than uniform, means that the feedback starts off as implicit prompts to aid self-discovery and slowly takes the form of increasingly more explicit clues, as needed. Through this graduated delivery, the more expert interlocutor (i.e. the tutor) engages in a negotiated estimation of how to provide no less and no more directive assistance than what is needed at any given time 'to encourage the learner to function at his or her potential level of ability' (p. 468). Contingent, rather than unconditional, means that the feedback is 'withdrawn as soon as the novice shows signs of self-control and ability to function independently' (p. 468).

Graduation and contingency were formalized by the researchers in a 13-point regulatory scale that was derived in a bottom-up analysis from the data (Lantolf and Aljaafreh, 1995, p. 622). It begins with most implicit or inductive prompts to encourage self-regulation, for instance, with the tutor asking the learner to read the essay and try to find errors before coming to the tutorial (level 0), or the tutor asking 'is there anything wrong in this sentence?' (level 3, shown in (7) above). The scale ends with increasingly more explicit and informative clues, for example with the tutor providing the correct form (level 10), a metalinguistic explanation (level 11), or new examples of the correct pattern (level 12). In example (7), the tutor only needed to graduate assistance up to level 6, by indicating the nature of the error rather broadly ('What the verb verb ... something wrong with the verb ... that you used. Okay, where? Do you see it?'), and the learner was able to come up with the correction on her own, first by pointing at the verb, then by uttering 'take'.

Over time, across episodes and tutorials, the microgenetic method should help capture how 'learning evolves through stages of decreasing reliance on the other person toward increasing reliance on the self' (p. 479), that is, from other-regulation to self-regulation. In other words, over time, assistance (i.e. negative feedback) ought to be more frequently placed on the implicit end of the regulatory scale. However, as Lantolf and Aljaafreh (1995) showed when inspecting the data longitudinally, these changes cannot be expected to be linear and smooth. Instead, microgenesis helps capture change that is dynamic, dialectical and at times regresses to earlier forms of mediation. As we have noted repeatedly across all chapters in this book, L2 development is always non-linear and dynamic.

Aljaafreh and Lantolf's proposal was tested in a quasi-experimental study by Nassaji and Swain (2000). Over four writing tutorial sessions, Nassaji acted as a tutor and provided feedback on article errors to two Korean ESL learners. The tutorials involved providing graduated and contingent or ZPD-tuned assistance to one of the writers, and random or ZPD-insensitive assistance to the other. In this latter condition, the tutor provided a prompt choosing a level randomly from the regulatory scale and then tried to avoid further collaboration or interaction on the issue. In the last tutorial, both learners completed a fill-in-the-gap version of each of the four essays they had discussed with the tutor, with each gap representing one of the article errors that had been discussed during their own sessions. On average, the learner who received the ZPD-tuned feedback was able to fill in the correct articles 83 per cent of the 28 total instances that had been negotiated in her sessions, whereas the learner who participated in the ZPD-insensitive tutorials was able to correctly provide only 40 per cent of her 20 randomly negotiated instances. Thus, these results lend some initial support to the proposal.

In most cognitive-interactionist discussions of L2 instruction, there is a felt tension that stems from dichotomies such as explicit and implicit instruction, deductive and inductive instruction, and instruction that integrates form with meaning versus that which isolates form from meaning. A benefit of exploring negative feedback, in particular, and L2 instruction, in general, within the Vygotskian framework of the ZPD is that these dichotomies blur and a continuum is conjured all along these dimensions, which can change within the same interactional activity dynamically as well as over multiple successive activities, as co-participants jointly facilitate the gradual and non-linear emergence of self-regulated mediation during L2 activity.

10.7 INTERACTION IS SOCIAL: CONVERSATION ANALYSIS AND SLA

If Vygotskian sociocultural theory offers SLA researchers a social respecification of cognition and puts consciousness at the centre of inquiry, the approach known as Conversation Analysis puts forward a novel social respecification of interaction and has its centre in the study of sociability as a mundane and orderly accomplishment. When applied to SLA problems, this framework characterizes L2 learning as primordially socio-interactional practice and focuses on the detailed analysis of naturally occurring spoken interactions, whether in casual and intimate conversation, in institutional and public talk, or in the instructional talk of classrooms and tutorials.

The field of sociology experienced a profound crisis in the United States in the 1940s, stimulating seminal work by sociologists Erving Goffman and Harold Garfinkel during the 1950s and 1960s. Goffman focused on the self, symbolic interaction and life as a theatre, whereas Garfinkel emphasized practical activity, interactionally created sequentiality and the local production of social organization. In the early 1960s Garfinkel coined the term 'ethnomethodology' to refer to his approach to the study of social order. The school of Conversation Analysis (CA) built on his ethnomethodological thinking, first through new ideas developed by Harvey Sacks and Emanuel Schegloff, both students of Garfinkel, and soon joined by Gail Jefferson, herself a student of Sacks. Although these scholars spent most of their careers in California, during the 1980s Jefferson relocated to the Netherlands, thus helping extend the geographical sphere of influence of the school. CA has now greatly expanded and is practised by a large and diverse interdisciplinary community in the United States, Europe and Australia, with a shared interest in studying the organization of talk-in-interaction.

In the context of L2 learning, CA began to be applied to L2 data first in Denmark by Alan Firth and Johannes Wagner, as they studied oral interactions among non-native speakers who used English as a lingua franca for business-related purposes in Europe. Although dissemination of their empirical work began in the early 1990s, it was a special issue in the *Journal of Pragmatics* (Wagner, 1996) and an oft-cited article in the *Modern Language Journal* (Firth and Wagner, 1997) that rapidly opened up these ideas to the European and North American SLA audiences, together with an early piece by Markee (1994), who had also broached the discussion of CA in North American SLA. In little more than ten years, CA-for-SLA, as it has been termed, has grown into its own area of study. Other leading contributors have joined Firth and Wagner, such as Numa Markee (1994, 2000) and Junko Mori (2007) in the United States, and Paul Seedhouse (2004, 2005) in the United Kingdom, and SLA scholars who were well known for other work, such as Gabriele Kasper (2006) and Anne Lazaraton (2002), have reoriented their careers and joined the research programme as well. The application of this framework to SLA has resulted in the rapid accumulation of edited volumes, special issues of journals and book-length L2-related treatments. Authoritative reviews of this burgeoning literature have been undertaken by Seedhouse (2005), Kasper (2006) and Mori (2007).

10.8 THE CA PERSPECTIVE IN A NUTSHELL

A goal of CA, and one that makes it related to but different from ethnomethodology, is the discovery of universal mechanisms by which organized talk is possible. That is, CA practitioners believe that 'context-sensitive social actions' offer evidence for the existence of 'a context-free machinery', which ultimately helps explain humans' capacity to engage in interaction and display their social actions in specific local contexts (Seedhouse, 2005, p. 167). The context-free machinery includes rules for **turn taking** (or how to keep, yield or take the floor), **repair** (or how to address trouble in talk) and **sequential design** (or how to make each new action-at-talk change, maintain or produce the next new action-at-talk, in sequentiality that is emergent but constrained by shared preferences among sanctioned choices). However, evidence of the context-free machinery is always sought in local interaction in situ, and this is something that CA shares with ethnomethodology. Language is social action, and this special stance is reflected in the use of the verb 'do' in CA, which you will find in many titles of CA studies: people do not use language to communicate; they do language, and they do communication.

A cornerstone of CA thinking is the **radically emic perspective**, explained by Markee and Kasper (2004) as follows:

> CA establishes an emic perspective ... by examining the details of ... the orientations and relevancies that participants display to each other through their interactional conduct ... Thus, participant orientations, relevancies, and intersubjectivity are not treated as states of mind that somehow lurk behind the interaction, but as local and sequential accomplishments that must be grounded in empirically observable conversational conduct.
>
> (p. 495)

This radically emic imperative of CA must not be confused with the emic perspective that ethnographers pursue as an ideal in their research (Headland et al., 1990). Not only is the CA concept of emic very different from the concept as conceived of in the ethnographic tradition, but it is also in epistemological tension with it. Ethnographers seek to attain an insider's view of the context and a deep understanding of what is relevant in it for participants, and they do this by becoming intimately familiar with participants and settings through long-term observation and participation, as well as by directly eliciting the participants' perspective through interviews and by gathering information about the wider context, such as institutional documents and cultural artefacts (Wolcott, 1999). A main goal is to give voice to participants in the research interpretations, and this is done via triangulation and member checks during the analyses and via polyphonic styles in the reporting that recognize and balance multiple etic (the researcher's) and emic (the insider's) perspectives. By contrast, CA forbids the analyst to engage in any *a priori* invocation of social structure, culture, power, ideology or any such interpretive categories that pre-existing theories or assumptions may make available, although it may allow all such categories if they are *a posteriori* interpretations closely grounded in the observable interactional conduct of the social agents at talk. We may want to think about it in terms of *witnessable* evidence, a term that I find useful and borrow from Livingston (2008). Likewise, interviews, participants' insights, or information retrieved from the wider context are precluded, since only witnessable evidence produced in the ongoing immediate interaction is allowed into the analysis. Thus, this CA radically emic imperative makes it difficult to investigate macro dimensions of the social context that many other L2 researchers find important. At the same time, however, it also has salutary consequences for disciplinary understandings of L2 learning, as we will see in the next two sections.

Another trademark of CA is the highly technical transcription conventions that analysts must use in order to capture the relevant details of a given interaction, which are needed to render observable or witnessable evidence of the actions-at-talk. For example, squared brackets [] indicate overlap between speakers; numbers in parenthesis (0.56) indicate timed pauses; segments inside parenthesis [h] indicate uncertainty in the transcription; underlinings show emphasis; colons ::: show lengthened vowel sounds; a left-facing arrow < indicates the beginning of rushed talk and a right-facing > arrow the beginning of talk that is slowed down; and upward ↑ or downward ↓ arrows indicate upward or downward intonation.

In the next two sections, I have chosen to highlight two contributions of CA-for-SLA and one doubt.

10.9 SOME CONTRIBUTIONS OF CA-FOR-SLA

A main insight of CA is that L2 interactions, just like any human interactions, are orderly accomplishments in doing communication, rather than random or deficient attempts at using the L2. Thus, what other approaches may take for evidence of linguistic problems, CA reconceptualizes as interactional resources. Donald Carroll (2005) illustrates this in a study of conversational data between three self-selected female peers in a second-year EFL classroom in Japan. He carefully inspected the phenomenon of adding an extra vowel at the end of certain words (e.g. *what-o* or *what-u, have-u, raining-u, dark-u*), which is typically interpreted by SLA researchers as an attempt to impose the consonant–vowel syllabic structure of L1 Japanese on English words, a case of negative L1 transfer (see Chapter 3). Carroll's CA analysis ascertained that the extra vowel was associated with several interactional actions, most of them related to its value as a 'displayed sense of incompleteness' (p. 229), which allowed a speaker to maintain or reestablish speakership. Thus, for example, it appeared at the end of utterances, timed to coincide with what could be an appropriate juncture for another speaker to take the floor. In such cases, all speakers oriented to the vowel signalling that there was more to come from the same speaker. This is how speaker S uses *raining-u*, and *like-u* as she produces the two-part comparison of what she doesn't like (rain) and what she does (blue skies) (p. 228):

(8)   S: yeah   (0.22) but (0.49) but I don't like(h) raining-u
             (0.14)
       K: [mm::::]
       A: [ah::h::] very <u>dark</u>-u
             (0.14)
       S: da- yeah [I::a I   ] I like-u
       A: [un un un   ]
       K: [a::h::   ]
             (0.19)
       S: I: I(h): huh (h)rike-u (0.14) brue sky

By looking at interactional practice as an accomplishment, CA changes the lens from the usual inspection of what L2 learners cannot or will not do, to a more affirming exploration of what they can indeed do as they 'do' interaction.

Cognitive-interactionist SLA researchers investigate L2 interactions as filled with meanings that they attribute to (from their perspective) commonsensical actions, such as misunderstanding a message or correcting an error, and commonsensical categories, such as being a non-native speaker, or being a student, or being a female (see Chapter 4). By contrast, the CA study of L2 interaction posits that actions and categories which outsiders, including researchers and teachers, may assume to be at work in an interaction have no constant value. Instead, they can be relevant or irrelevant to particular L2 users and their interlocutors in specific interactional events. The relevance of these actions and categories is co-produced by the participants locally, turn by turn, and it is adjudicated by the analyst via inspection of the available observable evidence in the interactional conduct, in agreement with the radically emic perspective that CA adopts. This position of CA has the potential to afford a healthy new lens that suspends and challenges many taken-for-granted constructs.

For example, the notion of error becomes obsolete in the CA approach, because nothing can be treated as error *a priori*. Instead, CA analysts talk about repairables, but only when the participants display evidence that they orient to something in the talk as a source of trouble for them. Indeed, much talk seems to proceed as if what grammarians call errors did not exist, as CA studies of L2 data have uncovered little if any evidence that interlocutors consistently orient towards 'errors' or invoke them in their interactional conduct. Likewise, negotiation for meaning is not necessarily a priority in L2–L2 talk-in-interaction, and Firth (1996) and many others have noted that speakers orient to 'normality' in most cases, for example by doing 'let it pass', which refers to frequent instances when a hearer 'lets the unknown or unclear action, word or utterance "pass" on the (common-sense) assumption that it will either become clear or redundant as talk progresses' (p. 243).

Similarly, the identity of speakers as 'native' or 'non-native' and as 'novice language learners' or 'expert language users' cannot be taken as fixed, as CA has demonstrated how such categories may be relevant in one interactional event and irrelevant in the next. This was shown by Yuri Hosoda (2006) in her analysis of 15 video- and audio-taped casual conversations involving 15 L2 Japanese speakers, who had been living in Japan between 6 and 20 years, and their L1 Japanese friends or acquaintances. She captured witnessable evidence supporting the interpretation that, on occasion, the L2 speakers 'orient to themselves as a "novice" in the language spoken in the interaction while they treat their interlocutors, at that moment, as a language expert' (p. 33). This occurred when an L2 speaker invited their L1 friend to correct or help with certain lexical items. These invitations were recognizable because they were performed via overt signals such as sound lengthening, rising intonation, explicit expressions of ignorance, gaze, raised eyebrows, and so on. However, Hosoda also observed many instances in which so-called ungrammaticalities were not oriented to by either speaker, an indication that differential language expertise was treated as irrelevant in such cases.

Co-participants in an interaction typically, but not always, co-orient to joint interactional action and interactional identities. In the study by Hosoda just discussed, for example, she found that momentary orientation to language novice or expert status was co-shared, as in all the cases without exception when an L2 speaker oriented to trouble with lexis 'the L1 speakers took on (relative) "expert" roles by supplying lexical items and pursuing L2 speakers' uptake' (p. 44). A slightly different picture emerged from a study by Salla Kurhila (2005), in which she analysed 14 hours of video- and audio-taped personal and institutional exchanges among about 100 different L2 speakers of Finnish and 20 L1 Finnish speakers, focusing on instances in which a non-native speaker oriented towards trouble with morphology, particularly Finnish case endings. In some instances, her results were in agreement with Hosoda's findings, and the orientation of the L2 speaker was also shared by the L1 speaker, who provided the target form in the next turn. In other instances in the data, however, in the presence of a same previous action by an L2 speaker, L1 speakers did not orient to these L2 speaker-initiated grammatical repairs and instead displayed understanding with head nods and acknowledgement tokens (*mhm, joo,* or 'yes' in Finnish). In these data, it was frequently L1 Finnish-speaking secretaries who did so. Kurhila suggested that the given L1 speaker in such a given interaction was orienting to the interactionally relevant action to keep the conversation moving, perhaps because their institutional roles of secretary took precedence over their role as linguistically expert interlocutors in those particular instances.

External contexts or settings, however, cannot be taken to 'impose' particular roles or restrictures on the interactional work of L2 speakers because, as Kurhila (2005) herself puts it, in any ongoing interaction 'each response talks a different set of identities and relationships into being' (p. 155). This has been shown to be the case even in the institutional context of teacher–student and student–student talk examined in CA studies of L2 classrooms. In one such study, Keith Richards (2006) concluded that in classroom settings the default institutional roles are teacher and student, but they are 'not binding' as discourse identities in the moment-by-moment organization of the interaction; instead they just play a 'pre-eminent position within the range of possible options' (p. 60) and this pre-eminence of the roles is constantly subject to interactionally achieved change. In sum, as Firth and Wagner (2007) put it, identity in CA is always 'a motile, liminal, achieved feature of the interaction' (p. 801).

10.10 LEARNING IN CA-FOR-SLA?

A doubt has been expressed by all reviewers of the efforts at applying the CA framework to SLA problems: It is unclear what CA findings may mean in practice vis-à-vis efforts at understanding L2 learning. This is because no *a priori* concept of 'learning' can be assumed, unless speakers in a given interaction happen to orient to learning (Seedhouse, 2005; Kasper, 2006; Mori, 2007). A strategy to address learning from a CA perspective has been to study interactions longitudinally, so as to be able to inspect whether over time L2 speakers can be seen to transform and expand resources displayed in past interactions, thus perhaps providing evidence of socio-interactional development in the L2.

Brouwer and Wagner (2004) illustrated the potential of this research strategy by inspecting repeated interview-like conversations over two and a half months between Tomoyo, a Japanese student in Denmark, and Viggo, her Danish acquaintance. The researchers noted that Tomoyo initially used rather general displays of trouble (*hvad siger du*, 'What do you say') but later she increasingly used more specific tokens (*hvad betyder X*, 'What does X mean'), better helping Viggo identify the source and initiate repair. She also gradually produced better timed and more varied acknowledgement tokens as well as more appropriately timed laughter as response to acknowledgement tokens from Viggo. Young and Miller (2004) undertook a more in-depth analysis of four weekly writing tutorials between Chuong, a Vietnamese ESL learner in college, and his tutor. They showed how by the third session Chuong became increasingly more active at turn taking and initiated more interactional actions associated with 'doing revision', such as producing an explanation (*this this very strong?*) and offering candidate language for the revisions. Very importantly, Young and Miller also made the point that the tutor herself changed over time in ways that were co-produced by tutor and tutee and facilitated the beneficial changes in the tutee. Hellermann (2006) tracked the growth in interactional competence witnessable over seven and a half months of instruction in the video- and audio-recorded interactions of two learners enrolled in a college ESL-sustained silent reading course. Eduardo, a 51-year-old immigrant from Mexico with limited schooling and literacy, gradually displayed ways in which he became more competent and slowly but surely began interacting and participating in the instructional events of the course. Abbey, a 21-year-old student born and schooled in China, needed much less time but also showed growth in her display of verbal and non-verbal actions during talk-at-interaction events in this classroom.

In the end, however, even when put in longitudinal perspective, the examination of interaction from a strictly CA perspective can take us only far enough to answer the question of When is L2 learning happening? while it faces difficulty answering the more traditional questions of What is L2 learning? and How does it happen? It is no coincidence, therefore, that in the three longitudinal studies we have just reviewed the researchers resorted to the help of additional theories that directly focus on learning, such as communities of practice (Brouwer and Wagner, 2004), situated learning (Young and Miller, 2004) or language socialization (Hellermann, 2006). It may be that, in the future, CA-for-SLA will need to blend other such theories and craft a theoretically hybrid intellectual space that enables a fuller exploration of L2 learning.

10.11 GRAMMAR IS SOCIAL: SYSTEMIC FUNCTIONAL LINGUISTICS

Systemic Functional Linguistics (SFL) is a school of linguistics that respecifies grammar as a social semiotic process, that is, as the social action of meaning-making, which always occurs in context and is driven by functions and purposes in the lives of communities. It investigates the relationship between meaning and form, content and wording, context and text, integrally. Instead of viewing these pairs as analytical dichotomies, it considers them inseparable, complementary counterparts that explain how people 'mean', how they construe their experience through meaning making. This is studied mainly via the analysis of phenomena beyond the clause that are instantiated in oral and written texts. The meaning-making potential entailed in the discourse-semantic and lexicogrammatical resources of a language is enabled by the interpretive expectations of use of the larger society and as they are instantiated in particular contexts of situation. When applied to SLA problems, SFL compels us to redefine additional language learning as semiotic development in an L2, or the development of flexible meaning-making L2 capacities across contexts.

SFL was founded in the 1960s by M. A. K. Halliday, a UK-born and Australia-adopted linguist. He completed his doctorate in Mandarin Chinese at the University of London and taught that language for several years, after which he was inducted into linguistics by the successors of the Prague School. In the mid-1970s he relocated in Australia, where he wrote many of his most influential writings, and he currently resides in Hong Kong. Given this intellectual trajectory, SFL can be said to have ties with European functionalism but to be decidedly international. It has become the most practised linguistic approach in Australia (and the only linguistic movement to have had a serious impact on national educational practices ever), but it also encompasses a geographically widespread and large research community, with an international association, an annual conference since 1974 and a flagship journal, *Functions of Language,* published by John Benjamins. In the view of some, SFL has grown to be the strongest competitor of Chomskyan linguistics, the formalist linguistic school *par excellence.*

In the context of L2 learning, a few researchers in North America have heralded the approach – in particular, Mary Schleppegrell (2004), Heidi Byrnes (2006) and Mariana Achugar and Cecilia Colombi (2008). All of them have argued that SFL offers SLA researchers unique advantages. Nevertheless, in SLA other schools of linguistics have been endorsed more strongly, for example, cognitive linguistics (which, like SFL, accords meaning a pivotal place in its theory of language) and corpus linguistics (which, also much like SFL, places language use beyond the sentence at the centre of the descriptive enterprise). And, yet, SFL has a much more explicit social orientation than cognitive linguistics or even corpus linguistics does. It is perhaps for this reason that it has greatly influenced other lines of critically oriented functional linguistic work, including social semiotics, the study of multimodality, Critical Discourse Analysis and ecolinguistics. SFL-inspired SLA research (e.g. Young and Nguyen, 2002; Schleppegrell, 2004; Mohan and Slater, 2006) has engaged in the in-depth description of the language resources associated with various academic registers that most people learn during schooling, explicating the challenges that they pose for L2 users. Particularly rich are descriptions of how the registers of history and science differ from everyday language. By comparison, studies of actual development of meaning-making capacities in the L2 are still rare. In the next section, we examine three emergent efforts in this direction.

10.12 LEARNING HOW TO MEAN IN AN L2

L2-oriented SFL scholars have focused on the ways in which users of a language gradually develop the capacity to transform oral or everyday language and mobilize it into the range of formal and written registers that are required for successful functioning in academic contexts. Cecilia Colombi and Mariana Achugar have applied this SFL view of academic language development to the context of the university education of Spanish heritage speakers in the United States. Many of these learners already possess strong oral expertise for meaning making in daily-life contexts, but they wish to expand their competencies and learn more specialized registers for future professional goals.

In a series of longitudinal studies reviewed by Achugar and Colombi (2008), Colombi tracked changes towards more academic writing in the essays written over nine months by Rosa, Roberto and Lucía, three Mexican-American college students enrolled in a Spanish course. She was able to demonstrate three kinds of positive change. First, over time Rosa, Roberto and Lucía made their writing more academic-sounding by using a higher proportion of content words (nouns, verbs, adjectives and adverbs), that is, by increasing their textual use of what is known as **lexical density**. This is in contrast to oral and informal discourse, which typically contains a higher number of function words (pronouns, demonstratives, articles, prepositions). Second, they also increasingly used more expressions that packaged and condensed a given meaning over grammatically incongruent wording, or what Hallidayans call **grammatical metaphor**. This can be illustrated in the English utterance *the withdrawal of assistance led to concern*. The nouns *withdrawal, assistance* and *concern* actually mean two actions ('to withdraw', 'to assist') and one quality ('being concerned'). More grammatically congruent pairings of form and meaning would be preferred in oral and everyday discourse, for example: *someone stopped helping* and *someone is concerned*. Third, and as part of the increase in the use of grammatical metaphor, towards the end of the nine-month period of study the essays written by Rosa, Roberto and Lucía showed a decrease in what is called by SFL scholars **grammatical intricacy**, that is, language that relies on subordination to express logical connections. To continue with our example, the verb *led to* does not really mean any action, like verbs usually do, but instead establishes a cause–effect connection between two ideas. In everyday language, the same logical relation could be expressed more congruently by means of subordination, via an adverbial clause that expresses temporal or logical relations: *when/because someone stopped helping, they got worried*. The grammatical intricacy of the essays declined over time as these writers gradually tapped grammatical metaphor to express logical connections between textual elements, instead of relying exclusively on subordination. In sum, by slowly engaging in greater lexical density, more abundant and varied use of grammatical metaphor, and lesser grammatical intricacy, these writers continued developing the kinds of flexible L2 repertoires that can be called upon in written, formal contexts of L2 use.

Another interesting application of SFL to the study of additional language learning can be found in the notion of **functional recasts**, proposed by Bernard Mohan in the context of content-based education for English language learners in Canada (see Mohan and Beckett, 2003; Mohan and Slater, 2006). Unlike the recasts studied by cognitive-interactionists, which focus on formal errors (see Chapter 4, section 4.11), functional recasts offer semantic paraphrases that edit a learner's discourse towards more formal ways of expressing a certain academic meaning. Specifically, teachers offer functional recasts to support learners in their efforts to achieve higher lexical density, more grammatical metaphor and less grammatical intricacy in their academic oral expression. This is shown in an excerpt from an ESL college classroom in Canada, involving a teacher and a student interacting during an oral presentation about the human brain (Mohan and Beckett, 2003, p. 428):

(9)   Student: To stop the brain's aging, we can use our bodies and heads. Like walking make the circulation of blood better …

    Teacher: So, we can prevent our brain from getting weak by being mentally and physically active?

We can see that the teacher reformulation transforms 'use our bodies' into *being physically active* and 'use our heads' into *being mentally active*, thus changing the student's congruent realizations (verbs that are actions and nouns that are entities) into grammatical metaphors that construe the same meanings as adverbs and adjectives. The researchers described the occurrence of such functional recasts in the content-based classroom as 'a complex, rapid-fire editing process with [the student] as author and [the teacher] as editor, both working to enhance the text that [the student] is creating' (pp. 430–1). Interestingly, they also noted that as learners experiment with the processes that result in higher lexical density and more abundant use of grammatical metaphor, results will vary, and the teacher may at times offer semantic paraphrases that push learners in the reverse direction towards more congruent language, thus 'undoing the learner's over-ambitious attempts at less congruent and more compact statements' (p. 428). Once again, then, and as every approach to L2 learning shows, development is not linear.

A third area of contribution by SFL scholars is perhaps lesser known among SLA researchers but also extremely interesting. It pertains to the study of social 'identities as indexed in expanding language choices' (Achugar and Colombi, 2008, p. 49). This is done by analysing interpersonal language resources that SFL scholars have identified as organized into **appraisal systems** (Martin, 2000). These resources help construct the user of the language as taking a stance, producing an evaluation and holding authority. Traditional resources may be hedging devices, for example by using modal verbs in certain ways, but the lexicogrammatical devices that construct appraisal are subtle and they extend over clauses, as meaning making usually does. Achugar (reported in Achugar and Colombi, 2008) tracked such changes in the answers that Marcelo, a graduate student in a bilingual Master of Fine Arts programme in southwest Texas, offered when she asked 'what does it mean [to you] that the program is bilingual?' at two different times, one year apart. As a first-year student, Marcelo was able to construct affect attitudes by expressing feelings (*me impresiona*, 'it impresses me') and drawing on references to personal experience in order to answer the question. As a second-year student, he used subjective evaluating devices (*yo creo que*, 'I think that') and even attempted to mention published authors (*no me acuerdo cómo se llamaba ni cómo se llamaba lo que escribió pero …*, 'I don't remember the name or the title, but …'). Achugar interprets these changes as indexing a developed sense of expertise and belonging to the academic community, an 'awareness of the resources available to present oneself as an authority and to be recognized as a member of [a] professional community' (Achugar and Colombi, 2008, p. 53).

In sum, the SFL approach offers much promise for SLA purposes. However, it remains to be seen whether SLA researchers will take more full advantage of the benefits of using it to illuminate the study of L2 learning.

10.13 LANGUAGE LEARNING IS SOCIAL LEARNING: LANGUAGE SOCIALIZATION THEORY

Language socialization theory respecifies language learning as fundamentally about social learning. This vibrant area of research has expanded greatly in its three decades of existence, as two authoritative reviews by Garrett and Baquedano-López (2002) and Duff (2007) amply show. It originated in the field of linguistic anthropology during the 1970s and early 1980s, when the seminal work of Elinor Ochs and Bambi Schieffelin led the way into richly contextualized studies of young children and their caregivers, mutually engaged in social routines that helped socialize the new members into the language, culture and values of their given community (e.g. Ochs and Schieffelin, 1984). The approach was then expanded by Shirley Brice Heath (1983) to include school–community differences in socialization and an explicit focus on literacy, not only orality. Many other researchers representing the second generation that began in the 1990s have continued to expand the socialization perspective with increasingly more work being conducted in L2 and multilingual contexts.

In their reviews, Garrett and Baquedano-López and Duff characterize the study of language socialization as preeminently ethnographic and longitudinal, preoccupied with the connection between language and culture, straddling micro and macro dimensions of context, and analytically centred around routines, rituals and other kinds of human activities that recur and are typical of a given community. These commentators also characterize the framework as influenced by European critical sociologists (Bourdieu and Giddens, especially) and increasingly more open to diverse sociocultural and poststructuralist critical theories. The theoretical expansion results from a concerted effort to be responsive to the strongly multiethnic, multicultural and multilingual makeup of our contemporary world and it reaffirms a continual interest to address 'the channels of mutual influence linking ideology, practice, and outcome' (Garrett and Baquedano-López, p. 355). Many of the titles of language socialization studies since the 2000s thus flag key terms, such as 'narrative', 'identity' and 'ideology', that are also associated with other sociocultural and poststructuralist approaches to the social study of language.

10.14 THE PROCESS OF LANGUAGE SOCIALIZATION: ACCESS AND PARTICIPATION

Much L2 socialization research has explored the kinds of cultural repertoire that make membership into a group possible, and the social processes that may support learners' appropriation of such repertoires. In doing so, this work has thrown into sharp relief the ways in which access to the new language and participation in the new community is not without struggles for L2 learners.

A common obstacle is when assumed shared knowledge is actually not shared. For example, Patricia Duff (2004) discovered that it was a typical practice in two grade 10 classes in a Canadian high school to draw on pop culture during animated teacher–student discussions. The teachers and the Canada-born students would make jokes, tell anecdotes and structure social studies debates around what they thought was common-knowledge references to *The Simpsons*, the British royal family, and so on. They seemed to use such talk effectively, in essence connecting relevant personal knowledge with academic subjects, an excellent educational practice that usually maximizes learning. However, for the ESL members of the two classes, who had lived in Canada for one to three years only and were largely unfamiliar with Canadian pop culture, such talk only served to silence them and weaken their learning of the subject matter. Interestingly, none of the participants in these classrooms showed much awareness of just how difficult these interaction events were: fast-paced, full of slang and with many speakers contributing at the same time. Instead, the silence of the ESL peers was interpreted by the teachers, the Canada-born students, and even the ESL students themselves, as shyness and limited language ability, attributes associated with dominant ideologies of 'being Asian' and 'being a newcomer'.

Second language socialization studies have further revealed that learning outcomes can be greatly improved when L2 learners are not construed as definitional novices and instead their invisible expertise is made visible during socializing events. For example, in a two-year study, Betsy Rymes (2003, 2004) focused on Rene, a Costa Rican boy who had arrived in the United States in kindergarten and was enrolled in second and eventually third grade in an elementary school in the southeastern United States. Rene was usually friendly and verbally outgoing but became visibly shy during the official reading lessons. Rymes showed that this shyness was interactionally created by a zealous teacher, who overacted as the expert with her excessive modelling of classroom activities, and by other already socialized students, who always beat Rene when competing for the floor. Unexpectedly, during the second year of study the boy was able to engage in the kinds of language use his teachers had been desperately trying to elicit from him. This happened when some space opened up for talking about things that were familiar to his world beyond the school. For example, he decoded successfully the word *chancy* in a phonics card game by drawing on his knowledge of *Chansey*, one of the characters in the immensely popular video game of Pokémon (Rymes, 2004). With the co-participation of other peers, who were also Hispanic immigrants and ostensibly shared inside knowledge of certain birthday customs, he also narrated to a surprised and interested Ms Spring (his white, middle-class ESL teacher) an animated face-in-the-cake story (2003, p. 397):

(10)   The first time I did it I … was like four years old. And then I took a bite, and then my dad stook my whole face in the ca:ke ((laughs slightly)) And then I started crying

Rymes emphasized that these productive moments usually happened when the students emerged as experts and the teacher was momentarily repositioned as a cultural novice in the interaction. She argued that these events where teacher–expert and learner–novice roles are reversed, or at least blurred, are important sites for language socialization and learning.

Second language socialization research has also clearly shown that access and participation are often restricted because members of a given group or community, the so-called 'experts', are variably knowledgeable, competent and willing as socialization partners. In a one-year study of the academic socialization of international students at a Canadian university, Naoko Morita (2004) investigated the experiences of six female Japanese students enrolled in a variety of Master's and doctoral courses. Among them, 23-year-old Nanako and 27-year-old Rie were doing a Master's degree in education. Both worried about their difficulties in participating in class discussions and actively sought the help of their instructors. One of the instructors whom Nanako approached responded in a supportive manner that, although without leading to any changes in Nanako's visible behaviour, greatly encouraged her and helped her learn better (p. 587):

> (11) If someone followed me in all my courses and simply observed me, she
> would have just thought that I was a quiet person. But my silence had
> different meanings in different courses. In Course E, the instructor made me
> feel that I was there even though I was quiet. In the other courses my
> presence or absence didn't seem to make any difference … I just sat there
> like an ornament.

The instructor whom Rie approached, on the other hand, explicitly construed her problems as a personal deficiency in language ability and invoked the good of the other students as a main reason for declining to make any adjustments in her teaching. After several proactive efforts, Rie had to resign herself and gave up on her hopes to recruit a willing socializing partner in this teacher: 'It was unfortunate that my presence was not respected' (p. 594). By contrast, she was able to negotiate successful participation in one of her other graduate courses, where her Japanese-Korean multicultural background was viewed as an asset: 'I could feel my own presence in this course' (p. 592). Nevertheless, it is important to remember that both expert and novice contributions are always co-constructed, not predetermined, and that their success or failure is also co-shared, rather than located in one or the other participant alone. For example, for Emiko, a 24-year-old Japanese student in the same study, an accommodating response by her instructor did not have the same benefits as it had for Nanako. Instead, Emiko felt initially more comfortable when her instructor agreed not to call on her during class discussions, but eventually her learning was short-changed because she felt cornered into the role of being the only silent member of the class.

10.15 THE OUTCOMES: WHAT IS LEARNED THROUGH L2 SOCIALIZATION?

By focusing on 'the process by which novices or newcomers in a community or culture gain communicative competence, membership, and legitimacy in the group' (Duff, 2007, p. 310), second language socialization studies help reconceptualize as social not only the process of language learning but also its outcomes. Namely, what is learned when people embark on additional language learning goes well beyond the mastery of a language, even if this is broadly conceived as including discourse, pragmatics and non-linguistic resources. It also encompasses 'appropriate identities, stances … or ideologies, and other behaviors associated with the target group and its normative practices' as well (p. 310).

Thus, for example, in a study abroad investigation, DuFon (2006) showed many interactional ways in which L2 learners of Indonesian were socialized by their host families into talking about and acting towards food. In the process, they learned a great deal of L2 vocabulary (*pedas*, 'spicy'; *asin*, 'salty') and formulas for how to compliment (*enak*, 'delicious') or directly criticize (*kurang enak*, 'not very tasty'; *hambar*, 'tasteless') the cook (both actions are apparently acceptable during Indonesian meals!). But they were also socialized into thinking of food as a central pleasure of life and some of these US learners moved towards this world-view, which was different from the more utilitarian food-as-nutrition stance they had brought with them from their home culture. Kyle, one of the study abroad students, reflected on these changes (p. 117):

(12)   My eating behavior has changed. Now I eat a lot in the morning, plus my eating etiquette has changed. Things that taste good taste really good. I kind of look at the food differently, with more respect.

The inseparability of language learning and the learning of normative ways of being and thinking is well illustrated in an ethnographic study conducted by Leslie Moore (2006), which documented L2 teaching practices during the first year of elementary schooling among the Fulbe, a multilingual Muslim majority ethnic group in the northern part of Cameroon, in west-central Africa. Fulbe children usually learn Fulfulde at home and acquire Arabic for religious purposes and French for education purposes during schooling, starting at age 6. Moore focused on the ways memorization (or guided repetition, as she prefers to call it) was used in the teaching of Arabic verses of the Qur'an, which occurred in Qur'anic schooling, and the teaching of French dialogues, which occurred in public schools. Memorization was used in both contexts because it is valued in Fulbe society as an excellent learning method, particularly suitable for children between the age of 6 and puberty, who are thought to possess a *taaskaare wuule* or virgin memory and to be *tabulae rasae* or blank slates (p. 116). However, her analysis of 90 hours of recordings over a school year showed that the method was used in subtly different ways in the two contexts. During the Qur'anic lessons, students were expected to learn from the models offered by teacher or *mallum* or by a more senior student appointed by the *mallum* to that role, never from each other. It was fully understood that they would not learn the verse contents, only the form. Appropriate learner behaviour included being attentive and mentally imitating and rehearsing the verses and (at a different pace for each student) eventually being able to faithfully perform the sacred text, adopting similar 'pronunciation, sequencing, volume, and embodiment' as the *mallum* (p. 115) and without making mistakes. If any errors occurred, the student would be interrupted and the *mallum* would repeat the full verse again without indicating the blame of the error in any way. That is, there were no correction moves of the kinds illustrated in Chapter 4, section 4.11. By contrast, during the memorization activities in the French dialogues, the pedagogical approach of teachers in the public schools was closer in all these respects to what is practised by many Western language teachers. Moore argues that these differences are linked to the distinct social learning goals of the lessons in each context. Namely, the Arabic teaching of the sacred Qur'anic verses seeks to socialize young children into traditional and ethnic Muslim and Fulbe values, such as respect, humility, reverence and discipline. By contrast, the French language taught in elementary schools is part of a national project to develop a Cameroonian modern identity, which is implicated in postcolonial French values of being *évolué* or civilized and rational, related to more general Western educational values.

This far-reaching view of the outcomes of language socialization, then, resonates with James Gee's (1990) description of language competence:

> In socially situated language use, one must simultaneously say the 'right' thing, do the 'right' thing, and in saying and doing express the 'right' beliefs, values, and attitudes.
>
> (p. 140)

While many researchers and teachers will agree with this definition of L2 competence, it raises the difficult question of whether the adoption of what a community or a group defines as 'right saying, doing and being' must be taken as the neutral, necessary and benign goal of L2 learning. If so, socialization could risk being just a more fashionable guise of the dangerous ideology of assimilation. It should be clear that this is not the intended goal of researchers who apply language socialization to L2 learning. Nevertheless, this difficult but important question is to some extent eschewed unless identity, ideology and power are brought to the fore. As we will see in the remainder of the chapter, this is precisely what identity theory can offer to SLA researchers.

10.16 SENSE OF SELF IS SOCIAL: IDENTITY THEORY

Identity theory is seldom directly examined as part of the official world of SLA. Nevertheless, the study of identity and L2 learning is one of the most vibrant research areas in the wider field of applied linguistics. Identity theory respecifies sense of self as socially constructed and socially constrained. Interest in this area began to grow when in 1993 Bonny Norton Peirce completed her dissertation on the identity struggles of five immigrant women in Canada and later published parts of the study in two extensively cited sources, an article in *TESOL Quarterly* (Norton Peirce, 1995) and a book (Norton, 2000). In 2002 a new journal was devoted to the area, the *Journal of Language, Identity, and Education*, published by Routledge. Since then, work on second language identity has only continued to intensify.

The vibrant interest that identity theory has spurred is visible in the many second language studies cited in three reviews by key contributors to this literature: Blackledge and Pavlenko (2004b), Norton (2006) and Block (2007). They note that the preferred contemporary theoretical prism to study identity in applied linguistics is poststructuralism and that narratives have become an important site to inspect identity in many L2 studies (Block, 2007, p. 867). They also warn us that identities must be understood as socially constructed and situated, always 'dynamic, contradictory, and constantly changing across time and place' (Norton, 2006, p. 502). Furthermore, they posit that people cannot freely choose who they want to be, but rather they must negotiate identity positions in the larger economic, historic, and sociopolitical structures that they inhabit and which inhabit them (Pavlenko and Blackledge, 2004b, p. 3). You will find that in their writings second language identity scholars use many words that denote this poststructuralist view of identity as dynamic and contested, for example, nouns such as *fissures, splits, splinterings, gaps* and *seepage*, and adjectives such as *shifting, fragmented, decentered* and *hybrid*. Finally, much second language identity research, although not all, is decidedly oriented towards macro dimensions of context and explicitly theorizes the social as a site of struggle in need of transformation. Much of it, therefore, explores ways in which scholarly knowledge can become a platform for advocating social justice for L2 learners (Norton Peirce, 1995; Pavlenko and Blackledge, 2004b).

The most influential model of second language identity theory has been formulated by Norton (Norton Peirce, 1995; Norton, 2000). One main concept is **investment**, or the notion that 'if learners invest in a second language, they do so with the understanding that they will acquire a wider range of symbolic and material resources, which will in turn increase the value of their cultural capital' (Norton Peirce, 1995, p. 17). The investment that a given learner makes in learning an L2 can only be understood by consideration of her identities, her desires and her changing social world, as all three contribute to the structuring of different investments at different times and across contexts. This is complemented by the claim that intertwined with their investments are L2 learners' affective and symbolic affiliations to various **communities of practice**. Some of them are real, immediate communities in which learners strive for acceptance or legitimate membership, such as the classroom communities in which Nanako, Rie and Emiko wanted to belong more fully, in the study by Morita (2004) discussed in section 10.14. Others are **imagined communities**, or communities that exist at present only in the imagination, and which learners forge on the basis of their past memberships and life history as well as on the projections they make for a better future (we will examine an example in the next section). A final key element of Norton's identity model is the notion of **the right to speak**. This right and the power to exercise it is unequally distributed, and often L2 learners find themselves positioned by others as speakers without that right. The theoretical influences on this model of identity, as Norton (2006) succinctly explains, span sociology (Pierre Bourdieu), feminism (Chris Weedon), cultural anthropology (Jean Lave and Etienne Wenger) and literary criticism (Mikhail Bakhtin). In the next two sections, I illustrate these and other concepts of second language identity theory with a selective sample of ways in which identity is relevant for two rather different kinds of context for L2 learning: circumstantial and elective.

10.17 L2 LEARNERS' IDENTITY AND POWER STRUGGLES: EXAMPLES FROM CIRCUMSTANTIAL L2 LEARNING

Circumstantial L2 learning involves situations where members of a language minority must learn the majority language for reasons over which they have little choice and which are typically associated to larger-scale world events, such as immigration, economic hardship, postcolonialism, war or occupation. Identity research in these contexts has shown that learners strive to construct positive identities for themselves from a position of marginalization, and that they do so by reference to the identity options available to them in the multiple and contradictory discourses of family, school, workplace, media and so on.

Particularly in institutional contexts where language minority learners enjoy little power, such as schools, they are seen to struggle to fashion and negotiate identities that may allow them to exercise their agency and be viewed positively by others. Many encounter only limited success in overcoming marginalization. This was shown by McKay and Wong (1996) in a two-year ethnography of the literacy and identity experiences by four adolescents, all recently arrived immigrants from Taiwan and China who were enrolled in seventh and eighth grade in a high school in California. Among them, Brad Wang was probably the least successful story. He was the only student from a lower socioeconomic background, and he experienced a spiral of dispiriting positionings that in effect ended his high-school career. For one, his verbal virtuosity in spoken and written Chinese and his prior attendance of one of the top middle schools in Shanghai were invisible to his teachers, but his lack of toys and material goods were patently visible to his peers. Being one of few Chinese mainlanders in the school, he attempted to find strength in Chinese nationalist discourses that construe mainlanders as superior to other Chinese (as did another student, who told one of the researchers, *zhengzong zhongguoren* or 'I am authentic Chinese', p. 589). However, outnumbered by the school cliques of Cantonese and Taiwanese students, this was an ineffective, isolating move. He was initially eager to catch up with English, but his desperate attempts to save face by feigning comprehension soon made him be labelled as dishonest by his teachers, who drew from the racialized discourse that blames immigrants who do not assimilate and learn English fast as unwilling and of lower moral values. In the end, he was imposed an identity as a low achiever. From that imposed identity, his great potential for literacy growth, obvious to the researchers, remained untapped by the teachers. Gradually Brad Wang began acting out and eventually dropped out.

It has also been shown that the discourses and narratives through which possible identities are available to L2 learners are always contradictory and heterogeneous, and that the identity positionings they help fashion are also subject to change. In another ethnographic study, Linda Harklau (2000) traced the experiences of Aeyfer, Claudia and Penny during their senior year of high school and their first year of college. Unlike the newcomers studied by McKay and Wong, these students were old-timers who had been in the United States between six and ten years. In high school they enjoyed favourable subject positions, partly drawn from 'broader U.S.

societal "Ellis Island" images of immigrants leaving their homes, enduring financial and emotional hardships, and through sheer perseverance succeeding in building a better life for themselves in America' (p. 46). Interestingly, teachers and students participated in the co-construction and perpetuation of this heroic immigrant identity. For example, whenever given a choice over the topic of their writing, the students repeatedly chose to write about their personal immigration story, in essence appropriating the 'Ellis Island' myth to their own advantage. This positive identity, however, coexisted with discourses of paternalism and deficiency, in teacher images of immigrant students who do their best but always struggle academically. The generally affirming experiences in high school changed radically when Aeyfer, Claudia and Penny entered a two-year community college and were tracked into ESL classes by virtue of their being classified as non-native speakers by the institution. Their readings and assignments now contained constant probes to narrate themselves in a space between 'your country' and 'the United States', which trapped these US-educated immigrants in their college teachers' imposed identity of the international student, the newcomer who needs to be socialized into new ways of being. Once again, the discourses were heterogeneous and the positionings ambivalent. For example, Harklau noted that these students' idea of 'their' country seemed to align with neither the distant social worlds they had left behind many years before nor 'the White, middle-class version of culture that they and their teachers referred to generically as "American"' (p. 56). Bored and frustrated as a result of such imposed identities, Aeyfer, Claudia and Penny eventually avoided re-enrolling in more ESL classes, once they discovered they were not compulsory.

Finally, second language identity research has shown that not only surrounding discourses and ideologies, but also actual and imagined communities of practice, help structure the investments and, consequently, the varied learning trajectories and learning outcomes that are observed in contexts of circumstantial L2 learning. Norton Peirce's (1993) analysis of Katarina's story clearly illustrates this point. Katarina was a Polish immigrant who had a Master's degree in biology and 17 years of teaching experience in her home country, but she knew no English (although she was trilingual in Polish, Russian and German) when she arrived in Canada with her husband and their six-year-old daughter. Katarina felt alienated, not her own self, when positioned as an immigrant by others and 'bitterly resisted being positioned as unskilled and uneducated' (p. 142). Despite her new changed context, she continued to view herself as a member of a community of well-educated professionals. Therefore, and as part of her quest to regain her past professional status in a new professional life, she invested in this imagined community by completing an 18-month computer course. In order to meet this goal, she found herself forced to work as a part-time homemaker, a job that did not match her professional training and in which she did not recognize herself. Eventually she also decided to drop her subsidized nine-month ESL course only four months into it, essentially choosing the study of computers over the study of English, even though English was also a necessary tool in the fashioning of a professional identity. This choice was structured by her greater investment in a well-educated self than in an English speaking self, which was part of her identity as a member of her imagined professional community: 'I choose computer course, not because I have to speak, but because I have to think' (p. 142). Katarina's English did improve quite a bit over time, but the improvement came out of being able to practise English in a low-stakes context that she only viewed as temporary and not a part of her 'normal' self, as she felt relaxed when speaking in English with the elderly she was caring for. In stark contrast, with English-speaking professionals, such as teachers and doctors, she found it difficult to speak. This observation was true of other women in the study and led Norton (2001) to note that 'the very people to whom the learners were most uncomfortable speaking English were the very people who were members of – or gatekeepers to – the learners' imagined communities' (p. 166). The question remains as to whether and how Katarina, and other women in positions like hers, will develop not only L2 fluency in low-stakes contexts but also the ability to claim the right to speak in the L2 in high-stakes contexts, which are likely to be related to the communities that they envision for their future selves.

10.18 CLOSE IMPACT OF IDENTITIES ON L2 LEARNING: EXAMPLES FROM ELECTIVE L2 LEARNING

Elective L2 learning is engaged by people who learn a language from a majority position of equal power and hence with no evident or immediate power struggles. Studies of identity in elective language learning contexts are less numerous than those conducted in contexts of circumstantial bilingualism, and they have mostly concentrated on tracing the experiences of foreign language learners when they enter into contact with the L2 community, typically during residence in the L2 environment.

Identity research in these contexts has shown that foreign language learners also have investments that are structured by their identities and that guide different learners to allocate energy and effort differently in their efforts to learn an L2. For example, as we mentioned in Chapter 9 (section 9.4), many foreign language learners embrace the emulation of an idealized native speaker as a goal. This idealized goal draws from the discourse of monolingualism dominant in much foreign language education, which holds that the best kind of linguistic competence is that which is attained by primary socialization (i.e. in a language given by birth) and which contains no impurity or trace of other languages (i.e. no codeswitching or code mixing, no transfer, no foreign accent) (see Ortega, 1999). Nevertheless, other foreign language learners may actually selectively resist emulating aspects of that idealization, precisely because they clash with their current sense of self. This was shown by Yumiko Ohara (2001) when she examined the pitch levels used by three groups of female Japanese speakers in the United States. Ohara recorded the women on a series of scripted tasks in both languages and undertook a phonetic analysis of pitch frequencies, then interviewed them. The five Japanese-dominant bilinguals (i.e. international graduate students from Japan) consistently produced higher pitch in Japanese than in English. At the other extreme of the spectrum, the five 'budding bilinguals' (p. 236), who were enrolled in a first-semester university course, showed no evidence of changing their pitch across their two languages, neither did they give any signs of being aware of any pitch issues in Japanese when they were interviewed. These findings support the contention that in Japanese a high-pitched voice is a recognizable marker of femininity and suggest that certain subtle indexical resources of identity, such as the association between pitch and femininity, may be beyond the grasp of learners in the beginning of the learning process. The most interesting finding, however, arose from the five English-dominant Japanese speaking females, who had at least four years of Japanese university study and one year of living in Japan. All five were acutely aware of the cultural significance of pitch. However, their agency to act upon this awareness was exercised differently. Three of them produced the expected higher pitch in Japanese. In their interviews, they explicitly mentioned accommodation as the main reason. They felt they needed a higher pitch if they wanted to sound Japanese and come across as polite to Japanese interlocutors. The other two females, however, did not change their pitch. In their interviews, they explicitly revealed their resistance to this one aspect of the L2 in the construction of their Japanese identities (p. 244):

(13)   Sometimes it would really disgust me, seeing those Japanese girls, they were not even girls, some of them were in their late twenties, but they would use those real high voices to try to impress and make themselves look real cute for men. I decided that there was no way I wanted to do that.

For elective language learners, as much as for circumstantial ones, the extent to which they can exercise their agency and be who they want to be in the L2 is constrained by the agency of other speakers, who, like them, also draw on ideologies rooted in their surrounding discourses. This was the argument developed by Meryl Siegal (1996) in her case study of Mary, a high-school teacher from New Zealand who in her mid-forties spent a year in Japan funded by her government. Mary was heavily invested in learning to be pragmatically appropriate in the L2 and fervently wanted to be the kind of person who is polite and does not offend while using her upper-intermediate Japanese. Although she consciously avoided using honorifics because she found them too difficult, she developed multiple strategies to fashion this new identity as a humble and feminine self during interactions with Japanese speakers. For example, she deployed many hesitancy markers (e.g. *anō*) in her talk, she occasionally adopted a singing voice to come across as cheerful and she covered her mouth when laughing. Despite such careful efforts, Siegal captured an interaction during office hours between Mary and one of her Japanese teachers, in which she inadvertently was rather massively inappropriate when speaking to a social superior. For example, she used the particle *deshō* profusely without being aware of its multifunctional meanings that made it inappropriate in the context and she closed the exchange with 'excuse me, thank you very much' (*chotto dōmo, sumimasen, arigatō gozaimasu*) in a singing voice that was appropriate for a service encounter but not for a meeting with a professor. All these choices were aggravated by the fact that her speech was stripped of honorifics, which are essential when speaking to a social superior in Japanese. Interestingly, even though she violated a number of pragmatic norms, about which she cared greatly, she remained wholly unaware of the potentially face-threatening effect of her talk. This was because her interlocutor apparently did not give her any overt feedback. Siegal suggested this response may have been motivated in the Japanese nationalist discourse of the *henna gaijin* or 'strange foreigners', which construes Japanese as a difficult language that foreigners cannot and need not master; it would be only an oddity for foreigners to learn Japanese things too well and become too Japanese.

Finally, studies show that the socially constructed categories of gender, race and class are relevant for elective L2 learning in that they affect foreign language learners' investments, desires and identity negotiations in a number of important ways. For example, sexism greatly pervaded the language learning experiences of a group of US women during study abroad in Russia (Polanyi, 1995). Ironically, it also encouraged them to stretch their L2 competence, as they learned to negotiate in the L2 'how to get out of humiliating social encounters, how to interpret the intentions of even polite-seeming educated young men, how to get themselves in one piece after an evening spent in fending off unwanted advances' (p. 289). Gendered racism put an end to Misheila's desire to learn any Spanish ever again, after a bitter study abroad period in Spain during which she found herself constantly verbally harassed by men (Talburt and Stewart, 1999, p. 169):

(14)   My observation is very negative. For me while I've been in Spain I notice that the African woman is a symbol of sexuality. When I walk in the streets I always receive comments on my skin and sexual commentaries, especially with old men and adolescents between the age of 15 and 20.

Class, by way of contrast, was a main identity force for Alice, a college French student in the United States who engaged in L2 learning as a project of social upward mobility and identity reconstruction. This case was carefully documented by Celeste Kinginger (2004) over four years. Alice was bought up by a working-class single mum who moved her two daughters through Ohio and Georgia, and later by her grandfather in rural Arkansas. She had experienced many hardships in life and felt different from her younger and more privileged college peers. She was invested in French for its symbolic promise to help her transcend and escape her difficult life. Kinginger described the many ways in which Alice drew from the US popular discourses of French as the language of love, culture and frivolity, which are reinforced by textbook materials and the media, and used this ideology to imagine a future French-speaking self that afforded her the opportunity to symbolically exchange trailer parks for châteaux, as it were. Despite many disappointments over four years of several study abroad stays, Alice was eventually able to succeed in her quest. In order to do so, she had to engage in deep renegotiations of identity and had to look for opportunities for learning in less than obvious places. In the end, however, she was able to complete her project of a new identity as a competent L2 French speaker and a future French language teacher. Learning French allowed her 'to upgrade her access to cultural capital, become a cultured person, and share her knowledge with others' (p. 240).

10.19 TECHNOLOGY-MEDIATED COMMUNICATION AS A SITE FOR SOCIALLY RICH L2 LEARNING

We cannot finish a chapter on the social dimensions of L2 learning without commenting on the learning of an additional language in virtual contexts, that is, in contexts mediated by technology, since so much of our contemporary lives are spent in networked communication that transcends space and time. As Kern (2006) chronicles in an authoritative review of L2 learning and technology, the full palette of social theories we have discussed in this chapter has been successfully applied to the study of this area, expanding the epistemological landscape and also establishing a metaphor of **technology as medium,** or technology that creates 'sites for interpersonal communication, multimedia publication, distance learning, community participation, and identity formation' (p. 192). Lam (2006), Sykes et al. (2008) and Thorne and Black (2007) offer good reviews of cutting-edge developments in the domain. This research shows that technologies put to the use of digital social networks can foster second language and literacy learning that is remarkably rich in social terms.

A stream of socioculturally oriented research about L2 learning and technology has concentrated on exploring the learning about target discourses and cultures that accrues from participation in online communication either with classmates or in geographically and culturally distant classroom communities. In some studies, an expansion of the socio-interactional competence in the L2 is documented. For example, Darhower (2002) analysed the discourse produced by two intact classes of fourth-semester Spanish students when they completed weekly in-class chat activities over a nine-week term. He noted that the foreign language was used for a much wider variety of interpersonal purposes than would have been possible in the official face-to-face classroom discourse, including teasing and joking, and even deploying profane language during half-humorous flaming. He argued that such language use has potential for the expansion of L2 sociolinguistic repertoires. In many other studies, foreign language students are seen to develop much cultural knowledge about the L2. This is true of so-called telecollaborations among geographically and culturally distant classroom communities (Belz and Thorne, 2006) but also of less structured and more casual L2–L1 online encounters (e.g. Tudini, 2007). Other benefits of these virtual engagements are that students are often able to confront stereotypes and prejudice and increase cultural self-awareness (e.g. O'Dowd, 2005). Technology-mediated crosscultural partnerships are also particularly prone to generate healthy doses of intercultural discomfort and tension (e.g. Basharina, 2007) that should be carefully addressed by language teachers.

Much of the insight we currently have about technology and language learning comes from another stream of research about the use of out-of-school technology by immigrant youth. The findings amply document processes by which technology can help minority L2 learners fashion positive identities that can counter the negative positionings available to them in the world of school. This is done in many cases through the development of online relationships in transnational communities. Lam (2000) documented the story of Almon, a teenage immigrant from Hong Kong who had resided in the US for five years. He felt unsure of his English skills and discriminated against in the context of a school culture that positioned him as an ESL learner and a low achiever. His engagement with instant messaging, penpal emailing and his creation of a webpage about his favourite teenage Japanese pop singer opened up a new world of peers on the internet, who helped him construct a new, confident identity in which Almon felt an expert in web design and Japanese pop culture and a competent user of English. In a later article, Lam (2004) reported on two young women, Yu Qing and Tsu Ying, who emigrated from China and had been in the US for three years. Even though they were B students, they felt uncomfortable speaking English in the cliquish life of school, where they were caught in between worlds, unable to access much interaction with their Anglo peers and intimidated by their American-born Chinese peers, with whom they shared the same ethnic background but little linguistic or cultural common ground. Experimenting with the internet and looking for ways to practise their English online, they discovered a chatroom where immigrant Chinese people from all over the world chatted in English. Yu Qing and Tsu Ying showed a tremendous level of engagement with this new community, joining daily for about three hours during the eight-month study. They freely and creatively used English and mixed it with Romanized Cantonese, using these resources to create rapport and construct a shared identity as bilingual English–Cantonese speakers with a shared experience of immigration. Lam noted that participation in this supportive virtual community helped them gain English fluency and boosted their confidence also in their school environment.

Finally, several studies have documented remarkable literacy engagement by L2 users who found in technology-mediated virtual communities the space for creative writing and self-expression that they could not find in the academic discourse of schoolwork. Black (2006) chronicles the success story of Tanaka Nanako (presumably a self-chosen pseudonym). She was a young Chinese girl from Shanghai whose family emigrated to Canada when she was 11. Being a great fan of anime, the world-popular Japanese animation, she soon discovered fanfiction, which are online sites in which fans of media series (e.g. *Star Trek*, Harry Potter, anime) post their own creative writing that spins off the officially authored stories. Nanako read anime fanfiction avidly before she finally created her own page at the age of 13. Soon thereafter she became a prolific fanfiction writer on the site. Black documents the many ways in which Nanako's writing of fanfiction afforded her a wealth of process writing experiences that included peer feedback and multiple revisions as well as space for the development of positive identities. For example, one of Nanako's posted stories (written in 14 chapters!) 'became wildly popular' and 'received over 1,700 reviews from readers' (2006, p. 177). One can only imagine the tremendous boost that she experienced in her identity as a person and an English writer. Likewise, Yi (2007) described the less dramatic but equally intense engagement with literacy in Korean by Joan, a Korean–English bilingual ninth-grader in a US school who was able to thrive as a creative and versatile writer with the support of a local digital community of about 25 Korean heritage youth in her same city. Finally, the production and consumption of online (and traditional) texts that draw on multimodal forms of meaning making, including language, images and sound, has also been identified as a particularly important site of language and literacy learning that multilingual users, particularly young ones, can exploit with positive results for their academic achievement as much as for their identity development (e.g. Kenner and Kress, 2003; Hull and Nelson, 2005).

10.20 NEVER JUST ABOUT LANGUAGE

As I hope to have made clear throughout this chapter, for many, perhaps most, people who undertake to learn an additional language, what is at stake is not only the odds that they succeed in acquiring the second language or even that they succeed in acquiring the literacy and professional competencies that they desire for themselves or that they may need to function in society. For many, perhaps most additional second language learners, it is about succeeding in attaining material, symbolic and affective returns that they desire for themselves. It is also about being considered by others as worthy social beings. If this is so, then we must conclude that people who undertake to learn an additional language are engaged in changing their worlds. We can say, in this sense, that L2 learning is always transformative.

Much goes into the definition of what must develop when L2 competence develops, if the insights from the social turn are heeded. As Norton (2006) succinctly put it:

> second language learners need to struggle to appropriate the voices of others; they need to learn to command the attention of their listeners; they need to negotiate language as a system and as a social practice; and they need to understand the practices of the communities with which they interact.
>
> (p. 504)

To this broad list, Norton has proposed we must also add the 'ability to claim the right to speak' (Norton Peirce, 1995, p. 23) and 'an awareness of how to challenge and transform social practices of marginalization' (p. 25). That is, part and parcel of becoming competent in an additional language is growing able to exercise agency and productive power (Kamberelis, 2001) and transform one's worlds in and through the L2. But L2 learners as much as the people who surround them can have different affiliative or antagonistic engagements, as Bhabha (1994, p. 3) calls them, and these will influence the uneven access to, and variegated outcomes of, L2 learning. The institutions in which people live, and the material, social and cultural histories they live with and through, add complexity to people's ability to change their worlds through and in the learning of an additional language. Social contexts for L2 learning are, in this view, sites of struggle and transformation. But once we become convinced that L2 learning is never just about language, and that it is always transformative, the predicament is not small.

For one, we learn that we cannot promise L2 learners that their plights, their marginalization or their desires will be solved, only if (and as soon as) they attain a good level of L2 competence. Just as learning an L2 is never only about language, so is being judged as a competent and valued social being never just a matter of sheer L2 competence, even under greatly expanded definitions that include gestures and concepts (Lantolf and Thorne, 2006) or normative ways of saying, doing and being (see section 10.15). Many studies show learners with higher linguistic competence being bypassed by gatekeepers in favour of others with lesser linguistic expertise precisely because of race (Toohey, 2001), gender (Willett, 1995) or lack of material and symbolic resources (McKay and Wong, 1996). These influences were more important than linguistic and even sociocultural competence in those contexts.

With the awareness that L2 learning it never just about language also comes the question of whether we should do something about it. If the project of learning an additional language is itself about transforming social worlds, shouldn't educators who serve L2 learners, and researchers who study them, support them in their transformative efforts? Critical applied linguists have suggested the answer is yes (Canagarajah, 2002; Pennycook, 2004; Heller, 2007). As noted, some poststructuralist identity authors also maintain that scholarly knowledge can become a platform for advocating social justice for L2 learners (Norton Peirce, 1995; Pavlenko and Blackledge, 2004b). Suggestions have been also made for how to work for transformation, both by developing resources for L2 learners from minority groups to learn to empower themselves and contest marginalization through and in L2 learning (Davis et al., 2005) and by helping L2 learners from majority groups to empower themselves and critically interrogate normative discourses also through and in L2 learning (Kramsch, 2006). The social turn in SLA continues to entice people who are interested in understanding additional language learning to venture and glimpse new possibilities for L2 learners in their social contexts.

10.21 SUMMARY

- Since the mid-1990s, there is an ongoing social turn in SLA that has its roots in social constructivism, socioculturalism and poststructuralism and posits that we can only understand L2 learning if we examine it fully embedded in its social context.

- Vygotskian sociocultural theory respecifies cognition as fundamentally social and proposes consciousness as the central function of human cognition and the main object of inquiry; language is used to create thought, it also transforms thought, and it is the source of learning.

- The main concepts to remember in Vygotskian sociocultural theory are: language as a symbolic tool; mediation through object, others and self;

social, private and inner speech; the emergence of self-regulation; and the Zone of Proximal Development.

- The Vygotskian approach to SLA conceives of L2 learning as joint activity in which construction of co-knowledge is enabled and in which self-regulation is facilitated and negotiated through different kinds of mediation.

- L2 learning is captured through the microgenetic method during meditated thought and talk in L2 and L1 and it is evaluated not as already attained development but as potential improvement towards self-regulation for the future.

- CA-for-SLA investigates the socio-interactional accomplishments of L2 learners as they do communication, and it reconceptualizes into interactional resources actions and solutions that other approaches may take for evidence of deficiency.

- By following the radically emic imperative of grounding interpretive claims in the observable or witnessable evidence of interactional actions, CA-for-SLA proposes that a number of categories (e.g. error, negotiation for meaning, learner identity, linguistic expertise) have no constant value but are made relevant or irrelevant anew in each local interaction and each turn-at-talk.

- Co-participants in an L2 interaction typically, but not always, co-orient to joint interactional action and interactional identities. The external contexts and settings make some orientations, identities and goals more available than others, but they do not completely determine them.

- Systemic Functional Linguistics respecifies grammar as a social semiotic process, that is, as the social action of meaning making. The framework has been applied to L2 learning more readily in order to describe the textual challenges of L2 learners but less often to investigate semiotic development in the L2.

- The development of academic repertoires can be studied by inspecting textual changes in lexical density, grammatical metaphor and grammatical intricacy longitudinally; all three qualities are related to semiotic processes involved in making formal language less grammatically congruent and more informationally dense than everyday language.

- Functional recasts and appraisal systems are two other areas in which some SFL-inspired efforts at studying semiotic development in an L2 have been made.

- Language socialization theory sees language learning and social learning as constitutive of each other; it investigates how, through social activity with willing experts, newcomers gain not only language knowledge but also membership and legitimacy in a given group or community.

- In L2 studies, language socialization researchers have concentrated on studying what kinds of access to the new language and what conditions of participation in the new community support or hinder L2 learners' appropriation of the linguistic and cultural resources needed to be accepted in a new context as a competent member.

- The outcomes of language socialization are far reaching and include normative ways of viewing the world. That is, by increasingly participating more actively in activities with others, learners acquire new ways of saying, doing and being.

- Identity theory reconceptualizes sense of self as socially constructed and socially constrained and shows how this construct helps explain different language learning trajectories and their outcomes.

- The main concepts to remember in identity theory are: investment, communities of practice, imagined communities and the right to speak.

- Identity, ideology and power are intertwined and help understand L2 learning.

- In contexts for circumstantial as well as elective L2 learning, learners struggle to fashion identities that allow them to exercise their agency and be viewed positively by others; possible identities are made available by surrounding discourses in social structures that yield unequal power; learners have some agency to negotiate, resist, accommodate or change their identities across time and space.

- Technology-based communication affords L2 learners rich opportunities for identity negotiation and reconstruction and social and cultural learning, as well as unprecedented support for literacy development.

- The social perspectives on L2 learning discussed in this chapter, and particularly among them the poststructuralist approaches, suggest that L2 learning is never just about language; for many, perhaps most, people who undertake to learn an additional language, it is about succeeding in attaining material, symbolic and affective returns that they desire for themselves and it is also about being considered by others as worthy social beings. In both cases, learners are engaged in changing their worlds, and thus L2 learning is always transformative.

10.22 ANNOTATED SUGGESTIONS FOR FURTHER READING

Thinking socially, rather than psychologically, is not an easy task. You can read Kubota's (2003) incisive allegoric story of Barbara to understand what I mean by this. In that article she shows that it is common to go through a difficult and unfinished personal transformation in our understanding of the ineluctably social construction of all knowledge and discourse, including the knowledge and discourse of L2 learning. A specific danger is to read studies of L2 learning that inspect the problems from a radical, socially respecified perspective and, nevertheless, to miss the point and reinterpret what we read through our accustomed ways of thinking. Therefore, I urge you to enter the readings with an open mind and a holistic outlook and, at the same time, to pay close attention to detail as you delve into this literature.

For each of the topics discussed, the authoritative reviews cited at the beginning of each exposition can help you gain a good sense of the area and lead you to work beyond the limited selection that could be accommodated in the chapter. If you are the kind of reader who benefits from first looking into concrete examples of studies and only then reading the reviews, I can offer the following reading suggestions. Empirical studies can consolidate your view of Vygotskian sociocultural theory, and Frawley and Lantolf (1985), Donato (1994) and Nassaji and Swain (2000) are particularly interesting and easy to read for this purpose. For CA-for-SLA, reading the oft-cited Firth and Wagner (1997) is a must, followed up by the hybrid L2 CA studies by Hellermann (2006) and Richards (2006). The best short cut for applications of Systemic Functional Linguistics to L2 learning is Achugar and Colombi (2008), who also offer particularly helpful tables summarizing much relevant research. For language socialization theory, I recommend you read Gregory et al. (2007). This richly textured study of 6-year-old Sahil and his grandmother Razia in Bangladeshi London will help you connect the various themes reviewed in the sections you read about this approach. A good introduction to identity theory would be to read the empirical studies by Norton Peirce (1995), McKay and Wong (1996) and Kinginger (2004), in that order, as they complement one another and will strengthen your understanding of the approach. With respect to technology-mediated L2 learning, Lam (2004) offers an excellent example for how the framework of second language socialization can be creatively employed to study technology, and Black (2006) makes a convincing case for the truly unprecedented opportunities for L2 learning and identity transformation that social technology can offer youth. Finally, the studies collected in the important book by Pavlenko and Blackledge (2004a) can serve as a nice bridge between identity theory and critical applied linguistics.

References

Abe, J. A. A. (2005) The predictive validity of the Five-Factor Model of personality with preschool age children: a nine year follow-up study. *Journal of Research in Personality, 39*, 423–42.

Abbot-Smith, K., and Tomasello, M. (2006) Exemplar-learning and schematization in a usage-based account of syntactic acquisition. *Linguistic Review, 23*, 275–90.

Achugar, M., and Colombi, M. C. (2008) Systemic Functional Linguistic explorations into the longitudinal study of the advanced capacities: the case of Spanish heritage language learners. In L. Ortega and H. Byrnes (eds), *The longitudinal study of advanced L2 capacities* (pp. 36–57). New York: Routledge.

Ackerman, P. L. (2003) Aptitude complexes and trait complexes. *Educational Psychologist, 38*(2), 85–93.

Albert, A., and Kormos, J. (2004) Creativity and narrative task performance: an exploratory study. *Language Learning, 54*, 277–310.

Aljaafreh, A., and Lantolf, J. P. (1994) Negative feedback as regulation and second language learning in the zone of proximal development. *Modern Language Journal, 78*, 465–83.

Ammar, A., and Spada, N. (2006) One size fits all? Recasts, prompts and the acquisition of English possessive determiners. *Studies in Second Language Acquisition, 28*, 543–74.

Andersen, R. W. (1983) Transfer to somewhere. In S. M. Gass and L. Selinker (eds), *Language learning* (pp. 177–201). Rowley, MA: Newbury House.

Andersen, R. W. (1984a) The One to One Principle of interlanguage construction. *Language Learning, 34*, 77–95.

Andersen, R. W. (1984b) What's gender good for, anyway? In R. W. Andersen (ed.), *Second languages: a cross-linguistic perspective* (pp. 77–100). Rowley, MA: Newbury House.

Andersen, R. W. (1993) Four operating principles and input distribution as explanations for underdeveloped and mature morphological systems. In K. Hyltenstam and A. Vigorb (eds), *Progression and regression in language* (pp. 309–39). New York: Cambridge University Press.

Andersen, R. W., and Shirai, Y. (1996) The primacy of aspect in first and second language acquisition: the pidgin–creole connection. In W. C. Ritchie and T. K. Bhatia (eds), *Handbook of second language acquisition* (pp. 527–70). San Diego, CA: Academic Press.

Anderson, J. R. (1983) *The architecture of cognition*. Cambridge, MA: Harvard University Press.

Anderson, J. R. (2007) *How can the human mind occur in the physical universe?* New York: Oxford University Press.

Aoyama, K., Guion, S. G., Flege, J. E., Yamada, T., and Akahane-Yamada, R. (2008) The first years in an L2–speaking environment: a comparison of Japanese children and adults learning American English. *International Review of Applied Linguistics, 46*, 61–90.

Aston, G. (1986) Trouble-shooting in interaction with learners: the more the merrier? *Applied Linguistics, 7*, 128–43.

Baars, B. J., and Franklin, S. (2003) How conscious experience and working memory interact. *TRENDS in Cognitive Sciences, 7*(4), 166–72.

Bachman, L. F., and Palmer, A. S. (1996) *Language testing in practice: designing and developing useful language tests.* Oxford: Oxford University Press.

Baddeley, A., D. (2007) *Working memory, thought and action.* Oxford: Oxford University Press.

Baddeley, A. D., and Hitch, G. (1974) Working memory. In G. H. Bower (ed.), *The psychology of learning and motivation: advances in research and theory* (vol. 8, pp. 47–89). New York: Academic Press.

Bailey, K. M. (1991) Diary studies of classroom language learning: the doubting game and the believing game. Unpublished ERIC document no. ED367166.

Bailey, P., Onwuegbuzie, A. J., and Daley, C. E. (2000) Correlates of anxiety at three stages of the foreign language learning process. *Journal of Language and Social Psychology, 19*, 474–90.

Baker, S. C., and MacIntyre, P. D. (2000) The role of gender and immersion in communication and second language orientations. *Language Learning, 50*, 311–41.

Bardovi-Harlig, K. (1995) The interaction of pedagogy and natural sequences in the acquisition of tense and aspect. In F. R. Eckman, D. Highland, P. Lee, J. Mileham and R. Weber (eds), *Second language acquisition theory and pedagogy* (pp. 151–68). Mahwah, NJ: Lawrence Erlbaum.

Bardovi-Harlig, K. (1999) Exploring the interlanguage of interlanguage pragmatics: a research agenda for acquisitional pragmatics. *Language Learning, 49*, 677–713.

Bardovi-Harlig, K. (2000) *Tense and aspect in second language acquisition: form, meaning, and use* (vol. 50, supplement 1, *Language Learning* Monograph Series). Malden, MA: Blackwell.

Barsalou, L. W. (2008) Grounded cognition. *Annual Review of Psychology, 59*, 617–45.

Basharina, O. K. (2007) An activity theory perspective on student-reported contradictions in international telecollaboration. *Language Learning and Technology, 11*(2), 82–103.

Basturkmen, H., Loewen, S., and Ellis, R. (2002) Metalanguage in focus on form in the communicative classroom. *Language Awareness, 11*, 1–13.

Batistella, E. L. (1996) *The logic of markedness.* New York: Oxford University Press.

Baumeister, R. F., and Vohs, K. D. (eds) (2004) *Handbook of self-regulation: research, theory, and application.* New York: Guilford.

Beck, M., Schwartz, B., and Eubank, L. (1995) Data, evidence and rules. In L. Eubank, L. Selinker, and M. S. Smith (eds), *The current state of interlanguage: studies in honor of William E. Rutherford* (pp. 177–95). Amsterdam: John Benjamins.

Beebe, L., and Zuengler, J. (1983) Accommodation theory: an explanation for style shifting in second language dialects. In N. Wolfson and E. Judd (eds), *Sociolinguistics and second language acquisition* (pp. 195–213). Rowley, MA: Newbury House.

Belz, J. A., and Thorne, S. L. (eds) (2006) *Internet-mediated intercultural foreign language education.* Boston, MA: Heinle and Heinle.

Bhabha, H. (1994) *The location of culture.* New York: Routledge.

Bialystok, E. (1997) The structure of age: in search of barriers to second language acquisition. *Second Language Research, 13*, 116–37.

Bialystok, E. (2001) *Bilingualism in development: language, literacy, and cognition.* New York: Cambridge University Press.

Bialystok, E., and Hakuta, K. (1999) Confounded age: linguistic and cognitive factors in age differences for second language acquisition. In D. P. Birdsong (ed.), *Second language acquisition and the critical period hypothesis* (pp. 161–81). Mahwah, NJ: Lawrence Erlbaum.

Bialystok, E., and Sharwood-Smith, M. (1985) Interlanguage is not a state of mind: an evaluation of the construct for second language acquisition. *Applied Linguistics, 6*, 101–17.

Bickerton, D. (2007) Language evolution: a brief guide for linguists. *Lingua, 117*(3), 510–26.

Bigelow, M., delMas, R., Hansen, K., and Tarone, E. (2006) Literacy and oral recasts in SLA. *TESOL Quarterly, 40*, 665–89.

Birdsong, D. P. (1992) Ultimate attainment in second language acquisition. *Language, 68*, 705–55.

Birdsong, D. P. (ed.) (1999a) *Second language acquisition and the critical period hypothesis*. Mahwah, NJ: Lawrence Erlbaum.

Birdsong, D. P. (1999b) Introduction: whys and why nots of the critical period hypothesis for second language acquisition. In D. P. Birdsong (ed.), *Second language acquisition and the critical period hypothesis* (pp. 1–22). Mahwah, NJ: Lawrence Erlbaum.

Birdsong, D. P. (2005) Nativelikeness and non-nativelikeness in L2A research. *International Review of Applied Linguistics, 43*, 319–28.

Birdsong, D. P. (2006) Age and second language acquisition and processing: a selective overview. *Language Learning, 56*, 9–49.

Birdsong, D. P., and Molis, M. (2001) On the evidence for maturational constraints on second-language acquisition. *Journal of Memory and Language, 44*, 235–49.

Black, R. W. (2006) Language, culture, and identity in online fanfiction. *E-learning, 3*(2), 170–84.

Bley-Vroman, R. (1983) The comparative fallacy in interlanguage studies: the case of systematicity. *Language Learning, 33*, 1–17.

Bley-Vroman, R. (1990) The logical problem of foreign language learning. *Linguistic Analysis, 20*, 3–49.

Block, D. (1996) Not so fast: some thoughts on theory culling, relativism, accepted findings and the heart and soul of SLA. *Applied Linguistics, 17*, 63–83.

Block, D. (2003) *The social turn in second language acquisition*. Washington, DC: Georgetown University Press.

Block, D. (2007) The rise of identity in SLA research, post Firth and Wagner (1997). *Modern Language Journal, 91*, 863–76.

Boekaerts, M., de Koning, E., and Vedder, P. (2006) Goal-directed behavior and contextual factors in the classroom: an innovative approach to the study of multiple goals. *Educational Psychologist, 41*, 33–51.

Bongaerts, T. (1999) Ultimate attainment in L2 pronunciation: the case of very advanced late learners of Dutch as a second language. In D. P. Birdsong (ed.), *Second language acquisition and the critical period hypothesis* (pp. 133–59). Mahwah, NJ: Lawrence Erlbaum.

Braidi, S. (1999) *The acquisition of second-language syntax*. New York: Arnold.

Braidi, S. (2002) Reexamining the role of recasts in native-speaker/nonnative-speaker interactions. *Language Learning, 52*, 1–42.

Breen, M. (ed.) (2001) *Learner contributions to language learning: new directions in research*. New York: Longman.

Brouwer, C. E., and Wagner, J. (2004) Developmental issues in second language conversation. *Journal of Applied Linguistics, 1*(1), 29–47.

Brown, R. (1973) *A first language: the early stages*. Cambridge, MA: Harvard University Press.

Burgess, N., and Hitch, G. J. (2006) A revised model of short-term memory and long-term learning of verbal sequences. *Journal of Memory and Language, 55*, 627–52.

Byrnes, H. (2006) What kind of resource is language and why does it matter for advanced language learning? An introduction. In H. Byrnes (ed.), *Advanced language learning: the contribution of Halliday and Vygotsky* (pp. 1–28). New York: Continuum.

Byrnes, H., and Sinicrope, C. (2008) Advancedness and the development of relativization in L2 German: a curriculum-based longitudinal study. In L. Ortega and H. Byrnes (eds), *The longitudinal study of advanced L2 capacities* (pp. 109–38). New York: Routledge.

Cadierno, T. (2000) The acquisition of Spanish grammatical aspect by Danish advanced language learners. *Spanish Applied Linguistics, 4*, 1–53.

Cadierno, T. (2008) Learning to talk about motion in a foreign language. In P. Robinson and N. C. Ellis (eds), *Handbook of cognitive linguistics and second language acquisition* (pp. 239–75). New York: Routledge.

Call, M. L. S. (1985) Auditory short-term memory, listening comprehension, and the input hypothesis. *TESOL Quarterly, 19*, 765–81.

Canagarajah, A. S. (2002) *Critical academic writing and multilingual students.* Ann Arbor, MI: University of Michigan Press.

Cancino, H., Rosansky, E., and Schumann, J. H. (1978) The acquisition of English negatives and interrogatives by native Spanish speakers. In E. Hatch (ed.), *Second language acquisition: a book of readings* (pp. 207–30). Rowley, MA: Newbury House.

Candland, D. K. (1993) *Feral children and clever animals: reflections on human nature.* New York: Oxford University Press.

Carroll, D. (2005) Vowel-marking as an interactional resource in Japanese novice ESL conversation. In K. Richards and P. Seedhouse (eds), *Applying conversation analysis* (pp. 214–34). London: Palgrave/Macmillan.

Carroll, J. (1981) Twenty-five years of research on foreign language aptitude. In K. Diller (ed.), *Individual differences and universals in language learning aptitude* (pp. 83–118). Rowley, MA: Newbury House.

Carroll, M., Murcia-Serra, J., Watorek, M., and Bendiscioli, A. (2000) The relevance of information organization to second language acquisition studies: the descriptive discourse of advanced adult learners of German. *Studies in Second Language Acquisition, 22*, 441–66.

Carroll, S., Roberge, Y., and Swain, M. (1992) The role of feedback in adult second language acquisition: error correction and morphological generalization. *Applied Psycholinguistics, 13*, 173–89.

Carson, J., and Longhini, A. (2002) Focusing on learning styles and strategies: a diary study in an immersion setting. *Language Learning, 52*, 401–38.

Cenoz, J., Hufeisen, B., and Jessner, U. (2001) *Cross-linguistic influence in third language acquisition: psycholinguistic perspectives.* Clevedon, UK: Multilingual Matters.

Chapelle, C., and Green, P. (1992) Field independence/dependence in second-language acquisition research. *Language Learning, 42*, 47–83.

Chater, N., and Manning, C. D. (2006) Probabilistic models of language processing and acquisition. *TRENDS in Cognitive Sciences, 10*(7), 335–44.

Chaudron, C. (1977) A descriptive model of discourse in the corrective treatment of learners' errors. *Language Learning, 27*, 29–46.

Chaudron, C. (2006) Some reflections on the development of (meta-analytic) synthesis in second language research. In J. M. Norris and L. Ortega (eds), *Synthesizing research on language learning and teaching* (pp. 325–41). Amsterdam: John Benjamins.

Chun, D. M., and Payne, J. S. (2004) What makes students click: working memory and look-up behavior. *System, 32*, 481–503.

Clahsen, H. (2006) Dual-mechanism morphology. In K. Brown (ed.), *Encyclopedia of language and linguistics* (vol. 4, *Morphology*, pp. 1–5). Oxford: Elsevier.

Clément, R., Baker, S. C., and MacIntyre, P. D. (2003) Willingness to communicate in a second language: the effects of context, norms, and vitality. *Journal of Language and Social Psychology, 22,* 190–209.

Clément, R., Dörnyei, Z., and Noels, K. A. (1994) Motivation, self-confidence, and group cohesion in the foreign language classroom. *Language Learning, 44,* 417–48.

Clément, R., and Kruidenier, B. G. (1983) Orientations in second language acquisition: I. The effects of ethnicity, milieu and target language on their emergence. *Language Learning, 33,* 273–91.

Clément, R., Noels, K. A., and Deneault, B. (2001) Inter-ethnic contact, identity, and psychological adjustment: the mediating and moderating roles of communication. *Journal of Social Issues, 57,* 559–77.

Cobb, T. (2003) Analyzing late interlanguage with learner corpora: Quebec replications of three European studies. *Canadian Modern Language Review, 59,* 393–423.

Collins, L. (2002) The roles of L1 influence and lexical aspect in the acquisition of temporal morphology. *Language Learning, 52,* 43–94.

Collins, L. (2004) The particulars on universals: a comparison of the acquisition of tense–aspect morphology among Japanese- and French-speaking learners of English. *Canadian Modern Language Review, 61,* 251–74.

Cook, V. (1991) The poverty-of-the-stimulus argument and multicompetence. *Second Language Research, 7,* 103–17.

Cook, V. (1996) *Second language learning and language teaching* (2nd edition). London: Arnold.

Cook, V. (ed.) (2003) *Effects of the second language on the first.* Clevedon, UK: Multilingual Matters.

Cook, V. (2008) Multi-competence: black hole or wormhole for second language acquisition research? In Z. Han (ed.), *Understanding second language process* (pp. 16–26). Clevedon, UK: Multilingual Matters.

Coppieters, R. (1987) Competence differences between native and near native speakers. *Language, 63,* 544–73.

Corder, S. P. (1967) The significance of learners' errors. *International Review of Applied Linguistics, 5,* 161–70.

Cortázar, J. (1966 [1963]) *Hopscotch [Rayuela].* New York: Random House.

Cortes, V. (2006) Teaching lexical bundles in the disciplines: an example from a writing intensive history class. *Linguistics and Education, 17,* 391–406.

Costa, P. T., Jr, and McCrae, R. R. (1992) *Revised NEO Personality Inventory (NEO PI-R) and NEO Five-Factor Inventory (NEO-FFI): professional manual.* Odessa, FL: Psychological Assessment Resources.

Cowan, N. (1988) Evolving conceptions of memory storage, selective attention, and their mutual constraints within the human information-processing system. *Psychological Bulletin, 104*(2), 163–91.

Cowan, N. (2001) The magical number 4 in short-term memory: a reconsideration of mental storage capacity. *Behavioral and Brain Sciences, 24,* 87–114.

Cowan, N. (2005) *Working memory capacity.* Hove, UK: Psychology Press.

Crawford, J. (2000) *At war with diversity: US language policy in an age of anxiety.* Clevedon, UK: Multilingual Matters.

Crookes, G., and Schmidt, R. (1991) Motivation: reopening the research agenda. *Language Learning, 41,* 469–512.

Csizér, K., and Dörnyei, Z. (2005a) The internal structure of language learning motivation and its relationship with language choice and learning effort. *Modern Language Journal, 89,* 19–36.

Csizér, K., and Dörnyei, Z. (2005b) Language learners' motivational profiles and their motivated learning behavior. *Language Learning, 55*, 613–59.

Curtiss, S. (1977) *Genie: a psycholinguistic study of a modern-day 'wild child'.* New York: Academic Press.

Dagut, M., and Laufer, B. (1985) Avoidance of phrasal verbs: a case for contrastive analysis. *Studies in Second Language Acquisition, 11*, 241–55.

Daneman, M., and Merikle, P. M. (1996) Working memory and language comprehension: a meta-analysis. *Psychonomic Bulletin and Review, 3*, 422–33.

Darhower, M. (2002) Instructional features of synchronous computer-mediated communication in the L2 class: a sociocultural study. *CALICO Journal, 19*, 249–77.

Davies, A., Criper, C., and Howatt, A. P. R. (eds) (1984) *Interlanguage: papers in honour of S. Pit Corder.* Edinburgh: Edinburgh University Press.

Davies, A., and Elder, C. (eds) (2004) *Handbook of applied linguistics.* Malden, MA: Blackwell.

Davis, K. A., Cho, H., Ishida, M., Soria, J., and Bazzi, S. (2005) 'It's our kuleana': a critical participatory approach to language minority education. In L. Pease-Alvarez and S. R. Schecter (eds), *Learning, teaching, and community* (pp. 3–25). Mahwah, NJ: Lawrence Erlbaum.

Day, R., Chenoweth, N. A., Chun, A., and Luppescu, S. (1984) Corrective feedback in native–nonnative discourse. *Language Learning, 34*, 19–46.

de Bot, K. (1996) The psycholinguistics of the output hypothesis. *Language Learning, 46*, 529–55.

de Bot, K. (ed.) (2008) *Second language development as a dynamic process.* Special issue of *Modern Language Journal, 92*(2).

de Bot, K., Lowie, W., and Verspoor, M. (2006) *Second language acquisition: an advanced resource book.* New York: Routledge.

de Bot, K., Lowie, W., and Verspoor, M. (2007) A Dynamic Systems Theory approach to second language acquisition. *Bilingualism: Language and Cognition, 10*, 7–21.

de Graaff, R. (1997) The eXperanto experiment: effects of explicit instruction on second language acquisition. *Studies in Second Language Acquisition, 19*, 249–97.

de Guerrero, M. C. M. (1994) Form and functions of inner speech in adult second language learning. In J. P. Lantolf and G. Appel (eds), *Vygotskian approaches to second language research* (pp. 83–116). Norwood, NJ: Ablex.

de Guerrero, M. C. M. (2005) *Inner speech – L2: thinking words in a second language.* New York: Springer.

Dechert, H. W., and Raupach, M. (eds) (1989) *Transfer in language production.* Norwood, NJ: Ablex.

Dehaene, S., Dupoux, E., Mehler, J., Cohen, L., Paulesu, E., Perani, D., et al. (1997) Anatomical variability in the cortical representation of first and second language. *NeuroReport, 8*, 3809–15.

DeKeyser, R. (1997) Beyond explicit rule learning: automatizing second language morphosyntax. *Studies in Second Language Acquisition, 19*, 195–221.

DeKeyser, R. M. (2000) The robustness of critical period effects in second language acquisition. *Studies in Second Language Acquisition, 22*, 499–533.

DeKeyser, R. (2003) Implicit and explicit learning. In C. J. Doughty and M. H. Long (eds), *Handbook of second language acquisition* (pp. 313–48). Malden, MA: Blackwell.

DeKeyser, R. (ed.) (2007a) *Practicing in a second language: perspectives from applied linguistics and cognitive psychology.* New York: Cambridge University Press.

DeKeyser, R. (2007b) Skill acquisition theory. In B. VanPatten and J. Williams (eds),

Theories in second language acquisition: an introduction (pp. 97–112). Mahwah, NJ: Lawrence Erlbaum.

Dewaele, J.-M. (1998) Lexical inventions: French interlanguage as L2 versus L3. *Applied Linguistics, 19,* 471–90.

Dewaele, J.-M. (2001) Activation or inhibition? The interaction of L1, L2 and L3 on the language mode continuum. In J. Cenoz, B. Hufeisen, and U. Jessner (eds), *Cross-linguistic influence in third language acquisition: psycholinguistic perspectives* (pp. 69–89). Clevedon, UK: Multilingual Matters.

Dewaele, J.-M. (2002) Psychological and sociodemographic correlates of communicative anxiety in L2 and L3 production. *International Journal of Bilingualism, 6,* 23–39.

Dewaele, J.-M., and Furnham, A. (1999) Extraversion: the unloved variable in applied linguistics research. *Language Learning, 49,* 509–44.

Dewaele, J.-M., and Furnham, A. (2000) Personality and speech production: a pilot study of second language learners. *Personality and Individual Differences, 28,* 355–65.

Diessel, H., and Tomasello, M. (2005) A new look at the acquisition of relative clauses. *Language, 81,* 882–906.

Donato, R. (1994) Collective scaffolding in second language learning. In J. P. Lantolf and G. Appel (eds), *Vygotskian perspectives to second language research* (pp. 33–56). Norwood, NJ: Ablex.

Donato, R. (1998) Assessing foreign language abilities of the early language learner. In M. Met (ed.), *Critical issues in early second language learning: building our children's future* (pp. 169–97). Glenview, IL: Addison-Wesley.

Donitsa-Schmidt, S., Inbar, O., and Shohamy, E. (2004) The effects of teaching spoken Arabic on students' attitudes and motivation in Israel. *Modern Language Journal, 88,* 217–28.

Dörnyei, Z. (1994) Motivation and motivating in the foreign language classroom. *Modern Language Journal, 78,* 273–84.

Dörnyei, Z. (2001) New themes and approaches in second language motivation research. *Annual Review of Applied Linguistics, 21,* 43–59.

Dörnyei, Z. (2002) The motivational basis of language learning tasks. In P. Robinson (ed.), *Individual differences and instructed language learning* (pp. 137–57). Amsterdam: John Benjamins.

Dörnyei, Z. (2005) *The psychology of the language learner: individual differences in second language acquisition.* Mahwah, NJ: Lawrence Erlbaum.

Dörnyei, Z. (2007) The L2 motivational self system. Paper presented at the American Association for Applied Linguistics, Costa Mesa, CA, 21–24 April.

Dörnyei, Z., and Csizér, K. (2005) The effects of intercultural contact on tourism and language attitudes and language learning motivation. *Journal of Language and Social Psychology, 24,* 327–57.

Dörnyei, Z., Csizér, K., and Németh, N. (2006) *Motivational dynamics, language attitudes and language globalisation: a Hungarian perspective.* Clevedon, UK: Multilingual Matters.

Dörnyei, Z., and Kormos, J. (2000) The role of individual and social variables in oral task performance. *Language Teaching Research, 4,* 275–300.

Dörnyei, Z., and Ottó, I. (1998) Motivation in action: a process model of L2 motivation. *Working Papers in Applied Linguistics of Thames Valley University, 4,* 43–69.

Dörnyei, Z., and Schmidt, R. (eds) (2001) *Motivation and second language acquisition.* Honolulu, HI: University of Hawai'i, National Foreign Language Resource Center.

Dörnyei, Z., and Skehan, P. (2003) Individual differences in second language learning. In C. J. Doughty and M. H. Long (eds), *Handbook of second language acquisition* (pp. 589–630). Malden, MA: Blackwell.

Dörnyei, Z., and Ushioda, E. (eds) (2008) *Motivation, language identity and the L2 self.* Clevedon, UK: Multilingual Matters.

Doughty, C. J. (1991) Second language instruction does make a difference: evidence from an empirical study of ESL relativization. *Studies in Second Language Acquisition, 13*, 431–69.

Doughty, C. J. (2001) Cognitive underpinnings of focus on form. In P. Robinson (ed.), *Cognition and second language instruction* (pp. 206–57). New York: Cambridge University Press.

Doughty, C. J., and Long, M. H. (eds) (2003) *Handbook of second language acquisition.* Malden, MA: Blackwell.

Doughty, C. J., and Varela, E. (1998) Communicative focus on form. In C. J. Doughty and J. Williams (eds), *Focus on form in classroom second language acquisition* (pp. 114–38). New York: Cambridge University Press.

Duff, P. A. (1993) Syntax, semantics and SLA: the convergence of possessive and existential constructions. *Studies in Second Language Acquisition, 15*, 1–34.

Duff, P. A. (2004) Intertextuality and hybrid discourses: the infusion of pop culture in educational discourse. *Linguistics and Education, 14*(3/4), 231–76.

Duff, P. A. (2007) Second language socialization as sociocultural theory: insights and issues. *Language Teaching, 40*, 309–19.

Duff, P. A. (2008) *Case study research in applied linguistics.* New York: Routledge.

DuFon, M. A. (2006) The socialization of taste during study abroad in Indonesia. In M. A. DuFon and E. Churchill (eds), *Language learners in study abroad contexts* (pp. 91–119). Clevedon, UK: Multilingual Matters.

Dufva, M., Niemi, P., and Voeten, M. J. M. (2001) The role of phonological memory, word recognition, and comprehension skills in reading development: from preschool to grade 2. *Reading and Writing, 14*, 91–117.

Dufva, M., and Voeten, M. J. M. (1999) Native language literacy and phonological memory as prerequisites for learning English as a foreign language. *Applied Psycholinguistics, 20*, 329–48.

Dulay, H., Burt, M., and Krashen, S. D. (1982) *Language two.* New York: Oxford University Press.

Eckman, F. R. (1977) Markedness and the contrastive analysis hypothesis. *Language Learning, 27*, 315–30.

Eckman, F. R. (2004) From phonemic differences to constraint rankings: research on second language phonology. *Studies in Second Language Acquisition, 26*, 513–49.

Eckman, F. R., Bell, L., and Nelson, D. (1988) On the generalization of relative clause instruction in the acquisition of English as a second language. *Applied Linguistics, 9*, 1–20.

Edwards, D. J. (2004) The role of languages in a post-9/11 United States. *Modern Language Journal, 88*, 268–71.

Ehrlich, S., Avery, P., and Yorio, C. (1989) Discourse structure and the negotiation of comprehensible input. *Studies in Second Language Acquisition, 11*, 397–414.

Ehrman, M. E. (1990) The role of personality type in adult language learning: an ongoing investigation. In T. S. Parry and C. W. Stansfield (eds), *Language aptitude reconsidered* (pp. 126–78). Englewood Cliffs, NJ: Prentice Hall Regents/Center for Applied Linguistics.

Ehrman, M. E. (1996) *Understanding second language learning difficulties.* Thousand Oaks, CA: Sage.

Ehrman, M. E. (1998) The Modern Language Aptitude Test for predicting learning success and advising students. *Applied Language Learning, 9*(1/2), 31–70.

Ehrman, M. E., and Leaver, B. L. (2003) Cognitive styles in the service of language learning. *System, 31*, 393–415.

Eisenstein, M. R. (ed.) (1989) *The dynamic interlanguage: empirical studies in second language variation.* New York: Plenum Press.

Elliott, A. R. (1995) Foreign language phonology: field independence, attitude, and the success of formal instruction on Spanish pronunciation. *Modern Language Journal, 79,* 530–42.

Ellis, N. C. (1993) Rules and instances in foreign language learning: interactions of implicit and explicit knowledge. *European Journal of Cognitive Psychology, 5,* 289–319.

Ellis, N. C. (1996) Sequencing in SLA: phonological memory, chunking, and points of order. *Studies in Second Language Acquisition, 18,* 91–126.

Ellis, N. C. (1998) Emergentism, connectionism and language learning. *Language Learning, 48,* 631–64.

Ellis, N. C. (2002a) Frequency effects in language processing. *Studies in Second Language Acquisition, 24,* 143–88.

Ellis, N. C. (2002b) Reflections on frequency effects in language acquisition: a response to commentaries. *Studies in Second Language Acquisition, 24,* 297–339.

Ellis, N. C. (2005) At the interface: dynamic interactions of explicit and implicit language knowledge. *Studies in Second Language Acquisition, 27,* 305–52.

Ellis, N. C. (2006a) Language acquisition as rational contingency learning. *Applied Linguistics, 27,* 1–24.

Ellis, N. C. (2006b) Selective attention and transfer phenomena in L2 acquisition: contingency, cue competition, salience, interference, overshadowing, blocking, and perceptual learning. *Applied Linguistics, 27,* 164–94.

Ellis, N. C. (2007) The associative-cognitive CREED. In B. VanPatten and J. Williams (eds), *Theories in second language acquisition: an introduction* (pp. 77–95). Mahwah, NJ: Lawrence Erlbaum.

Ellis, N. C. (2008) Usage-based and form-focused language acquisition. In P. Robinson and N. C. Ellis (eds), *Handbook of cognitive linguistics and second language acquisition* (pp. 372–405). New York: Routledge.

Ellis, N. C., and Larsen-Freeman, D. (2006) Language emergence: implications for applied linguistics – introduction to the special issue. *Applied Linguistics, 27,* 558–89.

Ellis, N. C., and Robinson, P. (2008) An introduction to cognitive linguistics, second language acquisition, and language instruction. In P. Robinson and N. C. Ellis (eds), *Handbook of cognitive linguistics and second language acquisition* (pp. 3–24). New York: Routledge.

Ellis, N. C., and Schmidt, R. (1998) Rules or associations in the acquisition of morphology? The frequency by regularity interaction in human and PDP learning of morphosyntax. *Language and Cognitive Processes, 13,* 307–36.

Ellis, R. (1985) *Understanding second language acquisition.* New York: Oxford University Press.

Ellis, R. (1989) Are classroom and naturalistic acquisition the same? A study of the classroom acquisition of German word order rules. *Studies in Second Language Acquisition, 11,* 305–28.

Ellis, R. (2003) *Task-based language learning and teaching.* New York: Oxford University Press.

Ellis, R. (2005) Measuring implicit and explicit knowledge of a second language: a psychometric study. *Studies in Second Language Acquisition, 27,* 141–72.

Ellis, R. (2008) *The study of second language acquisition* (2nd edition). Oxford: Oxford University Press.

Ellis, R., and Barkhuizen, G. (2005) *Analyzing learner language.* New York: Oxford University Press.

Ellis, R., Basturkmen, H., and Loewen, S. (2001) Learner uptake in communicative ESL lessons. *Language Learning, 51,* 281–318.

Ellis, R., Loewen, S., and Erlam, R. (2006) Implicit and explicit corrective feedback and the acquisition of L2 grammar. *Studies in Second Language Acquisition, 28,* 339–68.

Ellis, R., and Sheen, Y. (2006) Reexamining the role of recasts in second language acquisition. *Studies in Second Language Acquisition, 28,* 575–600.

Engle, R. W. (2002) Working memory capacity as executive attention. *Current Directions in Psychological Science, 11,* 19–23.

Ericsson, K. A., and Kintsch, W. (1995) Long-term working memory. *Psychological Review, 102,* 211–45.

Ericsson, K. A., and Simon, H. A. (1993) *Protocol analysis: verbal reports as data* (revised edition). Cambridge, MA: Bradford Books/MIT Press.

Erlam, R. (2005) Language aptitude and its relationship to instructional effectiveness in second language acquisition. *Language Teaching Research, 9,* 147–71.

Eubank, L., Selinker, L., and Sharwood Smith, M. (eds) (1995) *The current state of interlanguage: studies in honor of William E. Rutherford.* Amsterdam: John Benjamins.

Evans, V., Bergen, B. K., and Zinken, J. (2007) The cognitive linguistics enterprise: an overview. In V. Evans, B. K. Bergen, and J. Zinken (eds), *The cognitive linguistics reader* (pp. 2–36). London: Equinox.

Eysenck, H. J., and Eysenck, S. B. G. (1964) *Manual of the Eysenck Personality Inventory.* London: Hodder & Stoughton.

Ferris, D. R. (2004) The 'grammar correction' debate in L2 writing: where are we, and what do we go from here? (And what do we do in the meantime?) *Journal of Second Language Writing, 13,* 49–62.

Finkbeiner, M., Nicol, K. F. J., and Nakamura, K. (2004) The role of polysemy in masked semantic and translation priming. *Journal of Memory and Language, 51,* 1–22.

Firth, A. (1996) The discursive accomplishment of normality: on 'lingua franca' English and conversation analysis. *Journal of Pragmatics, 26,* 237–59.

Firth, A., and Wagner, J. (1997) On discourse, communication, and (some) fundamental concepts in SLA research. *Modern Language Journal, 81,* 285–300.

Firth, A., and Wagner, J. (2007) Second/foreign language learning as social accomplishment: elaborations on a reconceptualized SLA. *Modern Language Journal, 91,* 800–19.

Fitzpatrick, T., and Wray, A. (2006) Breaking up is not so hard to do: individual differences in L2 memorization. *Canadian Modern Language Review, 63,* 35–57.

Flege, J. E. (1987) A critical period for learning to pronounce foreign languages? *Applied Linguistics, 8,* 162–77.

Flege, J. E. (1999) Age of learning and second-language speech. In D. P. Birdsong (ed.), *Second language acquisition and the critical period hypothesis* (pp. 101–32). Hillsdale, NJ: Lawrence Erlbaum.

Flege, J. E., and MacKay, I. R. A. (2004) Perceiving vowels in a second language. *Studies in Second Language Acquisition, 26,* 1–34.

Flege, J. E., Munro, M. J., and MacKay, I. R. A. (1995) Factors affecting strength of perceived foreign accent in a second language. *Journal of the Acoustical Society of America, 97,* 3125–34.

Flege, J. E., Yeni-Komshian, G., and Liu, S. (1999) Age constraints on second-language acquisition. *Journal of Phonetics, 25,* 169–86.

Flynn, S., Foley, C., and Vinnitskaya, I. (2004) The cumulative-enhancement model for language acquisition: comparing adults' and children's patterns of development in first, second and third language acquisition of relative clauses. *International Journal of Multilingualism, 1*, 3–16.

Foster, P. (1998) A classroom perspective on the negotiation of meaning. *Applied Linguistics, 19*, 1–23.

Foster, P., and Ohta, A. S. (2005) Negotiation for meaning and peer assistance in second language classrooms. *Applied Linguistics, 26*, 402–30.

Fox, B. A., and Thompson, S. A. (2007) Relative clauses in English conversation: relativizers, frequency, and the notion of construction. *Studies in Language, 31*, 293–326.

Frawley, W., and Lantolf, J. P. (1985) Second language discourse: a Vygotskian perspective. *Applied Linguistics, 6*, 19–44.

Freeman, D. E., and Freeman, Y. S. (2001) *Between worlds: access to second language acquisition* (2nd edition). Boston, MA: Heinemann.

García Mayo, M. P., and García Lecumberri, M. L. (eds) (2003) *Age and the acquisition of English as a foreign language.* Clevedon, UK: Multilingual Matters.

Gardner, R. C. (1985) *Social psychology and second language learning: the role of attitudes and motivation.* London: Edward Arnold.

Gardner, R. C. (2001) Integrative motivation and second language acquisition. In Z. Dörnyei and R. Schmidt (eds), *Motivation and second language acquisition* (pp. 1–19). Honolulu, HI: National Foreign Language Resource Center.

Gardner, R. C., and Lambert, W. C. (1972) *Attitudes and motivation in second language learning.* Rowley, MA: Newbury House.

Gardner, R. C., Masgoret, A.-M., Tennant, J., and Mihic, L. (2004) Integrative motivation: changes during a year-long intermediate-level language course. *Language Learning, 54*, 1–34.

Gardner, R. C., Masgoret, A.-M., and Tremblay, P. F. (1999) Home background characteristics and second language learning. *Journal of Language and Social Psychology, 18*, 419–37.

Garrett, P. B., and Baquedano-López, P. (2002) Language socialization: reproduction and continuity, transformation and change. *Annual Review of Anthropology, 31*, 339–61.

Gaskill, W. H. (1980) Correction in native–non native speaker conversation. In D. Larsen-Freeman (ed.), *Discourse analysis in second language research* (pp. 125–37). Rowley, MA: Newbury House.

Gass, S. M. (1997) *Input, interaction, and the second language learner.* Mahwah, NJ: Lawrence Erlbaum.

Gass, S. M. (2001) Sentence matching: a re-examination. *Second Language Research, 17*, 421–41.

Gass, S. M., and Mackey, A. (2000) *Stimulated recall methodology in second language research.* Mahwah, NJ: Lawrence Erlbaum.

Gass, S. M., and Mackey, A. (2007) *Data elicitation for second and foreign language research.* Mahwah, NJ: Lawrence Erlbaum.

Gass, S. M., Mackey, A., and Ross-Feldman, L. (2005) Task-based interactions in classroom and laboratory settings. *Language Learning, 55*, 575–611.

Gass, S. M., and Selinker, L. (eds) (1983) *Language transfer in language learning.* Rowley, MA: Newbury House.

Gass, S. M., and Selinker, L. (eds) (1993) *Language transfer in language learning* (revised edition). Amsterdam: John Benjamins.

Gass, S. M., and Selinker, L. (2001) *Second language acquisition: an introductory course* (2nd edition). Mahwah, NJ: Lawrence Erlbaum.

Gass, S. M., and Varonis, E. M. (1994) Input, interaction, and second language production. *Studies in Second Language Acquisition, 16*, 283–302.

Gasser, M. (1990) Connectionism and universals of second language acquisition. *Studies in Second Language Acquisition, 12,* 179–99.

Gathercole, S. E., Service, E., Hitch, G. J., Adams, A.-M., and Martin, A. J. (1999) Phonological short-term memory and vocabulary development: further evidence on the nature of the relationship. *Applied Cognitive Psychology, 13,* 65–77.

Gee, P. (1990) *Social linguistics and literacies: ideology and discourses.* London: Taylor & Francis.

Georgakopoulou, A. (2006) Thinking big with small stories in narrative and identity analysis. *Narrative Inquiry, 16,* 129–37.

Goldschneider, J., and DeKeyser, R. M. (2001) Explaining the 'natural order of L2 morpheme acquisition' in English: a meta-analysis of multiple determinants. *Language Learning, 51,* 1–50.

Gollwitzer, P. M., and Sheeran, P. (2006) Implementation intentions and goal achievement: a meta-analysis of effects and processes. *Advances in Experimental Social Psychology, 38,* 249–68.

Gordon, R. G. (ed.) (2005) *Ethnologue: languages of the world* (15th edition, web version edition). Dallas, TX: SIL International.

Gottschaldt, K. (1926) Über den Einfluß der Erfahrung auf die Wahrnehmung von Figuren. *Psychologische Forschung, 12,* 1–87.

Granger, S., Hung, J., and Petch-Tyson, S. (eds) (2002) *Computer learner corpora, second language acquisition and foreign language teaching.* Amsterdam: John Benjamins.

Gregersen, T., and Horwitz, E. K. (2002) Language learning and perfectionism: anxious and non-anxious language learners' reactions to their own oral performance. *Modern Language Journal, 86,* 562–70.

Gregory, E., Arju, T., Jessel, J., Kenner, C., and Ruby, M. (2007) Snow White in different guises: interlingual and intercultural exchanges between grandparents and young children at home in east London. *Journal of Early Childhood Literacy, 7,* 5–25.

Gries, S. Th. (2008) Corpus-based methods in analyses of SLA data. In P. Robinson and N. C. Ellis (eds), *Handbook of cognitive linguistics and second language acquisition* (pp. 406–31). New York: Routledge.

Grigorenko, E. L. (2002) Foreign language acquisition and language-based learning disabilities. In P. Robinson (ed.), *Individual differences and instructed language learning* (pp. 95–112). Amsterdam: John Benjamins.

Grosjean, F. (1989) Neurolinguists, beware! The bilingual is not two monolinguals in one person. *Brain and Language, 36,* 3–15.

Hahne, A. (2001) What's different in second language processing? Evidence from event-related brain potentials. *Journal of Psycholinguistic Research, 30,* 251–66.

Hall, J. K. (1993) The role of oral practices in the accomplishment of our everyday lives: the sociocultural dimension of interaction with implications for the learning of another language. *Applied Linguistics, 14,* 145–66.

Han, Z. (2000) Persistence of the implicit influence of NL: the case of the pseudo-passive. *Applied Linguistics, 21,* 78–105.

Han, Z. (2004) *Fossilization in adult second language acquisition.* Clevedon, UK: Multilingual Matters.

Han, Z. (2006) Fossilization: can grammaticality judgment be a reliable source of evidence? In Z. Han and T. Odlin (eds), *Studies of fossilization in second language acquisition* (pp. 56–82). Clevedon, UK: Multilingual Matters.

Harklau, L. (2000) From the 'good kids' to the 'worst': representations of English language learners across educational settings. *TESOL Quarterly, 34,* 35–67.

Harley, B., and Hart, D. (1997) Language aptitude and second-language proficiency in classroom learners of different starting ages. *Studies in Second Language Acquisition, 19*, 379–400.

Harley, B., and Hart, D. (2002) Age, aptitude, and second language learning on a bilingual exchange. In P. Robinson (ed.), *Individual differences and instructed language learning* (pp. 301–30). Amsterdam: John Benjamins.

Harley, B., and Wang, W. (1997) The critical period hypothesis: where are we now? In A. M. B. de. Groot and J. F. Kroll (eds), *Tutorials in bilingualism: psycholinguistic perspectives* (pp. 19–51). Mahwah, NJ: Lawrence Erlbaum.

Harrington, M., and Sawyer, M. (1992) L2 working memory capacity and L2 reading skill. *Studies in Second Language Acquisition, 14*, 112–21.

Hatch, E. (1978) Discourse analysis and second language acquisition. In E. Hatch (ed.), *Second language acquisition: a book of readings* (pp. 401–35). Rowley, MA: Newbury House.

Hawkins, B. (1985) Is 'an appropriate response' always so appropriate? In S. M. Gass and C. Madden (eds), *Input in second language acquistion* (pp. 162–78). Rowley, MA: Newbury House.

Hawkins, R. (2001) *Second language syntax: a generative introduction.* Malden, MA: Blackwell.

Hawkins, R. (ed.) (2008) *Current emergentist and nativist perspectives on second language acquisition.* Special issue of *Lingua, 118*(4).

Headland, J., Pike, K., and Harris, M. (eds) (1990) *Emics and etics: the insider/outside debate.* Newbury Park, CA: Sage.

Heath, S. B. (1983) *Ways with words: language, life, and work in communities and classrooms.* New York: Cambridge University Press.

Heckhausen, H., and Kuhl, J. (1985) From wishes to action: the dead ends and short cuts on the long way to action. In M. Frese and J. Sabini (eds), *Goal-directed behaviour: the concept of action in psychology* (pp. 134–60). Hillsdale, NJ: Lawrence Erlbaum.

Heift, T. (2004) Corrective feedback and learner uptake in CALL. *ReCALL, 16*, 416–31.

Heller, M. (ed.) (2007) *Bilingualism: a social approach.* New York: Palgrave/Macmillan.

Hellermann, J. (2006) Classroom interactive practices for literacy: a microethnographic study of two beginning adult learners of English. *Applied Linguistics, 27*, 377–404.

Herschensohn, J. (2007). *Language development and age.* New York: Cambridge University Press.

Higgins, E. T. (2000) Making a good decision: value from fit. *American Psychologist, 55*, 1217–30.

Higgins, E. T. (2005) Value from regulatory fit. *Current Directions in Psychological Science, 14*, 209–13.

Horst, M. (2005) Learning L2 vocabulary through extensive reading: a measurement study. *Canadian Modern Language Review, 61*, 355–82.

Horwitz, E. (1988) The beliefs about language learning of beginning university foreign language students. *Modern Language Journal, 72*, 283–94.

Horwitz, E. K., Horwitz, M. B., and Cope, J. (1986) Foreign language classroom anxiety. *Modern Language Journal, 70*, 125–32.

Hosoda, Y. (2006) Repair and relevance of differential language expertise in second language conversations. *Applied Linguistics, 27*, 25–50.

Hsiao, T.-Y., and Oxford, R. L. (2002) Comparing theories of language learning strategies: a confirmatory factor analysis. *Modern Language Journal, 86*, 368–83.

Hu, X., and Liu, C. (2007) Restrictive relative clauses in English and Korean learners' second language Chinese. *Second Language Research, 23*, 263–87.

Huebner, T. (1979) Order-of-Acquisition vs Dynamic Paradigm: a comparison of method in interlanguage research. *TESOL Quarterly, 13*, 21–8.

Huebner, T. (1983) *A longitudinal analysis of the acquisition of English.* Ann Arbor, MI: Karoma.

Huebner, T. (1998) Linguistics, applied linguistics, and second language acquisition theories. In H. Byrnes (ed.), *Learning foreign and second languages* (pp. 58–74). New York: The Modern Language Association of America.

Hull, G. A., and Nelson, M. E. (2005) Locating the semiotic power of multimodality. *Written Communication, 22,* 224–61.

Hulstijn, J. H. (2003) Incidental and intentional learning. In C. J. Doughty and M. H. Long (eds), *Handbook of second language acquisition* (pp. 349–81). Malden, MA: Blackwell.

Hulstijn, J., and Laufer, B. (2001) Some empirical evidence for the involvement load hypothesis in vocabulary acquisition. *Language Learning, 51*, 539–58.

Hulstijn, J. H., and Marchena, E. (1989) Avoidance: grammatical or semantic causes? *Studies in Second Language Acquisition, 11*, 241–55.

Hyland, K., and Hyland, F. (2006) Interpersonal aspects of response: constructing and interpreting teacher written feedback. In K. Hyland and F. Hyland (eds), *Feedback in second language writing: contexts and issues* (pp. 206–24). Cambridge: Cambridge University Press.

Hyltenstam, K. (1977) Implicational patterns in interlanguage syntax variation. *Language Learning, 27*, 383–411.

Hyltenstam, K. (1984) The use of typological markedness conditions as predictors in second language acquisition: the case of pronominal copies in relative clauses. In R. W. Andersen (ed.), *Second languages: a cross-linguistic perspective* (pp. 39–58). Rowley, MA: Newbury House.

Hyltenstam, K. (1987) Markedness, language universals, language typology, and second language acquisition. In C. Pfaff (ed.), *First and second language acquisition processes* (pp. 55–78). Cambridge, MA: Newbury House.

Hyltenstam, K., and Abrahamsson, N. (2001) Age and L2 learning: the hazards of matching practical 'implications' with theoretical 'facts': comments on Stefka H. Marinova-Todd, D. Bradford Marshall, and Catherine Snow's 'Three misconceptions about age and L2 learning'. *TESOL Quarterly, 35*, 151–70.

Hyltenstam, K., and Abrahamsson, N. (2003) Maturational constraints in SLA. In C. J. Doughty and M. H. Long (eds), *Handbook of second language acquisition* (pp. 539–88). Malden, MA: Blackwell.

Ide, S., Hill, B., Carnes, M. Y., Ogino, T., and Kawasaki, A. (2005) The concept of politeness: an empirical study of American English and Japanese. In R. Watts, S. Ide, and K. Ehlich (eds), *Politeness in language* (2nd edition, pp. 281–98). Berlin: Mouton de Gruyter.

Inbar, O., Donitsa-Schmidt, S., and Shohamy, E. (2001) Students' motivation as a function of language learning: the teaching of Arabic in Israel. In Z. Dörnyei and R. Schmidt (eds), *Motivation and second language acquisition* (pp. 297–311). Honolulu, HI: National Foreign Language Resource Center.

International Dyslexia Association (1998) *Basic facts about dyslexia: what every layperson ought to know* (2nd edition). Baltimore, MD: Author.

Ioup, G. (2005) Age and second language development. In E. Hinkel (ed.), *Handbook of research in second language teaching and learning* (pp. 419–35). Mahwah, NJ: Lawrence Erlbaum.

Ioup, G., Boustagoui, E., Tigi, M., and Moselle, M. (1994) Reexamining the critical period hypothesis: a case of successful adult SLA in a naturalistic environment. *Studies in Second Language Acquisition, 16*, 73–98.

Ioup, G., and Weinberger, S. (eds). (1987) *Interlanguage phonology: the acquisition of a second language sound system.* Rowley, MA: Newbury House.

Ishida, M. (2004) Effects of recasts on the acquisition of the aspectual form *-te i-(ru)* by learners of Japanese as a foreign language. *Language Learning, 54,* 311–94.

Iwashita, N. (2003) Negative feedback and positive evidence in task-based interaction: differential effects on L2 development. *Studies in Second Language Acquisition, 25,* 1–36.

Izumi, S. (2002) Output, input enhancement, and the noticing hypothesis. *Studies in Second Language Acquisition, 24,* 541–77.

Izumi, S. (2003) Comprehension and production processes in second language learning: in search of the psycholinguistic rationale of the output hypothesis. *Applied Linguistics, 24,* 168–96.

Izumi, Y., and Izumi, S. (2004) Investigating the effects of oral output on the learning of relative clauses in English: issues in the psycholinguistic requirements for effective output tasks. *Canadian Modern Language Review, 60,* 587–609.

Jansen, L. (2008) Acquisition of German word order in tutored learners: a cross-sectional study in a wider theoretical context. *Language Learning, 58,* 185–231.

Jarvis, S. (2002) Topic continuity in L2 English article use. *Studies in Second Language Acquisition, 24,* 387–418.

Jarvis, S., and Odlin, T. (2000). Morphological type, spatial reference, and language transfer. *Studies in Second Language Acquisition, 22,* 535–56.

Jarvis, S., and Pavlenko, A. (2008) *Crosslinguistic influence in language and cognition.* New York: Routledge.

Jia, G., and Aaronson, D. (2003) A longitudinal study of Chinese children and adolescents learning English in the United States. *Applied Psycholinguistics, 24,* 131–61.

Jia, G., and Fuse, A. (2007). Acquisition of English grammatical morphology by native Mandarin-speaking children and adolescents: age-related differences. *Journal of Speech, Language and Hearing Research, 50,* 1280–99.

Jiang, N. (2004) Semantic transfer and its implications for vocabulary teaching in a second language. *Modern Language Journal, 88,* 416–32.

Jin, H. G. (1994) Topic-prominence and subject-prominence in L2 acquisition: evidence of English-to-Chinese typological transfer. *Language Learning, 44,* 101–22.

Johnson, J., and Newport, E. (1989) Critical period effects in second language learning: the influence of maturational state on the acquisition of English as a second language. *Cognitive Psychology, 21,* 60–99.

Johnson, J., Prior, S., and Artuso, M. (2000) Field dependence as a factor in second language communicative production. *Language Learning, 50,* 529–67.

Juffs, A. (2004) Representation, processing, and working memory in a second language. *Transactions of the Philological Society, 102,* 199–225.

Jung, E. H. S. (2004) Topic and subject prominence in interlanguage development. *Language Learning, 54,* 713–38.

Kamberelis, G. (2001) Producing heteroglossic classroom (micro)cultures through hybrid discourse practice. *Linguistics and Education, 12,* 85–125.

Kaplan, A. (1993) *French lessons: a memoir.* Chicago, IL: University of Chicago Press.

Karmiloff-Smith, K., and Karmiloff-Smith, A. (2001) *Pathways to language: from foetus to adolescent.* Cambridge, MA: Harvard University Press.

Karoly, P., Boekaerts, M., and Maes, S. (2005) Toward consensus in the psychology of self-regulation: how far have we come? How far do we have yet to travel? *Applied Psychology: An International Review, 54,* 300–11.

Kasper, G. (2006) Beyond repair: conversation analysis as an approach to SLA. *AILA Review, 19*, 83–99.

Kasper, G., and Schmidt, R. (1996) Developmental issues in interlanguage pragmatics. *Studies in Second Language Acquisition, 18*, 149–169.

Keck, C. M., Iberri-Shea, G., Tracy-Ventura, N., and Wa-Mbaleka, S. (2006) Investigating the empirical link between task-based interaction and acquisition: a meta-analysis. In J. M. Norris and L. Ortega (eds), *Synthesizing research on language learning and teaching* (pp. 91–131). Amsterdam: John Benjamins.

Keenan, E., and Comrie, B. (1977) Noun phrase acessibility and universal grammar. *Linguistic Inquiry, 8*, 63–99.

Kellerman, E. (1979) The problem with difficulty. *Interlanguage Studies Bulletin, 4*, 27–48.

Kellerman, E. (1983) Now you see it, now you don't. In S. M. Gass and L. Selinker (eds), *Language transfer in language learning* (pp. 112–34). Rowley, MA: Newbury House.

Kellerman, E. (1985) If at first you do succeed. In S. M. Gass and C. Madden (eds), *Input in second language acquisition* (pp. 345–53). Rowley, MA: Newbury House.

Kellerman, E., and Sharwood Smith, M. (eds) (1986) *Crosslinguistic influence in second language acquisition*. New York: Pergamon Press.

Kenner, C., and Kress, G. (2003) The multisemiotic resources of biliterate children. *Journal of Early Childhood Literacy, 3*(2), 179–202.

Kern, R. (2006) Perspectives on technology in learning and teaching languages. *TESOL Quarterly, 40*, 183–210.

Keshavarz, M. H., and Astaneh, H. (2004) The impact of bilinguality on the learning of English vocabulary as a foreign language (L3). *Bilingual Education and Bilingualism, 7*, 295–302.

King, K., and Mackey, A. (2007) *The bilingual edge: the ultimate guide to how, when and why to teach your child a second language*. New York: HarperCollins.

Kinginger, C. (2004) Alice doesn't live here anymore: foreign language learning and identity reconstruction. In A. Pavlenko and A. Blackledge (eds), *Negotiation of identities in multilingual contexts* (pp. 219–42). Clevedon, UK: Multilingual Matters.

Klee, C., and Ocampo, A. (1995) The expression of past reference in Spanish narratives of Spanish–Quechua bilingual speakers. In C. Silva-Corvalán (ed.), *Spanish in four continents: studies in language contact and bilingualism* (pp. 52–70). Washington, DC: Georgetown University Press.

Klein, E. C. (1995) Second versus third language acquisition: is there a difference? *Language Learning, 45*, 419–65.

Klein, W. (1998) The contribution of second language acquisition research. *Language Learning, 48*, 527–50.

Klein, W., and Perdue, C. (1997) The basic variety (or: Couldn't natural languages be much simpler?). *Second Language Research, 14*, 301–47.

Knudsen, E. I. (2004) Sensitive periods in the development of the brain and behavior. *Journal of Cognitive Neuroscience, 16*, 1412–25.

Kormos, J. (1999) The effect of speaker variables on the self-correction behaviour of L2 learners. *System, 27*, 207–21.

Kramsch, C. (2000) Second language acquisition, applied linguistics, and the teaching of foreign languages. *Modern Language Journal, 84*, 311–26.

Kramsch, C. (2006) From communicative competence to symbolic competence. *Modern Language Journal, 90*, 249–52.

Krashen, S. (1978) Individual variation in the use of the monitor. In W. Ritchie (ed.), *Second language acquisition research: issues and implications* (pp. 175–83). New York: Academic Press.

Krashen, S. (1985) *The input hypothesis*. London: Longman.

Krashen, S. (2004) *The power of reading: insights from the research* (2nd edition). Boston, MA: Heinemann.

Krashen, S., Long, M. H., and Scarcella, R. (1979) Accounting for child–adult differences in second language rate and attainment. *TESOL Quarterly, 13*, 573–82.

Krashen, S., and McField, G. (2005) What works? Reviewing the latest evidence on bilingual education. *Language Learner*, November/December, 7–10, 34. Retrieved 7 July 2008 from http://users.rcn.com/crawj/langpol/Krashen-McField.pdf.

Kroll, J. F., and de Groot, A. M. B. (1997) Lexical and conceptual memory in the bilingual: mapping form to meaning in two languages. In A. M. B. d. Groot and J. F. Kroll (eds), *Tutorials in bilingualism: psycholinguistic perspectives* (pp. 169–99). Mahwah, NJ: Lawrence Erlbaum.

Kroll, J. F., Sumutka, B. M., and Schwartz, A. I. (2005) A cognitive view of the bilingual lexicon: reading and speaking words in two languages. *International Journal of Bilingualism, 9*, 27–48.

Kubota, R. (2003) Unfinished knowledge: the story of Barbara. *College ESL, 10*(1/2), 11–21.

Kuhn, T. S. (1962/1996) *The structure of scientific revolutions* (3rd edition). Chicago, IL: University of Chicago Press.

Kurhila, S. (2005). Different orientations to grammatical correctness. In K. Richards and P. Seedhouse (eds), *Applying conversation analysis* (pp. 143–58). New York: Palgrave/Macmillan.

Lai, C., and Zhao, Y. (2006) Noticing and text-based chat. *Language Learning and Technology, 10*(3), 102–20.

Lally, C. G. (ed.) (2001) *Foreign language program articulation: current practice and future prospects*. Westport, CT: Bergin and Garvey.

Lam, W. S. E. (2000) L2 literacy and the design of the self: a case study of a teenager writing on the internet. *TESOL Quarterly, 34*, 457–82.

Lam, W. S. E. (2004) Second language socialization in a bilingual chat room: global and local considerations. *Language Learning and Technology, 8*(3), 44–65.

Lam, W. S. E. (2006) Re-envisioning language, literacy, and the immigrant subject in new mediascapes. *Pedagogies, 1*(3), 171–95.

Lamb, M. (2004) Integrative motivation in a globalizing world. *System, 32*, 3–19.

Langacker, R. W. (2008) Cognitive grammar as a basis for language instruction. In P. Robinson and N. C. Ellis (eds), *Handbook of cognitive linguistics and second language acquisition* (pp. 66–88). New York: Routledge.

Lantolf, J. P. (1996) SLA theory building: 'letting all the flowers bloom!' *Language Learning, 46*, 713–49.

Lantolf, J. P. (2006a). Language emergence: implications for applied linguistics – a sociocultural perspective. *Applied Linguistics, 27*, 717–28.

Lantolf, J. P. (2006b) Sociocultural theory and second language learning: state of the art. *Studies in Second Language Acquisition, 28*, 67–109.

Lantolf, J. P., and Aljaafreh, A. (1995) Second language learning in the Zone of Proximal Development: a revolutionary experience. *International Journal of Educational Research, 23*, 619–32.

Lantolf, J. P., and Appel, G. (eds) (1994) *Vygotskian approaches to second language research*. Norwood, NJ: Ablex.

Lantolf, J. P., and Thorne, S. L. (2006) *Sociocultural theory and the genesis of second language development*. New York: Oxford University Press.

Lantolf, J. P., and Thorne, S. L. (2007) Sociocultural theory and second language learning.

In B. VanPatten and J. Williams (eds), *Theories in second language acquisition: an introduction* (pp. 197–220). Mahwah, NJ: Lawrence Erlbaum.

Lardiere, D. (2007) *Ultimate attainment in second language acquisition: a case study.* Mahwah, NJ: Lawrence Erlbaum.

Larsen-Freeman, D. (1997) Chaos/complexity and second language acquisition. *Applied Linguistics, 18*, 141–65.

Larsen-Freeman, D. (2000) Second language acquisition and applied linguistics. *Annual Review of Applied Linguistics, 20*, 165–81.

Larsen-Freeman, D. (2006). The emergence of complexity, fluency, and accuracy in the oral and written production of five Chinese learners of English. *Applied Linguistics, 27*, 590–619.

Larsen-Freeman, D., and Cameron, L. (2008) Research methodology on language development from a complex systems perspective. *Modern Language Journal, 92*, 200–13.

Larsen-Freeman, D., and Long, M. H. (1991) *An introduction to second language acquisition research*. New York: Longman.

Laufer, B., and Eliasson, S. (1993) What causes avoidance in L2 learning: L1–L2 difference, L1–L2 similarity or L2 complexity? *Studies in Second Language Acquisition, 15*, 35–48.

Laufer, B., and Goldstein, Z. (2004) Testing vocabulary knowledge: size, strength, and computer adaptiveness. *Language Learning, 54*, 399–436.

Lazaraton, A. (2002) *A qualitative approach to the validation of oral language tests.* Cambridge: Cambridge University Press.

Lee, E., and Kim, H.-Y. (2007) On crosslinguistic variations in imperfective aspect: the case of L2 Korean. *Language Learning, 57*, 651–85.

Leeman, J. (2003) Recasts and L2 development: beyond negative evidence. *Studies in Second Language Acquisition, 25*, 37–63.

Lemhfer, K., Dijkstra, T., and Michel, M. C. (2004) Three languages, one echo: cognate effects in trilingual word recognition. *Language and Cognitive Processes, 19*, 585–611.

Lenneberg, E. H. (1967) *Biological foundations of language*. New York: John Wiley & Sons.

Leow, R. P. (1997) Attention, awareness, and foreign language learning. *Language Learning, 47*, 467–506.

Leow, R. P. (2001) Attention, awareness and foreign language behavior. *Language Learning, 51*, 113–55.

Leung, Y.-K. I. (2006) Verb morphology in L2A vs L3A: the representation of regular and irregular past participles in English–Spanish and Chinese–English–Spanish interlanguages. In S. Foster-Cohen, M. M. Krajnovic, and J. M. Djigunovic (eds), *EuroSLA Yearbook 6* (pp. 27–56). Amsterdam: John Benjamins.

Levelt, W. J. M. (1989) *Speaking: from intention to articulation*. Cambridge, MA: MIT Press.

Lieven, E., and Tomasello, M. (2008) Children's first language acquisition from a usage-based perspective. In P. Robinson and N. C. Ellis (eds), *Handbook of cognitive linguistics and second language acquisition* (pp. 168–96). New York: Routledge.

Lightbown, P. M., and Spada, N. (2006) *How languages are learned* (3rd edition). New York: Oxford University Press.

Likert, R. (1932) A technique for the measurement of attitudes. *Archives of Psychology, 140*, 1–55.

Lindemann, S. (2002) Listening with an attitude: a model of native-speaker comprehension of non-native speakers in the United States. *Language in Society, 31*, 419–41.

Livingston, E. (2008) Context and detail in studies of the witnessable social order: puzzles, maps, checkers, and geometry. *Journal of Pragmatics, 40*, 840–62.

Lochtman, K. (2002) Oral corrective feedback in the foreign language classroom: how it affects interaction in analytic foreign language teaching. *International Journal of Educational Research, 37*(3/4), 271–83.

Loewen, S., and Philp, J. (2006) Recasts in the adult L2 classroom: characteristics, explicitness and effectiveness. *Modern Language Journal, 90*, 536–56.

Logan, G. D. (1988) Toward an instance theory of automatization. *Psychological Review, 95*, 492–527.

Long, M. H. (1990) Maturational constraints on language development. *Studies in Second Language Acquisition, 12*, 251–86.

Long, M. H. (1996) The role of the linguistic environment in second language acquisition. In W. Ritchie and T. Bhatia (eds), *Handbook of second language acquisition* (pp. 413–68). New York: Academic Press.

Long, M. H. (2003) Stabilization and fossilization in interlanguage development. In C. J. Doughty and M. H. Long (eds), *Handbook of second language acquisition* (pp. 487–535). Malden, MA: Blackwell.

Long, M. H. (2006) *Problems in SLA*. Mahwah, NJ: Lawrence Erlbaum.

Long, M. H., Inagaki, S., and Ortega, L. (1998) The role of implicit negative feedback in SLA: models and recasts in Japanese and Spanish. *Modern Language Journal, 82*, 357–71.

Long, M. H., and Sato, C. J. (1984) Methodological issues in interlanguage studies: an interactionist perspective. In A. Davies, C. Criper, and A. Howatt (eds), *Interlanguage* (pp. 253–79). Edinburgh: Edinburgh University Press.

Loschky, L. (1994) Comprehensible input and second language acquisition: what is the relationship? *Studies in Second Language Acquisition, 16*, 303–23.

Loschky, L., and Bley-Vroman, R. (1993) Grammar and task-based methodology. In G. Crookes and S. M. Gass (eds), *Tasks and language learning: integrating theory and practice* (pp. 123–67). Clevedon, UK: Multilingual Matters.

Lyn, H., and Savage-Rumbaugh, E. S. (2000) Observational word learning in two bonobos (pan paniscus): ostensive and non-ostensive contexts. *Language and Communication, 20*, 255–73.

Lyster, R. (1998) Negotiation of form, recasts, and explicit correction in relation to error types and learner repair in immersion classrooms. *Language Learning, 48*, 183–218.

Lyster, R. (2004) Differential effects of prompts and recasts in form-focused instruction. *Studies in Second Language Acquisition, 4*, 399–432.

Lyster, R., Lightbown, P. M., and Spada, N. (1999) A response to Truscott's 'what's wrong with oral grammar correction'. *Canadian Modern Language Review, 55*, 457–67.

Lyster, R., and Mori, H. (2006) Interactional feedback and instructional counterbalance. *Studies in Second Language Acquisition, 28*, 321–41.

Lyster, R., and Ranta, L. (1997) Corrective feedback and learner uptake: negotiation of form in communicative classrooms. *Studies in Second Language Acquisition, 19*, 37–66.

McCafferty, S. G. (ed.) (2008) *Gesture and SLA: toward and integrated approach*. Special issue of *Studies in Second Language Acquisition, 30*(2).

McCrae, R. R. (1996) Social consequences of experiential openness. *Psychological Bulletin, 120*, 323–37.

McDonough, K. (2005) Identifying the impact of negative feedback and learners' responses on ESL question development. *Studies in Second Language Acquisition, 27*, 79–103.

McDonough, K. (2006) Interaction and syntactic priming: English L2 speakers' production of dative constructions. *Studies in Second Language Acquisition, 28*, 179–207.

McDonough, K., and Mackey, A. (2006) Responses to recasts: repetitions, primed production and linguistic development. *Language Learning, 56*, 693–720.

McGroarty, M. (2001) Situating second language motivation. In Z. Dörnyei and R. Schmidt (eds), *Motivation and second language acquisition* (pp. 69–91). Honolulu, HI: National Foreign Language Resource Center.

MacIntyre, P. D., and Charos, C. (1996) Personality, attitudes and affect as predictors of second language communication. *Journal of Language and Social Psychology, 15*, 3–26.

MacIntyre, P. D., Clément, R., Dörnyei, Z., and Noels, K. A. (1998) Conceptualizing willingness to communicate in an L2: a situational model of L2 confidence and affiliation. *Modern Language Journal, 82*, 545–62.

MacIntyre, P. D., and Gardner, R. C. (1994) The subtle effects of language anxiety on cognitive processing in the second language. *Language Learning, 44*, 283–305.

MacIntyre, P. D., and Noels, K. A. (1996) Using social-psychological variables to predict the use of language learning strategies. *Foreign Language Annals, 29*, 373–86.

MacIntyre, P. D., Noels, K. A., and Clément, R. (1997) Biases in self-ratings of second language proficiency: the role of language anxiety. *Language Learning, 47*, 256–87.

McKay, S. L., and Wong, S.-L. C. (1996) Multiple discourses, multiple identities: investment and agency in second-language learning among Chinese adolescent immigrant students. *Harvard Educational Review, 66*, 577–608.

Mackey, A. (1999) Input, interaction, and second language development: an empirical study of question formation in ESL. *Studies in Second Language Acquisition, 21*, 557–87.

Mackey, A. (ed.) (2007) *Conversational interaction in second language acquisition.* New York: Oxford University Press.

Mackey, A., Gass, S. M., and McDonough, K. (2000) How do learners perceive interactional feedback? *Studies in Second Language Acquisition, 22*, 471–97.

Mackey, A., and Goo, J. M. (2007) Interaction research in SLA: a meta-analysis and research synthesis. In A. Mackey (ed.), *Input, interaction and corrective feedback in L2 learning* (pp. 379–452). New York: Oxford University Press.

Mackey, A., Oliver, R., and Leeman, J. (2003) Interaction input and the incorporation of feedback: an exploration of NS–NNS and NNS–NNS adult and child dyads. *Language Learning, 53*, 35–66.

Mackey, A., and Philp, J. (1998) Conversational interaction and second language development: recasts, responses, and red herrings? *Modern Language Journal, 82*, 338–56.

Mackey, A., Philp, J., Egi, T., Fujii, A., and Tatsumi, T. (2002) Individual differences in working memory, noticing of interactional feedback, and L2 development. In P. Robinson (ed.), *Individual differences and instructed language learning* (pp. 181–209). Amsterdam: John Benjamins.

McLaughlin, B. (1987) *Theories of second language learning.* London: Arnold.

McLaughlin, B., and Heredia, R. (1996) Information-processing approaches to research on second language acquisition and use. In W. C. Ritchie and T. K. Bhatia (eds), *Handbook of second language acquisition* (pp. 213–28). New York: Academic Press.

MacWhinney, B. (2001) The competition model: the input, the context, and the brain. In P. Robinson (ed.), *Cognition and second language instruction* (pp. 69–90). New York: Cambridge University Press.

Majerus, S., Poncelet, M., Elsen, B., and van der Linden, M. (2006) Exploring the relationship between new word learning and short-term memory for serial order recall, item recall, and item recognition. *European Journal of Cognitive Psychology, 18*, 848–73.

Maratsos, M. P. (2000) More overregularizations after all: new data and discussion on Marcus, Pinker, Ullman, Hollander, Rosen, and Hu. *Journal of Child Language, 27*, 183–212.

Marinova-Todd, S. H., Marshall, D. B., and Snow, C. E. (2000) Three misconceptions about age and L2 learning. *TESOL Quarterly, 34*, 9–34.

Marinova-Todd, S. H., Marshall, D. B., and Snow, C. E. (2001) Missing the point: a response to Hyltenstam and Abrahamsson. *TESOL Quarterly, 35*, 171–6.

Markee, N. (1994) Toward an ethnomethodological respecification of second language acquisition studies. In E. Tarone, S. M. Gass, and A. Cohen (eds), *Research methodology in second language acquisition* (pp. 89–116). Hillsdale, NJ: Lawrence Erlbaum.

Markee, N. (2000) *Conversation Analysis*. Mahwah, NJ: Lawrence Erlbaum.

Markee, N., and Kasper, G. (2004) Classroom talks: an introduction. *Modern Language Journal, 88*, 491–500.

Martin, J. R. (2000) Beyond exchange: appraisal systems in English. In S. Hunston and G. Thompson (eds), *Evaluation in text: authorial stance and the construction of discourse* (pp. 142–75). Oxford: Oxford University Press.

Masgoret, A.-M., and Gardner, R. C. (2003) Attitudes, motivation, and second language learning: a meta-analysis of studies conducted by Gardner and associates. *Language Learning, 53*, 123–63.

Masoura, E. V., and Gathercole, S. E. (2005) Contrasting contributions of phonological short-term memory and long-term knowledge to vocabulary learning in a foreign language. *Memory, 13*, 422–9.

Master, P. (1987) *A crosslinguistic interlanguage analysis of the acquisition of the English article system*. Unpublished doctoral dissertation. University of California, Los Angeles.

Master, P. (1997) The English article system: acquisition, function, and pedagogy. *System, 25*, 215–32.

Mayberry, R. I. (2007) When timing is everything: age of first-language acquisition effects on second-language learning. *Applied Psycholinguistics, 28*, 537–49.

Mayberry, R. I., and Lock, E. (2003) Age constraints on first versus second language acquisition: evidence for linguistic plasticity and epigenesis. *Brain and Language, 87*, 369–84.

Meara, P. (1996) The dimensions of lexical competence. In G. Brown, K. Malmkjær, and J. Williams (eds), *Performance and competence in second language acquisition* (pp. 35–53). New York: Cambridge University Press.

Meara, P. (2007). Growing a vocabulary. In L. Roberts, A. Gürel, S. Tatar, and L. Mart (eds), *EuroSLA Yearbook 7* (pp. 49–65). Amsterdam: John Benjamins.

Meisel, J., Clahsen, H., and Pienemann, M. (1981) On determining developmental stages in natural second language acquisition. *Studies in Second Language Acquisition, 3*, 109–35.

Meunier, F., and Granger, S. (eds) (2008) *Phraseology in foreign language learning and teaching*. Amsterdam: John Benjamins.

Miller, G. A. (1956) The magical number seven, plus or minus two: some limits in our capacity for processing information. *Psychological Review, 63*, 81–97.

Mitchell, R., and Myles, F. (2004) *Second language learning theories* (2nd edition). New York: Arnold.

Modern Language Aptitude Test. (2000–2001) Second Language Testing, Inc. http://www.2lti.com/htm/Test_mlat.htm

Mohan, B., and Beckett, G. H. (2003) A functional approach to research on content-based language learning: recasts in causal explanations. *Modern Language Journal, 87*, 421–32. [Reprinted from *Canadian Modern Language Review, 58*, 133–55 (2001).]

Mohan, B., Leung, C., and Davison, C. (2001) *English as a second language in the mainstream*. New York: Longman/Pearson.

Mohan, B., and Slater, T. (2006). Examining the theory/practice relation in a high school science register: a functional linguistic perspective. *Journal of English for Academic Purposes, 5*, 302–16.

Montrul, S., and Slabakova, R. (2003) Competence similarities between native and near-native speakers. *Studies in Second Language Acquisition, 25*, 351–98.

Moody, R. (1988) Personality preferences and foreign language learning. *Modern Language Journal, 72*, 389–401.

Moore, L. C. (2006) Learning by heart in Qu'ranic and public schools in northern Cameroon. *Social Analysis, 50*(3), 109–26.

Mori, J. (2007) Border crossings? Exploring the intersection of second language acquisition, Conversation Analysis, and foreign language pedagogy. *Modern Language Journal, 91*, 849–62.

Morin, A., and Michaud, J. (2007). Review: self-awareness and the left inferior frontal gyrus: inner speech use during self-related processing. *Brain Research Bulletin, 74*, 387–96.

Morita, N. (2004) Negotiating participation and identity in second language academic communities. *TESOL Quarterly, 38*, 573–603.

Moyer, A. (1999) Ultimate attainment in L2 phonology: the critical factors of age, motivation, and instruction. *Studies in Second Language Acquisition, 21*, 81–108.

Muñoz, C. (ed.) (2006) *Age and the rate of foreign language learning.* Clevedon, UK: Multilingual Matters.

Musumeci, D. (1996) Teacher–learner negotiation in content-based instruction: communication at cross-purposes? *Applied Linguistics, 17*, 286–325.

Myers, I. B., and McCaulley, M. H. (1985) *Manual: a guide to the development and use of the Myers–Brigg Type Indicator.* Palo Alto, CA: Consulting Psychologists Press.

Myles, F., Mitchell, R., and Hooper, J. (1999) Interrogative chunks in French L2: a basis for creative construction? *Studies in Second Language Acquisition, 21*, 49–80.

Naiman, N., Frohlich, M., Stern, H., and Todesco, A. (1978) *The good language learner.* Toronto: Ontario Institute for Studies in Education.

Nakahama, Y., Tyler, A., and van Lier, L. (2001) Negotiation of meaning in conversational and information gap activities: a comparative discourse analysis. *TESOL Quarterly, 35*, 377–405.

Nassaji, H., and Swain, M. (2000) A Vygotskian perspective on corrective feedback in L2: the effect of random versus negotiated help on the learning of English articles. *Language Awareness, 9*, 34–51.

Nation, I. S. P. (2006) How large a vocabulary is needed for reading and listening? *Canadian Modern Language Review, 63*, 59–81.

Nation, I. S. P., and Waring, R. (1997) Vocabulary size, text coverage and word lists. In N. Schmitt and M. McCarthy (eds), *Vocabulary: description, acquisition and pedagogy* (pp. 6–19). New York: Cambridge University Press.

Nation, R., and McLaughlin, B. (1986) Novices and experts: an information processing approach to the 'good language learner' problem. *Applied Psycholinguistics, 7*, 41–56.

Nicholas, H., Lightbown, P. M., and Spada, N. (2001) Recasts as feedback to language learners. *Language Learning, 51*, 719–58.

Nikolov, M., and Mihaljević Djigunović, J. (2006) Recent research on age, second language acquisition, and early foreign language learning. *Annual Review of Applied Linguistics, 26*, 234–60.

Noels, K. A. (2001) Learning Spanish as a second language: learners' orientations and perceptions of their teachers' communication style. *Language Learning, 51*, 107–44.

Noels, K. A. (2005) Orientations to learning German: heritage language learning and motivational substrates. *Canadian Modern Language Review, 62*, 285–312.

Noels, K. A., Clément, R., and Pelletier, L. G. (1999) Perceptions of teachers' communicative style and students' intrinsic and extrinsic motivation. *Modern Language Journal, 83*, 23–34.

Noels, K. A., Pelletier, L., Clément, R., and Vallerand, R. (2000) Why are you learning a second language? Motivational orientations and self-determination theory. *Language Learning, 50*, 57–85.

Norris, J. M., and Ortega, L. (2000) Effectiveness of L2 instruction: a research synthesis and quantitative meta-analysis. *Language Learning, 50*, 417–528.

Norris, J. M., and Ortega, L. (2003) Defining and measuring SLA. In C. J. Doughty and M. H. Long (eds), *Handbook of second language acquisition* (pp. 717–61). Malden, MA: Blackwell.

Norris, J. M., and Ortega, L. (2006) The value and practice of research synthesis for language learning and teaching. In J. M. Norris and L. Ortega (eds), *Synthesizing research on language learning and teaching* (pp. 3–50). Amsterdam: John Benjamins.

Norton Peirce, B. (1993) *Language learning, social identity, and immigrant women.* Unpublished doctoral dissertation, University of Toronto, Toronto.

Norton Peirce, B. (1995) Social identity, investment, and language learning. *TESOL Quarterly, 29*, 9–31.

Norton, B. (2000) *Identity and language learning: gender, ethnicity and educational change.* Harlow, UK: Longman/Pearson Education.

Norton, B. (2001). Non-participation, imagined communities and the language classroom. In M. P. Breen (ed.), *Learner contributions to language learning: new directions in research* (pp. 159–71). New York: Pearson/Longman.

Norton, B. (2006) Identity and second language learning. In K. Brown (ed.), *Encyclopedia of language and linguistics* (2nd edition, vol. 5, pp. 502–7). Oxford: Elsevier.

Norton, B., and Toohey, K. (2001) Changing perspectives on good language learners. *TESOL Quarterly, 35*, 307–22.

Nunan, D. (2003) The impact of English as a global language on educational policies and practices in the Asia-Pacific region. *TESOL Quarterly, 37*, 589–613.

Obler, L. (1989) Exceptional second language learners. In S. M. Gass, C. Madden, D. Preston, and L. Selinker (eds), *Variation in second language acquisition: Psycholinguistic issues* (pp. 141–59). Clevedon: Multilingual Matters.

Obler, L., and Hannigan, S. (1996) The neuropsychology of second language acquisition and use. In W. Ritchie and T. Bhatia (eds), *Handbook of second language acquisition* (pp. 506–23). New York: Academic Press.

Ochs, E., and Schieffelin, B. (1984) Language acquisition and socialization: three developmental stories and their implications. In R. A. Schweder and R. Levine (eds), *Culture theory: essays on mind, self, and emotion* (pp. 276–320). Cambridge: Cambridge University Press.

O'Brien, I., Segalowitz, N., Collentine, J., and Freed, B. (2006) Phonological memory and lexical, narrative, and grammatical skills in second language oral production by adult learners. *Applied Psycholinguistics, 27*, 377–402.

Odlin, T. (1989) *Language transfer: cross-linguistic influence in language learning.* New York: Cambridge University Press.

Odlin, T. (2003) Cross-linguistic influence. In C. J. Doughty and M. H. Long (eds), *Handbook of second language acquisition* (pp. 436–86). Malden, MA: Blackwell.

Odlin, T., and Jarvis, S. (2004) Same source, different outcomes: a study of Swedish influence on the acquisition of English in Finland. *International Journal of Multilingualism, 1*, 123–40.

O'Dowd, E. M. (2003) Understanding the 'other side': intercultural learning in a Spanish–English e-mail exchange. *Language Learning and Technology, 7*(2), 118–44.

Ohara, Y. (2001) Finding one's voice in Japanese: a study of pitch levels of L2 users. In A.

Pavlenko, A. Blackledge, I. Piller, and M. Teutsch-Dwyer (eds), *Muiltilingualism, second language learning, and gender* (pp. 231–54). New York: Mouton de Gruyter.

Oliver, R. (1995) Negative feedback in child NS/NNS conversation. *Studies in Second Language Acquisition, 17*, 459–81.

Oliver, R. (1998) Negotiation of meaning in child interactions. *Modern Language Journal, 82*, 372–86.

Oliver, R., and Mackey, A. (2003) Interactional context and feedback in child ESL classrooms. *Modern Language Journal, 87*, 519–43.

Olshtain, E. (1983). Sociocultural competence and language transfer: the case of apology. In S. M. Gass and L. Selinker (eds), *Language transfer in language learning* (pp. 232–49). Rowley, MA: Newbury House.

O'Malley, J. M., and Chamot, A. U. (1990) *Learning strategies in second language acquisition.* Cambridge, New York: Cambridge University Press.

Onwuegbuzie, A. J., Bailey, P., and Daley, C. E. (1999) Factors associated with foreign language anxiety. *Applied Psycholinguistics, 20*, 217–39.

Ortega, L. (1999) Language and equality: ideological and structural constraints in foreign language education in the US. In T. Huebner and K. A. Davis (eds), *Sociopolitical perspectives in language policy and planning in the USA* (pp. 243–66). Amsterdam: John Benjamins.

Ortega, L. (2005) For what and for whom is our research? The ethical as transformative lens in instructed SLA. *Modern Language Journal, 89*, 427–43.

Ortega, L., and Byrnes, H. (2008) Theorizing advancedness, setting up the longitudinal research agenda. In L. Ortega and H. Byrnes (eds), *The longitudinal study of advanced L2 capacities* (pp. 281–300). New York: Routledge.

Ortega, L., and Long, M. H. (1997) The effects of models and recasts on the acquisition of object topicalization and adverb placement by adult learners of Spanish. *Spanish Applied Linguistics, 1*, 65–86.

Oshita, H. (2000) What is happened may not be what appears to be happening: a corpus study of 'passive' unaccusatives in L2 English. *Second Language Research, 16*, 293–324.

Osterhout, L., Allen, M., and McLaughlin, J. (2002) Words in the brain: lexical determinants of word-induced brain activity. *Journal of Neurolinguistics, 15*, 171–87.

Osterhout, L., Poliakov, A., Inoue, K., McLaughlin, J., Valentine, G., Pitkanen, I., et al. (2008) Second language learning and changes in the brain. *Journal of Neurolinguistics, 21.* doi: 10.1016/j.jneuroling.2008.01.001.

Oxford, R. L. (1990) *Language learning strategies: what every teacher should know.* New York: Newbury House/HarperCollins.

Oxford, R. L. (ed.) (1996) *Language learning strategies around the world: cross-cultural perspectives.* Honolulu, HI: National Foreign Language Resource Center.

Oxford, R. L., and Nyikos, M. (1989) Variables affecting choice of language learning strategies by university students. *Modern Language Journal, 73*, 291–300.

Oxford, R. L., and Shearin, J. (1994). Expanding the theoretical framework of language learning motivation. *Modern Language Journal, 78*, 12–28.

Oyama, S. (1976) A sensitive period in the acquisition of a non-native phonological system. *Journal of Psycholinguistic Research, 5*, 261–85.

Pallier, C., Poline, J.-B., LeBihan, D., Argenti, A.-M., Dupoux, E., and Mehler, J. (2003) Brain imaging of language plasticity in adopted adults: can a second language replace the first? *Cerebral Cortex, 13*, 155–61.

Panova, I., and Lyster, R. (2002) Patterns of corrective feedback and uptake in an adult ESL classroom. *TESOL Quarterly, 36*, 573–95.

Paribakht, T. S., and Wesche, M. (1997) Vocabulary enhancement activities and reading for meaning in second language vocabulary acquisition. In J. Coady and T. Huckin (eds), *Second language acquisition: a rationale for pedagogy* (pp. 174–200). New York: Cambridge University Press.

Patel, A. D., and Iversen, J. R. (2007) The linguistic benefits of musical abilities. *TRENDS in Cognitive Sciences, 11*, 369–72.

Patkowski, M. (1980) The sensitive period for the acqustion of syntax in a second language. *Language Learning, 30*, 449–72.

Pavesi, M. (1986) Markedness, discoursal modes, and relative clause formation in a formal and an informal context. *Studies in Second Language Acquisition, 8*, 38–55.

Pavlenko, A. (1999) New approaches to concepts in bilingual memory. *Bilingualism: Language and Cognition, 2*, 209–30.

Pavlenko, A., and Blackledge, A. (eds) (2004a) *Negotiation of identities in multilingual contexts.* Clevedon, UK: Multilingual Matters.

Pavlenko, A., and Blackledge, A. (2004b) New theoretical approaches to the study of negotiation of identity in multilingual contexts. In A. Pavlenko and A. Blackledge (eds), *Negotiation of identities in multilingual contexts* (pp. 1–33). Clevedon, UK: Multilingual Matters.

Pavlenko, A., and Jarvis, S. (2002) Bidirectional transfer. *Applied Linguistics, 23*, 190–214.

Peacock, M., and Ho, B. (2003) Student language learning strategies across eight disciplines. *International Journal of Applied Linguistics, 13*, 179–200.

Penfield, W., and Roberts, L. (1959) *Speech and brain mechanisms.* Princeton, NJ: Princeton University Press.

Pennycook, A. (2004) Critical applied linguistics. In A. Davies and C. Elder (eds), *Handbook of applied linguistics* (pp. 784–807). Malden, MA: Blackwell.

Perani, D. and Abutalebi, J. (2005) The neural basis of first and second language processing. *Current Opinion in Neurobiology 15*, 202–6.

Perdue, C. (ed.) (1982) *Second language acquisition by adult immigrants: a field manual.* Strasbourg: European Science Foundation.

Philp, J. (2003) Constraints on 'noticing the gap': nonnative speakers' noticing of recasts in NS–NNS interaction. *Studies in Second Language Acquisition, 25*, 99–126.

Piaget, J. (1974) *The language and thought of the child.* New York: New American Library.

Pica, T. (1985) Linguistic simplicity and learnability: implications for language syllabus design. In K. Hyltenstam and M. Pienemann (eds), *Modelling and assessing second language acquisition* (pp. 137–51). Clevedon, UK: Multilingual Matters.

Pica, T. (1992) The textual outcomes of native speaker/non-native speaker negotiation: what do they reveal about second language learning? In C. Kramsch and S. McConnell-Ginet (eds), *Text in context: crossdisciplinary perspectives on language study* (pp. 198–237). Lexington, MA: D. C. Heath.

Pica, T. (1994) Research on negotiation: what does it reveal about second-language learning conditions, processes, and outcomes? *Language Learning, 44*, 493–527.

Pica, T. (2002) Subject matter content: how does it assist the interactional and linguistic needs of classroom language learners? *Modern Language Journal, 86*, 1–19.

Pica, T., Holliday, L., Lewis, N., and Morgenthaler, L. (1989) Comprehensible input as an outcome of linguistic demands on the learner. *Studies in Second Language Acquisition, 11*, 63–90.

Pica, T., Kanagy, R., and Falodun, J. (1993) Choosing and using communication tasks for second language instruction and research. In G. Crookes and S. M. Gass (eds), *Tasks and language learning: integrating theory and practice* (pp. 9–34). Clevedon, UK: Multilingual Matters.

Pica, T., Young, R. F., and Doughty, C. J. (1987) The impact of interaction on comprehension. *TESOL Quarterly, 21*, 737–58.

Pienemann, M. (1984) Psychological constraints on the teachability of languages. *Studies in Second Language Acquisition, 6*, 186–214.

Pienemann, M. (1989) Is language teachable? Psycholinguistic experiments and hypotheses. *Applied Linguistics, 10*, 52–79.

Pienemann, M. (1998) *Language processing and second language development: processability theory.* Amsterdam: John Benjamins.

Pienemann, M. (ed.) (2005) *Cross-linguistic aspects of processability theory.* Amsterdam: John Benjamins.

Pienemann, M., Johnston, M. and Brindley, G. (1988) Constructing an acquisition-based procedure for second language assessment. *Studies in Second Language Acquisition, 10*, 217–243.

Pigada, M., and Schmitt, N. (2006) Vocabulary acquisition from extensive reading: a case study. *Reading in a Foreign Language, 18*(1).

Pinker, S. (1989) *Learnability and cognition: the acquisition of argument structure.* Cambridge, MA: MIT Press.

Piske, T., MacKay, I. R. A., and Flege, J. E. (2001) Factors affecting degree of foreign accent in an L2: a review. *Journal of Phonetics, 29*, 191–215.

Poehner, M. E., and Lantolf, J. P. (2005) Dynamic assessment in the language classroom. *Language Teaching Research, 9*, 233–65.

Polanyi, L. (1995) Language learning and living abroad: stories from the field. In B. Freed (ed.), *Second language acquisition in a study abroad context* (pp. 271–91). Amsterdam: John Benjamins.

Politzer, R., and McGroarty, M. (1985) An exploratory study of learning behaviours and their relationship to gains in linguistic and communicative competence. *TESOL Quarterly, 19*(1), 103–23.

Potter, J. (2000) Post cognitivist psychology. *Theory and Psychology, 10*, 31–7.

Pujol, J., Soriano-Mas, C., Ortiz, H., Sebastian-Galles, N., and Losilla, J. M. D. (2006) Myelination of language-related areas in the developing brain. *Neurology, 66*, 339–43.

Pulvermüller, F., and Schumann, J. H. (1994) Neurobiological mechanisms of language acquisition. *Language Learning, 44*, 681–734.

Purcell, E., and Suter, R. (1980) Predictors of pronunciation accuracy: a reexamination. *Language Learning, 30*, 271–87.

Rampton, M. B. H. (1990) Displacing the 'native speaker': expertise, affiliation, and inheritance. *English Language Teaching Journal, 44*, 97–101.

Ravem, R. (1968). Language acquisition in a second language environment. *International Review of Applied Linguistics, 6*, 175–85.

Reali, F., and Christiansen, M. H. (2007) Processing of relative clauses is made easier by frequency of occurrence. *Journal of Memory and Language, 57*, 1–23.

Reber, A. S. (1996) *Implicit learning and tacit knowledge: an essay on the cognitive unconscious* (2nd edition). Oxford: Oxford University Press.

Reid, J. M. (ed.) (1995) *Learning styles in the ESL/EFL classroom.* New York: Heinle and Heinle.

Richards, K. (2006) 'Being the teacher': identity and classroom conversation. *Applied Linguistics, 27*, 51–77.

Ringbom, H. (1987) *The role of the first language in foreign language learning.* Clevedon, UK: Multilingual Matters.

Ringbom, H. (1992) On L1 transfer in L2 comprehension and L2 production. *Language Learning, 42*, 85–112.

Ringbom, H. (2001) Lexical transfer in L3 production. In J. Cenoz, B. Hufeisen, and U. Jessner (eds), *Crosslinguistic influence on third language acquisition: psycholinguistic perspectives* (pp. 59–68). Clevedon, UK: Multilingual Matters.

Ringbom, H. (2007). *Cross-linguistic similarity in foreign language learning.* Clevedon, UK: Multilingual Matters.

Ritchie, W. C., and Bhatia, T. K. (eds) (1996) *Handbook of second language acquisition.* San Diego, CA: Academic Press.

Robinson, P. (1995) Attention, memory, and the 'Noticing' Hypothesis. *Language Learning,* 45, 283–331.

Robinson, P. (1997) Generalizability and automaticity of second language learning under implicit, incidental, enhanced, and instructed conditions. *Studies in Second Language Acquisition, 19,* 223–47.

Robinson, P. (2002) Learning conditions, aptitude complexes, and SLA: a framework for research and pedagogy. In P. Robinson (ed.), *Individual differences and instructed language learning* (pp. 113–33). Amsterdam: John Benjamins.

Robinson, P. (2005a) Aptitude and second language acquisition. *Annual Review of Applied Linguistics, 25,* 46–73.

Robinson, P. (2005b) Cognitive abilities, chunk-strength, and frequency effects in implicit artificial grammar and incidental L2 learning: replications of Reber, Walkenfeld, and Hernstadt (1991) and Knowlton and Squire (1996) and their relevance for SLA. *Studies in Second Language Acquisition, 27,* 235–68.

Robinson, P., and Ellis, N. C. (eds) (2008a) *Handbook of cognitive linguistics and second language acquisition.* New York: Routledge.

Robinson, P., and Ellis, N. C. (2008b) Conclusion: cognitive linguistics, second language acquisition and instruction: issues for research. In P. Robinson and N. C. Ellis (eds), *Handbook of cognitive linguistics and second language acquisition* (pp. 489–545). New York: Routledge.

Romaine, S. (1995). *Bilingualism* (2nd edition). Malden, MA: Blackwell.

Rosa, E. M., and Leow, R. P. (2004) Awareness, different learning conditions, and second language development. *Applied Psycholinguistics, 25,* 269–92.

Rosa, E. M., and O'Neill, M. D. (1999) Explicitness, intake, and the issue of awareness: another piece to the puzzle. *Studies in Second Language Acquisition, 21,* 511–56.

Ross, S., Yoshinaga, N., and Sasaki, M. (2002) Aptitude–exposure interaction effects on *wh*-movement violation detection by pre- and post-critical period Japanese bilinguals. In P. Robinson (ed.), *Individual differences and instructed language learning* (pp. 267–99). Amsterdam: John Benjamins.

Rubin, J. (1975) What the 'good language learner' can teach us. *TESOL Quarterly, 9,* 41–51.

Russell, J., and Spada, N. (2006) The effectiveness of corrective feedback for the acquisition of L2 grammar: a meta-analysis of the research. In J. M. Norris and L. Ortega (eds), *Synthesizing research on language learning and teaching* (pp. 133–64). Amsterdam: John Benjamins.

Rutherford, W. E. (1983) Language typology and language transfer. In S. M. Gass and L. Selinker (eds), *Language transfer in language learning* (pp. 358–70). Rowley, MA: Newbury House.

Rymer, R. (1993) *Genie: an abused child's flight from silence.* New York: HarperCollins.

Rymes, B. (2003) Eliciting narratives: drawing attention to the margins of classroom talk. *Research in the Teaching of English, 37,* 380–407.

Rymes, B. (2004) Contrasting zones of comfortable competence: popular culture in a phonics lesson. *Linguistics and Education, 14,* 321–35.

Sagarra, N. (2008) Working memory and L2 processing of redundant grammatical forms.

In Z. Han (ed.), *Understanding second language process* (pp. 133–47). Clevedon, UK: Multilingual Matters.

Samuda, V., and Bygate, M. (2008) *Tasks in second language learning.* New York: Palgrave/Macmillan.

Sato, C. (1990) *The syntax of conversation in interlanguage development.* Tübingen: Gunter Narr.

Saville-Troike, M. (2005) *Introducing second language acquisition.* New York: Cambridge University Press.

Sawyer, M., and Ranta, L. (2001) Aptitude, individual differences, and instructional design. In P. Robinson (ed.), *Cognition and second language instruction* (pp. 319–53). New York: Cambridge University Press.

Schachter, J. (1974) An error in error analysis. *Language Learning, 24*, 205–14.

Schachter, J., and Celce-Murcia, M. (1971) Some reservations concerning error analysis. *TESOL Quarterly, 11*, 441–51.

Schachter, J., and Rutherford, W. E. (1979) Discourse function and language transfer. *Working Papers in Bilingualism, 19*, 3–12.

Schegloff, E., Jefferson, G., and Sacks, H. (1977). The preference for self-correction in the organization of repair in conversation. *Language, 53*, 362–82.

Schleppegrell, M. J. (2004) *The language of schooling: a functional linguistics perspective.* Mahwah, NJ: Lawrence Erlbaum.

Schmidt, R. (1983) Interaction, acculturation, and the acquisition of communicative competence. In N. Wolfson and E. Judd (eds), *Sociolinguistics and language acquisition* (pp. 137–74). Rowley, MA: Newbury House.

Schmidt, R. (1990) The role of consciousness in second language learning. *Applied Linguistics, 11*, 129–58.

Schmidt, R. (1994) Deconstructing consciousness in search of useful definitions for applied linguistics. *AILA Review, 11*, 11–26.

Schmidt, R. (1995) Consciousness and foreign language learning: a tutorial on the role of attention and awareness in learning. In R. Schmidt (ed.), *Attention and awareness in foreign language learning* (pp. 1–63). Honolulu, HI: National Foreign Language Resource Center.

Schmidt, R. (2001) Attention. In P. Robinson (ed.), *Cognition and second language instruction* (pp. 3–33). New York: Cambridge University Press.

Schmidt, R., and Frota, S. (1986) Developing basic conversational ability in a second language: a case study of an adult learner of Portuguese. In R. R. Day (ed.), *Talking to learn: conversation in second language acquisition* (pp. 237–326). Rowley, MA: Newbury House.

Schmitt, N. (1998) Tracking the incremental acquisition of second language vocabulary: a longitudinal study. *Language Learning, 48*, 281–317.

Schmitt, N. (2000) *Vocabulary in language teaching.* Cambridge/New York: Cambridge University Press.

Schmitt, N. (ed.) (2002) *An introduction to applied linguistics.* New York: Arnold.

Schmitt, N. (ed.) (2004) *Formulaic sequences.* Amsterdam: John Benjamins.

Schneiderman, E. I., and Desmarais, C. (1988) The talented language learner: some preliminary findings. *Second Language Research, 4*(2), 91–109.

Schraw, G., and Ericsson, K. A. (2005) An interview with K. Anders Ericsson. *Educational Psychology Review, 17*, 389–412.

Schumann, J. H. (1976) Second language acquisition: the pidginization hypothesis. *Language Learning, 26*, 391–408.

Schumann, J. H. (1990) Extending the scope of the acculturation/pidginization model to include cognition. *TESOL Quarterly, 24*, 667–84.

Schumann, J. H. (1997) *The neurobiology of affect in language.* Malden, MA: Blackwell.

Schwartz, B. D. (1993) On explicit and negative data effecting and affecting competence and linguistic behaviour. *Studies in Second Language Acquisition, 15,* 147–63.

Schwartz, B. D. (1998) The second language instinct. *Lingua, 106,* 133–60.

Schwartz, B. D., and Sprouse, R. A. (2000) When syntactic theories evolve: consequences for L2 acquisition research. In J. Archibald (ed.), *Second language acquisition and linguistic theory* (pp. 156–85). Malden, MA: Blackwell.

Scott, M. L. (1994) Auditory memory and perception in younger and older adult second language learners. *Studies in Second Language Acquisition, 16,* 263–81.

Scovel, T. (1988) *A time to speak: a psycholinguistic inquiry into the critical period for human speech.* Rowley, MA: Newbury House.

Scovel, T. (2000) A critical review of the critical period research. *Annual Review of Applied Linguistics, 20,* 213–23.

Scovel, T. (2001). *Learning new languages: a guide to second language acquisition.* Boston, MA: Heinle and Heinle.

Sebastián-Gallés, N., Echeverría, S., and Bosch, L. (2005) The influence of initial exposure on lexical representation: comparing early and simultaneous bilinguals. *Journal of Memory and Language, 52,* 240–55.

Seedhouse, P. (2004) *The interactional architecture of the language classroom: a Conversation Analysis perspective.* Malden, MA: Blackwell.

Seedhouse, P. (2005) Conversation Analysis and language learning. *Language Teaching, 38,* 165–87.

Segalowitz, N. (2003) Automaticity and second languages. In C. J. Doughty and M. H. Long (eds), *Handbook of second language acquisition* (pp. 382–408). Malden, MA: Blackwell.

Seidlhofer, B. (2001) Closing a conceptual gap: the case for a description of English as a lingua franca. *International Journal of Applied Linguistics, 1,* 133–58.

Seidlhofer, B. (2004) Research perspectives on teaching English as a lingua franca. *Annual Review of Applied Linguistics, 24,* 209–39.

Selinker, L. (1972) Interlanguage. *International Review of Applied Linguistics, 10,* 219–31.

Selinker, L., and Baumgartner-Cohen, B. (1995) Multiple language acquisition: 'Damn it, why can't I keep these two languages apart?' *Language, Culture and Curriculum, 8,* 115–21.

Selinker, L., and Lakshmanan, U. (1992) Language transfer and fossilization: the Multiple Effects Principle. In S. M. Gass and L. Selinker (eds), *Language transfer in language learning* (pp. 197–216). Amsterdam: John Benjamins.

Service, E. (1992) Phonology, working memory and foreign-language learning. *Quarterly Journal of Experimental Psychology, 45A*(1), 21–50.

Service, E., and Kohonen, V. (1995) Is the relation between phonological memory and foreign language learning accounted for by acquisition? *Applied Psycholinguistics, 16,* 155–72.

Shanks, D. R. (2005) Implicit learning. In K. Lamberts and R. Goldstone (eds), *Handbook of cognition* (pp. 202–20). London: Sage.

Sharwood Smith, M. (1986). Comprehension versus acquisition: two ways of processing input. *Applied Linguistics, 7,* 238–56.

Sharwood Smith, M., and Kellerman, E. (1989) The interpretation of second language output. In H. W. Dechert and M. Raupach (eds), *Transfer in language production* (pp. 217–36). Norwood, NJ: Ablex.

Sheen, Y. (2004) Corrective feedback and learner uptake in communicative classrooms across instructional settings. *Language Teaching Research, 8,* 263–300.

Sheen, Y. (2006) Exploring the relationship between characteristics of recasts and learner uptake. *Language Teaching Research, 10,* 361–92.

Sheen, Y. (2007) The effect of focused written corrective feedback and language aptitude on ESL learners' acquisition of articles. *TESOL Quarterly, 41*, 255–83.

Sheeran, P. (2002) Intention–behavior relations: a conceptual and empirical review. In W. Stroebe and M. Hewstone (eds), *European Review of Social Psychology* (vol. 12, pp. 1–30). New York: John Wiley & Sons.

Shehadeh, A. (2001) Self- and other-initiated modified output during task-based interaction. *TESOL Quarterly, 35*, 433–57.

Shehadeh, A. (2002) Comprehensible output, from occurrence to acquisition: an agenda for acquisitional research. *Language Learning, 52*, 597–647.

Shirai, Y., and Ozeki, H. (eds) (2007) *The L2 acquisition of relative clauses in East Asian languages*. Special issue of *Studies in Second Language Acquisition, 29*(2).

Shook, D. J. (1994) FL/L2 reading, grammatical information, and the input-to-intake phenomenon. *Applied Language Learning, 5*, 57–93.

Siegal, M. (1996) The role of learner subjectivity in second language sociolinguistic competency: Western women learning Japanese. *Applied Linguistics, 17*, 356–82.

Singleton, D. (1987) Mother and other tongue influence on learner French: a case study. *Studies in Second Language Acquisition, 9*, 327–45.

Singleton, D. (2001) Age and second language acquisition. *Annual Review of Applied Linguistics, 21*, 77–89.

Singleton, D. (2003) Critical period or general age factor(s)? In M. P. García Mayo and M. L. García Lecumberri (eds), *Age and the acquisition of English as a foreign language* (pp. 3–22). Clevedon, UK: Multilingual Matters.

Singleton, D. (2005) The critical period hypothesis: a coat of many colours. *International Review of Applied Linguistics, 43*, 269–85.

Skehan, P. (1986) The role of foreign language aptitude in a model of school learning. *Language Testing, 3*, 188–221.

Skehan, P. (1998). *A cognitive approach to language learning.* Oxford: Oxford University Press.

Skehan, P. (2002) Theorising and updating aptitude. In P. Robinson (ed.), *Individual differences and instructed language learning* (pp. 69–93). Amsterdam: John Benjamins.

Skehan, P., and Foster, P. (2001) Cognition and tasks. In P. Robinson (ed.), *Cognition and second language instruction* (pp. 183–205). New York: Cambridge University Press.

Slevc, L. R., and Miyake, A. (2006) Individual differences in second language proficiency: does musical ability matter? *Psychological Science, 17*, 675–81.

Slobin, D. I. (1973) Cognitive prerequisites for the development of grammar. In C. A. Ferguson and D. I. Slobin (eds), *Studies of child language development* (pp. 175–208). New York: Holt, Rinehart & Winston Inc.

Slobin, D. I. (1996) From 'thought and language' to 'thinking for speaking'. In J. J. Gumperz and S. C. Levinson (eds), *Rethinking linguistic relativity* (pp. 70–96). Cambridge: Cambridge University Press.

Smith, L. B., and Thelen, E. (2003) Development as a dynamic system. *TRENDS in Cognitive Sciences, 7*(8), 343–8.

Smith, N., and Tsimpli, I.-M. (1995) *The mind of a savant: language learning and modularity.* London: Blackwell.

Snow, C. E., Burns, M. S., and Griffin, P. (eds). (1998). *Preventing reading difficulties in young children.* Washington, DC: National Academy Press.

Snow, C., and Hoefnagel-Höhle, M. (1977) Age differences in the pronunciation of foreign sounds. *Language and Speech, 20*, 357–65.

Snow, C., and Hoefnagel-Höhle, M. (1978) The critical period for second language acquisition: evidence from second language learning. *Child Development, 49*, 1112–28.

Sorace, A. (1993) Incomplete vs. divergent representations of unaccusativity in near-native grammars of Italian. *Second Language Research, 9*, 22–48.

Spada, N., and Lightbown, P. M. (1993) Instruction and the development of questions in the L2 classroom. *Studies in Second Language Acquisition, 15*, 205–21.

Spada, N., and Lightbown, P. M. (1999) Instruction, first language influence, and developmental readiness in second language acquisition. *Modern Language Journal, 83*, 1–22.

Sparks, R. (2006) Is there a 'disability' for learning a foreign language? *Journal of Learning Disabilities, 39*, 544–57.

Speciale, G., Ellis, N. C., and Bywater, T. (2004) Phonological sequence learning and short-term store capacity determine second language vocabulary acquisition. *Applied Psycholinguistics, 25*, 293–321.

Spielmann, G., and Radnofsky, M. L. (2001) Learning language under tension: new directions from a qualitative study. *Modern Language Journal, 85*, 259–78.

Spolsky, B. (1995) Prognostication and language aptitude testing. *Language Testing, 12*, 321–40.

Sridhar, S. N. (1994) A reality check for SLA theories. *TESOL Quarterly, 28*, 800–805.

Stansfield, C. W., and Reed, D. J. (2004) The story behind the Modern Language Aptitude Test: an interview with John B. Carroll. *Language Assessment Quarterly, 1*(1), 43–56.

Stauble, A. E. (1978). The process of decreolization: a model for second language development. *Language Learning, 28*, 29–54.

Steinberg, F. S., and Horwitz, E. K. (1986) The effect of induced anxiety on the denotative and interpretive content of second language speech. *TESOL Quarterly, 20*, 131–6.

Sternberg, R. J. (2002) The theory of successful intelligence and its implications for language-aptitude testing. In P. Robinson (ed.), *Individual differences and instructed language learning* (pp. 13–43). Amsterdam: John Benjamins.

Sternberg, R. J., and Grigorenko, E. L. (1997) Are cognitive styles still in style? *American Psychologist, 52*, 700–712.

Stockwell, R., Bowen, J., and Martin, J. (1965) *The grammatical structures of English and Spanish*. Chicago, IL: University of Chicago Press.

Storch, N. (2002) Patterns of interaction in ESL pair work. *Language Learning, 52*, 119–58.

Stuart-Fox, D., and Moussalli, A. (2008) Selection for social signalling drives the evolution of chameleon colour change. *PLoS Biol, 6*(1), 0022–9. doi:10.1371/journal.pbio.0060025.

Sugaya, N., and Shirai, Y. (2007) The acquisition of progressive and resultative meanings of the imperfective aspect marker by L2 learners of Japanese: transfer, universals, or multiple factors? *Studies in Second Language Acquisition, 29*, 1–38.

Svirsky, M. A., Chin, S. B., and Jester, A. (2007) The effects of age at implantation on speech intelligibility in pediatric cochlear implant users: clinical outcomes and sensitive periods. *Audiological Medicine, 5*, 293–306.

Svirsky, M., and Holt, R. (2005) Language acquisition after cochlear implantation of congenitally deaf children: effect of age at implantation. Paper presented at the 149th Meeting of the Acoustical Society of America, 16–20 May, Vancouver.

Swain, M. (1985) Communicative competence: some roles of comprehensible input and comprehensible output in its development. In S. M. Gass and C. G. Madden (eds), *Input in second language acquisition* (pp. 235–53). Rowley, MA: Newbury House.

Swain, M. (1995) Three functions of output in second language learning. In G. Cook and B. Seidlhofer (eds), *Principle and practice in applied linguistics: studies in honour of H. G. Widdowson* (pp. 125–44). New York: Oxford University Press.

Swain, M. (2000) The output hypothesis and beyond: mediating acquisition through collaborative dialogue. In J. P. Lantolf (ed.), *Sociocultural theory and second language learning* (pp. 97–114). New York: Oxford University Press.

Swain, M. (2006) Verbal protocols: what does it mean for research to use speaking as a data collection tool? In M. Chalhoub-Deville, C. Chapelle, and P. A. Duff (eds), *Inference and generalizability in applied linguistics: multiple perspectives* (pp. 97–113). Amsterdam: John Benjamins.

Swain, M., and Lapkin, S. (1995) Problems in output and the cognitive processes they generate: a step towards second language learning. *Applied Linguistics, 16*, 371–91.

Swain, M., and Lapkin, S. (2000) Task-based second language learning: the uses of the first language. *Language Teaching Research, 4*, 253–76.

Sykes, J., Oskoz, A., and Thorne, S. L. (2008) Web 2.0, synthetic immersive environments, and mobile resources for language education. *CALICO Journal, 25*, 528–46.

Taguchi, N. (2007) Chunk learning and the development of spoken discourse in a Japanese as a foreign language classroom. *Language Teaching Research, 11*, 433–57.

Takahashi, S. (1996) Pragmatic transferability. *Studies in Second Language Acquisition, 18*, 189–223.

Talburt, S., and Stewart, M. (1999) What's the subject of study abroad? Race, gender, and 'living culture'. *Modern Language Journal, 83*, 163–75.

Tallerman, M. (ed.) (2005) *Language origins: perspectives on evolution.* New York: Oxford University Press.

Tarallo, F., and Myhill, J. (1983) Interference and natural language processing in second language acquisition. *Language Learning, 33*, 55–73.

Thomas, M. (1990) Acquisition of the Japanese reflexive zibun by unilingual and multilingual learners. In H. Burmeister and P. L. Rounds (eds), *Variability in second language acquisition: proceedings of the tenth meeting of the second Language Research Forum* (vol. 2, pp. 701–718). Eugene, OR: University of Oregon.

Thorne, S. L., and Black, R. (2007) Language and literacy development in computer mediated contexts and communities. *Annual Review of Applied Linguistics, 27*, 133–60.

Tocalli-Beller, A., and Swain, M. (2007) Riddles and puns in the ESL classroom: adults talk to learn. In A. Mackey (ed.), *Conversational interaction in second language acquisition* (pp. 143–67). New York: Oxford University Press.

Tomlin, R., and Villa, V. (1994) Attention in cognitive science and SLA. *Studies in Second Language Acquisition, 16*, 183–204.

Toohey, K. (2001) Disputes in child L2 learning. *TESOL Quarterly, 35*, 257–78.

Toth, P. (2006) Processing instruction and a role for output in second language acquisition. *Language Learning, 56*, 319–85.

Towell, R., and Dewaele, J.-M. (2005) The role of psycholinguistic factors in the development of fluency amongst advanced learners of French. In J.-M. Dewaele (ed.), *Focus on French as a foreign language: multidisciplinary approaches* (pp. 210–39). Clevedon, UK: Multilingual Matters.

Truscott, J. (1999) What's wrong with oral grammar correction. *Canadian Modern Language Review, 55*, 437–56.

Tseng, W.-T., Dörnyei, Z., and Schmitt, N. (2006) A new approach to assessing strategic learning: the case of self-regulation in vocabulary acquisition. *Applied Linguistics, 27*, 78–102.

Tucker, G. R. (1999) The applied linguist, school reform, and technology: challenges and opportunities for the coming decade. *CALICO Journal, 17*(2), 197–221.

Tudini, V. (2007) Negotiation and intercultural learning in Italian native speaker chat rooms. *Modern Language Journal, 91*, 577–601.

Tulving, E. (2002) Episodic memory: from mind to brain. *Annual Review of Psychology, 53*, 1–25.

Ullman, M. T. (2001) The neural basis of lexicon and grammar in first and second language: the declarative/procedural model. *Bilingualism: Language and Cognition, 4*, 105–22.

Ullman, M. T. (2004) Contributions of memory circuits to language: the declarative/procedural model. *Cognition, 92*, 231–70.

Ushioda, E. (2001) Language learning at university: exploring the role of motivational thinking. In Z. Dörnyei and R. Schmidt (eds), *Motivation and second language acquisition* (pp. 93–125). Honolulu, HI: National Foreign Language Resource Center.

Valdés, G. (2001) *Learning and not learning English: Latino students in American schools.* New York: Teachers College Press.

Van den Branden, K. (1997) Effects of negotiation on language learners' output. *Language Learning, 47*, 589–636.

Van den Branden, K. (ed.) (2006). *Task-based language teaching: from theory to practice.* New York: Cambridge University Press.

van Geert, P. (1998) A dynamic systems model of basic developmental mechanisms: Piaget, Vygotsky, and beyond. *Psychological Review, 105*, 634–77.

van Lier, L. (1994) Forks and hope: pursuing understanding in different ways. *Applied Linguistics, 15*, 328–47.

Vann, R., and Abraham, R. (1990) Strategies of unsuccessful language learners. *TESOL Quarterly, 24*, 177–97.

VanPatten, B. (2002) Processing instruction: an update. *Language Learning, 52*, 755–803.

VanPatten, B. (2004) Input and output in establishing form–meaning connections. In B. VanPatten, J. Williams, S. Rott, and M. Overstreet (eds), *Form–meaning connections in second language acquisition* (pp. 29–47). Mahwah, NJ: Lawrence Erlbaum.

VanPatten, B., and Williams, J. (eds) (2007) *Theories in second language acquisition: an introduction.* Mahwah, NJ: Lawrence Erlbaum.

Vansteenkiste, M., Lens, W., and Deci, E. L. (2006) Intrinsic versus extrinsic goal contents in self-determination theory: another look at the quality of academic motivation. *Educational Psychologist, 41*, 19–31.

Verhoeven, L., and Vermeer, A. (2002) Communicative competence and personality dimensions in first and second language learners. *Applied Psycholinguistics, 23*, 361–474.

Verspoor, M., Lowie, W., and Van Dijk, M. (2008) Variability in second language development from a Dynamic Systems perspective. *Modern Language Journal, 92*, 214–31.

von Stutterheim, C. (1991) European research on second language acquisition. In B. F. Freed (ed.), *Foreign language acquisition research and the classroom* (pp. 135–54). Lexington, MA: D. C. Heath and Company.

von Stutterheim, C., and Klein, W. (1987) A concept-oriented approach to second language studies. In C. W. Pfaff (ed.), *First and second language acquisition* (pp. 191–205). Rowley, MA: Newbury House.

Wagner, J. (ed.) (1996) *Conversational analysis of foreign language data.* Special issue of *Journal of Pragmatics, 26*(2).

Wallace, B., Ross, A., Davies, J. B., and Anderson, T. (2007) *The mind, the body and the world: sychology after cognitivism.* London: Imprint Academic.

Watson, R. A. (1995) *The philosopher's demise: learning French.* Columbia, MO: University of Missouri Press.

Wayland, R. P., and Gion, S. G. (2004) Training English and Chinese listeners to perceive Thai tones: a preliminary report. *Language Learning, 54*, 681–712.

Weber-Fox, C. M., and Neville, H. J. (2001) Sensitive periods differentiate processing for open and closed class words: an ERP study in bilinguals. *Journal of Speech, Language, and Hearing Research, 44,* 1338–53.

Wei, L. (ed.) (2000) *The bilingualism reader.* London: Routledge.

Wells, G. (1985) *Language development in the pre-school years.* Cambridge: Cambridge University Press.

Wells, G. (1999) Using L1 to master L2: a response to Antón and DiCamilla's 'socio-cognitive functions of L1 collaborative interaction in the L2 classroom'. *Modern Language Journal, 83,* 248–54.

Wesche, M. (1981) Language aptitude measures in streaming, matching students with methods, and diagnosis of learning problems. In K. Diller (ed.), *Individual differences and universals in language learning aptitude* (pp. 119–39). Rowley, MA: Newbury House.

White, L. (2003) *Second language acquisition and universal grammar.* New York: Cambridge University Press.

White, L., and Genesee, F. (1996) How native is near-native? The issue of ultimate attainment in adult second language acquisition. *Second Language Research, 12,* 233–65.

Wilks, C., and Meara, P. (2002) Untangling word webs: graph theory and the notion of density in second language word association networks. *Second Language Research, 18,* 303–24.

Willett, J. (1995) Becoming a first grader in a second language: an ethnographic study of second language socialization. *TESOL Quarterly, 29,* 473–503.

Williams, Jessica (1999) Learner-generated attention to form. *Language Learning, 49,* 583–625.

Williams, Jessica (2001) The effectiveness of spontaneous attention to form. *System, 29,* 325–40.

Williams, John N. (1999) Memory, attention, and inductive learning. *Studies in Second Language Acquisition, 21,* 1–48.

Williams, John N. (2005) Learning without awareness. *Studies in Second Language Acquisition, 27,* 269–304.

Williams, John N., and Lovatt, P. (2003) Phonological memory and rule learning. *Language Learning, 53,* 67–121.

Williams, S., and Hammarberg, B. (1998) Language switches in L3 production: implications for a polyglot speaking model. *Applied Linguistics, 19,* 295–333.

Willing, K. (1988) *Learning styles in adult migrant education.* Adelaide, Australia: National Curriculum Resource Centre of the Adult Migrant Education Program.

Wilson, M. (2002) Six views of embodied cognition. *Psychonomic Bulletin and Review, 9,* 625–36.

Wode, H. (1976) Developmental sequences in naturalistic L2 acquisition. *Working Papers on Bilingualism, 11,* 1–31.

Wolcott, H. (1999) *Ethnography: a way of seeing.* Walnut Creek, CA: AltaMira.

Wong Fillmore, L. (1979) Individual differences in second language acquisition. In C. Fillmore, D. Kempler, and W. Wang (eds), *Individual differences in language ability and language behavior* (pp. 203–28). New York: Academic Press.

Wray, A. (2002) *Formulaic language and the lexicon.* New York: Cambridge University Press.

Yano, Y., Long, M. H., and Ross, S. (1994) The effects of simplified and elaborated texts on foreign language reading comprehension. *Language Learning, 44,* 189–219.

Yashima, T. (2002) Willingness to communicate in a second language: the Japanese EFL context. *Modern Language Journal, 86,* 55–66.

Yashima, T., Zenuk-Nishide, L., and Shimizu, K. (2004) The influence of attitude and affect on willingness to communicate and second language communication. *Language Learning, 54,* 119–52.

Yi, Y. (2007) Engaging literacy: a biliterate student's composing practices beyond school. *Journal of Second Language Writing, 16,* 23–39.

Young, R. F. (1991) *Variation in interlanguage morphology.* New York: Peter Lang.

Young, R. F., and Miller, E. R. (2004) Learning as changing participation: discourse roles in ESL writing conferences. *Modern Language Journal, 88,* 519–35.

Young, R. F., and Nguyen, H. T. (2002) Modes of meaning in high school science. *Applied Linguistics, 23,* 348–72.

Yu, M.-C. (2004) Interlinguistic variation and similarity in second language speech act behavior. *Modern Language Journal, 88,* 102–19.

Zobl, H. (1980) The formal and developmental selectivity of L1 influence on L2 acquisition. *Language Learning, 30,* 43–57.

Zobl, H. (1982) A direction for contrastive analysis: the comparative study of developmental sequences. *TESOL Quarterly, 16,* 169–83.

Author index

References to tables are indexed as, for example, 22t.

Aaronson, D. 144
Abbot-Smith, K. 104
Abe, J.A.A. 196
Abrahamsson, N. 25, 30
Abutalebi, Jubin 21–2
Achugar, Mariana 234–5, 236, 254
Albert, A. 196
Aljaafreh, A. 225–6
Andersen, Roger 33, 54, 113, 116–17, 127, 144
Anderson, John 84
Aoyama, K. 17
Appel, G. 218, 220
Astaneh, H. 48
Aston, G. 77

Baars, Bernard 90, 95, 98t
Bachman, L.F. 196
Baddeley, Alan 90, 91
Bailey, K.M. 214
Bailey, P. 201
Baker, S.C. 203, 215
Bakhtin, Michael 242
Baquedano-López, P. 237
Bardovi-Harlig, K. 57, 127, 128, 140, 143
Barkhuizen, G. 144
Barsalou, L.W. 104, 108
Basturkmen, H. 70
Batistella, E.L. 37
Baumeister, R.F. 212
Baumgartner-Cohen, B. 50
Beck, M. 71
Beckett, G.H. 235–6
Beebe, L. 51
Belz, J.A. 248
Bhabha, H. 250
Bhatia, T.K. 11
Bialystok, Ellen 24, 43, 83, 85
Bickerton, Derek 3
Bigelow, M. 81, 162

Birdsong, David 18t, 19, 20t, 28, 30
Black, R.W. 249, 254
Blackledge, A. 242, 251, 254
Bley-Vroman, Robert 24, 65, 158
Block, D. 216, 242
Boekaerts, M. 211
Bongaerts, Theo 23, 28, 202
Bourdieu, Pierre 242
Bot, Kees de 11, 105, 108, 109, 143
Braidi, S. 11
Breen, M. 215
Brice Heath, Shirley 237
Brouwer, C.E. 232, 233
Brown, Roger 110–11
Burgess, Neil 91
Burt, Marina 124
Byrnes, H. 139, 140

Cadierno, T. 47–8
Call, M. S. L. *see* Scott, Mary Lee
Cameron, L. 114
Canagarajah, A.S. 251
Cancino, H. 35, 119, 144
Candland, D.K. 13
Carpenter, Patricia 92–3
Carroll, Donald 229–30
Carroll, John 149–51, 154, 166
Carroll, M. 46
Carroll, Suzanne 75
Carson, J. 214
Celce-Murcia, M. 44–5
Cenoz, Jasone 48, 54
Chamot, Anna 209, 210, 211, 215
Chapelle, C. 205
Charos, C. 197
Chater, N. 103, 109
Chaudron, Craig 73, 81
Christiansen, M.H. 130
Chun, D.M. 155

Clahsen, Harald 130–2
Clément, Richard 173–4, 175–6, 179, 180, 181, 190, 202, 203, 204
Collins, L. 44
Colombi, Cecilia 234–5, 236, 254
Comrie, B. 129–30
Cook, Vivian 5, 9, 26, 30, 50, 54, 90–1, 141
Coppieters, R. 19, 20t
Corder, S.P. 140, 143
Cortázar, Julio 9
Costa, P.T., Jr. 194t, 195
Cowan, Nelson 90, 91, 93, 95, 96
Crookes, G. 175
Csizér, K. 171, 179, 180, 184, 185, 187, 190, 204
Curtiss, S. 13

Dagut, M. 40
Daneman, Meredyth 92–3
Darhower, M. 248
Davies, A. 7, 143
Davis, K.A. 251
Day, R. 72
de Bot, Kees 11, 105, 108, 109, 143
de Graaff, R. 160
de Groot, Annette 89
de Guerrero, María 221
de Saussure, Ferdinand 217
Dechert, H.W. 54
Deci, Edward 175
Dehaene, Stanislas 21
DeKeyser, Robert 19, 81, 85–7, 108, 124, 125, 158
Dewaele, Jean-Marc 50, 90, 194t, 197–8, 199, 215
Diessel, H. 130
Mihaljevi Djigunovi , J. 30
Donato, Richard 223–4, 254
Donitsa-Schmidt, S. 181–2, 183, 190
Dörnyei, Zoltán 171, 175, 178, 179, 180, 184, 185, 186–8, 190, 204, 208, 211, 215
Doughty, Catherine 7, 11, 60, 74t, 95
Duff, Patricia 46, 144, 237–8, 239
DuFon, M.A. 240
Dufva, Mia 153, 154
Dulay, Heidi 124

Eckman, Fred 38
Edwards, D.J. 190
Ehrlich, S. 78
Ehrman, M.E. 166, 195, 206, 207–8, 215
Eisenstein, M.R. 143
Elder, C. 7
Eliasson, S. 40
Elliott, A.R. 202

Ellis, Nick 85, 90, 95, 96, 102, 103, 104, 105, 108, 109, 113, 114–15, 125, 137
Ellis, Rod 11, 51, 70, 74–5, 81, 138, 139, 144
Engle, Randall 93, 108–9
Ericsson, K. Anders 91, 94, 108
Erlam, Rosemary 161
Eubank, L. 143
Evans, V. 104
Eysenck, H.J. & S.B.G. 193, 194t

Ferris, D.R. 81
Finkbeiner, M. 89
Firth, Alan 227, 231, 232, 254
Flege, James 19, 22–3, 24, 25, 26
Flynn, Suzanne 49
Foster, Pauline 77
Franklin, S. 90, 95, 98t
Frawley, W. 221–2, 254
Freeman, D.E. & Y.S. 11
Freud, Sigmund 217
Frota, S. 63, 64, 73, 80
Furnham, Adrian 197–8, 199, 215
Fuse, A. 124–5, 144

Ganschow, Leonore 152–3, 154
García Lecumberri, M. 17, 30
García Mayo, M.P. 17, 30
Gardner, Robert 168, 170–1, 172t, 174–5, 184, 188, 196, 200–1, 202, 215
Garfinkel, Harold 227
Garrett, P.B. 237
Gaskill, W.H. 72
Gass, Susan 11, 54, 64–5, 67, 80, 81, 94, 96, 144
Gasser, M. 105
Gathercole, S.E. 156–7
Gee, James 241
Genesee, F. 20
Georgakopoulou, A. xiii
Goffman, Erving 227
Goldschneider, J. 124, 125
Goo, J.M. 66
Gordon, R.G. 2
Gottschaldt, K. 205
Granger, Sylvianne 42
Green, P. 205
Gregersen, T. 201–2
Gregory, E. 254
Grigorenko, Elena 154, 196, 205–6
Groot, Annette de 89
Grosjean, François 30
Guion, S.G. 43

Hahne, Anja 21
Hakuta, Kenji 24

Halliday, M.A.K. 233–4
Hammarberg, Bjorn 49–50
Han, Z. 134–5, 144
Hannigan, S. 154–5
Harklau, Linda 243–4
Harley, B. 158–9
Harrington, Michael 90, 93, 156
Hart, D. 158–9
Hatch, Evelyn 60
Hawkins, B. 77
Hawkins, R. 11, 112, 143
Headland, J. 228
Heckhausen, H. 184
Heift, T. 81
Heller, M. 251
Hellermann, J. 232–3, 254
Heredia, R. 85, 108, 117–18
Herschensohn, Julia 30
Higgins, E. Tory 186
Hitch, Graham 90, 91
Ho, B. 210
Hoefnagel-Höhle, Marian 16
Holt, Rachael 14, 25
Horst, Marlise 94
Horwitz, Elaine 200–2, 215
Hosoda, Yuri 231
Hsiao, T.-Y. 210
Hu, X. 130
Huebner, Thom 36, 118–19, 140, 144
Hulstijn, Jan 40–1, 94, 95, 109
Hyland, K. & F. 81
Hyltenstam, K. 25, 30, 32, 121

Ide, S. 57
Inbar, O. 181, 182–3, 184
Ioup, Georgette 14–16, 19, 143, 144
Iversen, J.R. 167
Iwashita, N. 81
Izumi, Shinichi 63, 69, 97
Izumi, Y. 69

Jansen, L. 139
Jarvis, Scott 36, 41–2, 43, 49, 50, 54
Jefferson, Gail 227
Jia, G. 124–5, 144
Jiang, Nan 89
Jin, H.G. 45
Johnson, Jacqueline 18t, 19, 158, 206
Juffs, Alan 156
Jung, E.H.S. 45
Just, Marcel 92–3

Kamberelis, G. 250
Kaplan, Alice 147, 148, 169t, 170, 171, 192t, 208

Karmiloff-Smith, K. & A. 3
Karoly, P. 211
Kasper, Gabriele 143, 228, 232
Keck, C.M. 66
Keenan, E. 129–30
Kellerman, Eric 38–9, 54, 112, 118
Kern, R. 248
Keshavarz, M.H. 48
King, K. 30
Kinginger, Celeste 247–8, 254
Kintsch, Walter 91, 108
Klee, C. 33
Klein, Elaine 48
Klein, Wolfgang 122, 123t, 126, 141
Knudsen, E.I. 13
Kormos, Judit 196, 198–9
Kramsch, Claire 7, 251
Krashen, Stephen 16–17, 59–60, 94, 124, 136–7,
  160, 198
Kroll, Judith 89
Kruidenier, B.G. 173–4, 181, 190
Kubota, R. 253–4
Kuhl, J. 184
Kuhn, T.S. xiii
Kurhila, Salla 231–2

Lai, C. 81
Lakshmanan, U. 136
Lam, W.S.E. 249, 254
Lamb, M. 180–1, 190
Lambert, Wallace 168
Lantolf, James 218, 219, 220, 221–2, 224–6,
  251, 254
Lapkin, Sharon 64, 70
Lardiere, D. 134, 135, 144
Larsen-Freeman, Diane 11, 103, 104, 105, 114,
  137, 141, 215
Laufer, Batia 40, 88, 95, 109
Lazaraton, Anne, 228
Lave, Jean 242
Leaver, B.L. 206, 207–8, 215
Lenneberg, E.H. 12
Leont'ev, Aleksei 218
Leow, Ron 97
Levelt, W.J.M. 69
Lieven, E. 115, 116
Lightbown, Patsy 10–11, 35–6, 138
Likert, R. 170
Lindemann, S. 78
Liu, C. 130
Livingston, E. 229
Lochtman, K. 73
Lock, E. 14
Loewen, S. 97

Logan, G.D. 91
Long, Michael 7, 11, 16–17, 60–2, 64, 66, 72, 73, 74t, 80, 136, 143
Longhini, A. 214
Loschky, Lester 60, 65, 81
Lovatt, P. 157
Luria, Alexander 218
Lyn, H. 3
Lyster, Roy 72, 73, 74t, 75, 76, 81

MacIntyre, P.D. 197, 200–1, 202, 203, 215
MacKay, I.R.A. 26
Mackey, Alison 30, 65, 66–7, 75–6, 81, 94, 97, 138, 144, 157–8, 162
Majerus, S. 91
Manning, C.D. 103, 109
Maratsos, M.P. 112
Marchena, E. 40–1
Marinova-Todd, Stefka 22, 24
Markee, Numa 228
Martin, J.R. 236
Marx, Karl 217
Masgoret, A.-M. 172t, 188
Masoura, E.V. 156–7
Master, Peter 36
Mayberry, Rachel 14
McCaulley, M.H. 193–4
McCrae, R.R. 194t, 195, 196
McDonough, Kim 67, 81, 97
McField, G. 60
McGroarty, M. 184, 210–11
McKay, S.L. 243, 251, 254
McLaughlin, Barry 11, 85, 108, 117–18, 137, 160
Meara, Paul 88–9
Meisel, Jürgen 130–2, 139
Michaud, J. 221
Miller, E.R. 232, 233
Miller, G.A. 92t
Mitchell, R. 11
Miyake, A. 167
Mohan, Bernard 235–6
Molis, Michelle 18t, 19
Montrul, S. 20
Moody, R. 194t, 195
Moore, Leslie 240–1
Mori, H. 76, 81
Mori, Junko 232
Morin, A. 221
Morita, Naoko 239, 242
Moyer, Alene 23, 28, 202
Muñoz, C. 17, 30
Musumeci, D. 77
Myers, I.B. 193–4

Myles, F. 11, 116

Naiman, N. 208
Nakahama, Y. 77
Nassaji, H. 226–7, 254
Nation, Paul 88, 109, 160
Neville, Helen 21
Newport, Elissa 18t, 19, 158
Nicholas, H. 74
Noels, Kimberly 175–6, 177–8
Norris, J.M. 66, 75, 138, 144
Norton, B. 242, 250
Norton Peirce, Bonny 241, 242, 244–5, 250, 251, 254
Nyikos, M. 210

Obler, L. 154–5
O'Brien, I. 157
Ocampo, A. 33
Ochs, Elinor 237
Odlin, Terence 33, 41–2, 49, 52, 54
Ohara, Yumiko 245–6
Ohta, Amy 77
Oliver, R. 64, 74t, 75–6
Olshtain, Elite 47
O'Malley, J.M. 209, 210, 211
Onwuegbuzie, A.J. 201
Ortega, Lourdes 66, 74t, 75, 138, 140, 141, 144, 245
Osterhout, Lee 21, 22
Ottó, I. 184
Oxford, Rebecca 175, 209–10, 211, 215
Oyama, Susan 17, 18

Pallier, Christophe 21
Palmer, A.S. 196
Panova, I. 73
Paribakht, Sima 88
Patel, A.D. 167
Patkowski, Mark 17, 19
Pavesi, M. 139
Pavlenko, Aneta 50, 54, 89, 242, 251, 254
Payne, J.S. 155
Peacock, M. 210
Pelletier, Luc 175–6
Penfield, W. 12
Pennycook, A. 251
Perani, Daniela 21–2
Perdue, Clive 122, 123t
Philp, Jenefer 97, 162
Piaget, Jean 55, 220
Pica, Teresa 61, 64, 67, 68, 77, 80, 117
Pienemann, Manfred 35, 130–3, 138, 144
Pigada, M. 109

Piske, T. 24
Poehner, M.E. 224
Polanyi, L. 247
Politzer, R. 210–11
Potter, J. 103
Pujol, J. 24
Pulvermüller, F. 24
Purcell, E. 202

Radnofsky, M.L. 192
Ranta, Leila 73, 74t, 166
Raupach, M. 54
Ravem, R. 35
Reali, F. 130
Reber, Arthur 99–100
Reid, Joy 206–7
Richards, Keith 232, 254
Ringbom, Håkan 42–3, 49, 54
Ritchie, W.C. 11
Roberts, L. 12
Robinson, Peter 90, 95, 96, 100–2, 105, 108, 113, 125, 137, 151, 160, 162–3, 164, 166
Romaine, S. 4
Ross, S. 159
Rubin, Joan 208–9
Russell, J. 72, 75
Rutherford, William 44, 54
Ryan, Richard 175
Rymer, R. 13
Rymes, Betsy 238

Sacks, Harvey 227
Sato, C. 126, 143, 144
Savage-Rumbaugh, E.S. 3
Saville-Troike, M. 11
Sawyer, Mark 90, 93, 156, 166
Scarcella, Robin 16–17
Schachter, Jacqueline 40, 44–5, 54
Schegloff, Emanuel 68, 73, 227
Schieffelin, Bambi 237
Schmidt, Richard 55–8, 59, 60, 63–4, 73, 78, 80, 85, 95, 96, 97, 105, 108, 115, 117, 143, 144, 175, 190
Schmitt, Norbert 7, 89, 109
Schumann, John 24, 58–9, 134, 135, 144
Schwartz, B.D. 72, 111, 137
Scott, Mary Lee 155–6
Scovel, Tom 11, 22, 29, 30
Sebastián-Gallés, Núria 25, 26
Seedhouse, Paul 232
Segalowitz, Norman 83, 85, 108
Seidlhofer, Barbara 140–1
Selinker, Larry 11, 34, 50, 54, 110, 134, 136, 140, 143

Service, Elisabet 155
Shanks, David 98t, 99, 100
Sharwood Smith, M. 54, 60, 83, 112, 118
Sheen, Younghee 74–5, 81, 161
Shehadeh, Ali 68–9
Shirai, Y. 116, 127
Siegal, Meryl 246–7
Simon, Herbert 94, 108
Singleton, David 17, 27, 29, 33
Sinicrope, C. 139
Skehan, Peter 151, 152, 163, 164, 166
Slabakova, R. 20
Slevc, L.R. 167
Slobin, Dan 47, 113
Smith, Linda 104–5, 109
Snow, Catherine 16, 24, 153
Snow, Richard 162
Sorace, A. 19–20, 135
Spada, Nina 10–11, 35–6, 72, 75, 138
Sparks, Richard 152–3, 154
Spielman, G. 192
Spolsky, B. 166
Sprouse, R.A. 111
Sridhar, S.N. 140
Stauble, A.E. 119, 120t
Steinberg, F.S. 201
Sternberg, Robert 151, 196, 205–6
Stewart, M. 247
Storch, Neomy 77
Sugaya, N. 116
Suter, R. 202
Svirsky, Mario 14, 25
Swain, Merrill 62–3, 64, 70, 81, 218, 222–3, 226–7, 254

Takahashi, S. 47
Talburt, S. 247
Tallerman, M. 3
Thelen, Esther 104–5, 109
Thomas, Margaret 50
Thorne, S.L. 218, 219, 220, 221, 222, 248, 251
Tocalli-Beller, A. 222–3
Tomasello, Michael 104, 115, 116, 130
Tomlin, R. 95, 96
Toohey, K. 251
Toth, P. 69
Towell, R. 90
Truscott, J. 72
Tseng, W.-T. 211–12, 215
Tucker, Richard 217
Tulving, Endel 87–8, 108

Ullman, M.T. 25
Ushioda, E. 184–5, 190

Vallerand, Robert 175–6
Van den Branden, Kris 67–8
van Geert, Paul 105
VanPatten, Bill 11, 113
Vansteenkiste, M. 175, 176
Varela, E. 74t
Varonis, Evangeline 64–5, 67, 81
Verhoeven, Ludo 194t, 195–6, 215
Vermeer, Anne 194t, 195–6, 215
Verspoor, M. 113
Villa, V. 95, 96
Voeten, M.J.M. 153
Vohs, K.D. 212
von Stutterheim, C. 126
Vygotsky, Lev 218, 220, 224

Wagner, Johannes 227, 232, 233, 254
Wallace, B. 103
Waring, R. 88
Watson, Richard 147–8, 153–4, 169t, 170, 171, 176, 192t
Wayland, R.P. 43
Weber-Fox, C.M. 21
Weedon, Chris 242
Wei, L. 4
Weinberger, S. 143

Wells, G. 152
Wenden, Anita 215
Wenger, Etienne 242
Wesche, Marjorie 88, 151, 154, 164, 166
White, Lydia 7, 11, 20, 111, 112
Wilks, C. 88
Willett, J. 251
Williams, Jessica 11, 69, 70, 75–6, 81
Williams, John 43–4, 102, 108, 157, 160
Williams, Sarah 49–50
Willing, Ken 206
Wilson, M. 104
Wode, Henning 33
Wolcott, H. 229
Wong Fillmore, Lily 114, 115t, 144
Wong, S.-L.C. 243, 251, 254

Yano, Y. 64
Yashima, Tomoko 179–80, 196, 204, 215
Yi, Y. 249–50
Young, R.F. 51, 232, 233
Yu, M.-C. 47

Zhao, Y. 81
Zobl, Helmut 32, 35, 54, 160
Zuengler, J. 51

Subject index

Entries referring to specific groups of language users are constructed in the following ways: [L1-L2] speakers, e.g. Spanish-English speakers, or [Language] L2 speakers, e.g. English L2 speakers. Entries for individual informants are constructed as follows: [Name] (L1-L2 speaker), e.g. Julie (English-Arabic speaker). References to tables are entered as, for example, 22t.

accents 15, 22–3, 202
accommodation 246
Acculturation Model 58–9
accuracy-speed trade-off 197–200
accuracy vs. emergence 132
accuracy vs. progress 40, 117–18, 138
acquisition *see* L1 acquisition; L2 acquisition
additional languages, acquisition of *see* L2
    acquisition
adolescents 15, 16–17
adults, rate of acquisition 16–17
affect 163, 192–3, 211–12
age factors 12–30
    age of onset 7–8, 25–6
    critical/sensitive period 12–14, 20–3, 23–8
    interpretation of evidence 23–8
    and language aptitude 155–6, 158–9
    rate of acquisition 16–17, 26
    ultimate attainment 8, 17–20, 22–3, 26–7, 28
Alberto (Spanish-English speaker) 58–9, 134
Alice Kaplan (English-French speaker) 146,
    147, 169t, 170, 192t, 208, 247–8
Almon (Cantonese-English speaker) 249
amotivation 177
analytical ability 158–9, 161
anaphora 15–16
animacy 43–4
animal communication 2–3
animal learning, critical/sensitive periods 13
anxiety 197, 200–2
appraisal systems 236
aptitude *see* language aptitude
Aptitude Complex Hypothesis 162–3
aptitude-treatment interactions 164
Arabic L2 speakers 14–16, 181–3, 240–1

articles 36–7, 43–4, 116–17, 118–19, 161
artificial grammars 99–100
artificial languages 43–4, 85–7
Aspect Hypothesis 127–9
associative learning 100–2, 103
attention 63–4, 93–6, 98t, 99
Attitude/Motivation Test Battery (AMTB)
    168–70
attitudes 170–5, 178–83
    to minority languages 173–5
    of native-speaker interlocutors 78, 231,
        238–9
    perfectionism 201–2
    to speakers of target language 170–1, 173–5,
        176, 180–1
    to target language 56, 58–9, 170, 246,
        247–8
automatic processing 83, 84–7, 90
Autopractan (miniature language) 85–7
avoidance 39–41, 138
awareness 96–9, 153

Basic Variety 122–4
Berber-Dutch speakers 67–8
bidirectional transfer 50
Big Five Model of Personality 194–5
bilingualism
    bilingual acquisition 4–5
    definition 4
    effect on brain function 21–2, 25–7
    lexical representation 89
    and memory capacity 155–6
    and multicompetence 9, 27, 140–1
bonobos, use of language 3
Brad Wang (Chinese-English speaker) 243–5

brain
　　activation patterns 20–2, 90
　　changes in structure 24–5
　　control of speech production 22
　　development of functions 12–14
　　effect of bilingualism 21–2, 25–7
Bristol Language Project 152

Catalan L2 speakers 25
central executive 83–4
child language acquisition *see* L1 acquisition
children
　　formula-based learning 114, 115t
　　rate of acquisition 16–17, 28, 114
chimpanzees, use of language 3
Chinese-English speakers 18t, 19, 40, 44–5,
　　124–5, 134–5, 243–5
Chinese-Japanese speakers 50
Chinese L2 speakers 45
circumstantial bilingualism/learning 243–5
clarification requests 61–2, 68, 71
class, and identity 247–8
classroom contexts 69–76, 161, 175, 177, 178,
　　209, 210, 229–30
　　discussions 237–9
cochlear implants, and language acquisition 14,
　　25
codeswitching 49–50
cognition 82–109
　　and affect 211–12
　　attention 63–4, 93–6, 98t, 99
　　automatic processing 83, 84–7, 90
　　awareness 96–9
　　controlled processing 83–4, 90
　　definition 82
　　emergentism 102–5
　　field-dependence vs. field-independence
　　　205–6
　　implicit/explicit interface 136–8, 158
　　information processing 82–102
　　memory 83, 87–93, 150t, 151, 153, 154–9,
　　　161
　　personality 193–200
cognitive-interactionist approach 55, 64–6,
　　226–7, 230
communities of practice 242, 244–5
competence 250–1 *see also* morphosyntax;
　　phonology
　　communicative competence 203
　　definition 110, 241
　　discourse competence 56–7
　　multicompetence 9, 27
　　pragmatic competence 57, 246–7
　　testing 15–16

Comprehensible Input Hypothesis 59–60
Comprehensible Output Hypothesis 62–3,
　　67–9
computer-mediated communication 248–50
concept-oriented approach 126, 141
confidence 202–3
confirmation checks 61–2, 68
conflict-dominance orientation 183
consonants, final stops 37–8
Contrastive Analysis 31, 111
controlled processing 83–4, 90, 163
Conversation Analysis 68, 227–33
correlational approach 146–7, 188
Counterbalance Hypothesis 76
Critical Applied Linguistics 254
Critical Period Hypothesis 12–14, 20–3, 24 *see*
　　also age factors
crosslinguistic influences 31–54
　　avoidance 39–41
　　bidirectional transfer 50
　　expression of motion 47–8
　　interlanguages 34, 51–2
　　interlingual identification 32–4
　　L3 acquisition 48–50
　　and learning difficulty 31–4
　　markedness 37–8, 129–30, 138–9
　　pragmatic transfer 46–7, 57
　　and rate of acquisition 34–7, 41–4, 48–50
　　semantic transfer 41–2
　　transferability 38–9
Crucial Similarity Measure 33

data analysis
　　correlations 18–19, 146–7, 188, 198, 201,
　　　203–4
　　emergence benchmark 131–2
　　task effects 77
data collection *see also* tests
　　coding of negotiation moves 64–5, 73–5
　　dual-task conditions 86–7, 98t
　　grammaticality judgements 18–20, 101–2
　　interviews 209
　　Likert scales 170, 174, 195–6, 200–1, 209–10,
　　　211–12
　　matched-guise tasks 174
　　neuroimaging 20–2
　　picture description tasks 67–8
　　post-tests 157, 161
　　self-corrections 199
　　think-aloud protocols 97, 209
　　transcription conventions 229
　　working memory tasks 91–3, 155–6, 157
dative alternation 100–2
deaf children, language acquisition 14, 25

developmental sequence 51, 52
    articles 36–7, 118–19
    and crosslinguistic differences 34–7, 45–6
    definition 110
    L1 acquisition 3–4, 34, 112–13
    morphology 124–9, 139–40
    negation 119–21
    questions 35–6, 114, 115–16, 132–3
    syntax 129–33, 138–9
    tense and aspect 112, 117, 126–9, 221–2,
        223–4
    word order 130–3, 138
devoicing 37–8
digital span recall tasks 92t
domain-specificity *see* modularity, nativism
dual-task conditions 86–7, 98t
Dutch-English speakers 38–9, 40–1, 197
Dutch-French speakers 197–8
Dutch L2 speakers 195–6
dynamic motivation 183–5
dynamic systems (emergentism) 104–5

educational policy 8, 28, 206
effective instruction 8, 75 *see also* teaching
        methods
effort 169–70
elective bilingualism 7–8
elective learning 245–8
elicitations (negotiation of form) 72 *see also*
        prompts
elicited imitation tasks 92t
Embedded Figures Test 205–6
emergence 131–2
emergentism 102–5, 113–14, 137
English-Arabic speakers 14–16
English as a foreign language contexts (EFL
        contexts) 178–81, 201–2, 210, 229–30
English-Chinese speakers 45
English-French speakers 19–20, 32, 33, 43,
        62–3, 146–7, 153–4, 161, 164, 169t, 170,
        192t, 208, 247–8
English-German speakers 37–8, 46
English-Hebrew speakers 47
English-Japanese speakers 50, 245–7
English-Korean speakers 45
English L2 speakers
    developmental sequence 18t–19, 35–7, 45,
        51, 52, 114, 115–16, 124–7, 132–3,
        232–3
    immigrant identities 243–5, 248–51
    literacy and rate of acquisition 153
    motivation 179–81
    pragmatic transfer 47
    speaking style 199

English-Russian speakers 247
English-Spanish speakers 116–17, 177–8,
        234–5
English-Swedish speakers 49–50
enjoyment 169t, 170, 176
Error Analysis 31
ethnomethodology 227, 228–9
European Science Foundation Project 122–4
evidentiality 33
evolution, human language 2–3
exceptional learners 14–16, 23, 28, 154–5
explicit correction 71, 225–7
explicit grammar instruction 161
explicit learning 158–61
extraversion 196–200
extrinsic motivation 176
Eysenck's model of personality 193, 194t,
        197–8

feedback 71–6, 161, 162–3, 225–7
feral children 13
field-dependence vs. field-independence 205–6
field sensitivity 206, 214
Finnish-English speakers 41–3, 49, 153, 155
Finnish L2 speakers 231
first language acquisition *see* L1 acquisition
Five-Factor Model of Personality 194–5
fluency 197–200
Fong (Chinese-English speaker) 134–5
foreign accents *see* accents
foreign language aptitude *see* language aptitude
Foreign Language Classroom Anxiety Scale
        (FLCAS) 200
foreign language contexts 6, 17, 178–83, 200,
        201–2, 204, 209, 210, 229–30
formula-based learning 114–16
fossilization 133–6 *see also* ultimate attainment
French-English speakers 32, 35–6, 44
French L2 speakers 19–20, 32, 33, 43, 146–7,
        153–4, 161, 164, 169t, 170, 192t, 208,
        223–4, 247–8
Fulfulde-Arabic speakers 240–1
functional recasts 235–6
Fundamental Difference Hypothesis 24, 158

Ge (Hmong-English speaker) 118–19
gender, and identity 245–6
gender, grammatical 43–4
Geng (Chinese-English speaker) 134–5
German-English speakers 37–8
German-French speakers 43
German L2 speakers 130–2, 138, 139, 155
    English L1 37–8, 46
globalization, effect on attitudes 180, 184

'good language learner' research studies 208–11
grammar, acquisition of 100–2, 112–24, 136–40, 157
grammatical metaphor vs. grammatical intricacy 235
grammatical sensitivity 150t, 151, 152
grammaticality judgements 18–20, 101–2

Hebrew-Arabic speakers 181–3
Hebrew-English speakers 40, 47
Hebrew L2 speakers 47
heritage learning contexts 6, 234–5, 250
Hmong-English speakers 118–19
Hokkien-English speakers 134
Hopscotch (1963) 9
Hungarian-English speakers 179, 180, 199

identity 173, 181, 192–3, 231–2, 236, 240–1, 248–51
identity theory 241–8
imagined communities 242
immersion schools 62–3, 70, 76, 159
immigrants 122–4, 130–2, 195–6, 243–5, 248–51
implicit learning 99–102, 158–61
Implicit Tallying Hypothesis 96
incidental learning 94–5, 100–2
individual differences
    affect 163, 192–3
    analytical ability 158–9, 161
    anxiety 197, 200–2
    attitudes 56, 58–9, 170–5, 178–83
    attitudes to target language 56, 58–9, 170, 246, 247–8
    exceptional learners 14–16, 23, 28, 154–5
    gender issues 245–6, 247
    'good language learners' 208–10
    language aptitude 9, 145–67
    learner readiness 138–9
    learning strategies 208–11
    learning styles 206–8
    memory capacity 89–93, 150t, 151, 161
    motivation 9, 163, 168–91
    multidimensional aptitude 161–3
    openness to experience 196
    orientations 171–5, 176–83, 198–200
    personality 56, 193–200
    phonological awareness 153
    socio-educational factors 24
    sociocultural factors 174, 210–11, 237–41
    willingness to communicate (WTC) 202–5
    working memory 90–1
Indonesian-English speakers 180–1

information processing 82–109, 163
information structure 44–6
inner speech 220, 221
input 59–60, 114–16
Input, Processing and Output Anxiety Scales (IPOAS) 200–1
Input Processing Theory 113
instructed learners 6
    Fong (Chinese-English speaker) 134–5
    Geng (Chinese-English speaker) 134–5
    Laura (English-Arabic speaker) 16
    Patty (Hokkien-English speaker) 134
integrativeness 170–1, 186–7
Interaction Hypothesis 60–2
interaction, in Conversation Analysis 227–33
interdisciplinarity, SLA research 7
interface (implicit/explicit knowledge) 136–8
interference *see* crosslinguistic influences
interlanguages 110–44 *see also* L2 acquisition
    Basic Variety 122–4
    cognitivist-emergentist theories 113–14
    crosslinguistic influences 34, 51–2
    definition 6, 110
    formula-based learning 114–16
    grammaticalization 122–4
    markedness 129–30
    overgeneralization 117, 118–19, 135
    parallels with L1 development 112–13
    restructuring 117–18
    simplification 116–17
    U-shaped learning 39, 117–18
    variability 119–21
interlingual identification 32–4
interlocutors, effect on interaction 77–8, 231
international posture (international orientation) 179–80
interviews 209
intrinsic motivation 175–8
introversion, and speaking style 198–200
investment 169t, 170, 242
Italian-German speakers 138

Japanese-English speakers 40, 55–8, 59, 78, 100–2, 117, 229–30
Japanese L2 speakers 50, 116, 231, 245–7
Joan (Korean-English speaker) 250
Jorge (Spanish-English speaker) 119–21
Julie (English-Arabic speaker) 14–16

Katarina (Polish-English speaker) 244–5
knowledge 83, 87
    implicit/explicit interface 136–8
    vocabulary 88–9
Korean-English speakers 18t, 19, 22–3, 226

Korean-Japanese speakers 50
Korean L2 speakers 45

L1 acquisition *see also* bilingualism
  critical/sensitive period 12–14, 25–6
  developmental sequence 3–4, 34, 112–13
  and language aptitude 152, 153
  learning mechanisms 158
  monolingual bias 5–6
  similarities with L2 acquisition 34
  willingness to communicate (WTC) 202
L2 acquisition *see also* bilingualism;
      multilingual acquisition
  age of onset 7–8
  crosslinguistic influences *see* crosslinguistic
      influences
  definition 5
  grammar 100–2, 112–24
  individual differences *see* individual
      differences
  interlanguages *see* interlanguages
  language activation 26–7, 50
  and learning disabilities 152–4
  and literacy 153, 162
  markedness 37–8, 129–30
  native speaker as benchmark 27, 140–1
  rate of acquisition *see* rate of acquisition
  social dimensions *see* social dimensions of L2
      acquisition
  technology-mediated communication
      248–50
  theories *see* theories of language
      development
  ultimate attainment 8, 17–20, 22–3, 26–7,
      28, 133–6
  universals 9, 136
  use of first language 70
L2 Motivational Self System 185–8
L2 speakers *see also* individual differences
  attitudes of native speakers to 78
  codeswitching 49–50
  definition 6
  perceptions of target language 33–4, 38–9
  perfectionism 201–2
L3 acquisition *see* multilingual acquisition
language activation (language dominance)
    26–7, 50
language aptitude 9, 145–67
  age factors 155–6, 158–9
  correlation of L1 and L2 ability 152
  definition 149
  grammatical sensitivity 150t, 151, 152
  and intelligence 151
  and learning disabilities 152–4

memory capacity 150t, 151, 154–8
multidimensional aptitude 161–3
  and musical ability 167
  and personality 195
  phonetic coding ability 150t, 154
  and rate of acquisition 149–51, 153
language evolution 2–3
Language Learning Orientation Scale (LLOS)
    175–8
language mediation 219–24
language-related episodes 70
language socialization theory 236–41
languaging 222–3
lateralization, brain function 12
Laura (English-Arabic speaker) 16
learner-initiated focus on form 70 *see also*
    negotiation of form
learner language *see* interlanguages
learner perceptions 33–4
learner readiness 138–9
learning contexts 55–81
  classroom contexts 209, 210, 229–30
  classrooms 69–76, 159, 175, 177, 178
  conversational interaction 72–3
  foreign language contexts 6, 17, 178–83, 200,
      201–2, 204, 209, 210, 229–30
  heritage languages 250
  heritage learning contexts 6, 234–5
  immersion schools 62–3, 70, 76, 159
  naturalistic learners 15–16, 33, 55–8, 118–19
  post-colonial speech communities 52
  and rate of acquisition 17
  sociocultural factors 174, 210–11, 237–41
  study abroad 240, 246–8
  technology-mediated communication
      248–50
  and willingness to communicate 203–4
learning disabilities, effect on L2 acquisition
    152–4
learning languages *see* L1 acquisition; L2
    acquisition
learning outcomes 239–41
learning strategies 208–11
Learning Style Model 207–8
learning styles 206–8
lexical density 235
lexical transfer 49
lexicalization 163
Likert scales 170, 174, 195–6, 200–1, 209–10,
    211–12
Linguistic Coding Differences Hypothesis
    152–3, 154
linguistic environment *see* learning contexts
linguistic transfer *see* crosslinguistic influences

linguistic universals *see* universals
literacy, effect on language learning 153
LLOS (Language Learning Orientation Scale) 175–8
long-term memory 87–9

Magyar-English speakers 179, 180, 199
Mandarin-English speakers *see* Chinese-English speakers
markedness 37–8, 129–30, 138–9
Mary (English-Japanese speaker) 246–7
media orientation 179, 180
mediation, role of language 219–24
memory 83, 87–93, 150t, 151, 153, 154–9, 161
metalinguistic explanations 161
methodology *see also* data analysis; data collection; SLA research
    artificial grammars 99–100
    cognitive-interactionism 55, 64–6, 226–7, 230
    cognitivist approach 111
    concept-oriented approach 126
    Contrastive Analysis 31, 111
    Conversation Analysis 228–9
    correlational approach 146–7, 188
    Error Analysis 31
    ethnomethodology 227, 228–9
    formal linguistic approach (nativism) 111
    'good language learner' studies 209–11
    Likert scales 195–6
    measuring awareness 96–8
    meta-analysis 66
    microgenetic method 224, 226
    Performance Analysis 31
    reliability 188–9, 196, 212
    Systemic Functional Linguistics (SFL) 233–4
    task design 65, 86–7, 91–3, 98t, 99, 174
    triangulation 161, 211
    validity 93, 97, 100, 149, 151, 177, 193, 201, 207
microgenetic method 224, 226
migrant workers 130–2
miniature languages 85–7
minorities, and linguistic identity 243–5, 248–51
minority languages 8, 28, 173–4
Modern Languages Aptitude Test (MLAT) 149–51
modularity 111, 137
monolingual language acquisition *see* L1 acquisition
morphology
    developmental sequence 117, 124–9, 139–40
    ultimate attainment 133

morphosyntax
    developmental sequence 32, 34–7
    rate of acquisition 41–4
    ultimate attainment 17–20
motion, expression of 47–8
motivation 9, 86, 163, 168–91
    attitudes 56, 58–9, 170–5
    circumstantial vs. elective learning 243–8
    conflict-oriented vs. peace-oriented 182, 183
    definition 168
    dynamic motivation 183–5
    L2 Motivational Self System 185–8
    self-determination theory 175–8
multicompetence 9, 27, 140–1
multidimensional aptitude 161–3
multilingual acquisition 4, 181–3 *see also* bilingualism; L2 acquisition
    crosslinguistic influences 48–50
musical ability, and language aptitude 167
myelination 24–5
Myers-Briggs Type Indicator (MBTI) 193–4, 195

native speakers
    attitudes to L2 speakers 78, 231, 238–9
    as models for L2 learners 27, 140–1, 245
    embroiderers 78
    passing off as 14, 16, 202
nativism 111 *see also* domain-specificity, modularity
naturalistic learners 122–4
    definition 6
    Alberto (Spanish-English speaker) 58, 134
    Ge (Hmong-English speaker) 118–19
    Julie (English-Arabic speaker) 15–16
    Philip (English-French speaker) 33
    Wes (Japanese-English speaker) 55–8, 59, 78, 117
negation 32, 35, 119–21
negative attitudes
    of native speakers 78
    to target language 59, 246, 247–8
negative feedback 71–6, 161, 225–7
negative transfer 31–42, 230 *see also* crosslinguistic influences
negotiation for meaning 61–2, 64–9, 71, 76, 77–8
negotiation of form 69–76
NEO Five-Factor Inventory (NEOFFI) 195
neuroimaging 20–2
non-word repetition span tasks 92t
Nora (Spanish-English speaker) 114, 115t
Norwegian-English speakers 35
noticing 162, 163

Noticing Hypothesis 58, 63–4, 95–7, 99
Noun Phrase Accessibility Hierarchy 129–30

One to One Principle 113, 116–17, 127
openness to experience 163, 196
Operating Principles 113
orientations 171–5, 176–83, 198–200
Output Hypothesis 62–3, 67–9
overextension 41–2, 112
overgeneralization 117, 118–19, 135

pattern recognition 162, 163
Patty (Hokkien-English speaker) 134
peace orientation 183
PEN model (Psychotism, Extraversion and
    Neuroticism) 193, 194t
Performance Analysis 31
personality 56, 193–200, 195
Philip (English-French speaker) 33
phonetic coding ability 150t, 154
phonological awareness 153
phonological loop, working memory 90
phonology
    critical/sensitive period 22–3
    tone languages 43
    voicing 37–8
phrasal verbs 40–1
picture description tasks 67–8
Pidginization Hypothesis 58–9 *see also*
    Acculturation Model
pitch, and gender identity 245–6
politeness 46–7, 57, 77, 246–7
post-colonial speech communities 52
post-tests 157, 161
poststructuralism 217–18
power, and identity 243–8
power law of learning 85
pragmatics 46–7, 57, 246–7
prejudice 8, 78
prepositions 41–2
principles of language
    Crucial Similarity Measure 33
    One to One Principle 113, 116–17
    Operating Principles 113
    Transfer to Somewhere principle 33
private speech 220, 221–2
probabilistic learning 103–4
Process Model of L2 Motivation 184
Processability Theory 132–3
processing 82–109, 163
prompts 73–5, 76, 225–6
pronouns 32, 50, 161
pronunciation 15, 22–3, 202
psychotypology 38–9

Pushed Output Hypothesis 62–3, 67–9

Quechua-Spanish speakers 33
questions 35–6, 114, 115–16
Qur'anic recitation, teaching methods 240–1

racism 247
radically emic perspective, Conversation
    Analysis 228–9
rate of acquisition 8, 16–17, 26, 114
    effect of crosslinguistic differences 34–7,
        41–4
    effect of grammar instruction 139–40
    foreign language contexts 17
    L3 acquisition 48–50
    and language aptitude 149–51, 153
    and memory capacity 155, 156–7
Rayuela (1963) 9
reaction times 87
reading span tasks 92–3
recasts 72, 73–4, 162–3, 235–6
reflexives 50, 223–4
relative clauses 52, 129–30, 138–9
    avoidance 40
reliability 188–9, 196, 212
Rene (Spanish-English speaker) 238
repair 68–9, 228, 230–1, 232
representation 83, 87 *see also* memory
requests 47
research questions 7–8
restructuring 117–18
Richard Watson (English-French speaker)
    146–7, 153–4, 169t, 170, 192t
right to speak 242, 250
Russian L2 speakers 247

Sarah Williams (English-Swedish speaker) 49
satellite-framed languages 47–8
second language acquisition *see* L2 acquisition
second language acquisition research *see* SLA
    research
second language contexts 6
self-determination theory 175–8
self-initiated repair 68–9
self-perception 201–2
self-regulation theory 211–12, 219–21
Self-Regulatory Capacity in Vocabulary
    Learning Scale 211–12
semantic transfer 41–2, 49
sensitive period, language acquisition 13–14,
    20–3, 23–8
sentence repetition tasks 92t
sequential design 228
sexism 247

shared variance (*r²*) 146
SILL (Strategy Inventory for Language Learning) 209–10
simplification 116–17
skill acquisition theory 84–7, 137
SLA research 4–5 *see also* methodology
  cognitive-interactionist studies 64–79
  Conversation Analysis 227–8, 229–33
  critical reviews 175
  definition 1–2
  emergentism 102–5
  focus on English L2 users 6–7
  'good language learner' studies 208–11
  interdisciplinarity 7
  interlanguages 118–33, 134–6, 139–40
  language aptitude 149–52, 153–9, 160–1, 162, 163
  meta-analyses 66–7, 75–6, 125, 138, 188
  monolingual bias 5–6
  morpheme studies 124–5
  motivation 173–5, 177–83, 184–5, 187–8
  personality 195–6, 197–9
  questions 7–8
  skill acquisition theory 85–7, 88–9, 90–1, 100–2
  sociocultural studies 218–19, 221–4, 225–7
  Systemic Functional Linguistics (SFL) 234–6
  teaching methods 139–40, 225–7
  technology-mediated communication 248–50
  willingness to communicate (WTC) 203–4
social dimensions of L2 acquisition 9, 216–54
  and age-related effects 24
  circumstantial learning 243–5
  communities of practice 231, 242, 244–5
  Conversation Analysis 227–33
  elective learning 245–8
  feedback 225–7
  gender issues 245–6, 247
  identity 173, 181, 192–3, 231–2, 236, 240–1, 248–51
  identity theory 241–8
  language socialization theory 236–41
  and learning outcomes 239–41
  poststructuralism 217–18
  social constructivism 217
  sociocultural context 174, 210–11, 237–41
  sociocultural theory 217, 218–27
  Systemic Functional Linguistics (SFL) 233–6
  technology-mediated communication 248–50
  Zone of Proximal Development 224–5
social speech 220, 222–4
Spanish-Catalan speakers 25

Spanish-English speakers 18t, 19, 35, 36–7, 58–9, 114, 115t, 119–21
Spanish L2 speakers 33, 116–17, 127, 128t, 177–8
  heritage speakers 234–5
speaking style 196–200
speech perception, tests 15
speed-accuracy trade-off 197–200
stop consonants 37–8
Strategy Inventory for Language Learning (SILL) 209–10
study abroad 240, 246–8
subject-prominent languages 44–6
Swedish-English speakers 36, 40, 41–3, 49
Swedish L2 speakers 32, 49–50
symbolic learning 100–2
synopsis-ectasis continuum 207
syntax 112–24
  anaphora 15
  dative alternation 100–2
  developmental sequence 129–33, 138–9
  and memory capacity 157–8
  relative clauses 129–30
  teaching methods 136–40
  tense and aspect 44, 112, 117, 123t, 126–9
  ultimate attainment 134–5
  word order 130–3, 138
Systemic Functional Linguistics (SFL) 233–6

Tanaka Nanako (Chinese-English speaker) 249
task design 65, 86–7, 91–3, 98t, 99, 174
  task-essentialness 65, 67, 74t
Teachability Hypothesis 138–9
teaching methods 8, 235–6
  classroom discussions 237–9
  grammar 136–40
  and language aptitude 162–4
  negative feedback 72, 73–6, 161, 225–7
  Qur'anic recitation 240–1
  recasts 72, 73–4, 162–3
  use of technology-mediated communication 248
  writing 225–7, 232
technology-mediated communication 248–50
tense and aspect 44, 123t
  developmental sequence 112, 117, 126–9, 221–2, 223–4
tests
  Attitude/Motivation Test Battery (AMTB) 168–70
  Embedded Figures Test 205–6
  implicit learning 100
  Language Learning Orientation Scale (LLOS) 175–8

tests – *contd*
  learning style profiles 206–7
  Modern Languages Aptitude Test (MLAT)
    149–51
  morphosyntactic processing 86–7
  personality 193–6
  post-tests 157, 161
  Self-Regulatory Capacity in Vocabulary
    Learning Scale 211–12
  Strategy Inventory for Language Learning
    (SILL) 209–10
theories of language development *see also*
    methodology
  Acculturation Model 58–9
  Aptitude Complex Hypothesis 162–3
  Aspect Hypothesis 127–9
  Comprehensible Input Hypothesis 59–60
  Conversation Analysis 228
  Counterbalance Hypothesis 76
  concept-oriented approach 126, 141
  critical/sensitive period 12–14, 20–3, 23–8
  emergentism 102–5, 113–14, 137
  Fundamental Difference Hypothesis 158
  identity theory 241–8
  Implicit Tallying Hypothesis 96
  information processing 82–109
  Input Processing Theory 113
  Interaction Hypothesis 60–2
  L2 Motivational Self System 185–8
  language socialization theory 236–41
  Learning Style Model 207–8
  Linguistic Coding Differences Hypothesis
    152–3, 154
  Markedness Differential Hypothesis 38
  and models of personality 193–5
  nativism 111
  Noticing Hypothesis 58, 63–4, 95–7, 99
  One to One Principle 127
  Operating Principles 113
  Process Model of L2 Motivation 184
  Processability Theory 132–3
  Pushed Output Hypothesis 62–3, 67–9
  self-determination theory 175–8
  self-regulation theory 211–12, 219–21
  skill acquisition theory 84–7, 137
  and sociocultural theory 217, 218–27
  Systemic Functional Linguistics (SFL) 233–6
  Teachability Hypothesis 138–9
  Universal Grammar (UG) 111, 137
  usage-based learning 104, 113–14, 137
think-aloud protocols 97, 209
tone languages 43
topic-prominent languages 44–6
transfer *see* crosslinguistic influences

Transfer to Somewhere principle 33
transferability 38–9
triangulation 161, 211
Tsu Ying (Cantonese-English speaker) 249
Turkish-Swedish speakers 32
turn taking 228, 232

U-shaped learning 39, 117–18
ultimate attainment 8, 17–20, 22–3, 26–7, 28,
    133–6
unaccusativity 135
underuse 41–2
Universal Grammar (UG) 111, 137
universals 2, 9, 136
usage-based learning 104, 113–14, 137

validity 93, 97, 100, 149, 151, 177, 193, 201, 207
variability 105, 113–14, 119–21 *see also*
    individual differences
verb-framed languages 47–8
verbs
  acquisition of morphology 117, 126–9
  phrasal verbs 40–1
  tense and aspect 44, 112, 117, 123t, 126–9,
    221–2, 223–4
  transfer of meaning 38–9
vocabulary knowledge 88–9, 155, 156–7, 208
voicing 37–8

Wes (Japanese-English speaker) 55–8, 59, 78,
    117
willingness to communicate (WTC) 202–5
word-final consonants 37–8
word order 130–3, 138
word span tasks 92t
working memory 89–93, 155–6, 157
writing 225–7, 232, 234–5, 249–50

xenophilic orientation 179, 180

young learners
  Jorge (Spanish-English speaker) 119, 120t, 121
  Nora (Spanish-English speaker) 114, 115t,
    144, 221
  Tanaka Nanako (Chinese-English speaker)
    249
  ten young Chinese children 114
  Rene (Spanish-English speaker) 238
  Yu Qing (Cantonese-English speaker) 249

ZISA project (Zweitsprachwerb Italienischer,
    Portugiesischer und Spanischer Arbeiter
    project) 130–2
Zone of Proximal Development 224–5